The Living God

Julia A. Lamm

THE LIVING GOD: SCHLEIERMACHER'S THEOLOGICAL APPROPRIATION OF SPINOZA

The Pennsylvania State University Press
University Park, Pennsylvania

An earlier version of Chapter 1 appeared in *The Journal of Religion* 74, no. 4 (October 1994): 476–505. © 1994 by the University of Chicago.

Library of Congress Cataloging-in-Publication Data

Lamm, Julia A., 1961–
    The living God : Schleiermacher's theological appropriation of Spinoza / Julia A. Lamm.
        p.   cm.
    Includes bibliographical references.
    ISBN 0-271-01540-3 (alk. paper)
    1. God—History of doctrines—18th century. 2. God—History of doctrines—19th century. 3. Schleiermacher, Friedrich, 1768–1834 —Contributions in doctrine of God. 4. Spinoza, Benedictus de, 1632–1677—Influence. 5. Kant, Immanuel, 1724–1804—Influence.
    I. Title.
    BT101.S144L36   1996
    231′.092—dc20   95-33949
                                                                                               CIP

Copyright © 1996 The Pennsylvania State University
All rights reserved
Printed in the United States of America
Published by The Pennsylvania State University Press,
University Park, PA 16802-1003

It is the policy of The Pennsylvania State University Press to use acid-free paper for the first printing of all clothbound books. Publications on uncoated stock satisfy the minimum requirements of American National Standard for Information Sciences—Permanence of Paper for Printed Library Materials, ANSI Z39.48-1992.

Contents

Acknowledgments	vii
Abbreviations	ix
INTRODUCTION	1
1. THE EARLY ESSAYS ON SPINOZA, 1793–1794	13
2. BERLIN AND THE *SPEECHES ON RELIGION*, 1799–1801	57
3. SPINOZISM, PANTHEISM, AND CHRISTIAN DOGMATICS: EXPLANATIONS AND REVISIONS, 1821–1830	95
4. LIMITS AND METHOD: THE COINCIDENCE OF DIVINE CAUSALITY AND THE NATURE-SYSTEM	127
5. THE FIRST PART OF THE *GLAUBENSLEHRE* AND SCHLEIERMACHER'S POST-KANTIAN SPINOZISM	159
6. THE SECOND PART OF THE *GLAUBENSLEHRE* AND SCHLEIERMACHER'S LIVING GOD	199
Bibliography	229
Index of Names	236
Subject Index	239

In loving memory of my mother
Grace Jordan McGinniss
1930–1994

Acknowledgments

I thank, first of all, B. A. Gerrish, who is as conscientious an adviser as he is a scholar and professor. It was his interest in Schleiermacher and the *Pantheismusstreit* that inspired my dissertation "The 'Living God': Schleiermacher's Doctrine of God and the Spinozist Revival in Germany" for the University of Chicago. This book is a revision of that earlier work. I am also grateful to the other faculty members of the Chicago Divinity School, most especially Bernard McGinn and David Tracy, who, as the two readers on my committee, helped me to strengthen my argument. Albert L. Blackwell of Furman University and William C. McFadden, S.J., of Georgetown University both very generously undertook close readings of the book manuscript and offered invaluable criticisms and comments. William D. Blattner of Georgetown University clarified some of the finer points of Spinoza's thought and eighteenth-century German philosophical language for me.

I thank Georgetown University and its Theology Department for providing me with research and travel grants, and I especially thank my friends and colleagues in the department for their patience and support over the past six years.

All translations of Schleiermacher's two essays on Spinoza, *Spinozismus* and *Kurze Darstellung des Spinozistischen Systems* are my own. Dawn DeVries, Friederike Eigler, and B. A. Gerrish all checked the translations along the way, and their comments have been of immense help.

An earlier version of Chapter 1 appeared as "Schleiermacher's Post-Kantian Spinozism: The Early Essays on Spinoza, 1793–94" in the *Journal of Religion* 74, no. 4 (October 1994): 476–505. I am grateful to The University of Chicago Press for granting permission to publish parts of it here.

And last, but really first, my most profound gratitude goes to my family: my sister, Jane Lamm Carroll, and my brother, James D. Lamm, have been faithful in their support throughout the entire process of research and writing this book. Most supportive of all was my mother, Grace Jordan McGinniss, to whom this book is dedicated. Her death came too early, and we miss her.

Abbreviations

ASL   *Aus Schleiermachers Leben in Briefen.* 2d ed. Vols. 1 and 2. Berlin: Reimer, 1860–63. Translated by Frederica Maclean Rowan under the title *The Life of Schleiermacher as Unfolded in His Autobiography and Letters,* 2 vols. London: Smith, Elder, 1860. *ASL* is cited by volume and page. The Rowan translation will be cited as "*Letters*" by volume and page numbers.

CF   F.D.E. Schleiermacher. *The Christian Faith.* English translation of *Glaubenslehre* (1830/31). Translated and edited by H. R. Mackintosh and J. S. Stewart. Edinburgh: T. and T. Clark, 1928. Since 1976, published in the United States by Fortress Press, Philadelphia.

Expl.   "Explanations" to the third (1821) edition of the *Reden.* Reference will be to Speech number and explanation number; supplementary reference will be to translator ("Oman") by page number.

Gl.   F.D.E. Schleiermacher. *Der christliche Glaube nach den Grundsätzen der evangelischen Kirche im Zusammenhange dargestellt.* First edition (1821/22). 2 vols. Edited by Hermann Peiter. Berlin: Walter de Gruyter, 1984. Second edition (1830/31). 2 vols. 7th ed. Edited by Martin Redeker. Berlin: Walter de Gruyter, 1960. The first edition will be cited as "$Gl.^1$" by proposition number and paragraph number or "p.s." and postscript number, if applicable; when necessary, supplementary reference will be to "Peiter" by volume and page numbers. The second edition will be cited as "$Gl.^2$" by proposition number and paragraph number or "p.s." and postscript number, if applicable; reference to the German edition will be to "Redeker" by volume and page numbers; reference to the English translation will be to "*CF*" by page number. General reference in passing to this work will be to "*Glaubenslehre.*"

KGA   *Friedrich Daniel Ernst Schleiermacher: Kritische Gesamtausgabe.*

Edited by Hans-Joachim Birkner, Gerhard Ebeling, Hermann Fischer, Heinz Kimmerle, and Kurt-Victor Selge. Berlin: Walter de Gruyter, 1980– . *KGA* is cited by part, volume, and page numbers.

R   F.D.E. Schleiermacher. *Über die Religion. Reden an die Gebildeten unter ihren Verächtern.* The critical edition of the first (1799) edition is in *KGA* 1/2:185–326. A critical edition of the second (1806) and third (1821) editions is in *Friedrich Schleiermacher's Reden Ueber die Religion,* ed. G. Ch. Pünjer. Braunschweig: C. A. Schwetschke, 1879. The first edition will be cited as "R^1" by the original manuscript page number, given in the margins of both the *KGA* and Pünjer editions, in order to facilitate cross reference. The second and third editions will be cited as "R^2" and "R^3" by page number in Pünjer, or if applicable as "Pünjer" by page number. General reference in passing to this work will be to "*Reden.*" R^1 has been translated by Richard Crouter under the title *On Religion: Speeches to its Cultured Despisers.* Cambridge: Cambridge University Press, 1988. R^2 and R^3 have been translated by John Oman, also under the title *On Religion: Speeches to Its Cultured Despisers.* New York: Harper & Row, 1958; reprint, Louisville, Ky.: Westminster/John Knox Press, 1994. Reference will be to translator by page number; supplementary reference will be to German edition by page number.

INTRODUCTION

Are you better able to conceive of God as a person than as natura naturans?

—F.D.E. Schleiermacher to F. H. Jacobi,
30 March 1818

For the entire span of his career, this was Friedrich D. E. Schleiermacher's basic response to unrelenting charges that his doctrine of God was not Christian but Spinozistic and pantheistic. Of Schleiermacher's debut publication, *Reden über die Religion* (1799), his ecclesiastical superior Fr. S. G. Sack wrote, "I can acknowledge the book, now that I have read it through with deliberation, as nothing more than a spirited apology for pantheism, a rhetorical presentation of the Spinozistic system."[1] More than two decades later, similar criticisms were raised in response to the first edition of Schleiermacher's Christian dogmatics, the *Glaubenslehre* (1821–22).[2]

---

1. *ASL* 3:276, trans. in Albert L. Blackwell, "The Antagonistic Correspondence of 1801 between Chaplain Sack and His Protégé Schleiermacher," *Harvard Theological Review* 74, no. 1 (1981): 113.
2. See Christian Friedrich Böhme, review of *Der christliche Glaube*, in *Allgemeine Literatur-Zeitung*, May 1823, 49–72; Johann Friedrich Ferdinand Delbrück, *Erörterungen einiger Hauptstücke in Dr. Friedrich Schleiermachers christliche Glaubenslehre* (Bonn, 1827); and Isaaco Rust, *De nonnullis, quae in theologia nostrae aetatis dogmatica desiderantur* (Erlangen, 1828). Cited by James Duke and Francis Fiorenza, trans., in *On the "Glaubenslehre": Two Letters to Dr. Lücke* (see note 4).

Schleiermacher defended himself initially by claiming he was not interested in Benedict de Spinoza's philosophy, only in his piety: "The mind and heart of this great man seemed deeply influenced by piety, even though it were not Christian piety."[3] Later, he dissociated himself from the name of Spinoza altogether and insisted that he "had looked neither to the right nor to the left for the help of any philosopher, but had quite simply inquired about the feeling common to all pious Christians."[4] Yet throughout the ongoing controversy Schleiermacher remained steadfast in his conviction that between anthropomorphism and the deification of nature there is a "third alternative."[5]

Critics have continued to maintain that Schleiermacher's view of God, whose causality is "equal in scope to the nature-system," suggests an impersonal causality virtually indistinguishable from the natural order. Whatever their differences, Schleiermacher's various critics do seem to agree on two fundamental issues, both of which have to do with the stability of central Christian doctrines. First, the critics concur that Schleiermacher's doctrine rejects the traditional Christian theistic belief in a transcendent, personal God.[6] Second, the critics concur that Schleiermacher's doctrine of God

---

3. Explanation 3 to the second Speech; Oman, 104.

4. *On the "Glaubenslehre": Two Letters to Dr. Lücke,* ed. and trans. James Duke and Francis Fiorenza (Chico, Calif.: Scholars Press, 1981), 49. Hereafter cited as *"On the 'Glaubenslehre'"* by page number.

5. Schleiermacher to Jacobi, 30 March 1818, ASL 2:352; *Letters* 2:283. This response to the opposition Jacobi sets up between Christian theism and pantheism or atheism goes back twenty-five years to Schleiermacher's two essays on Spinoza, which were based on Jacobi's *Über die Lehre des Spinoza* (see Chapter 1).

6. Karl Barth: "Is this neuter really God, the God of piety, the God of which the doctrine of faith treats.... God is *given* to us in feeling. Not given to us externally, as Schleiermacher assures us at length. But surely a neuter that is posited and given is obviously not Spirit, not God, but, no matter how abstract, a thing.... One cannot equate this relationship with the older Reformed view of God or the general Christian concept of the omnipotence of God. It is one thing to call God omnipotent and quite another to call omnipotence God." *The Theology of Schleiermacher: Lectures at Göttingen,* ed. Dietrich Ritschl, trans. Geoffrey W. Bromiley (Grand Rapids, Mich.: William B. Eerdman's, 1982), 217. Richard R. Niebuhr: "The present-day reader can scarcely deny that the appearance of immanentism in Schleiermacher's thought remains. *The Christian Faith* lacks an adequate expression of the transcendence of God." *Schleiermacher on Christ and Religion: A New Introduction* (New York: Scribner's, 1964), 191. Samuel David Smith III: "No matter what his intention, Schleiermacher fails to make any radical distinction which can be described in the language of faith between the Creator and creation. He lacks the sense of discontinuity and transcendence which is so central a part of traditional Christian declaration." "A Study of the Relation between the Doctrine of Creation and the Doctrine of Revelation through the Created Universe in the Thought of John Calvin, Friedrich Schleiermacher and Paul Tillich" (Ph.D. diss. Vanderbilt University, 1965), 143.

endangers the traditional theistic understanding of the individual's relationship with God, thereby robbing the human person of dignity and freedom; Schleiermacher's God is not a God who responds to prayers and justifies individual persons.[7] While critics are often correct in recognizing Spinozistic and pantheistic strains in Schleiermacher's thought, they rarely take the effort to trace out the subtleties of what that might mean. My criticism of the critics is similar to Friedrich Heinrich Jacobi's criticism of Pierre Bayle's rejection of Spinoza: although he may not have been entirely wrong about Spinoza's propositions, Bayle "did not understand *sufficiently whence they come,* . . . he did not *appreciate* their premises."[8]

It is not, however, just Schleiermacher's critics who highlight his affinities with Spinoza. Even those generally supportive of Schleiermacher seem to take his Spinozism for granted.[9] Rarely, however, has this Spinozism been

---

7. Karl Barth: "There was for him no bondage of the will in the sense of the reformers, no sin that meant real and effective lostness, no word of truth that was more than one of many possible expressions of subjective experience, no justification that was not viewed as an infusion of righteousness after the manner of Roman Catholics." *Theology of Schleiermacher,* 102. Vincenzo Vitiello: the intention is to "*decentralize* man"; "Schleiermacher's religious anti-humanism goes so far as to assert that the infinite chaos, in which without any doubt each point represents a world, is, in reality, precisely as such, the most suitable symbol of religion. In this 'anti-humanism' the determination of the religious is more profound, essential, and original, than the very figure of God." "The Otherness of God: Schleiermacher and Barth," in *Schleiermacher's Philosophy and the Philosophical Tradition,* ed. Sergio Sorrentino (Lewiston: Edwin Mellen Press, 1992), 134. Walter Moore: "The individual man and particular events are being lost sight of in the execution of the one decree for the world. . . . Schleiermacher has presented an unconvincing view of the significance of my personal history." "Schleiermacher as a Calvinist: A Comparison of Calvin and Schleiermacher on Providence and Predestination," *Scottish Journal of Theology* 24, no. 2 (1971): 182.

8. Jacobi, *Über die Lehre des Spinoza,* in *The Spinoza Conversations between Lessing and Jacobi: Text with Excerpts from the Ensuing Controversy,* ed. Gérard Vallée, trans. G. Vallée, J. B. Lawson, and C. G. Chapple (Lanham, Md.: University Press of America, 1988), 104. Hereafter cited as *"Spinoza Conversations"* by page number. See Pierre Bayle, *Dictionnaire historique et critique* (5th edition, 1740), translated by Richard H. Popkin under the title *Historical and Critical Dictionary: Selections* (Indianapolis: Bobbs-Merrill, 1965).

9. John Cobb: "Schleiermacher requires little more than that the universe as a whole be understood as a living and infinite unity on which each of its parts must be seen as absolutely dependent. Specifically, Schleiermacher finds fully acceptable the philosophy of Spinoza." *Living Options in Protestant Theology* (Philadelphia: Westminster Press, 1962), 131. Charles Hartshorne and William L. Reese: "Schleiermacher had indeed turned decisively away from classical theism toward pantheism, but he failed to safeguard the full reality of the Many, as free and temporal, within the One." *Philosophers Speak of God* (Chicago: University of Chicago Press, 1953; reprint, Chicago: Midway, 1976), 267. Schubert Ogden: "Already with Schleiermacher, classical theism was definitely abandoned for an outlook that, in all essentials and regardless of its author's intention, is quite close to Spinoza's pantheism." *The Reality of God* (New York: Harper & Row, 1977), 52.

substantiated.[10] In the English language no full-scale study of the relation between Schleiermacher and Spinoza has been written; and where their relation has been given careful consideration, only a section or at the most an occasional chapter is devoted to the subject.[11] Very often, those scholars who defend Schleiermacher against charges of pantheism do so without taking into consideration his supposed Spinozism. This is problematic insofar as *pantheism* is too obscure a term, and one is therefore forced to formulate a definition such as "an identification of God and world."[12] Yet to clear Schleiermacher of such a position is not to address the more subtle and interesting question of his supposed Spinozism. What is needed is a study of how Schleiermacher understood and appropriated Spinoza, particularly with regard to the doctrine of God, and how such appropriation may or may not have affected his formulations of traditional Christian doctrines. The question of his pantheism is an abstraction from the question of his Spinozism, which itself must be distinguished from any conscious adaptation of Spinoza's philosophy.

At the very least, it can be said that whatever influences Spinoza may have had on Schleiermacher's doctrine of God, they were not, at least in the major theological works, direct. In his two early philosophical essays on Spinoza, Schleiermacher's only access to Spinoza was through Jacobi.

---

10. Understandably, more has been written in German than in English. Wilhelm Dilthey recognizes Spinoza as an important early influence on Schleiermacher, and he made portions of Schleiermacher's essays on Spinoza available in his *Leben Schleiermachers* (Berlin, 1870); curiously, Dilthey argues that Shaftesbury was a greater influence than Spinoza, but he offers little evidence to support that claim. See "Shaftesbury und Spinoza," in *Leben Schleiermachers*, in *Gesammelte Schriften*, vol. 13, pt. 1, pp. 166–79 (Göttingen: Vandenhoeck & Ruprecht, 1970). Theodor Camerer argues that Schleiermacher's *Dialektik* completes Spinoza's system, but he is concerned primarily with Schleiermacher's philosophy, not his theology. See *Spinoza und Schleiermacher: Die kritische Lösung des von Spinoza hinterlassenen Problems* (Stuttgart & Berlin, 1903). Most recently, Günter Meckenstock offers a detailed analysis of Schleiermacher's early essays on Spinoza, but the scope of his study is limited to the early writings and does not extend to Schleiermacher's later theology. See *Deterministische Ethik und kritische Theologie: Die Auseinandersetzung des frühen Schleiermacher mit Kant und Spinoza, 1789–94* (Berlin: Walter de Gruyter, 1988).
11. The best work in English on Spinoza and Schleiermacher is in Albert L. Blackwell, *Schleiermacher's Early Philosophy of Life: Determinism, Freedom, and Phantasy* (Greenville, S.C.: Scholars Press, 1982); see also Richard B. Brandt, *The Philosophy of Schleiermacher: The Development of His Theory of Scientific and Religious Knowledge* (New York: Greenwood Press, 1968).
12. See, for example, Friedrich Beisser, *Schleiermachers Lehre von Gott: Dargestellt nach seinen "Reden" und seiner "Glaubenslehre"* (Göttingen: Vandenhoeck & Ruprecht, 1970), 42–43, and John E. Thiel, *God and World in Schleiermacher's Dialektik and Glaubenslehre: Criticism and the Methodology of Dogmatics* (Bern: Peter Lang, 1981), 151.

In the *Reden* he makes no references to Spinoza's writings; in the *Glaubenslehre*, he makes no references to Spinoza at all. Therefore any connections between Spinoza's system of thought and Schleiermacher's are delicate and must be carefully drawn. With this in mind, I employ four terms: *Spinozism*, as defined in the conversations between Jacobi and Lessing; *neo-Spinozism*, as exemplified by Herder and his translation of Spinoza's substance into substantial force and as reflected in an organic worldview; *post-Kantian Spinozism*, as Schleiermacher's unique appropriation of Spinoza, characterized by the four themes of monism, determinism, realism, and nonanthropomorphism, and characterized also by his adaptation of the dictum *One and All*; *Spinozan*, as an adjective that indicates certain genuine parallels between Schleiermacher's thought and Spinoza's, regardless of whether or not they are intended.[13] Some of the Spinozan, neo-Spinozist, post-Kantian Spinozist and even Spinozist themes present in Schleiermacher's early works were carried through into his mature theological system. Granted, the lines of influence, never very direct, became even less so: neo-Spinozism had since waned, and Schleiermacher had long since left the romantic circle in Berlin; criticisms from other theologians and church representatives had served to temper Schleiermacher's enthusiasm for Spinoza and encouraged him to be more judicious in his appeals; the method of his Christian dogmatics (different, for instance, from that employed in the *Dialektik*) precluded, so he claimed, any endorsement of any philosophy and put other limits on what could be said about God. Nevertheless, Schleiermacher was the first to attempt a Christian doctrine of God within the limits set to reason by Kant's philosophy, and in Spinoza he found clarifications and distinctions that were key to overcoming obstacles he found in Kant.

Anticipating accusations that he was a *determinist*, Schleiermacher once wrote of himself that "he is satisfied with the name of determinist, provided only that he is promised that no proposition of any other determinist will be attributed to him that is not clearly contained in what he himself has said or will say."[14] Most likely, Schleiermacher would have said the same thing about his supposed Spinozism, but the proviso is a daunting one, and to date his critics have not attended to it. If the qualified ways in which, as well as the reasons why, Schleiermacher appropriated Spinoza are under-

---

13. As far as is possible, I shall resist drawing direct comparisons between the propositions of Schleiermacher and Spinoza, since that would be another study altogether. At some points, however, it will prove to be unavoidable.

14. Schleiermacher, *Über die Freiheit* (1790/92), in *KGA* 1/1:244; translated by Albert L. Blackwell under the title *On Freedom* (Lewiston Edwin Mellen, 1992), p. 29. Blackwell's translation is cited as *"On Freedom"* by page number.

stood, then the usual charges of Spinozism and pantheism do not hold. The focal issues are what precisely Schleiermacher meant by a *living* but not necessarily *personal* God, and what according to such a view of the deity is the status of the individual. Schleiermacher moved from a personal to a living God, which stands in contradistinction from, on the one side, a "lifeless and blind necessity" in nature and, on the other side, the anthropomorphized God of previous dogmatics and popular religion. Schleiermacher offered a *third alternative* that, he was convinced, while not perhaps presently accepted as "orthodox," is certainly at least an "inspired heterodoxy" that would one day be recognized as truly orthodox.[15] I argue that Schleiermacher's notion of a *living God,* while indeed influenced by his appropriation of Spinoza and neo-Spinozism, is developed in the *Glaubenslehre* in such a way that it is free from the charges of pantheism commonly made against it. In support of this thesis I develop eight subtheses.

First, Schleiermacher's appropriation of Spinoza is best understood as a post-Kantian Spinozism characterized by four themes: organic monism, ethical determinism, higher realism, and a nonanthropomorphic, nonanthropocentric view of God. Schleiermacher came to age philosophically during the fallout of the two great intellectual events of eighteenth-century Germany—the publication of Kant's *Critiques* (1781, 1788, 1790) and the Pantheist Controversy (1783–86) between Jacobi and Moses Mendelssohn. In coming to terms with the critical philosophy of Kant and the revival of Spinoza, Schleiermacher laid the foundation for certain philosophical and theological commitments that remained with him throughout his career, even though they would undergo considerable revision and refinement. We must therefore go back to these earliest essays on Kant and Spinoza in order to understand how Schleiermacher's appropriation of Spinoza was actually a simultaneous appropriation of Spinoza and Kant.

Second, the question of Spinozism cannot be collapsed into that of pantheism, since that would grossly oversimplify Spinoza's philosophy; however, in his development of an explicitly Christian doctrine of God, Schleiermacher did allow what he considered to be an acceptable form of pantheism that corresponds to his appropriation of Spinoza. What he understood by an acceptable form of pantheism is highly qualified and has very little to do with his critics' presuppositions about pantheism.

Third, the themes of his appropriation of Spinoza, which can be traced from his early essays on Spinoza through the *Reden* to the *Glaubenslehre,* can be roughly summarized as follows: (1) A denial that the divine transcen-

---

15. See Schleiermacher, *On the "Glaubenslehre,"* 53.

dence entails that God be understood as some personal, extramundane, infinite individual that has intellect and will analogous to human intellect and will. For Spinoza this was captured in the phrase *natura naturans*, for Schleiermacher in *lebendige Gottheit*. (2) A denial of a temporal creation by some extramundane cause. For Spinoza, this assumed the principle of *nihil ex nihilo*, which Schleiermacher defended in 1793–94; for the mature Schleiermacher, it meant a significant qualification of the Christian principle of *creatio ex nihilo*, hence a revision of the doctrine of creation. (3) A view of nature as interdependent, as a causal nexus, in relation to which humanity is not an exception. Everything has a like cause, which is to say it can be explained in terms of the finite world, and thus the traditional interpretation of miracles is rejected. For Schleiermacher this intimate connection of natural causality and divine causality was expressed in the doctrine of preservation. (4) A deterministic ethics. This is not explicit in the *Glaubenslehre*, since Dogmatics does not include Ethics, but it is suggested in Schleiermacher's understanding of partial freedom and dependence, utter dependence, and the eternal divine decree. (5) A basic disposition of delight and acceptance, marked by an absence of resentment; in Schleiermacher this was captured by the term *pietas*, a sensibility which includes a resistance to anthropomorphism and anthropocentrism, as well as a spirit of consent. While Schleiermacher's appropriation of Spinoza played a role in his development of each of these points, Spinoza was never the sole determinant; in some cases, such as ethical determinism, Spinoza aided Schleiermacher in further clarifying a position he had already held; in other cases, the Spinoza he appropriated was a Platonized Spinoza.

Fourth, these themes do indeed lead to a significant revision of certain traditional Christian doctrines (namely, creation, evil, Christology, justification by faith, and the divine attributes); rather than undermining the stability of Christian doctrines, such revisions are intended by Schleiermacher to make those doctrines more credible, even though perhaps less comforting.

Fifth, the main thesis necessarily includes a method of interpretation of the *Glaubenslehre* not, to my knowledge, taken in other discussions of Schleiermacher's doctrine of God but nevertheless called for by Schleiermacher's own methodology. In short, focus must be on what he calls the first form of dogmatic propositions ("descriptive of human states") *and* on part 2 as the heart of his doctrine of God.[16] If these methodological criteria

---

16. See *Gl.*² §30; *CF* 125. Propositions in the secondary forms, including statements on the divine attributes, although certainly important, are correctives and qualifiers to understanding the sense of divine causality. Part 1, as an abstraction from part 2, sets conceptual

Diagram 1. Three Forms of Dogmatic Propositions in the *Glaubenslehre* (See §30)

	First Form of Proposition	Second Form of Proposition	Third Form of Proposition
	Descriptions of Our Religious Self-Consciousness	*Conceptions of Divine Attributes*	*Utterances Regarding the Constitution of the World*
Part 1	Doctrines: *Creation *Preservation	Doctrines: *God is Eternal *God is Omnipresent *God is Omnipotent *God is Omniscient	Doctrines: Original Perfection of World Original Perfection of Man
Part 2 Consciousness of Sin	Doctrines: Original Sin Actual Sin	Doctrines: God is Holy God is Just The Mercy of God	Doctrine: Evil
Consciousness of Grace	Doctrines: The Person of Christ The Work of Christ *Regeneration Sanctification	Doctrines: *The Divine Love *The Divine Wisdom	Doctrines: Election, the Holy Spirit, Holy Scripture, Ministry of the Word, Baptism, the Lord's Supper, Power of the Keys, Prayer, the Visible Church, Return of Christ, Resurrection of the Flesh, Last Judgment, Eternal Blessedness

*Denotes doctrines on which this study will focus

are taken seriously, it would follow that there are two candidates for determining the extent to which Schleiermacher's doctrine of God, with its Spinozan elements, can be said to undermine positive Christian doctrines: the Christological doctrines and the doctrine of justification by faith. Because of its decisive role in Protestant theology and because it focuses on the relation of the individual soul to the divine causality, it is the doctrine of justification by faith that I apply to test whether Schleiermacher's appro-

---

limits to what can be said and thus prevents the entrance of alien elements into the system. See Diagram 1.

priation of Spinoza does indeed undermine central Christian doctrines by taking away God's transcendence and consequently human dignity.

Sixth, this method of interpretation will show what Schleiermacher meant by a living but not necessarily personal God, and how the individual stands in relation to such a God. It will also show how Schleiermacher departed decisively from Spinoza, namely, on the question of divine intentionality. What is more, discussion of divine intentionality does not appear only at the end of the *Glaubenslehre,* under the proposition on the divine wisdom, nor is it only introduced in part 2. On the contrary, elements of it are found also in part 1, which means there is not a radical break between the two parts, as some maintain; there are not two separate systems, one philosophical and the other theological. Part 1, as a description of the general relationship between God and the world, can fairly be said to be more Spinozistic than part 2. Nevertheless the fact remains that part 1 also contains the notion of divine intentionality; part 1 sets the limits to, and must be read in the context of, part 2. The underlying principles are consistent in both parts.

Seventh, Schleiermacher's appropriation of Spinoza was filtered through the revival of Spinoza in late-eighteenth-century Germany, which means that it was essentially aesthetic in character; Spinoza's uncompromising monism is thus translated into an aesthetic monism that allows for genuine individuality, novelty, beauty, and goodness. It is most especially in this sense that Schleiermacher's Spinoza is a Platonized Spinoza. In his Christian dogmatics, the aesthetic becomes the redemptive.

Eighth, Schleiermacher appropriated Spinoza's thought by means of his own unique interpretation of the ancient dictum *One and All.* This interpretation of the *One and All* also marks what Gadamer refers to as Schleiermacher's "transposition of the Platonic dialectic."[17] Just as Schleiermacher's appropriation of Spinoza was simultaneously an appropriation of Kant, so too was it simultaneously an appropriation of Plato. This means that Schleiermacher is never just a Kantian, a Spinozist, or a Platonist. How Schleiermacher appropriated various systems into his own system is what makes his thought uniquely his own.

My argument proceeds along the following lines. Chapter 1 identifies and describes the four post-Kantian Spinozist themes as they are first developed in two early essays on Spinoza, *Spinozismus* and *Kurze Darstellung des Spinozistischen Systems* (1793–94). Chapter 2 demonstrates how these

17. Hans-Georg Gadamer, "Schleiermacher Platonicien," *Archives de Philosophie* 32 (1969): 28–39.

four themes, along with Schleiermacher's own adaptation of the dictum *One and All,* are developed in the first edition of the *Reden* (1799). Chapter 3 analyzes how Schleiermacher defines "Spinozism" and "pantheism" and the degree to which he accepts these labels for himself as he makes the transition to writing a Christian dogmatics (1821). The focus is on Schleiermacher's responses to his critics both in his "Explanations" to the *Reden* and in the revisions he makes between the first and second editions of his *Glaubenslehre.* Chapter 4 proceeds to part 1 of the *Glaubenslehre* and analyzes the methodological limits Schleiermacher assigns to language about God. This becomes the framework for understanding the influence his early appropriation of Spinoza might have had on his Christian dogmatics and for judging the degree to which he might be considered a Spinozist. Chapter 5 continues the discussion of part 1 by tracing through the four post-Kantian Spinozist themes and determining how they may or may not have been modified by the dogmatic enterprise. And last, Chapter 6 turns to part 2 of the *Glaubenslehre* and examines what light certain Christian doctrines (particularly justification, the divine love, and the divine wisdom) shed on what Schleiermacher means by a *living God.*

Because my concern is Schleiermacher's *theological* appropriation of Spinoza (i.e., the degree to which Schleiermacher's specifically Christian doctrine of God is influenced by Spinoza and neo-Spinozism), I focus almost exclusively on three main texts: the two early essays on Spinoza, *Spinozismus* and *Kurze Darstellung des Spinozistischen Systems;* the first three editions of *Über die Religion: Reden an die Gebildeten unter ihren Verächtern,* including the "Explanations" attached to the 1821 edition; and both editions of *Der christliche Glaube nach den Grundsätzen der evangelischen Kirche im Zusammenhange dargestellt,* including marginal notes. If the subject of my study were more far-ranging—that is, if it had to do with Schleiermacher's appropriation of Spinoza rather than Schleiermacher's *theological* appropriation of Spinoza—then it would have to include examination of the *Grundlinien einer Kritik der bisherigen Sittenlehre* and the *Dialektik.*[18] Since I am interested in Schleiermacher's development of a specifically Christian doctrine of God, I focus chiefly on his two major theological works.

Schleiermacher found in Spinoza a kindred soul, a great thinker of deep piety, whose general impulses—when put within the limits of piety, cor-

---

18. Schleiermacher, *Grundlinien einer Kritik der bisherigen Sittenlehre* (1803), in *Schleiermachers Werke* (Leipzig, 1928; reprint, Aalen: Scientia Verlag, 1967); *Dialektik* (1811, 1814, 1818, 1822, 1828, 1831), in *Schleiermachers Werke,* ed. Ludwig Jonas (Berlin: Reimer, 1839). In English there are three good comparisons of the *Glaubenslehre* and the *Dialektik:* Paul

rected by the critical philosophy, translated into modern terminology, and informed by the new science—aided Schleiermacher in formulating a doctrine of God that defies the strict opposition set up by Jacobi; it is the *third alternative*. This strain of Spinozism did not necessarily produce the tensions in Schleiermacher's Christian dogmatics. If anything, it helped him address the major inconsistencies of certain traditional Christian doctrines and make revisions that although not orthodox, he deemed more intelligible and reverent.

Frederick Mehl, "Schleiermacher's Mature Doctrine of God as Found in the *Dialektik* of 1822 and the Second Edition of *The Christian Faith* (1830–31)" (Ph.D. diss., Columbia University, 1961); Gerhard Spiegler, *The Eternal Covenant: Schleiermacher's Experiment in Cultural Theology* (New York: Harper & Row, 1967); John E. Thiel, *God and World* (see note 12).

1

THE EARLY ESSAYS ON SPINOZA, 1793–1794

> *This is thus the true transition from Leibnizianism to Spinozism.*
>
> —F.D.E Schleiermacher, *Spinozismus*

The evidence suggests that the first time Schleiermacher read F. H. Jacobi's *Über die Lehre des Spinoza* (On Spinoza's doctrine) was in 1787, very shortly after he had left the Pietist seminary in Barby (by mutual agreement with the faculty there) and matriculated at the University of Halle.[1] Yet it was Schleiermacher's second encounter with Jacobi's presentation of Spinoza that proved to be decisive.[2] Sometime in the winter months of 1793–94, after a temporary move to Berlin in September 1793 and presumably before his final set of theological exams in March 1794, Schleiermacher wrote two essays on Spinoza—*Spinozismus* (Spinozism) and *Kurze Darstellung des Spinozistischen Systems* (Brief presentation of the Spinozistic system).[3] Since Schleiermacher did not have direct access to Spinoza's works,

---

1. See correspondence between Schleiermacher and his father: J.G.A. Schleiermacher to F.D.E. Schleiermacher, 17 May 1787 (*Brief* 69), and F.D.E. Schleiermacher to J.G.A. Schleiermacher, 14 August 1787 (*Brief* 80), in *KGA* 5/1:79, 92.
2. In April 1794 he explained to his friend Carl Gustav von Brinckmann that he kept Jacobi's book so long because he studied Spinoza so extensively. Schleiermacher to Brinckmann, mid-April 1794 (*Brief* 256), in *KGA* 5/1:344.
3. Both *Spinozismus* and *Spinozistisches System* are found in *KGA*, part 1, vol. 1. Hereafter each is cited by short title and page number.

much of his task lay in determining, as he puts it in *Spinozistisches System,* what "in Spinoza is different from Jacobi's presentation of it" (580). He went about this task by setting up dialogues between Jacobi, Kant, Leibniz, and Spinoza. In the process, he developed his own distinctive post-Kantian Spinozism. At the same time that he used Spinoza to respond to Kant, he also appropriated Spinoza into a Kantian framework.[4] To understand this, we must go back to the intervening years (1787–92) when, as a student of Johann August Eberhard and later in Drossen and Schlobitten, Schleiermacher immersed himself in Kant's critical philosophy.

During these years, Schleiermacher unquestionably viewed himself as a Kantian. Indeed, throughout his career he endeavored to do his theological thinking within the limits set by Kant's critical philosophy, but at no time was he so preoccupied with Kant as in the first decade of his career when he attempted to situate himself in relation to three prevailing responses to Kant.[5] The first option, represented by Eberhard, was a flat rejection of Kant in the form of retrenchment into the orthodoxy of the Wolffian school of philosophy. The second option, represented by Johann Gottfried Herder, was a more subtle rejection, not only of Kant but also of the whole Enlightenment obsession with reason; Herder's approach developed a genuinely new alternative in philosophy. The third option, represented by Karl Leonhard Reinhold and Johann Gottlieb Fichte, was an enthusiastic acceptance of the critical philosophy that sought to carry through Kant's program more consistently than Kant himself had. Because Schleiermacher's own response to Kant was a combination of the last two options, it is not enough to say that Schleiermacher was a Kantian, since he went beyond Kant. Nor is it enough to say that Schleiermacher was a post-Kantian, for the same could be said of Reinhold or Fichte. Schleiermacher may be distinguished from other post-Kantians on the basis of his appeal to Spinoza as a way of correcting what he found to be misguided in Kant. For this reason he is best understood as a post-Kantian Spinozist.

From 1789 to 1792, Schleiermacher focused his intellectual energies on Kant's *Critique of Practical Reason* (1788). Through a series of essays, notes, and dialogues, Schleiermacher grappled with questions of

---

4. As Meckenstock says, "Doch ist unverkennbar, daß seine Fragestellung selbst sehr stark durch die kritische Philosophie Kants veranlaßt und geprägt ist." *Deterministische Ethik,* 198.

5. See Henry E. Allison, *The Kant-Eberhard Controversy* (Baltimore: Johns Hopkins University Press, 1973), 4–6.

moral philosophy. In the process, he evolved from being a conscientious student and devoted follower of Kant to being an independent, creative thinker in his own right. This earliest development of his thought culminated in the constructive essay *Über die Freiheit (On Freedom)*, in which he attempted to carry forth the principles of critical philosophy as given in Kant's first *Critique* by rejecting the main tenets of the second *Critique*. Although he had begun to criticize Kant's postulates of freedom, immortality, and God as early as 1789,[6] in *Über die Freiheit* he presented his own determinist ethical theory as an alternative. Convinced that Kant's notion of transcendental freedom posits an unnecessary gap between desire and freedom, Schleiermacher developed a new understanding of freedom in the context of "the doctrine of the necessary interconnection of actions with the universal chain of causes and effects,"[7] or *determinism*. Schleiermacher came to discover that the gap between freedom and desire in the second *Critique* was really an extension of the gap between noumena and phenomena in the first *Critique*,[8] and he found the key to repairing this second Kantian dualism when he reread Jacobi's *Über die Lehre des Spinoza* in 1793. Spinoza's teaching regarding the relation of finite things to the infinite aided Schleiermacher in repairing the gap between phenomena and noumena, and Spinoza's teaching on the relation between thought and extension aided him in further repairing the gap between desire and freedom insofar as it confirmed the solution Schleiermacher had already arrived at in *Über die Freiheit*. These two teachings presume a third, namely Spinoza's understanding of the infinite. Schleiermacher's reflections on this third marked his return to theology.[9] The *post-Kantian Spinozism* that Schleiermacher constructed in his two essays on Spinoza has four defining characteristics: an *organic monism*, an *ethical determinism*, a *critical realism*, and a *nonanthropomorphic view of God*. Insofar as these four themes can still be found in his mature doctrine of God as set forth in the *Glaubenslehre,* the post-Kantian Spinozism developed in these early essays on Spinoza can be said to be foundational albeit not solely determinative for Schleiermacher's thought.

6. See *Über das höchste Gut* and *Notizen zu Kant*, in *KGA* 1/1:81–128 and 129–34.
7. *On Freedom*, 49.
8. For further discussion, see Julia A. Lamm, "The Early Philosophical Roots of Schleiermacher's Notion of *Gefühl*, 1788–94," *Harvard Theological Review* 87, no. 1 (1994): 67–105.
9. On what he judged to be the three chief doctrines of Spinoza's philosophy, see *Spinozismus*, 523.

The Philosophical Context

Spinoza and Spinozism in Germany

During his lifetime and for nearly a century after his death in 1677, Spinoza was maligned as an atheist and immoralist.[10] Henry Oldenburg, who had begun a correspondence with him in August 1661, politely summarized the reaction of many readers: "You appear to set up a fatalistic necessity for all things and actions; if such is conceded and asserted, people aver, that the sinews of all laws, of virtue, and of religion, are severed, and that all rewards and punishment are vain.... If we are driven by fate, and all things follow a fixed and inevitable path laid down by the hard hand of necessity, they do not see where punishment can come in."[11] Inquiries less civil than Oldenburg's, like that of Lambert de Velthuysen, simply accused Spinoza of being an atheist: *"In order to shun the reproach of superstition, he seems to me to have thrown off all religion.... [W]ith covert and disguised arguments I [Spinoza] teach atheism."*[12] As both letters suggest, the criticism almost always stemmed from the fear that in denying freedom and a personal God Spinoza had undermined all morality.

Such fears and condemnations gained further voices long after Spinoza's death. Perhaps the most vicious and most famous appeared in 1697 with the first edition of Pierre Bayle's *Dictionnaire*. Bayle (1647–1706) begins his description of Spinoza with two curt statements: "a Jew by birth, and afterwards a deserter from Judaism, and lastly ... a systematic atheist who employed a totally new method."[13] The themes are familiar: Spinoza's doctrine of God is a "monstrous absurdity" because it is not "distinguished from matter and ... acts necessarily and in accordance with the full extent

---

10. For a history of the reception of Spinoza in Germany, see David Bell, *Spinoza in Germany from 1670 to the Age of Goethe* (London: The Institute of German Studies, University of London, 1984); Max Grunwald, *Spinoza in Deutschland: Gekrönte Preisschrift* (Berlin, 1897); Moses Krakauer, "Zur Geschichte des Spinozismus in Deutschland während der ersten Hälfte des achtzehnten Jahrhunderts" (Ph.D. diss., University of Breslau, 1881); Thomas McFarland, *Coleridge and the Pantheist Tradition* (Oxford: Clarendon Press, 1969), 53–106, 261–66; Winfried Schröder, *Spinoza in der deutschen Frühaufklärung* (Würzburg: Königshausen & Neumann, 1987); and Gérard Vallée, introduction, in *Spinoza Conversations*, 1–62.

11. Henry Oldenburg, London, to B. de Spinoza, 16 December 1675, in *Works of Spinoza*, trans. R.H.M. Elwes (New York: Dover, 1955), 2:299–300. Elwes's translation is hereafter cited as "Elwes" by volume and page number.

12. Lambert de Velthuysen, Utrecht, to B. de Spinoza, 24 January 1671, quoted in letter from Spinoza, The Hague, to Isaac Orobio, [Utrecht], n.d., 1671, in Elwes 2:365, 366.

13. Bayle, *Historical and Critical Dictionary*, trans. Popkin, 288.

of his powers" (315); his denial of free will is also absurd because it is inconceivable that an infinitely holy God would not have created us with free will and equally inconceivable that we would then not be responsible for our own actions. Bayle's general attack is twofold. On a philosophical level, he ridicules Spinoza's intellectual stature. Even his weakest adversaries, Bayle contends, have overthrown the atheist's hypothesis since it runs counter to the most common notions. Yet Bayle unwittingly incriminates himself by appealing to the very "common notions" that Spinoza finds so delusory: "Is it not some consolation in misfortune to flatter oneself that the prayers that are addressed to God will be answered and that in any case he will reward us for our patience and will furnish us with a magnificent compensation?" (316). On a personal level, Bayle is even harsher in his criticisms, portraying Spinoza as pernicious, impious, unethical, and rude. Bayle's attacks, both philosophical and personal, do not have the evidence to support them. Sound arguments can indeed be made for Spinoza's "atheism"—arguments that at least grasp and address Spinoza's agenda and do not engage in vilification. Yet all the evidence shows that, as Bayle himself acknowledges but dismisses, "he was sociable, affable, honest, obliging, and of a well-ordered morality" (295).[14]

Reasonable or not, Bayle's assessment set the tone for the various interpretations of Spinoza to follow. Such derisive rejection, prevalent among the *philosophes,* appeared most definitively in the work of one of the founders of the German Enlightenment, Christian Wolff (1669–1754), who, in his *Theologia naturalis* (1737), wrote, "Spinozism, not far removed from atheism, is as harmful as atheism, and in a certain respect even more harmful than atheism."[15] This initial wave of German animosity took a turn in the third quarter of the eighteenth century, when Spinoza began to receive more sympathetic treatment in the thought of Gotthold Ephraim Lessing (1729–81) and the early works of Herder. However, not until the famous *Pantheismusstreit* (Pantheist Controversy) that erupted between Mendelssohn and Jacobi in 1783 did attitudes toward Spinoza shift significantly.[16]

14. For a discussion of Spinoza's life, see Yirmiyahu Yovel, *Spinoza and Other Heretics,* vol. 1, *The Marrano of Reason* (Princeton, N.J.: Princeton University Press, 1989).
15. Christian Wolff, *Theologia naturalis,* proposition 716. Quoted in and translated by McFarland, *Coleridge and the Pantheist Tradition,* 75.
16. The documents are presented in Heinrich Scholz, ed., *Die Hauptschriften zum Pantheismusstreit zwischen Jacobi und Mendelssohn* (Berlin: Reuther & Reichard, 1916). They are translated (in part) in *Spinoza Conversations,* which is a good translation, but unfortunately omits the very sections that Schleiermacher used in his two essays on Spinoza. Discussions of the controversy are found in Lewis White Beck, *Early German Philosophy: Kant and His Predecessors* (Cambridge: Harvard University Press, 1969); Frederick C. Beiser, *The Fate of*

A renewed interest in Spinoza's thought resulted, and a deep affinity with Spinoza's sensibilities was discovered.

In July 1783, two and a half years after Lessing's death, Jacobi, on hearing of Mendelssohn's intention to write something on their mutual friend, decided to make public a conversation he had had with Lessing. In a letter addressed to Elise Reimarus but clearly intended for Mendelssohn, Jacobi writes, "I confide it to you here *sub rosa,* that Lessing was in his final days a firm Spinozist" (*Spinoza Conversations,* 79). His concern, he claims, is that Mendelssohn be aware of Lessing's Spinozism so that he may proceed cautiously in his own writing. As Jacobi relates it, the conversation between himself and Lessing, which took place in Lessing's home in July 1780, began in response to Goethe's poem "Prometheus." After Lessing read Jacobi's copy of the poem, the conversation proceeded as follows:

> *L:* I find it good.... The point of view in which the poem is cast is my own point of view.... The orthodox concepts of the divinity are no longer for me; I cannot stand them. *Hen kai Pan!* [One and All] I know naught else. That is also the tendency in this poem; and I must admit, I like it very much.
>
> *J:* Then you would indeed be more or less in agreement with Spinoza.
>
> *L:* If I am to call myself by anybody's name, then I know none better.

The conversation continued the following day:

> *J:* You surprised me and I felt confused. Dismay it was not. I certainly did not expect to find you a Spinozist or pantheist; and still less did I expect that you would put it to me directly and so frankly and clearly. I had come chiefly in the hope of receiving your help against Spinoza....
>
> *L:* Then there is no help for you. Why don't you become his friend openly? There is no other philosophy but the philosophy of Spinoza.

Reason: German Philosophy from Kant to Fichte (Cambridge: Harvard University Press, 1987); B. A. Gerrish, "The Secret Religion of Germany: Christian Piety and the Pantheism Controversy," *Journal of Religion* 67, no. 4 (October 1987): 437–55; McFarland, *Coleridge and the Pantheist Tradition;* and John H. Zammito, *The Genesis of Kant's "Critique of Judgment"* (Chicago: University of Chicago Press, 1992).

J: That may be true. For if a determinist wants to be consistent, he must become a fatalist; all else will follow as a matter of course.
L: I can see we understand each other.

(85–86)

Jacobi then, at Lessing's request, discusses what he takes to be the "*spirit of Spinozism*" and further proceeds to offer his own criticism of Spinoza. In brief, Jacobi defined Spinozism as being based on the principle *a nihilo nihil fit* (from nothing nothing comes), from which it follows that there is only an immanent, inherent cause of the universe, devoid of reason and will. The result is fatalism and atheism, a complete denial of human freedom and of a personal God.

Unlike Bayle's assessment, Jacobi's is a generally fair (at times astute, at other times misleading) interpretation of Spinoza's thought. Bayle, Jacobi says, may not have been too wrong about Spinoza's conclusions, but "he did not understand *sufficiently whence they come*, . . . he did not *appreciate* their premises as the author had" (104). Also unlike Bayle's criticism, Jacobi's does not involve any personal attacks. It is not that Spinoza himself was an atheist, but that his system leads to atheism. "In fact," Jacobi writes, "Spinoza urged such piety and wisdom far more heartily that did *Nathan*. He too worshipped a providence, even if to him it was the same as the very order of nature, which arises of necessity from its own eternal laws; he too related everything to God" (154).[17] Jacobi's quarrel then is not with Spinoza himself, nor is it a reactionary assault. Nevertheless, the dangers to which Spinoza's thought can lead are for him clear and must be guarded against.

Mendelssohn, in his *Morgenstunden* (also published in 1785), did not deny that Lessing was a Spinozist, although he took great pains to argue that this in no way diminished his friend's character. He named Lessing the "champion" of Spinozism, just as he had been the champion of "any persecuted doctrine."[18] His understanding of Spinozism, however, is of a "refined Spinozism"(65, 73, 130–31), which, in the end, is not significantly different from traditional theism insofar as it included a strong sense of providence and of a "perfect harmony between the doctrine of intentions and that of efficient causes" (69). Consequently, this refined Spinozism is not a form of fatalism but "is totally compatible with the truths of religion and morality" (73). It still allows for, in Vallée's words, "the objective

---

17. "Nathan" is a reference to Lessing's play, *Nathan the Wise* (1779).
18. See *Spinoza Conversations*, 65, 72.

existence of the manifold outside God, posited by a free act of creation"(37–38).

The consequences of the controversy between Jacobi and Mendelssohn went quite beyond what either had intended or desired. Arising as it had during a general movement away from the philosophical views and rationalistic methods of the German Enlightenment, the *Pantheismusstreit* issued in a resurgence of interest in Spinoza's thought.[19] Although for Jacobi Spinoza represented all that was wrong with rationalism, for others he provided an alternative to more conventional understandings of God. Goethe, Lessing, Herder, and Jacobi each presented his own form of resistance to such rationalism, a resistance that would eventually lead, in the 1790s, to romanticism. Perhaps the greatest product of this Spinozan renaissance is Johann Gottfried Herder's *God, Some Conversations,* first published in 1787.

Herder describes the universe as a causal nexus of living forces that "functions organically."[20] The universe is a system of microcosms within macrocosms, all of which are internally related.[21] Herder considers this worldview to reflect the "spirit of Spinozism" (137) insofar as it is the translation of Spinoza's *substance* into *substantial force:* "Had [Spinoza] developed the conception of power as he did that of matter, then he would necessarily, and as a consequence of his own system, have come to the conception of forces which are active in matter, as well as in organs of thought" (123).[22] God is the infinite Force that is the presupposition of all forces: "The eternal, primal power, *the force of all forces,* is but one"(ibid., emphasis added). This means, for Herder as for Spinoza, that God is immanent in the world, not external to it. Herder makes it clear that the word *God* is not merely a "collective name" (121). God and the world cannot be identified; rather, everything depends on God (144, 132). As the substan-

---

19. Vallée points out that until Jacobi the *Ethics* had been neglected and most references to Spinoza had been based on his *Theologico-Political Treatise.* See Vallée's introduction to *The Spinoza Conversations,* 32 n. 77.

20. Johann Gottfried Herder, *God, Some Conversations,* trans. Frederick H. Burkhardt (New York: Veritas, 1940; reprint, Indianapolis: Bobbs-Merrill, 1962), 172. "The whole of God's world becomes a realm of immaterial forces in which none is unrelated to others, because it is only by reason of the relationship and reciprocal activity between them all that the appearances and changes of the world come about" (109).

21. "For the organ itself is also a system of forces which in their inner connection serve a single ruling one." Ibid., 174.

22. "If he had chosen the conception of force and activity, then everything would have been easier for him, and his system would have been much more clear and unified." Ibid., 108; cf. 109.

tial Force that grounds all forces, God is not the childish, anthropomorphized God of conventional theology (129). Yet this is not to say that because there are no final causes there is not wisdom and goodness in the infinite, immanent, divine Force: "But with every activity [force] makes its subsequent activity easier. And, since it cannot do this otherwise than by implanted, internal laws of harmony, wisdom and goodness which . . . are benevolently forced upon every creature, impressed upon it, . . . therefore you see everywhere a progress out of chaos into order, an inner increase and enhanced beauty of forces in ever-widening limits according to ever more observed laws of harmony and order" (189). In short, for Herder, as for Lessing and Goethe, Spinozism is not atheism.

By the time Schleiermacher entered the discussion in 1793–94, a decade after its inception, neo-Spinozism was already widespread among philosophical and literary circles in Germany, but it was as vague and indefinite as it was pervasive. Consider, for example, three basic yet fundamentally different interpretations of Spinozism. Jacobi's, the harshest view, accused Spinozism of leading to a thoroughgoing atheism and fatalism. Then there was Mendelssohn's *refined Spinozism,* which did little to distinguish Spinozism in any significant way from traditional theism. Finally, there were appropriations of Spinoza by Lessing and Herder. Lessing, according to Jacobi's account, had been attracted to Spinoza's nonanthropocentrism, his denial of free will, and his notion of the *One and All;* at the same time, he had continued to maintain a belief in divine providence. Herder translated Spinoza's *substance* into *substantial force,* thereby wresting away the putative, now-dead God of deism and Protestant orthodoxy and salvaging a living God.

To determine, therefore, the degree to which Schleiermacher can be said to have been a Spinozist, we need to know what sort of Spinozism is meant. Since in 1793–94 it was primarily in response to Jacobi that Schleiermacher formed his own understanding of Spinoza, and since as late as 1818 Schleiermacher would still find Jacobi to be an important intellectual force with which to contend, a more detailed examination of Jacobi's *Über die Lehre des Spinoza* is in order.

Jacobi's Philosophy of Faith

Jacobi's consuming desire was to expose the dangers of rationalism and speculative thought and to present his own philosophy as an alternative to it. In his view, absolutized reason (reason left to itself and arbitrarily systematized) leads to nihilism. That is to say, it leads to a denial of an objective reality, of human freedom, and of a personal God—the test cases for traditional theism. This, he insists, is the logical consequence of Kant's transcendental idealism, as is evidenced in Fichte's philosophy. In his "Open Letter to Fichte" (1799), Jacobi writes, "If . . . an essence is to become an object completely comprehended by us, then we must negate, destroy it in thought objectively—as existing of itself—in order to allow it to become completely our own creation subjectively, a mere scheme. Nothing may remain in it and constitute an essential part of its concept that were not our action, now a mere representation of our productive imagination."[23] Everything becomes the ego, since "pure reason" derives everything from itself, and thus the human spirit becomes a "world creator." To become that, however, "it must destroy itself in essence in order to arise, to have itself solely in concept; in the concept of a pure absolute emerging from and entering into, originally—from nothing, to nothing, for nothing, into nothing."[24] This nihilistic move is what Jacobi calls *inverted Spinozism*: rather than substance, consciousness is primary, the only "real" existent. Transcendental idealism, then, is the "representation of a materialism without matter, or of a *mathesis pura*, in which pure and empty consciousness imagines mathematical space."[25]

Such unyielding criticism of any form of materialism began more than fifteen years before this letter to Fichte and prompted both Jacobi's conversations with Lessing and the ensuing controversy with Mendelssohn. Jacobi had at that time set up an opposition in which there was no room for compromise. On the one side there is Spinozism, which results necessarily in materialism, hence fatalism, hence atheism; on the other side is theism, which views nature in terms of "miracles, mysteries and signs" and thus allows for freedom and a personal God. The stakes are high, for the choice

---

23. F. H. Jacobi, "Open Letter to Fichte," in *Philosophy of German Idealism*, ed. Ernst Behler (New York: Continuum, 1987), 127.
24. Ibid.
25. Ibid., 123. By materialism, whether as a pantheism or as rationalism ("inverted Spinozism"), Jacobi means a worldview that denies purpose, freedom, and direction; it denies, in other words, an intelligent, free, and purposeful God. There is nothing that transcends lifeless matter or the ego. Everything is arbitrary and in the end inconsequential. This is why the notion of "final causes" is so central to the discussion at hand: for Jacobi, there must be a personal God who can intervene in the course of nature and bring about certain desired effects through an act of thought (derivatively, human beings can control their actions through free will); for Spinoza, no volition can be ascribed to God, the notion of "purpose" being but a figment of human imagination; for Herder and Schleiermacher, there is purpose, but it is given immanently in the course of nature, not through the distinction of ends and means.

is between a God who is a mere postulate and a *living God;* morality itself depends on which is chosen. Jacobi is convinced that if there is not a transcendent, personal God, then there are no final causes, only efficient ones; it follows that the mind can only observe and accompany the "mechanism of efficient powers" (*Spinoza Conversations,* 89).

In response, therefore, to Lessing's question, What is the "*spirit* of Spinozism"? Jacobi describes seven characteristics, which I shall use as criteria to judge whether or not Schleiermacher can be said to be *Spinozist*. (1) It assumes the principle *a nihilo nihil fit,* which seems to deny the doctrine of *creatio ex nihilo;* this implies that (2) there is no transition between the supernatural and the natural, which is to say, there is no transcendent God operating on a finite world, rather everything must come from some other finite thing, which must itself have an efficient cause; consequently (3) there is only an immanent, inherent cause, "eternally unchangeable *in itself,* which, taken together with all that followed from it, would be One and the Same" (87). It follows from all this that (4) there is an infinite regress of causes, and that (5) the immanent cause has neither intellect nor will; because "of its transcendental *unity* and constant absolute infinity, it cannot have any object of thinking and willing" (87). Finally, (6) the "spirit of Spinozism" denies final causes (extramundane causes willed by an intelligent divine being to bring about some effect in relation to particular events and persons), and thus (7) it is deterministic.

Jacobi's own choice is, of course, for "*an intelligent personal first cause of the world*" (88), but Lessing admits that he covets neither free will nor a transcendent God. "Human prejudice," Lessing explains, "has it that we consider the idea [of free will] as primary and supreme, and want to derive everything from it since everything, including representations, is dependent upon higher principles" (89). Lessing felt much more at home with the nonanthropocentric orientation of Spinoza. The notion of a free will did not provide him the reassurance that it did Jacobi, and he found the notion of a personal, infinitely perfect God to be, in Jacobi's words, "such *infinite boredom* that the very thought of it caused him pain and dread" (98). He had had enough of the orthodox doctrine of God and preferred instead the *Hen kai Pan,* the *One and All.* If he did entertain any thought of a personal deity, it was, according to Jacobi, in terms of "the soul of the universe" (97).

When Lessing asks his friend how he could believe anything but Spinozism, Jacobi proclaims his suspicion not only of Spinozism but of all speculative systems. Arbitrary connections between ideas are made without any correspondence to reality. Strict rationalism is in the end nihilism: there is no self, no other, no objectively existing world. Again, the triumph of speculative reason, whether in the form of materialism (Spinoza) or idealism (Fichte), brings with it the destruction of freedom and of theism. When Lessing further asks if this fear of skepticism does not result in a rejection of philosophy, Jacobi insists, "I draw back from a philosophy that makes a total scepticism necessary"; he continues, "I love Spinoza because he, more than any other philosopher, has led me to believe firmly that certain things cannot be explained; things that we therefore cannot disregard but must take as we find them" (94). Jacobi thus uses Spinozism as the "springboard" for his own philosophy of faith. Toward the end of *Über die Lehre des Spinoza,* in a letter to Mendelssohn dated 4 April 1785, he argues that true philosophy is an attempt "to unveil, to reveal *existence,*" and in this endeavor philosophical explanation is ever only a means to the ultimate goal, which itself can never be explained; that goal is "whatever is insoluble, whatever is immediate, whatever is simple" (96).

What is required is a leap of faith, a leap that involves an immediate certainty that "*the representation itself [is] in conformity with the thing represented*" (120). It needs no proof because such faith, or feeling, is the immediate certainty that there is a reality outside and independent of our understanding. Such a conviction does not arise through our cognition alone; rather, it is what allows for any convictions that we may have based on rational grounds.[26] Contrary to Fichte, Jacobi maintains that only in being aware of other real things and of a Thou do we become aware of ourselves. All knowledge thus depends originally on this faith, which is an immediate knowledge of the revelation of nature. Reason must remain true to this faith, this immediate certainty, if it is not to run the danger of becoming speculative, thus "*degenerate,*" hence nihilistic. Underlying this understanding of faith is Jacobi's fierce determination to defend his notion of a personal God—what he calls the *living God* who "can manifest himself only in *that which is alive* and can make himself known to that which is alive only *through love which has been quickened*" (*Spinoza Conversations,* 121). To this Schleiermacher responds that Spinoza presents us with a third alternative in which no leap of faith is needed.

Schleiermacher's Essays on Spinoza

Schleiermacher's two essays on Spinoza differ significantly in syle. The first part of *Spinozismus* consists of the simple copying down, with barely a

---

26. For an analysis of Jacobi's understanding of *Glaube,* see B. A. Gerrish, "Faith and Existence in the Philosophy of F. H. Jacobi," in *Witness and Existence: Essays in Honor of*

marginal comment, of Jacobi's forty-four paragraphs describing Spinoza's system.[27] In the second part Schleiermacher directs his attention to the text of the Jacobi-Mendelssohn correspondence and "interweaves" his own observations, thereby amending the forty-four paragraphs and thus bringing the two parts closer together. *Spinozismus*, therefore, is not so much a formal essay as it is a series of extended notes, with no given order, on selected quotations from Jacobi's *Über die Lehre des Spinoza*. *Spinozistisches System*, a more formal essay than *Spinozismus*, is outlined according to three general categories: polemical theology, constructive theology, and cosmology. Schleiermacher's original intention seems to have been simply to discern which elements in Jacobi's presentation could genuinely be attributed to Spinoza's system and which were actually the consequences of Jacobi's own biases. The essay, however, quickly becomes constructive in character. Schleiermacher shifts from simple analysis to defending Spinoza against Jacobi's accusations and comparing Spinoza's system with those of Kant and Leibniz. In the process of attempting to locate the central principle in Spinoza's thought, Schleiermacher comes to reject Jacobi's contention that there is no "other system that agrees with Spinozism as well as Leibniz's system does" (*Spinoza Conversations*, 92). He argues instead that Spinoza stands against Leibniz and with Kant.

This is typical of Schleiermacher's overall tack. Even where he is in general agreement with Jacobi's concerns (e.g., in the struggle against sheer speculative thought, the espousal of a viable realism after Kant's transcendental idealism, the articulation of the notion of a living God), Schleiermacher reverses Jacobi's assessments of Spinoza. Spinoza is close to Kant, not Leibniz; Spinoza represents the opposite, not the essence, of rationalism and materialism; Spinoza's *natura naturans*, while not personal, is indeed a *living* God. Where Schleiermacher disagrees with Jacobi's concerns (e.g., on the issues of free will, final causes, a personal God), Schleiermacher defends Spinoza. He argues, in effect, that Spinoza actually stands in close alliance with Kant, that Leibniz was mostly wrong, and that Spinoza's thought (when translated into "modern" philosophical and scientific language) offers a more coherent system than does that of Leibniz, Kant, or Jacobi. The implication is that, using Spinoza, Kant can be taken in a direction other than that taken by Fichte.

Schleiermacher thus constructs a form of Spinozism that undercuts the strict opposition set up by Jacobi between, on the one side, atheism, panthe-

---

Schubert M. Ogden, ed. Philip E. Devenish and George L. Goodwin (Chicago: University of Chicago Press, 1989), 106–39.

27. These are found in Jacobi's letter to Mendelssohn, 26 April 1785. See Scholz, *Hauptschriften*, 141–65.

ism, and determinism, and on the other side, Christian theism and free will. It can be said to be *Spinozist* insofar as it fits Jacobi's definition of the "spirit of Spinozism" and insofar as he clearly identifies it with what he takes to be Spinoza's general worldview. It is clearly *neo-Spinozist* insofar as, with Herder and others, he translates Spinoza's *natura naturata* into a dynamic organism of forces and powers. It is *Spinozan* insofar as it does indeed contain certain parallels with Spinoza's philosophy, although it remains questionable whether Schleiermacher actually borrowed these principles from Spinoza or simply found confirmation and clarification in Spinoza. First and foremost, however, it is a *post-Kantian Spinozism* characterized by Schleiermacher's own rendition of *organic monism, ethical determinism, critical realism,* and *nonanthropomorphism;* as such, it is uniquely his own and can neither be strictly identified with Spinoza's system nor reduced to some crude form of pantheism. An important hermeneutical key to this post-Kantian Spinozism is his adaptation of the ancient dictum *One and All.*

An Organic Monism

"There has to be an Infinite, within which everything finite exists" (*Spinozistisches System,* 564). This *principle of inherency,* Schleiermacher decides, must be the chief proposition of Spinoza's system, that from which all its other principles are derived. In analyzing the implications of this principle, Schleiermacher seems to be driven by three concerns. His first concern is to convince Jacobi that Spinoza's philosophy represents a "middle way," not "pure atheism" (563). Toward that end, he needs to explain both Spinoza's rejection of an extramundane cause and his reformulation of the divine attributes. Schleiermacher's second concern is to show that Kant's critical philosophy stands in essential agreement with Spinoza's system. Toward that end, he draws an analogy between Kant's *noumenon* and Spinoza's *infinite substance,* arguing that "Kantianism seems to me, when it understands itself, to be on Spinoza's side" (570). Schleiermacher's third concern, inconsistent with his second, is to overcome Kant's dualisms through an application of Spinoza's monism. In the end, he winds up displacing Kant's noumenon with Spinoza's infinite and entirely replacing Kant's theory of individuality with one suggested by Spinoza. The result is an appropriation of Spinoza's uncompromising monism into his own form of organic monism.

According to Spinoza, there is only one substance, God, which as absolutely infinite is also indivisible. All else is a modification of this one substance. Therefore modes, or finite things, "can neither be, nor be conceived without substance; wherefore they can only be in the divine nature, and can only through it be conceived. For substances and modes form the sum total of existence, therefore, without God nothing can be, or be conceived."[28] God has an infinite number of attributes, only two of which we can know, namely, thought and extension. Extended substance is infinite and contains, contrary to what most say, no finite, separate parts. There are no separate substances that follow their own laws, rather all that comes to pass does so "solely through the laws of the infinite . . . necessity of [God's] essence."[29] Spinoza thus emphasizes a strict, causal monism that allows no violation of the unity of nature or nature's laws. Regarding *natura naturata* (finite existence), a thing "cannot exist or be conditioned to act, unless it be conditioned for existence and action by a cause other than itself, which also is finite, and has a conditioned existence."[30] There is an unbroken chain of like causes, which extends to infinity. Regarding *natura naturans* (God as a free cause), "God is the immanent, not the transitive, cause of all things."[31] This, of course, entails a fundamental reconceptualization of God and God's attributes. While Spinoza agrees with his scholastic predecessors in affirming that God is always active in

28. *Ethics*, 1.15, proof; Elwes 2:55. N.B. references to the *Ethics* of Spinoza are by part and proposition number, and "proof," "note," "corollary," or "definition," as needed.
29. *Ethics* 1.15, note; Elwes 2:59.
30. *Ethics* 1.28; Elwes 2:67.
31. *Ethics* 1.18, in *The Collected Works of Spinoza*, trans. and ed. Edwin Curley (Princeton, N.J.: Princeton University Press, 1985), 1:428. Curley's translation is hereafter cited as "Curley" by volume and page number. H. F. Hallett explains that "causality, according to Spinoza, is not a temporal relation, not such as was destructively analysed by Hume and defended by Kant; it consists not in regularity or temporal sequence but in agency immanent in deed. Empirical transeunt causes . . . possess something of this real power, though in a privative and derivative form . . . ; but so far as they are transeunt, so that the effect lies beyond the cause, they are evidently devoid of it. The causality of God suffers no such defect, and his effects, therefore, are integral with their cause, which is immanent in them. The two poles of divine creation, *Natura naturans* and *Natura naturata* are indiscerptible, though not co-ordinate, transeunt, or alternative. *Natura naturata* is dependent upon and subordinate to *Natura naturans*, which in turn necessarily actualizes itself as *Natura naturata*." "Substance and Its Modes," in *Spinoza: A Collection of Critical Essays*, ed. Marjorie Grene (Garden City, N.Y.: Anchor Books, 1973), 149. According to Alan Donagan, "Transient causes cause the happening of their effects. Since the causes of finite happenings are themselves happenings, every transient cause is itself an effect of another transient cause, as the laws of transient causation show by their form; for they all imply that, for every effect that has a transient cause, there is an infinite series of temporally prior transient causes and effects. It is otherwise with immanent causes. . . . Not only are self-caused things immanent causes, but nothing except what is self-caused can be an immanent cause for itself, no effect of an immanent cause can be an immanent cause." *Spinoza* (Chicago: University of Chicago Press, 1988), 63.

thought because of God's self-knowledge, he differs from them in claiming that God is also active in an infinite number of ways.[32] No longer is God's power or omnipotence understood anthropomorphically as the power of some divine ruler who considers various possibilities and then creates or annuls laws arbitrarily; the divine causality is better understood as an immanent power or force *(vīs* or *Kraft),* always already active in and through the laws of nature.

Jacobi says that the problem with this view of God is that it renders both the notion of an "absolute individual" (a real, individuated finite thing) and the notion of an "individual absolute" (an extramundane, intelligent God) meaningless.[33] In denying that God is an extramundane cause, Spinoza also denies final causes, or causation through thought; as a consequence understanding and will "are only subordinate powers, and belong to *created,* not to *creating,* nature" *(Spinozismus,* 545). In other words, the infinite is reduced to the finite, which is understood as a blind, mechanistic system of efficient causes, without purpose or freedom. Jacobi thus sets up another absolute opposition, insisting that "between the system of final causes and the system of purely efficient causes" there is no middle system (545). Although Schleiermacher claims to find nothing to fault in this assessment, he quickly points out a weakness in Jacobi's argument. In fact, in both *Spinozismus* and *Spinozistisches System,* he proceeds to defend Spinoza and to construct the "middle system" thought by Jacobi to be impossible.

As he struggled to understand and defend Spinoza, Schleiermacher appropriated three fundamental principles for his own thought: the principle of inherency, the principle *ex nihilo nihil fit,* and the principle of an infinitely active (living) God. Schleiermacher judged the principle *ex nihilo nihil fit* to be a corollary to the principle of inherency: "The infinite thing produces finite things and what belongs to them not in a transitive [*vorübergehende*] way, not insofar as one is destroyed through the others, but only insofar as they all belong to eternal unchanging existence. In the transitive way, as

---

32. "As it follows from the necessity of the divine nature (as all admit), that God understands himself, so also does it follow by the same necessity, that God performs infinite acts in infinite ways. . . . [Further] God's power is identical with God's essence in action; therefore it is as impossible for us to conceive God as not acting, as to conceive him as non-existent." *Ethics* 2.3, note; Elwes 2:84. See Harry Austryn Wolfson, *The Philosophy of Spinoza: Unfolding the Latent Processes of His Reasoning* (1934; reprint, New York: Schocken Books, 1969), 2:16–17.

33. "An absolute individual is just as impossible as an individual absolute." *Spinozismus,* 530.

changeable in the causal relation, finite things produce one another. Spinoza certainly depends not only on *ex nihilo nihil fit*, but also on *nihil ex nihilo fit;* each thing must have something from which it originates, that is, each thing must be viewed as an effect" (529; cf. *Spinozistisches System*, 575). There are two possible ways of viewing the infinite, "inasmuch as it is at one moment considered apart from finite things per se but in the next moment is represented in inextricable connection with them" (*Spinozistisches System*, 567). Although, due to his Kantian commitments, he is uncomfortable speaking of the "inner attributes" of God, Schleiermacher seems to go along with Spinoza's explanation. God has neither will (since no new relation to unchanging being can emerge) nor intellect (since God cannot be said to have representations or judgments). If in God will were separated from intellect, or potentiality from actuality, then it would follow that God could be inactive. Because potentialities cannot be conceived apart from actualities,[34] the notion of final causes must also be rejected. This became for Schleiermacher the most fundamental criterion of what we can properly say of God: however the "infinite Being" is conceived, it cannot be conceived as inactive. For Schleiermacher as for Spinoza, a reconceptualization of divine power and agency is needed. Schleiermacher, however, avoids the specifics of Spinoza's metaphysics and, in developing his own terminology, draws from critical philosophy and neo-Spinozism: we cannot speak of the inner attributes of God, only of the activity of God through the finite world; we cannot speak of substance, only of substantial force.

According to Schleiermacher, Spinoza's *principle of inherency* opposes two other possible explanations of the relationship between the Infinite and the finite: it rejects the theistic doctrine *creatio ex nihilo*, and it resists an atheistic positing of finite things existing solely in themselves. Schleiermacher wonders why Spinoza had not chosen this latter approach; he dismisses Jacobi's criticisms of it; but he does not himself explicitly pursue it. His assumption is that, had Spinoza accepted it, he would have had to "deny [the infinite's] existence completely, or to assign to it the role that Aristotle taught him [namely, that of eternal, immovable prime mover, remote from the world]" (*Spinozistisches System*, 564). Since Spinoza clearly had an infinite, and since his infinite is not the unrelated and transcendent prime mover of Aristotle, Schleiermacher concludes that this approach is clearly not applicable. Schleiermacher's interest therefore turns to the differences between the theistic notion of an extramundane cause

---

34. See *Spinozistisches System*, 563–64, and *Spinozismus*, 534. Cf. Spinoza, *Ethics*, 1.17, note; 1.32, cor. 2; and 1.33, note 2.

and Spinoza's principle that nothing comes from nothing. It is in regard to this controversy that he begins to dissolve Jacobi's association of Spinoza with Leibniz and to construct his own alliance with Spinoza and Kant.

Schleiermacher utterly rejects Leibnizian "monadology" in favor of Spinoza, whom he judges "to be successful in every respect" (569).[35] The theory of an infinite monad that created the finite world errs on at least three counts. If the infinite monad is viewed as having created the finite monads, then the theory violates the principle *ex nihilo nihil,* and Schleiermacher agrees with Spinoza that the unity of nature cannot be compromised. If the infinite monad is viewed as having "created the world from the finite monads, then they would still have been inactive before all and thus would have been as good as nonexistent" (570), and inactivity cannot be ascribed to the living God, nor does it have a place in Schleiermacher's organic universe. If, finally, one does grant an infinite monad, there is nothing on which to base the assumption that it would "not belong to the world" (570), hence such a claim would trespass the limits placed on reason.

Not only is Spinoza "victorious" over Leibniz, but he is also right where Kant is wrong. Despite Kant's decisive breakthrough in philosophy, he still makes the fundamental error of allowing "one to think of an unconditioned outside of the sequence [of conditioned things]" (570). If Kant really understood himself, Schleiermacher argues, he would recognize with Spinoza that there is nothing outside of the totality of the conditioned.[36] Kant certainly knows that his unconditioned can neither "sustain the eternal regress" nor "explain the beginning of finite things"; he also knows that his extramundane reality did not create the sense world. Schleiermacher concludes,

> Is this extramundane reality the cause of the sense world for Kant? By no means. The sense world is merely a product of the world of intelligence and of human beings, and the world of noumena is the cause of the sense world in precisely the same way that Spinoza's infinite substance is the cause of finite things. How is Kant therefore forced, or even merely occasioned, to accept the extramundane thing as cause of the world of intelligence? Does he know whether the category of causality is at all applicable to noumena? Does he know whether that world is a conditioned world, in addition to which he

---

35. In rejecting Leibniz, Schleiermacher is also rejecting the Leibnizian-Wolffian school he had been trained in at the University of Halle.

36. Spinoza, unlike the scholastics, did allow infinite series, as is evidenced by the refrain, "... and so on *ad infinitum.*" See Wolfson, *Philosophy of Spinoza,* 2:67–68.

needs to seek an unconditioned? Clearly, *Kant arrives at his conclusion through nothing other than an inconsequential residue of old dogmatism, and in this respect Kant is actually a Spinozist.* (*Spinozistisches System,* 570; emphasis added)

By nearly identifying Kant's noumena and Spinoza's infinite substance, Schleiermacher not only thinks he has achieved the sought-for union of their two systems, he also thinks he has found the solution to Kant's main dualism. Elsewhere he writes, "The Spinozistic relation of the noumenon to phenomenon nearly fuses with the Kantian" (*Spinozismus,* 526). In other words, just as the finite inheres in the infinite, so phenomena can be understood to inhere in noumena, or better, noumenon. Although he almost immediately recognizes the severe tension in his analogy, that very tension gives him an insight that will constitute one of the main elements of his post-Kantian Spinozism—namely, with Spinoza's monistic principle of inherency the Kantian dualism between phenomena and noumena can be resolved.

Given that the infinite is not outside the totality of the finite, what more can be said of this underlying reality? Once again, Schleiermacher proceeds to show, first, where Leibniz fails and, second, where Spinoza and Kant succeed. He wants to continue the comparison between Spinoza's infinite substance and Kant's noumenal world but is careful to remember that the comparison is a limited one, "otherwise Spinoza would have to have invented the critical philosophy before Kant" (*Spinozistisches System,* 573). The fundamental agreement nevertheless remains: "For both . . . the [infinite thing], the real and essential, the *a priori,* the *an sich* contains the essence and existence of the finite. . . . In completely different ways, both saw the necessity to attribute to the things of our perception another existence that lies outside our perception"(573). Kant's mistake rests in having violated his own critical philosophy by positing a plurality of noumena. According to Schleiermacher, we can only speak of the world as noumenon, that is, in the singular: *"the noumenon, the world as noumenon"* (574). In speaking of the world as noumenon, however, we cannot go any further, as Schleiermacher thinks Spinoza had, and maintain a positive unity. We would then be claiming more knowledge than we should, since we can have no representation of the unity of phenomena (*Spinozismus,* 526).

Where it becomes even more difficult to show agreement between his two philosophers, Schleiermacher redeems his comparison by translating Spinoza's "obscure terminology" into modern language. For instance, if Spinoza had had access to the principles of critical idealism, Schleiermacher says he would not have misplaced the attributes of thought and extension outside of ourselves; instead, he would have recognized them as being "in" us and as having to do with our way of thinking: "*The sole difference between Spinoza and Kant rests on this point*" (*Spinozistisches System*, 575; emphasis added). What here modernizes Spinoza's thought is the turn to the subject. Schleiermacher, however, is less successful in modernizing Jacobi's paragraph on "the inherence of finite things in the infinite" (575). On this point, he admits, Spinoza "seems completely to deviate from Kant, and in this expression the correctness of the comparison of his infinite with the Kantian noumenon seems to be destroyed" (575). Ideally, Schleiermacher's exposition of this paragraph should clarify three as yet unsolved problems in his comparison of Kant and Spinoza: the idea of inherency itself, the nature of the relation between the infinite and finite, and how, given that relationship, individuality can still be maintained.

After faltering somewhat in trying to address these points philosophically, Schleiermacher employs the metaphor of a tree.[37] And so, Schleiermacher says, "we come again to the Spinozistic relation" (*Spinozismus*, 527). The universe, here represented by a tree, is comprised of infinitely many things and of an infinite succession of these things. This fluctuation of becoming in the tree continues on to infinity; there is no cause outside of the tree. There are two attributes, fluidity and solidity, each of which has two modes. These attributes and their modes are related in various ways throughout the tree but always remain bound together. One can only be perceived through the varying relations to, and mixtures with, the other. The idea of individuality necessarily emerges where there is a cohering of motion, force, and mass, but the individual parts (e.g., bark, leaves, etc.) are never separate entities; they are always and only part of the whole and cannot be understood otherwise. Their boundaries are ambiguous and can have many configurations. At the same time, the whole cannot be known apart from the relations of the parts, only through the whole series of its parts. "In this way," Schleiermacher says, "finite things inhere in the infinite" (*Spinozistisches System*, 577).

This metaphor is not unlike that offered by Spinoza to explain the relationship between part and whole. In a letter to Oldenburg devoted entirely to this very issue, Spinoza argues that the mind works in such a way as to form separate ideas, and that a separate idea is then assumed to be a whole in itself, not the part that it really is. Consider, he says, a worm in the

---

37. He uses this metaphor twice: at this point in the argument in *Spinozistisches System* (576–77), and in his third annotation in *Spinozismus* (526–27).

blood system: "This little worm would live in the blood, in the same way as we live in a part of the universe, and would consider each particle of blood, not as a part, but as a whole. He would be unable to determine, how all the parts are modified by the general nature of blood, and are compelled by it to adapt themselves, so as to stand in a fixed relation to one another."[38] There are no real parts for Spinoza because everything is a mode of the infinite substance, which is indivisible.[39]

It is interesting that both Schleiermacher and Spinoza use an organism metaphor to explain the relation of part and whole. In doing so, both are making the same point—namely, what appears to be a part is really always and only connected and interdependent; it *is* insofar as it contributes to the whole, and the whole *is* only through its parts. There is, however, an important difference between Schleiermacher's understanding of organism and Spinoza's, and the difference is a crucial one. Schleiermacher's metaphor of the tree presupposes a modern notion of force that would have been foreign to Spinoza. For Spinoza, *force* or *power* (*vīs*) has to do with a thing's *conatus*, that by which a thing perseveres in its existence.[40] For Schleiermacher and the neo-Spinozists, who presume a Newtonian universe interpreted through subsequent discoveries in biology and chemistry, *force* (*Kraft*) has more to do with dynamic movement, active matter, gravitational pull, self-expansive power, electrical charge, chemical transformation, and the like.[41] This difference has far-reaching implications. First, it means that the neo-Spinozist understanding of the organic relation between part and whole allows for genuine plurality and novelty; in other words,

---

38. Spinoza to Oldenburg, n.d., 1665; Elwes 2:291. According to Lee C. Rice, "Spinoza's point is not that the worm *errs* in viewing the particles as individuals: the error lies rather in accounting for their individuation . . . in terms of isolation from the whole: the individuals are not substances in the traditional meaning of that term. . . . To be an individual is to be a center of action connected in various ways with a network of other individuals." "Spinoza on Individuation," in *Spinoza: Essays in Interpretation,* ed. Maurice Mandelbaum and Eugene Freeman (LaSalle, Ill.: Open Court, 1975), 205.

39. "The simplest bodies are separable only by abstraction from the complexes that they constitute." Lucia Lermond, *The Form of Man: Human Essence in Spinoza's "Ethic"* (Leiden: E. J. Brill, 1988), 26.

40. See *Ethics* 2.45, note; 3.7; and 4.4, proof; Elwes 2:118, 136, 191.

41. On the effects of science on the intellectual climate of the late eighteenth and early nineteenth centuries, see Brandt, *Philosophy of Schleiermacher;* Marjorie Hope Nicolson, *Newton Demands the Muse: Newton's "Opticks" and the Eighteenth Century Poets* (Princeton: Princeton University Press, 1946); H. B. Nisbet, *Herder and the Philosophy and History of Science* (Cambridge: The Modern Humanities Research Association, 1970); and Zammito, "Kant Against Eighteenth-Century Hylozoism," in *The Genesis of Kant's "Critique of Judgment,"* chap. 9.

it opens up to an aesthetic worldview. The whole is an infinite, dynamic, extended system of inherent causes and internal relations, which, because of its continual transformations, hangs together in an intricate, complex, and sometimes unpredictable fashion. As an aesthetic worldview, the neo-Spinozist organic understanding of the relation of part to whole includes aesthetic judgments based on criteria of complexity, harmony, and novelty. Second, the new understanding of force allows for genuine individuality in a way that Spinoza's does not because it abandons the substance-based interpretation of individuality. Schleiermacher thus agrees with Spinoza that finite things are not individual substances;[42] rather than deny the very concept of individuality, however, he redefines it in terms of relationality. Individuality is "nothing other than the cohesion, the identical combination of forces of a certain measure at a single point" (*Spinozistisches System*, 574). His development of this idea is a refutation of Kant's noumenological interpretation of individuality and personhood.

Whereas Schleiermacher's metaphor of the tree falls short of adequately addressing the three points mentioned above (the idea of inherency, the nature of the relation between the infinite and finite, and the status of the individual), he expands on these themes in greater depth toward the end of *Spinozismus*. In responding to Jacobi's charge that in Spinoza's system there are no real individuals, only the "I continue" of the sole substance and the ensuing struggle of everything finite "in and with the infinite" (*Spinozismus*, 547), Schleiermacher formulates what he takes to be the key question: "How and why do I view the objects which appear externally in experience as things which are separated from one another; how do I thereby come to connect the manifold to the objective unity, and on what does it depend, that I connect . . . these manifold together?" (548). Schleiermacher thinks that both Leibniz and Kant, in their attempts to argue for some objective ground of individuality, were unsuccessful in answering this question, and he is thus willing to follow Spinoza in the attempt to find subjective grounds of individuality. He begins his own explanation with a fairly straightforward account of what he judges to be Spinoza's position:

> The attributes of substance are thought and extension, and two modes necessarily belong to each of these. The substance is one and

---

42. Interestingly, Schleiermacher touches on this in *Über die Freiheit* when he undertakes a historical survey of the notion of freedom. The pantheist (he does not specify who might fit under this category) holds that "no particular substance lies at the basis of our faculties but that our whole ego belongs to the one necessary Substance. They therefore had to maintain that the grounds determining changes in our egos were to be encountered not in the substance they denied but in the Substance they granted." *On Freedom*, 105.

is separable only in thought, however in itself it is *re vera* inseparable. The parts into which you can analyze it in thought must be analogous, and each must have in itself all attributes of the substance—it must have in itself something extended and thinking, movement and rest, understanding and will—otherwise it could be no part of substance . . . ; hence, there are still no individuals. (550–51)

In a very subtle way, however, Schleiermacher's explanation of Spinoza becomes his own appropriation of Spinoza insofar as the relation between substance and its modes is described in terms of force, at least implicitly so. His focus is on movement: "The modifications of movement are not only the degree of [the substance] simply, but also the relation of the same to the mass" (551). An individual or "mass," therefore, would be a joining point of modifications of movement: "A determined mass must be therefore in each moment of the point of union more of these modifications, and so you call it an individual" (551). In other words, an individual is the result of a relation of forces. There is no noumenal substance behind an individual thing.

The association between "modification of movement" and "force" becomes explicit in the next annotation, where Schleiermacher responds to Jacobi's conclusion that "force is generally for [Spinoza] the living essence of God Godself" (554). Initially confused by this and thrown into self-doubt regarding his own interpretation, Schleiermacher modestly offers some "preliminary thoughts" (555). He explains that "the proper and differentiated life force (*Lebenskraft*) can be proper and differentiating in no other degree than that in which generally something proper and differentiating can accrue to things" (555). He then goes on to recognize this life force as belonging to infinite substance: "This proper force which accrues to finite things can therefore be wholly nothing other than the force of infinite substance which is communicated to each particle of the same" (555). Infinite substance, better understood as infinite force, is that which continually and actively manifests itself in and through the finite world by communicating its force to finite forces. This *Lebenskraft* cannot be conceived of as being in anyway outside of or apart from the finite world. It *is* insofar as it presents itself in the finite. Its activity is completely presented in the finite world, but it can in no way be reduced to the finite since it sustains finite things and determines whatever differentiation they have. Schleiermacher continues, the force of infinite substance "has the aim to bring about a certain perseverence of the mass in its character; just as certainly, however, the force of all remaining finite things combined has the aim to move each mass out of its character, and these forces constitute with each taken together only one and the same force" (555). What individuates finite things is continually changing, but such change only yields new finite forces, which are then reconfigured into other individuals. Hence Schleiermacher can say that the "scientific formulation" of the proposition that there can be no absolute individual is what he calls the "flux of all things" (531). The doctrine of the flux of things refers to how "an individual divides into or unites in itself several things, and also in that often something is said to exist, even though both matter and form have totally changed" (*Spinozistisches System,* 567). There are no gaps in the system of causes. All finite causes are interrelated, each depends on the infinite cause, and the infinite force is completely given in the whole of finite causes. Schleiermacher seems satisfied with this exposition; in a later annotation he writes, "The force and everything that belongs to it accrues from the eternity of substance" (*Spinozismus,* 557).

It is in terms of this concept of the universe as an active, living system dependent on the unceasing activity of the infinite that Schleiermacher's worldview can be said to be monistic: the infinite is found only in the totality of the flux of finite things; there is no individual or personal absolute outside this system of relations; the essence of things has to do with their relations; the human is no exception to the laws of nature. It is a monism modified by the critical philosophy of Kant and by the new science. This is what Schleiermacher means by his *transition to Spinozism:* "[Leibniz's] personal deity is now certainly no cause of the world. . . . This is thus the *true transition from Leibnizianism to Spinozism.* The withdrawal of this world soul into itself, the union of death with resurrection, I cannot conceive of other than as an alternating production and destruction of the organic components of the whole [*Umfang*], i.e., of finite, not absolute, individuals—thus, once more, Spinozism" (532; emphasis added). Schleiermacher admits that this system is to be contrasted with that of final causes. For Jacobi, however, such an admission, along with its denial of a personal God, can only mean determinism, that is to say, fatalism and atheism. For Schleiermacher, too, it means what he calls a *complete determinism.* Elsewhere, referring to himself in the third person, he writes, "He is satisfied with the name of determinist, provided only that he is promised that no proposition of any other determinist will be attributed to him that is not clearly contained in what he himself has said or will say" (*On Freedom,* 29).

A Complete Determinism

Jacobi assesses the ethical implications of Spinoza's "naturalism" as follows: "If there are only efficient but no final causes, then the thinking faculty has merely the role of spectator in all of nature; its only role is to accompany the mechanism of efficient powers" (*Spinozismus*, 527). Because it allows no causation through thought, naturalism necessarily yields "straightforward *unreserved* fatalism."[43] Yet this assessment, Schleiermacher contends, marks where Jacobi is most wrong in his interpretation and where Spinoza prevails. Schleiermacher ventures "to prove the contrary out of Spinoza's propositions" (*Spinozismus*, 529) by explaining Spinoza's position on final causes and then by showing how this does not lead to fatalism. In the process, he returns to the problem of the Kantian gap between freedom and desire,[44] and he finds in Spinoza's teaching on the relation between thought and extension not only another corrective to Kant, but also a confirmation and clarification of the ethical determinism he had already begun to develop two years earlier in *Über die Freiheit*.

There are, for Spinoza, no final causes for the same reason that there is no extramundane cause: they would violate the principle *ex nihilo nihil*.[45] In the relationship of finite things, everything must have a like cause, or a relation of like causes, from which it comes forth. Thus a transformation in thought cannot originate in extension, nor can a transformation in extension be attributed to an act of thought. The concern, once again, is that nothing arbitrary be thought to arise that would annul the continuum of

---

43. F. H. Jacobi, *David Hume über den Glauben, oder Idealismus und Realismus* (Breslau, 1787; facsimile edition, New York: Garland Publishing, 1983), Preface to the 1815 edition, p. 116.

44. For more on this problem, see Paul Guyer, "Feeling and Freedom: Kant on Aesthetics and Morality," *The Journal of Aesthetics and Art Criticism* 48 (1990): 137–46.

45. I offer here Schleiermacher's summary. For Spinoza's own position, see *Ethics*, appendix to part 1, where he argues that the common notion of final causes arose from the assumption that "God made all things for man," from the need to justify narrow prejudices of good and bad, and from ignorance regarding the causes of things. "In their endeavour to show that nature does nothing in vain, i.e., nothing which is useless to man, they only seem to have demonstrated that nature, the gods, and men are all mad together." Elwes 2:76. To counter such ignorance and self-centeredness, Spinoza insists "that nature has no particular goal in view, and that final causes are mere human figments." Elwes 2:77. Final causes—along with notions of goodness, badness, beauty, deformity—are abstract notions, that is, "mere modes of imagining, and do not indicate the true nature of anything, but only the constitution of the imagination." Elwes 2:80. The perfection, or reality, of things is determined "only from their own nature and power." Elwes 2:81.

nature. Schleiermacher notes that Spinoza does acknowledge final causes *if* such causes be understood as psychological concepts[46] or as some transcendental notion, such as goodness.[47] Whatever *direction* an act or transformation may have results from its various relations and causal operations: "The action receives direction only when it, as it were, goes through other things; the number of these things determines their degree, while their connection determines their direction in the most real sense" (536). Direction, in other words, does not come from some intention or end outside these finite causes. As Schleiermacher's explanation implies, the intensity of direction is proportionate to the degree of complexity in relations.

Given this discussion alone, it is not at all clear the degree to which Schleiermacher follows Spinoza in denying final causes. Elsewhere, both in his earlier essay *Über die Freiheit* (1792) and in his famous *Reden über die Religion* (1799), he does discuss the notion of final causes at some length.[48] If these other discussions are taken into account, certain key principles can be recognized that lend insight into the present discussion. For instance, the principle *ex nihilo nihil* remains a constant in Schleiermacher's understanding of causality, just as the determination of things by their relations with other things remains fundamental to his views of nature and of the ethical life. It could even be said that he is similar to Spinoza in understanding final causes as psychological, although for Schleiermacher "psychological" is not necessarily a derogatory term. Indeed, as Albert L. Blackwell illustrates so well, he will come to hold a very subtle and powerful understanding of the role of religious imagination.[49] Nevertheless, in these two essays on Spinoza Schleiermacher remains on the whole noncommittal concerning final causes.

What is clear, however, is his conviction that Spinoza's denial of final causes does not result in fatalism. Jacobi, he writes, "had a natural tendency to make the fatalism of Spinoza as crass as possible" (*Spinozistisches System*, 580). Everything is not simply reducible to the mechanisms of the body, because there is a parallelism between thought and extension. Although Schleiermacher does not himself use the term *parallelism,* the basic

---

46. "The operation of a representation is never *ad extra*, and the mechanism that becomes real through its concepts ... is only a psychological one. Thus far certainly Spinoza too concedes final causes." *Spinozismus,* 532.

47. "The idea of design, intention and goodness finds no place here, outside of a transcendental goodness that consists purely in the completeness that, as it happens, is essential to the infinite." Ibid., 534.

48. See *On Freedom,* 137ff.; *Reden,* trans. Crouter, 98, 126, 147.

49. See Blackwell, *Schleiermacher's Early Philosophy of Life,* 205–95.

concept itself is not new to him. Indeed, he had already formulated his own version of it in *Über die Freiheit,* where he argued that there is what he referred to as an "interchange" (*Abwechseln*), "reciprocity" (*Wechselwirkung*), or "interconnection" (*Zusammenhang*) between the succession of ideas and the laws governing motion. "The series, according to both laws of change, continue uninterrupted alongside one another, but *through freedom* reciprocally *intermesh* and are brought into connection" (*On Freedom,* 133). In both series the same change occurs, albeit "regarded from another point of view and in another relationship" (132–33). The rules of determinism still hold, but freedom is not thereby forfeited. The difference between fatalism and determinism is that whereas for the former "the subject is unalterably determined to the action," for the latter "the subject *is brought to* the action" (107). An action arises out of the preceding series of actions (which coinheres with a preceding series of concepts) and out of the system of forces that come to bear in the present situation; freedom is expressed through the manner in which we actively appropriate both the preceding series and the present situation, relating them to each other and bringing thought and action to a point of coinherence.

Schleiermacher continues these same themes in *Spinozismus* and *Spinozistisches System,* except that in appropriating Spinoza's theory of parallelism he gives his own position more clarity and definition. Schleiermacher explains that in Spinoza's theory of parallelism, every transformation, whether of thought or of extension, includes a new relation to the other. That is, everything finite is seen from two sides, thought and extension, so that everything that happens in extension takes place in consciousness, and, conversely, thinking matter is extended matter. There is, Schleiermacher says, a *necessary coincidence* between the two even though there is no causal relation between them: "Because both refer to the *whole relationship,* everything that is in the presentation is also in the representation, and everything that is in the representation is in the presentation. I am therefore justified in saying: Thought and sensation are nothing but concepts of extension, motion and velocity; I could also say, extension, velocity and motion are nothing other than presentation of mind, volition and faculty. This is how I think in this respect Spinoza wants to have his system understood" (*Spinozismus,* 530; emphasis added).[50] The key to Schleiermacher's appropriation of Spinoza's theory of parallelism is found in the phrase *whole*

---

50. Spinoza explains the matter more succinctly: "Mind and body are one and the same thing, conceived first under the attribute of thought, secondly, under the attribute of extension." *Ethics,* 3.2, note; Elwes 2:131. Cf. *Ethics* 2.7.

relationship, which expresses the monistic and deterministic worldview, although Spinoza's monism and determinism are modified through the idea of force (velocity and motion). This view, as Schleiermacher adapts it, rejects the dualism implied by Kant's notion of transcendental freedom and Jacobi's notion of free will. There is no deep gulf between mind and body, freedom and desire, thought and matter, but that is not to say, contrary to Jacobi's interpretation, that there is a reduction of everything to matter. Matter is never a static "stuff," and thought is never an isolated idea; rather, matter becomes spiritualized and thought is always embodied. Extension, to repeat Schleiermacher's statement, is always the "presentation of mind." Jacobi is therefore too one-sided in presuming that for Spinoza extension is only a thing and thought only a copy of a thing, for if "both are bound up with each other in the strictest sense," then it follows that "what occurs in thought must also occur in extension" (*Spinozistisches System,* 578). In a complete determinism, thought is not secondary or passive, yet neither is it solely determinative.

When translated from metaphysics into morality (reflecting Jacobi's real reason for rejecting Spinoza), the parallelism between thought and extension means that the mind is not a mere "spectator" of the body. There is a relationship, although not a direct causal one, between reason and action. A representation (the idea of a presentation, in this case, of an action) can be followed by a judgment. This alone, however, cannot be the cause of a transformation in act: "Representation does not extend to the actual action in the strictest sense of the word [i.e., causality] but surely it extends to the *resolution* [*Entschluß*], insofar as it is thought as pure judgment and embraces pain and pleasure in itself" (*Spinozismus,* 528; emphasis added). This stands in direct opposition to Kant's position, which Zammito summarizes: "Purpose is the *relation* between a concept and an object whereby the concept acts as cause of the actuality (existence) of the object."[51] For Schleiermacher, Kant's position is really a violation of truly practical reason since the concept would be a noumenal cause. Although both Kant and Jacobi suppose that the only alternative would be the reduction of concepts to matter, Schleiermacher insists there is indeed another alternative, one that calls for a new way of viewing the relation between concept (representation) and act or desire (presentation). The alternative view he has in

---

51. Zammito, *Genesis of Kant's "Critique of Judgment,"* 91. In the third *Critique* Kant writes, "An end is the object of a concept so far as this concept is regarded as the cause of the object (the real ground of its possibility); and the causality of a *concept* in respect of its Object is finality." *The Critique of Judgement,* part 1, trans. James Creed Meredith (Oxford and New York: Oxford University Press, 1986), 61.

mind centers on what Schleiermacher calls *resolution,* which is judgment combined with desire. Because of resolution, "morality loses nothing" (*Spinozismus,* 530). Judgment, as the moral expression of reason, can still inform action, but it never functions as a separate faculty beyond the system of determining conditions. Our actions, since they are never isolated, are determined by preceding and presently existing sets of relations, and our judgments are never divorced from affections and desires.

Schleiermacher's appeal to the term *Entschluß* is another example of how his encounter with Spinoza's thought lends clarity and definition to his own ethical determinism. In *Über die Freiheit* Schleiermacher wrote about a unifying activity between the faculty of representation and the faculty of desire, between thought and action, between freedom and desire; at that point, he had termed this joining activity *Gefühl.* In *Spinozismus* and *Spinozistisches System,* he substitutes the term *Gefühl* with *Entschluß,* but the moral activity he is describing remains essentially the same. This shift is evidently due to his being influenced by Spinoza's terminology: Spinoza's *decretum* (decision) is translated by Jacobi as *Entschluß* (decision or resolution). The difference between the earlier essay on freedom and the two essays on Spinoza is that Spinoza's theory of parallelism does lend Schleiermacher's deterministic ethics more definite contours. *Entschluß,* developed against the backdrop of Spinoza's theory of parallelism, involves a complete and necessary coincidence between the series of representations/ideas and the series of presentations/actions, whereas in its earlier rendition as *Gefühl* the coinherence of the two series depended on the degree to which the moral agent cultivates and exercizes the capacity for moral discernment.

Schleiermacher says that it is because of *Entschluß* that "Spinoza was a fatalist in no other understanding than in that which I call *complete determinism*" (532; emphasis added). By *determinism* he means that everything, including thought, must have preceding and similar causes. In other words, there is no noumenal cause, such as transcendental freedom, that is immune to the causal nexus. In describing this determinism as *complete* (*volkommen*), Schleiermacher underscores that our choices always involve every aspect of our experience and thus involve desire along with judgment.[52] Together, desire and judgment determine our moral character in that they are expressions of our *impulses* (*Triebe*), which in turn are the

---

52. *Vollkommen* could also be translated as "perfect" insofar as it alludes to the ethics of perfectibility that Schleiermacher espouses. As John Wallhauser explains it, Schleiermacher seeks a mediating third type of ethics to correct the dangers posed by, on the one hand, a merely descriptive ethic of feeling (Aristotle) and, on the other hand, a sheerly normative ethic of obligation (Kant, Fichte). The preferred third type (represented by Plato and Spinoza)

unique combination of various forces and modes of the underlying force (*Grundkraft*) that come together at a particular point in a particular time.⁵³ The will, Schleiermacher informs Jacobi, is the intellect occupied with impulse.⁵⁴ In other words, considered as a separate faculty, there is no will at all, much less a free one. Whereas "Leibniz declares desire as the true product of the will, Spinoza [declares it to be] actually only the consciousness of striving" (*Spinozismus*, 532). Because we are conscious of our actions, Spinoza writes, we form a general idea—namely, *will*—"whereby we explain all particular volitions."⁵⁵ To understand this is to know the difference, for both Schleiermacher and Spinoza, between sophistry and science. Schleiermacher quotes Jacobi, who in turn is paraphrasing Spinoza in saying that *will* "is a clumsy word which excites sophists and annoys true scientists" (*Spinozismus*, 536).

This understanding of *will* is essential for Schleiermacher's post-Kantian Spinozism, for Schleiermacher purposely appropriates what he takes to be Spinoza's intention into the modern mindset and language. He suggests that Spinoza, dissatisfied with the understanding of will in his own day, would be at home in late-eighteenth-century philosophical discourse: "Would Spinoza passionately disclaim our modern terminology (faculty of representation and faculty of desire)? By no means. At that time faculty (*Vermögen*) and power (*Kraft*) were confused, and faculty was applied to the ground of explanation, to the true cause of the actuality of being-able-to" (536). Once again, he discerns no separate faculty that can bring about deliberate actions apart from other relations, apart from our imagination, our desire, our impulses—all of which are expressions of the cohesion of underlying powers and forces. Schleiermacher thus judges Kant's transcendental freedom to be unacceptable and opts instead for his own appropriation of Spinoza's qualified understanding of freedom. Like Spinoza, Schleiermacher sees the ethical life as, to a significant degree at least, the

---

unifies the first two. According to Wallhauser, "Schleiermacher opposes an ethics derived from the concrete given as well as one derived from an abstract transcendence of reason. The empirical and the rational need to be brought into harmonious relation with one another. Schleiermacher's alternative to those traditions is an ethics of the indwelling of reason in nature, transforming and elevating nature into new being." "Schleiermacher's Critique of Ethical Reason: Toward a Systematic Ethics," *Journal of Religious Ethics* 17, no. 3 (Fall 1988): 30.

53. See *Spinozismus*, 537. See also *Spinozistisches System*, 578: "Every individual thing is an aggregate of different mixtures of immediate and mediated modes in relation to all other similar things."

54. See *Spinozismus*, 537.

55. *Ethics*, 2.49, note; Elwes 2:124. Cf. *Ethics* 3.2, note.

attempt to describe, understand, and order systems of relations and causes without pretending to extricate oneself from them. The difference between Spinoza and Schleiermacher is yet again to be found in the latter's appeal to *force*. The moral agent, like the rest of the organic world, is best described in terms of the relation of forces, except that forces are now identified as desires, concepts, and their interrelations.

At issue is the concept of causality itself. Spinoza offers Schleiermacher a sophisticated understanding that, once modernized, fits well with his organic monism. Kant and Jacobi, whatever their differences, share a view of nature as a mechanistic system in which causality is primarily efficient (external, mechanical). Jacobi, for instance, refers to "the mechanism of efficient powers," which stands over and against final causes (527). Likewise, Kant recognizes only two types of causality, *efficient* (causality through the "mere mechanical laws of nature"[56]) and *final* (causality "determined by [an agent's] idea of a whole made possible through that idea"[57]). Needless to say, Kant subordinates efficient causes to final causes. In the end, however, Kant's transcendental freedom, intended to be a final cause, really acts as an efficient cause.[58] Schleiermacher thus views Kant and Jacobi as sharing with the fatalists a mechanistic, blind view of nature, except that, unlike the fatalists, they place the natural causal system under the purview of thought.

With the development of his organic monism, Schleiermacher has already rejected a mechanical view of nature and along with it a simplistic, binary understanding of causality. Although he does not use the language of causality, an understanding of a complex, organic system of causation is implied in his appropriation of what he terms Spinoza's principle of inherency and its concomitant principle of the flux of all things. To say all finite things inhere in the infinite is to say the infinite is the *immanent* cause of everything finite. To refer to the flux of all things is to acknowledge that there are internal and external, remote and immediate causes. In modernizing Spinoza's principles through the notion of force, Schleiermacher also translates the language of causality into the language of force. Change occurs,

---

56. Immanuel Kant, *Critique of Judgement*, part 2, 42.
57. Ibid., 20–21.
58. According to Kant, "Thus reason, which with its ideas always became transcendent when proceeding in a speculative manner, can be given for the first time an objective, although still only practical, reality; its transcendent use is changed into an immanent use, whereby reason becomes, in the field of experience, *an efficient cause through ideas.*" *Critique of Practical Reason*, trans. Lewis White Beck (New York: Liberal Arts Press, 1956), 49, emphasis added.

and individuals are formed, neither through purely external efficient causes nor through intervening final causes, but through the exchange of force. The system of forces is such that there is never just one cause; rather, there is a nexus of causes, and every cause or force is dependent on the infinite, grounding force.

Schleiermacher extends this view of causality as force to the field of moral activity. For him, an organic monism *is* a complete determinism, only from a different point of view. Hence, what is true of a finite thing is also true of a moral action, is also true of a moral agent: "The so-called essence of things—that by which we mark out their identity—is only a relationship" (*Spinozistisches System*, 567–68). Critics of ethical determinism conclude that a moral anthropology such as this degrades or loses the human individual, the moral person. Kant needed freedom (a freedom, in part, from desire) to retain a strong sense of individuality over against the forces of nature; Fichte appealed to the ego as creator of nature and its forces; Jacobi insisted on a personal God who is not a passive observer of the mechanisms of nature. Against such views, Schleiermacher says that "reason individualizes us least of all" (574). Hence the question of individuation returns, although this time it is more specific. The concern has to do with the nature of moral personhood. Schleiermacher extends his organic monism to moral anthropology and offers a monistic interpretation of human nature that views life as an organic whole and seeks integration of the many aspects that compose an individual's life.

Just as, when discussing the problem of individuation in general, Schleiermacher uses Spinoza in order to undermine a substance-based understanding of individuality, so he also uses Spinoza to correct Kant's noumenological concept of a person, most notably a moral person. Because Kant insisted that the human person is not subject to the rules of the natural causal system, his moral theory depends on a philosophical anthropology that distinguishes between the noumenological and phenomenological selves. According to Kant, Schleiermacher says, the phenomenological person is defined by the "unity of self-consciousness," whereas the noumenological person is defined by an "identity of substance" (*Spinozismus*, 542). Kant's notion of transcendental freedom depends on this distinction. Yet the result is another untenable dualism. Schleiermacher offers an alternative anthropology: "There is, however, also yet another possible case, namely, that no noumenon grounds the I of consciousness for itself alone, rather this I is only a fleeting, solely time-dependent quality of an other thing. This case strikes a chord more in the Spinozistic [teachings]—The noumenological concept of personality is therefore an empty concept and what remains left over is only the phenomenological" (542–43). Schleiermacher thus returns to an earlier theme: Kant's moral philosophy violates the principles of critical philosophy insofar as it is closer to theoretical reason than to truly practical reason. With Spinoza he insists that human nature is no exception to nature's nature. To be truly practical, our processes of moral discernment must be understood to operate in the sphere of natural causation, and therefore the importance of desires must be acknowledged: "By no means, however, can I now also conclude further: each moral subject must be a person in noumenological meaning, since action in accordance with laws, and so being an end in itself, and proposing ends for oneself, [all this] is nothing other than a certain identity of the rules of desire" (544). This reference to the "rules of desire" marks Schleiermacher's most rebellious stance against Kant. For Kant, there is no desire or feeling that lies beyond the force of the moral law;[59] freedom is the power of will to intervene in and alter the causal system of desires. For Schleiermacher, *will*, *maxims*, and *ends* are abstractions from fundamental desires.[60] Unless desire is included as an integral part of the process of moral discernment, rather than as a hindrance to it, the question of how we can be motivated to act according to the law or to choose the good can never be answered.

In defending Spinoza against Jacobi's charge of fatalism, Schleiermacher therefore finds an ally in his attempt to repair the gaps in Kant's philosophy—that between phenomena and noumena, and that between desire and freedom. With regard to his ethical theory, Spinoza's influence was not such that his philosophical system converted Schleiermacher to determinism, since Schleiermacher had already arrived at that position when, as a student, he ran up against the limitations of Kant's moral anthropology. Hence in *Über die Freiheit*, written one to three years before he reread Jacobi's *Über die Lehre des Spinoza*, Schleiermacher had already distinguished determinism from fatalism and defended it against criticisms by "freewillers," offered a highly developed epistemological theory of the relation between moral concepts and actions, abandoned Kant's noumenological understanding of the moral agent, and fundamentally redefined freedom in terms compatible with the natural causal system. His encounter with Spinoza's

---

59. According to Kant, "no kind of feeling, (even) under the name of a practical or moral feeling, may be assumed as prior to the moral law and as its basis." *Critique of Practical Reason*, 77. "The moral law determines the will directly and objectively in the judgment of reason. Freedom, the causality of which is determinable merely through the law, consists, however, only in the fact that it limits all inclinations, including self-esteem, to the condition of obedience to its pure law." Ibid., 81.
60. See *Spinozismus*, 537; cf. *On Freedom*, 17–18, 74.

determinism confirmed many of the directions his reflections had already taken, and he was able to develop these reflections further through an adaptation of some of Spinoza's terminology (e.g., *Entschluß*) as well as an appropriation of some underlying philosophical principles (e.g., parallelism). Moreover, Spinoza seemed to supply him with a sophisticated understanding of causality, which he used to counter Kant's rather simplistic understanding of freedom as an efficient cause. There is, however, one essential point that Spinoza's philosophy introduced to Schleiermacher's monism and determinism that is not found in the essays predating *Spinozismus* and *Spinozistisches System*—namely, the situating of the finite in the infinite.[61] Schleiermacher's encounter with Spinoza gave him an ontological framework that allowed him to develop his monistic and deterministic worldview into a post-Kantian realism and ultimately led him back to theological questions.

Realism and the Feeling for Being

The test case for the transition to Spinozism lies in the claim that there cannot be an individual absolute, which is itself another formulation of the chief proposition, "*There has to be an Infinite, within which everything else exists*" (*Spinozistisches System*, 564). The problem, Schleiermacher concedes, is that this proposition would seem to derive the infinite from our ideas. In other words, it can be mistaken as a form of idealism:

> To be sure, it is quite likely that [Spinoza] ran into the confusion of the logical ground with the real ground, and therefore of logical being for real being, for which so many other philosophers are blamed. (564)

> Finally, the proposition that the order and interconnection of things is the very same as the interconnection and order of concepts and vice versa seems to facilitate this confusion [between thought and reality] even more. (565)

> [O]ne can easily be misled to return to this opinion: Spinoza's infinite thing is only a general thing. (568)

---

61. In the essays that predate *Spinozismus* and *Spinozistisches System* Schleiermacher criticized Kant for making God and immortality postulates of practical reason, thus making religion subservient to morality. See *Über das höchste Gut* (1789) and *An Cecilie* (1790), in *KGA* 1/1:81–128 and 189–212.

Schleiermacher insists that Spinoza neither confuses the two kinds of connection (he only "substitutes one for the other") nor deduces the real world from the logical. "The logical being of things must be derived out of movement and rest, and it consists in the way this derivation and connection is carried out" (566); "intelligence could not . . . have become the cause of substance" (*Spinozismus*, 535). Such explanations, however, similar to those given for the denial of an extramundane cause and of free will, do not sufficiently address the issue at hand.

A better explanation can be found in Schleiermacher's insistence that Spinoza's infinite, which cannot be found outside the totality of finite things, is not an empty abstraction, a "general thing." Since the predicate of uniqueness does not apply, no determinate concept of God can be formed: "Spinoza's refusal to call God an individual came from the fact that this would have led again to the idea of distinguishing God from finite things and thinking of God outside of finite things" (*Spinozistisches System*, 569). Considered in the abstract, apart from finite things, the infinite would thus seem to be "nothing but the being shared by them, the totally indeterminate [being], pure matter, as Jacobi says" (567). For Jacobi (as for Kant) this totally indeterminate substance of Spinoza is nothing more than some lifeless substrate of finite things. Schleiermacher prefers to refer to Spinoza's infinite as "unrepresentable matter" (*die unvorstellbare Materie*), for as he understands Spinoza, it is neither an object of perception nor a general concept.[62] This preference in terminology is based on a distinction between *content* (according to which the Infinite is called "unrepresentable matter") and *form* (according to which it is called "the unconditioned"). His appeal to this distinction is another attempt on Schleiermacher's part to interpret Spinoza through Kantian terminology, an attempt which Meckenstock rightly assesses as being "misleading and blurred."[63] Yet it is important to discern Schleiermacher's intention here, however flawed his execution. In

---

62. He also says at this point that it cannot be intuited, which seems to contradict what he says in *Spinozismus*. Probably what he is rejecting here is the possibility of having a sensible intuition, as opposed to an intellectual intuition, of the infinite. For the many ways in which the term "intuition" was used in late-eighteenth-century Germany, see Moltke S. Gram, "Intellectual Intuition: The Continuity Thesis," *Journal of the History of Ideas* 42 (1981): 287–304.

63. Meckenstock, *Deterministische Ethik*, 206. Beiser offers a similar assessment of Reinhold's attempt to improve Kant's theory of representation by focusing on the distinction between form and content. See *Fate of Reason*, 255. At the beginning of his Transcendental Aesthetic, Kant writes, "That in the appearance which corresponds to sensation I term its *matter;* but that which so determines the manifold of appearance that it allows of being ordered in certain relation, I term the *form* of appearance." *Critique of Pure Reason*, trans. Norman Kemp Smith (New York: St. Martin's Press, 1965), 65–66.

referring to the distinction between content and form, he reiterates his earlier point that the "real ground" in Spinoza is not derived from the "logical ground"; he does this by stressing the independence of the "object" or "matter" (the concretely existing entity) from the form it acquires in the representing subject. Of course, the infinite is not an object per se—not only is it not an object in the series of conditioned things, it is also not an infinite object outside of that series. Hence the form it takes is the negation of any specific form—it is the "unconditioned."

The infinite "is not to be found outside the sequence [of finite things], but only in the entire totality of it" (*Spinozistisches System*, 567). Mendelssohn, Schleiermacher complains, "could not comprehend that nothing subsists outside of finite things and that nonetheless only the Infinite really subsists. He means that finite things would have real existence, and their *sum* [*Zusammen*], as he calls the Infinite, much against the spirit of Spinoza, could only be something collective and thus could only exist in a thinking subject" (*Spinozismus*, 535). This is not a fair reading of Mendelssohn, for it is taken from a part of a letter in which Mendelssohn was trying to understand what Jacobi was saying of Spinoza.[64] What is important for present purposes, however, is Schleiermacher's interpretation of *Zusammen* and his contrasting it with *Inbegriff* (totality) and *Umfang* (encompassing whole). In these essays on Spinoza, both terms, *Inbegriff* and *Umfang*, refer to an actual, organic, complex, intricate, and living whole. Conceptually, the sheer physicality of it, its embodiment, is based on forces and powers, not substance. Recall that Schleiermacher has already introduced the term *Umfang* in speaking of the transition from a personal godhead to Spinozism: "The withdrawal of this world soul into itself, the union of death with resurrection, I cannot conceive of other than as an alternating production and destruction of the *organic components of the whole* [*Umfang*], i.e., of finite, not absolute, individuals—thus, once more, Spinozism" (*Spinozismus*, 532; emphasis added). As this passage suggests, the *Umfang* is not a product of the mind but has real existence prior to it; it is the unifying ground of the organic world, of the causal nexus that includes the operations of the mind. Contrary to what Jacobi and Kant think, it is not some lifeless substrate but is living in the most essential way. *Inbegriff* likewise means totality, but again its grounding is real, not just ideal; it is prior to its parts; *Inbegriff* means the embodiment, the organic unity of all finite

---

64. See *Spinoza Conversations*, 113–14. According to Zammito, Mendelssohn is attempting to illustrate where Jacobi misrepresents Spinoza. See *Genesis of Kant's "Critique of Judgment,"* 232.

things and transformations, the actually existing unconditioned. As opposed to this, *Zusammen* means sum, a mere collective or abstraction the mind forms out of the manifold of finite things.[65] The difference, therefore, between *Umfang* and *Inbegriff*, on the one hand, and *Zusammen*, on the other, is fundamentally the difference between a form of critical realism and subjective idealism, and it presses home the distinction between the finite and the infinite. The finite cannot constitute a totality without the infinite, nor can finite things exist in themselves. The actually existing infinite, found only in the totality, embodiment, or whole of finite existence, is manifested in both thought and extension and is the ground of the continuum between them.

The realism Schleiermacher is developing here is meant to be post-Kantian, which is to say in part that it is not a naive realism that presupposes the world *is* just as we experience it to be. Recall that he sees the sole difference between Kant and Spinoza as resting in the fact that Spinoza understood space and time to be "outside" us, rather than "in" us as the attributes of thought and extension. In applying Kantian insight to Spinoza, Schleiermacher undertakes his own constructive thought:

> If one now replaces attributes of the divinity with characteristics of the beholder, then this means that absolute matter is able to take the form of every *faculty of representation;* it possesses along with complete immediate unrepresentability an infinite (mediate) representability. What Hemsterhuis and with him Jacobi philosophize about the different views of the world according to the *receptivity of the organs* belongs to just this point. They are both quite near to critical idealism on this issue without knowing it. (*Spinozistisches System*, 575; emphasis added)[66]

The beginning of this passage represents Schleiermacher's first actual attempt to speak theologically with the limits set by critical philosophy with-

---

65. The distinction being made here was a fairly common one for the time, yet once again Schleiermacher appropriates it through an unlikely combination of disparate interpretations. An aggregate or composite is that in which the parts can exist without the whole, and although the whole needs parts in order to be what it is, it does not need particular parts. In other words, there are no necessary connections between the parts themselves or between the parts and the whole. A whole, or *totum*, however, is that in which the parts cannot exist without the whole, and the whole cannot exist without those particular parts. There is a necessary and internal connection, such that parts and whole define each other.

66. Jacobi enlisted François Hemsterhuis (1721–90) in his fight against Spinozism by giving Lessing three of his books to read. To Jacobi's disappointment, Lessing found Hemster-

out reducing God, as he thought Kant had, to being a mere postulate of practical reason. Schleiermacher's concern is to counter Jacobi's claim that if the infinite lacks determinateness and individuality, then our representations of it must really be representations of nothingness.[67] Insofar as the infinite is not an individual absolute, it is not an object and therefore cannot be delineated as objects can be because it is not conditioned as objects are conditioned. Our relation to it is not one of subject to object but one of inherency or, better, immediacy. And what is immediate to us, what is not an object of perception, is not able to be represented by us (although it can be *felt* or *intuited*). Hence it has "complete immediate unrepresentability." Insofar as the infinite is actively present in everything finite, it is also mediated to us through finite things, and it inevitably, albeit always inaccurately, takes on the form of the conditioned in our faculty of representation. For example, we attribute to the ground force the characteristics of the forces that depend on it, but the ground force can never be identified with or limited by any particular force. As universally present to and mediated through the finite, it can take on infinite representations, none of which suffices. Elsewhere Schleiermacher says that it has no representation itself because all representations subsist in it (*Spinozistisches System*, 567); it is the condition of the possibility of any representation.

Meckenstock criticizes this passage as an example of how Schleiermacher's theology is at the service of his cosmology,[68] but Schleiermacher's point here is not to find an explanation for the finite world. On the contrary, given the (Spinozan) principle of inherency, and given the (Kantian) limits placed on reason, his point is to explore how we may be said to experience the infinite and how that experience is related to our faculty of representation. His answer is found in the second part of the passage, namely in the phrase *receptivity of the organs,* which he attributes to Jacobi and Hemsterhuis. In appealing to this phrase he emphasizes both that we exist in a state of receptivity to "real being," and that the point of contact is an organic one. This receptivity of the organs is therefore part of his critical realism. In relation to the finite, it expresses the continuum between the self and nature. Impressions are received from the outside, and we are so

---

huis's *Aristée* (1779) to be "pure Spinozism." *Spinoza Conversations*, 99. Hemsterhuis emphasized the *organe moral* and *sentiment interne*. See Heinz Moenkemeyer, *François Hemsterhuis* (Boston: Twayne Publishers, 1975). Hemsterhuis was best known for his Platonism.

67. See George Di Giovanni, "From Jacobi's Philosophical Novel to Fichte's Idealism: Some Comments on the 1789–99 'Atheism Dispute,'" *Journal of the History of Philosophy* 27 (January 1989): 80, 98.

68. See Meckenstock, *Deterministische Ethik*, 209; cf. 202, 208.

constituted as to appropriate them. The finite world really exists before we conceive it: "A concept must always have an object, as Spinoza himself clearly says: if distinct, individual consciousness is a result of the individualization of particular things, then what can its object be except the extended object? For what else individual and determinate is there?" (*Spinozistisches System*, 579). The conscious, thinking subject, in other words, emerges from the objective world, not vice versa. In relation to the infinite, it expresses the receptive element in the relation of inherency: "The body can indeed in various ways receive [*annehmen*] properties from its relationships to the Infinite and through them from the Infinite itself" (*Spinozismus*, 531).

Schleiermacher, in struggling for clarity on this theme, turns his attention to Jacobi's first presentation of Spinoza's system, found in a letter to Hemsterhuis. Jacobi writes, "*Being* is not an *attribute*, not something derived from some power or other; it is what underlies all attributes, properties, and powers, that which is signified through the word *substance*, and before which nothing can be supposed but which is presupposed by everything" (534; Scholz, *Hauptschriften*, 124). Schleiermacher thinks Jacobi has failed to grasp an important philosophical distinction, and he proceeds to defend Spinoza's position by modernizing the terminology:

> The confusion of the words *Being* and *Substance* cannot be foreign to those who are already familiar with Spinoza through the preceding paragraphs. Spinoza actually wants to say so much. Being is the first condition of all attributes; thus it is interconnected precisely with the pure original matter and accrues to it prior to all attributes: the original matter is the *Actually Existing*, extension (in which all further attributes would have to inhere) is the presentation of this Actually Existing, while consciousness, the thinking one, is the *original feeling for this Being*.[69]

Although it is not clear that Schleiermacher is any less confused than Jacobi on this point, he makes three crucial moves. First, by virtually identifying

---

69. *Spinozismus*, 534; emphasis added. "Die Verwechselung der Wörter *Seyn* und *Substanz* kann dem, welcher schon durch die Paragraphen mit Spinoza bekannt ist nicht fremd seyn. Spinoza will eigentlich soviel sagen. Das Seyn ist die erste Bedingung aller Eigenschaften, es hängt also genau mit dem reinen Urstof zusammen, und komt diesem vor allen Eigenschaften zu: Der Urstof ist das Seyende, die Ausdehnung ist die Darstellung dieses Seyenden, an welcher alle fernern Eigenschaften inhäriren müßen, das Bewußtseyn, das Denkende ist das ursprüngliche Gefühl dieses Seyns. Alles das hängt auch so, und von diesem Gesichtspunkt ausgegangen sehr genau zusammen." Note that *das Seyende* is singular; hence the Heideg-

original matter with the *Actually Existing,* Schleiermacher is denying that Spinoza's infinite substance is either just a product of the mind or some lifeless substrate; the more static terms—*being, substance, matter*—are replaced by the more active (but difficult to translate) term *Actually Existing.* Second, on account of the parallelism between presentation and representation, we are immediately related to the infinite by virtue of being both extended (bodily) beings and thinking beings. Third, in relation to the infinite the receptive organ is identified as *feeling (Gefühl)*—not perception, understanding, or reason. The modifier *original* is important in that it distinguishes this *feeling* from particular feelings, emotions, or sentiments *(Empfindungen)*.[70] Schleiermacher draws a connection between *original matter (Urstoff)*, which is prior and indeterminate, and *original feeling*, which is prior to other modes of knowing and, unlike those other modes, is indeterminate.

This explanation has moved the conversation further from Spinoza, but what is interesting and, for Jacobi and Schleiermacher, important, is that consciousness or the attribute of thought, as the immediate re-presentation of Being, is taken to be the original feeling for this being. This explains how the infinite can be immediately "known" or "felt" without an accompanying representation. This is an example of what Schleiermacher envisions when he considers how critical philosophy would change Spinoza. Thought, as attribute, is now "in us" as immediate consciousness, which is now, for the first time in his analysis, described as *feeling for being:* it is our awareness of, and point of connection with, the infinite. Schleiermacher expands on this in the next annotation in *Spinozismus,* where he gains further insight into the significance of *das Gefühl des Seyns.* Jacobi says that in every concept there is "(1) something absolute and original, which constitutes the thought independently of its object; (2) something added and transient, which manifests a relation and is the result of this relation" (*Spinozismus,* 535; Scholz, *Hauptschriften,* 125). Schleiermacher interprets this as another reason why the infinite is not to be conceived as merely a universal and why the objective world is not a mere derivative from the mind: "The representations of finite things cannot have been in the intelligence before the finite things and therefore cannot be the cause of finite things" (*Spinozismus,* 535). This summarizes an emerging realism in terms

---

gerian distinction between *Being (Sein)* and particular beings or *entities (die Seienden)* cannot be read back into Schleiermacher's text.

70. Schleiermacher had already begun to formulate this important distinction in *Über die Freiheit.*

already used to articulate monism and determinism: an extramundane cause did not think the world into being; our thoughts are not the sole or direct causes of our actions; the world is not merely a product of our thought; the affirmation of an infinite results from our receptivity to the infinite through feeling, not from our generalizing about particulars.

Even more significant, especially in retrospect, is the "sudden insight" the quotation from Jacobi gives into "the illustration of relations of the Infinite to finite things" (535). Having suggested that Mendelssohn could not understand that nothing exists outside the infinite and that still only the infinite really exists, Schleiermacher now explains how this infinite is not just a universal or collective of finite things:

> My illustration is not from the object of space but is taken from that of time, however the application is easy and natural. The genuinely true and real in the soul is the feeling for being, the immediate concept as Spinoza calls it. This concept, however, is never itself perceived; rather, only particular concepts and particular expressions of the will are perceived, and apart from these nothing exists in the soul, at any moment of time. Can one say for this reason that the individual concepts would have their separated, individual existence? No; nothing actually exists but the feeling for being: the immediate concept. The particular concepts are only its manifestations. (535)

Whereas discursive modes of knowing arise out of our receptivity to what is particular, an immediate mode of knowing arises out of our receptivity to the infinite, and just as particular finite things inhere in the infinite, so representations inhere in original feeling.

In these early and elusive references to *feeling,* a term which would become so important to his mature theology, Schleiermacher appropriates many philosophical strains at once. He seems to borrow the term from Jacobi, although not entirely with Jacobi's meaning; in relation to the term *being,* Schleiermacher clearly also understands it to be a form of Spinoza's "immediate concept," what in the *Ethics* is referred to as "intuition."[71] This actually reveals some misunderstanding on Schleiermacher's part, for there is only a loose semblance between Spinoza's *intuition* and Schleier-

---

71. According to Spinoza, intuition "proceeds from an adequate idea of the absolute essence of certain attributes of God to the adequate knowledge of the essence of things." *Ethics* 2:40, note 2; Elwes 2:113.

macher's *feeling*. Both terms are intended to convey immediate forms of knowledge, that is, they are nondiscursive modes of awareness; neither has a sensible ideatum. For Spinoza, however, *intuition*, as the third kind of knowledge, gets its ideas from God since it is part of the infinite intellect; intuition is an immediate insight into the essence of things. For Schleiermacher, the *feeling for being* never occurs apart from the perceptible, although it is not knowledge of the perceptible; just as the infinite is not found outside of the totality of the finite, so the feeling for being does not occur apart from experiences of finite things. The difference between the two thinkers could also rest in the fact, as has already been noted, that Schleiermacher resisted the rationalistic details of Spinoza; more than likely in this case, given the indirect access, Schleiermacher probably simply did not know the details of what Spinoza meant by *intuition*. What is important is that he takes the term *feeling* to be Spinozan and models his own definition accordingly. The role it plays is similar, but not identical, to Jacobi's term *faith* (*Glaube*), which is the "conviction" or "immediate certainty which not only needs no proof but even totally excludes all proofs,"[72] and as such serves as the springboard for the necessary mortal leap. Schleiermacher's notion of *feeling* is similar to Jacobi's in that it too is an affirmation of the real: "Nothing is found in the thinking subject by itself; it is never original but rather is always but a copy, an inner assertion, a confirmation (mens affirmat), as it were, of that which is found in extension" (*Spinozistisches System*, 579). Unlike Jacobi's *faith*, however, Schleiermacher's *feeling* is the immediate intuition of the infinite *in the finite*. No leap of faith is necessary because the gap between the finite and the infinite, between phenomena and noumena, has been closed by his organic monism, thus making a new form of realism possible. In this sense, the term also has Platonic undertones, for in borrowing the phrase *receptivity of the organs* from Hemsterhuis, Schleiermacher also introduces a strand of Platonism to his emerging Spinozism. Much like that of the eighteenth-century Scottish Enlightenment, Schleiermacher's organic, aesthetic monism (with its stress on internal relations) and his critical realism (with its stress on immediate forms of knowledge) is Platonic in character. In his *Reden*, written five years after these essays on Spinoza, Schleiermacher would come to

---

72. *Spinoza Conversations*, 120. According to B. A. Gerrish, "Belief [interchangeable with *feeling* or *faith*] is rather the confidence that accompanies cognition, or is presupposed in cognition. . . . Belief, then, remains as the conviction of reality, the confidence, attached to both kinds of cognition." "Faith and Existence," 123.

refer to his position as a *higher realism* and would continue to associate this with Spinoza.[73]

A Nonanthropomorphic God

At the heart of the Lessing-Jacobi conversations on Spinoza is the issue of a personal God. Lessing finds the notion "boring"; Jacobi cannot think of God as otherwise. Jacobi's God is what he calls a "living God," which is to say, God is personal, utterly transcendent, intelligent. Jacobi's "living God," in other words, represents the opposite of the supposed materialism and atheism of Spinozism. Schleiermacher argues for what he, too, will come to call a "living God," but for him this is indeed the God described by neo-Spinozism when neo-Spinozism recognizes limits set forth by critical philosophy. To explain how we can "know" or be related to such a God, Schleiermacher adapts Jacobi's notion of the *feeling for being*. We cannot, he says, cognize God, the Infinite, because we can only know mediately that which is individual; hence we "know" the infinite only immediately (without representation) through our contact with the finite. That immediate knowledge is the feeling for being, the original feeling, for Schleiermacher.

For Schleiermacher, as for Spinoza, God cannot be understood as being outside the totality of finite things; God cannot be an individual. That much is given in his organic monism, the implication of which does indeed seem to be a denial of God defined strictly as a personal God. Schleiermacher, however, never refuses to call God "personal," but he always remains insistent that we must be extremely cautious in how we assign that term. For example, he, like Spinoza, argues that will and intellect cannot be divided in God (or God would somehow have to be thought of as being inactive), and for this reason such notions as *creatio ex nihilo* and *final causes* are rejected or at least radically redefined. Yet these are the very doctrines Jacobi uses as the litmus test for understanding God as personal: "But my credo is not to be found in Spinoza. *I believe in an intelligent personal first cause of the world*" (*Spinoza Conversations*, 88). The re-

---

73. "And how will the triumph of speculation, the completed and rounded idealism, fare if religion does not counterbalance it and allow it to glimpse a *higher realism* than that which it subordinates to itself so boldly and for such good reason? . . . Respectfully offer up with me a lock of hair to the manes of the holy rejected Spinoza! The high world spirit permeated him, the infinite was his beginning and end." Crouter, 103–4.

sponse to Jacobi that Schleiermacher formulates in these early essays on Spinoza would remain fundamentally the same throughout the decades. Indeed a quarter-century later, after the two had commenced a formal correspondence, Schleiermacher wrote to Jacobi:

> If you form to yourself a living conception of a person, must not this person of necessity be finite? Can an infinite reason and an infinite will really be anything more than empty words, when reason and will, by differing from each other, also necessarily limit each other? And if you attempt to annul the distinction between reason and will, is not the conception of personality destroyed by the very attempt?[74]

Schleiermacher's preoccupation with the question of a personal God was also to play a central role in the controversy surrounding his *Reden über die Religion*. Although from 1799 to 1806 Schleiermacher's main conversation partner (and harshest critic) on such matters would be his ecclesiastical supervisor, F.S.G. Sack, there is a sense of Jacobi looming in the background.

---

74. Schleiermacher to Jacobi, 30 March 1818, in *Letters* 2:283.

2

BERLIN AND THE *SPEECHES ON RELIGION*, 1799–1801

> *The usual conception of God as one single being outside of the world and behind the world is not the beginning and the end of religion.*
>
> —F.D.E. Schleiermacher, *On Religion*

Shortly after completing the second part of *Spinozismus,* in the spring of 1794, Schleiermacher passed his ministerial examinations, was ordained in the Reformed Church, and took a pastorate in Landsberg. Two years later he returned to Berlin, where he served as the Reformed chaplain at Charité Hospital, a position which freed him to pursue his intellectual interests and to immerse himself in the social and literary circle of the early romantic movement.[1] The early period of German romanticism was characterized by a yearning and passion for the infinite; by a view of nature as an organic, dynamic, living whole; by a celebration of novelty, particularly creative genius; by an emphasis on intuition and feeling, as opposed to rationalism;

---

1. See Oskar Walzel, *Deutsche Romantik* (Leipzig: B. G. Teubner, 1923); translated by Alma Elie Lussky under the title *German Romanticism* (New York: G. P. Putnam's Sons, 1932). For Schleiermacher's contribution to this movement, see Jack Forstman, *A Romantic Triangle: Schleiermacher and Early German Romanticism* (Missoula, Mont.: Scholars Press, 1977), and Kurt Nowak, *Schleiermacher und die Frühromantik: Eine literaturgeschichtliche Studie zum romantischen Religionsverständnis und Menschenbild am Ende des 18. Jahrhunderts in Deutschland* (Göttingen: Vandenhoeck & Ruprecht, 1986).

by a seeking of multiplicity and higher forms of complexity; and by an understanding of the individual as a microcosm of the universe. With respect to all these characteristics the romantics felt a deep affinity with both Plato and Spinoza, but it was the renaissance of the latter's philosophy that seemed especially to fire their imaginations. This, then, was the milieu in which Schleiermacher composed his influential *Reden über die Religion* (*On Religion: Speeches to Its Cultured Despisers*).

On 21 November 1797, Schleiermacher's twenty-ninth birthday was marked by a surprise visit from Friedrich Schlegel, Henriette Herz, and Count Alexander von Dohna, who together encouraged him to write a book on religion by his thirtieth birthday.[2] The result was a work consisting of five "Speeches," moving in theme from the more abstract to the more concrete: from Speech 1, an "Apology" which suggests another approach in discerning what religion in general is, to Speech 5, an account of the main intuition of Christianity. At the same time that the *Reden* inspired the leading figures of the early romantic movement, they also attracted the attention and suspicion of the church authorities. A decade-old Edict of Religion required state censorship to ensure the orthodoxy of religious publications. It therefore fell to Fr. S. G. Sack, Schleiermacher's immediate church superior and an old family friend, to censor the *Reden,* which had been submitted anonymously for publication.[3] Schleiermacher found himself in the uncomfortable position of having to discuss his controversial work with Sack without acknowledging his own authorship. The second Speech, "On the Essence of Religion," became the focus of conflict insofar as it challenged more conventional views of a personal God and immortality and was, in Sack's words, "nothing more than a spirited apology for pantheism, a rhetorical presentation of the Spinozistic system."[4] Schleiermacher would, in 1806, undertake a substantial revision of the second Speech, but he retained both his appeal to Spinoza and his nonconventional views.

The second Speech is therefore critical for any consideration of Schleiermacher's development of the doctrine of God insofar as it has been the focus of charges relating to Schleiermacher's supposed pantheism and Spinozism. The focus by Schleiermacher's critics on the second Speech has not been unwarranted, since indeed it is there that Schleiermacher further develops the four main themes of his post-Kantian Spinozism. First, the

2. See Forstman, *Romantic Triangle,* 65–66.
3. See Blackwell, "Antagonistic Correspondence."
4. Ibid., 113.

basic tenets of his *organic monism* are carefully and deliberately pulled together under what he terms *system,* which he opposes to metaphysics. Second, his *complete determinism* of the earlier essays is the backdrop against which he draws the contrast between true religion and conventional morality. Schleiermacher is now addressing Fichte more than Kant, but the issues are the same—namely, determinism, freedom, and individuality. Third, his stance against Fichte's speculative idealism also indicates a further development of the *critical realism* Schleiermacher struggled to articulate in his essays on Spinoza. The realism implicit in the earlier essays is now made explicit; he now refers to it as a *higher realism,* and he ties it directly to Spinoza. As in 1794, this critical realism involves feeling and intuition, but in 1799 these terms become the hinge of his whole worldview. Fourth, the question of a personal God receives new attention in the aftermath of the *Reden.* As a result, Schleiermacher's own position, now more clearly explained, becomes more controversial, at least from the orthodox point of view as represented by Sack. In the correspondence between Sack and Schleiermacher in 1801, the question of how we conceptualize God (whether as personal or as nonpersonal) becomes a test case of the effect of Schleiermacher's post-Kantian Spinozism on his Christian doctrine of God.

A System of Intuitions: Religion and the Critique of Systems

In trying to sustain his readers' interest as he begins the second Speech, Schleiermacher suggests that his question is actually a modern formulation of the one posed by Simonides in Cicero's *De natura deorum:* not "What are the gods?" but "What is religion?" He knows that, rather than being able to instill religion in his readers, he can only hope to draw forth whatever religion is already there.[5] He does, however, want to be sure that if the cultured despisers continue to disparage religion, they should at least argue with the actual foe and not with some imposter: "You do not like religion; we started from that assumption. But in conducting an honest battle against it, which is not completely without effort, you do not want to have fought against a shadow like the one with which we have struggled.

---

5. How religion is taught is the subject of the third Speech, "On Self-Formation for Religion."

Religion must indeed be something integral that could have arisen in the human heart, something thinkable from which a concept can be formulated about which one can speak and argue" (Crouter, 100; R^1 47). In order to present religion as something respectable to the despisers, as something not alien to their own spirit,[6] Schleiermacher describes religion as that which "gives" *system*.[7] In thus connecting religion and system, Schleiermacher plays on the despisers' love for irony by developing an unusual understanding of *system*. "You are not accustomed," he acknowledges, "to connect the concept of something infinite with the term *system*, but rather the concept of something that is limited and completed in its limitation" (Crouter, 106; R^1 59). In fact, Schleiermacher shares with his romantic friends a deep suspicion of philosophical and theological systems, of any pretense to derive a whole system of thought from a single principle.[8] Schleiermacher's own brand of circumspection was influenced both by his philosophical convictions—the Kantian limits placed on the claims of pure reason, the Platonic reminder that knowledge proceeds from ignorance—and by his religious formation in Moravian piety.

In the Spinoza essays of 1793–94, Schleiermacher used the word *system* no fewer than seven times; in each case it carried a neutral connotation and referred to some system of thought. For instance, it had been his concern in

---

6. See Speech 1, where he writes, "I wish to lead you to the innermost depths from which religion first addresses the mind. I wish to show you from what capacity of humanity religion proceeds." Crouter, 87; R^1 20.

7. There are two understandings of system operating here: system as imposed (idealism, morals); system as discovered (piety). Just as, in reading the *Reden*, one must be careful to distinguish between religion and true religion, so one must also distinguish between system and true system.

8. Schleiermacher's suspicion far antedates his exposure to German romanticism. As early as 1789 he admitted to his father, "Still I had always been far from system seeking. . . . I do not believe that I shall bring it at any time to a fully formed system, so that all questions that can be raised could be answered, decisively and in connection with all the rest of my knowledge; I have, however, always believed of this, that investigations and probings, the patient listening to all witnesses and all parties, would be the only means by which to attain a sufficient ground of certainty and, before all things, to attain a sure border between that over which we take a necessary part, and must be able to stand accountable to ourselves and to each other, and that which can be left undecided without detriment to our peace and happiness. So, I view quietly the jousting of the philosophical and theological athletes, . . . learning something from both." Schleiermacher, Drossen, to his father, 23 December 1789 (*Brief* 131), in *KGA*, pt. 5, vol. 1, p. 183. According to Blackwell, "It is Schleiermacher's conviction that, despite the felt need of reason for unity and completeness, our knowledge in all spheres remains always partial. Philosophic wisdom therefore consists in learning to live with incompleteness, learning to accept it gracefully as an inevitable condition of human life." *Schleiermacher's Early Philosophy of Life*, 53.

Spinozistisches System to ascertain which propositions "held" Spinoza's thought together in its systematic presentation. In *Spinozismus*, he argued that the abuses of systematizing result in sophistry, which he set in opposition to science or, more specifically, to the scientific formulation "the flux of all things." This dichotomy between sophistry and science anticipated the one he makes in the *Reden* between system and speculation, the former relating to religion and the latter to metaphysics and morals. Religion, Schleiermacher argues, has too often been confused with metaphysics and morals. All three have a common object, "namely, the universe and the relationship of humanity to it" (Crouter, 97; R^1 41). Religion, however, "must treat this subject matter completely differently, express or work out another relationship of humanity to it, have another mode of procedure or another goal" (Crouter, 98; R^1 42). This other relationship is one of part to an organic whole, an intimate connection between the finite and the infinite. Its mode of procedure consists in passivity (in which the mind discovers but does not create) and in oscillation (between the One and All, between losing oneself and finding oneself). Its goal is nothing less than union with the infinite.

In 1799, the metaphysical system Schleiermacher wishes to refute is the philosophy of Fichte, which he refers to variously as "transcendental Philosophy," "rounded idealism," or speculation. A philosophical system such as Fichte's "classifies the universe and divides it into this being and that, seeks out the reasons for what exists, and deduces the necessity of what is real while spinning the reality of the world and its laws out of itself" (Crouter, 98; R^1 43).[9] This criticism is reminiscent of that put forth by Jacobi, who viewed Fichte's subjective idealism as the logical consequence of Kant's transcendental idealism, hence as the "inverted Spinozism" in which thought rather than matter becomes primary, the result being nihilism. Like Jacobi, Schleiermacher calls into question the legitimacy of such philosophical egocentrism. Just before his tribute to Spinoza, he writes, "Idealism will destroy the universe by appearing to fashion it; it will degrade it to a mere allegory, to an empty silhouette of our own limitedness" (Crouter 103–4; R^1 54). Although Fichte thought he was carrying through Kant's critical philosophy, by Schleiermacher's estimate he actually violates it: "Into this realm, therefore, religion must not venture too far. It must

---

9. For more on the relationship between Schleiermacher and Fichte, see Günter Meckenstock, "Schleiermachers Auseinandersetzung mit Fichte," and Giovanni Moretto, "The Problem of the Religious in the Philosophical Perspectives of Fichte and Schleiermacher," in Sorrentino, ed., *Schleiermacher's Philosophy and the Philosophical Tradition*.

not have the tendency to posit essences and to determine natures, to lose itself in an infinity of reasons and deductions, to seek out *final causes,* and to proclaim eternal truths" (Crouter, 98; R^1 43; emphasis added). Unlike Jacobi, Schleiermacher views morality and its positing of final causes as committing the same error. Morality is an imposed and arbitrary system because it "develops a system of duties out of human nature and our relationship to the universe; it commands and forbids actions with unlimited authority" (ibid.) Such criticism could be directed against Kant, Jacobi, and Fichte, since all three argue in their own ways for a freedom that Schleiermacher finds incoherent in the face of what he has called "complete determinism."

Schleiermacher has more than just philosophers in mind when he contrasts religion with metaphysics and morals. After all, in the *Reden,* unlike the earlier essays on Spinoza, his audience is the cultured despisers of Berlin, whom he is trying to convince that what they take to be religion (the sterile and rigid structures of conventional Christianity, or the emptiness of deism) is not really religion. What they so despise about religion, the complacency of its middle-class practitioners, Schleiermacher identifies as the extinguisher of true religion. The inborn spark of religious capacity is dampened by bourgeois preoccupations. In the third Speech, "On Self-Formation for Religion," Schleiermacher writes,

> But if only it were not begrudged [each person] to yield to this drive [to let oneself be penetrated by every impression] in comfortable inactive rest, for, from the standpoint of bourgeois life, this is indolence and laziness. Design and purpose must be in everything; prudent and practical people must always accomplish something, and when the spirit can no longer serve, they are fond of exercising the body; work and play, only no quiet, submissive contemplation. (Crouter, 147; R^1 148)

He also criticizes the "mania for system" behind claims of church authority, a mania founded on superstition and intolerance. "Modern Rome, godless but consistent, hurls anathemas and excommunicates heretics; ancient Rome, truly pious and religious in a lofty style, was hospitable to every god and so it became full of gods" (Crouter, 108; R^1 64).

Next to metaphysics and morals, therefore, Schleiermacher presents religion "as the necessary and indispensable third . . . , as their natural counterpart" (Crouter, 102; R^1 52). Unlike the other two, religion is "the sensibility and taste for the Infinite" (Crouter, 103; R^1 53). A closer examination of what religion is in relation to metaphysics and morality will reveal a definite line of development from Schleiermacher's organic monism and complete determinism of 1794 to his "system of intuitions" (*System von Anschauungen*) of 1799. The four main objects in which the religious intuition recognizes system are nature, humanity, history, and the reflective self. Since the first of these (nature) has mainly to do with his discussion of metaphysics and the relationship of the infinite to the finite, it will be considered under one section (*organic monism*); the other three (humanity, history, and the self) become issues in his refutation of conventional morality and thus will be treated under another section (*complete determinism*).

Organic Monism: True System versus Metaphysics

Judging from what religion is not, certain conclusions may be drawn about what Schleiermacher means by "system," for religion and system are the two sides of the same coin. Religion is not deductive, but descriptive and inductive. Rather than determining essences, it recognizes what relations it can. It understands "the principles according to which like must be related to like and the particular subordinated to the universal" (Crouter, 99; R^1 45).[10] Religion, properly understood, does not create its own system of "derivation and connection" (Crouter, 106; R^1 58) and impose these on the universe; rather, it recognizes the system in the universe—its interconnectedness, its causal nexus. Religion alone can recognize system, since religion looks to the infinite whole and its relations. But religion, it must be remembered, does not assemble a system, because it is itself a part of that whole. In his revision of 1806, Schleiermacher further clarifies how religion, as a system, contrasts with that of the "false systematizers": "Religion is certainly a system, if you mean that it is formed according to an inward and necessary connection" (Oman, 50; R^2 61); it corresponds to nature and is "not the result of caprice and tradition" (Oman, 52; R^2 64). Religion distinguishes itself by the fact that it "gives" true system because it is "immediate and true for itself" (Crouter, 106; R^1 58).[11] Schleiermacher is close here to both *Jacobi*, insofar as religion involves a revealing of existence, and *Spinoza*, insofar as system includes necessary causes and connections.

---

10. In this sense he is like Spinoza, who maintains that we must know the causes of emotions before we can order them according to reason; therein is our freedom.

11. "Why, for so long, did speculation *give* you deceptions instead of a system, and words instead of real thoughts?" Crouter, 103; R^1 54; emphasis added.

In order to illustrate the difference between what he means by religion as true system and arbitrary systems, Schleiermacher bids his readers to elevate themselves above the common "mania for system" to that "infinite dimension of sensible intuition," the starry sky. Those who create finite systems (including the transcendental philosophers who deduce their own worlds of thought) are likened to those childish minds who "connect" the stars to make pictures of dogs, or bears, or big dippers. Of them Schleiermacher says, "But you know that there is no semblance of a system in that, that still other stars are discovered between these pictures, that even within their limits everything is undetermined and endless, and that the pictures themselves remain something purely arbitrary and highly changeable" (Crouter, 106–7; R^1 60). There is nothing necessary in such picturing. Another is free to image the stars differently, according to that person's imagination. Imagination is necessary to thinking as the bridge, so to speak, between sensory experience and understanding, but it is caprice to impose this back, for instance, onto the stars, to claim that is how they in fact are, and to require others to see it thus. In other words, we cannot make a universal out of particulars. To do so would be to mistake as real what is only an abstraction from the real, or to make finite what is infinite.

Ironically, the only appropriate symbol is that of "infinite chaos." Chaos seems a peculiar symbol for religion since, like intuition, it by definition is incompatible with system.[12] Here again, Schleiermacher uses an unexpected meaning of a term in order to disrupt the despisers' assumptions, gain their attention, and seduce them into his way of thinking: "This infinite chaos, where of course every point represents a world, is as such actually the most suitable and highest symbol of religion. In religion, as in this chaos, *only the particular [Einzelne] is true and necessary;* nothing can or may be proved anything else. Everything universal under which the particular is supposed to be treated, each collection and combination of this sort, either exists in a different territory, if it is to be referred to the inner and essential realm, or is only the work of playful imagination and freest caprice. . . . Individual persons [*Jeder*] may have their own arrangement and their own rubrics; the particular can thereby neither win nor lose" (Crouter, 107; R^1 60–61; emphasis added). Chaos turns out to be an apt symbol for religion because it helps to explain both aspects of the *One and All*, perhaps the chief tenet of Schleiermacher's post-Kantian Spinozism.

---

12. Vincenzo Vitiello interprets this appeal to chaos as part of Schleiermacher's "intention to *decentralize* man. . . . Schleiermacher's religious anti-humanism goes so far as to assert that the infinite chaos, in which without any doubt each point represents a world, is, in reality, precisely as such, the most suitable symbol of religion." "Otherness of God," 134. Gerhard

Regarding the *All:* "Chaos" maintains individuality and genuine plurality insofar as "only the particular is true and necessary." Schleiermacher chides the despisers, "You lack the basic feeling for the *infinite, whose symbol is multiplicity and individuality.* Everything finite exists only through the determination of its limits, which must, as it were, 'be cut out of' the infinite. Only thus can a thing be infinite and yet be self-formed within these limits; otherwise you lose everything in the uniformity of a universal concept" (Crouter, 103; R^1 53; emphasis added). This text gives evidence for certain aspects of Schleiermacher's post-Kantian Spinozism: everything is determined by limits and relations; everything comes from, is part of, the infinite. Yet it also underscores why his Spinozism can only be called a monism in a qualified way, as an organic or aesthetic monism. It is not a strict monism according to which there is no real individuation and everything finite is merely an appearance of the one, undifferentiated substance. Nor is it an absolute monism according to which all transcendence is collapsed into immanentism, the result being what Jacobi refers to as materialism.[13] There is for Schleiermacher genuine plurality—an especially important concept for the romantics. Thus his is never a simple monism: in rejecting any form of dualism it also rejects any notion of absolute identity of substance in which particularity gets lost. As opposed to a strict or absolute monism, organic monism rests in the insistence that the internal and external cannot be sundered. Schleiermacher's post-Kantian Spinozism does not lose sight of the individual, as many claim Spinozistic or monistic worldviews do. That is why, in part, *system* is a much more adequate term than *monism:* it better explains the status of finite things. It is related to that earlier monism which distinguished *Zusammen* as the sum of finite things, from *Umfang,* as the infinite embracing whole of real finite things. Schleiermacher still, in 1799, resists the temptation to lose "everything in the uniformity of a universal concept." Finite things can be infinitely imaged, thus no one universal idea applies; the whole is more than the aggregate of finite things. Thus the *One* is distinguished from the *All* of the finite world but is never known apart from the finite.

Regarding the *One:* "Chaos" is always dialectically related to the absolute unity. Intuition, which distinguishes the system of religion from other

---

Spiegler interprets Schleiermacher's appeal to the notion of chaos, which is always viewed in dialectical relation to identity, as a boundary concept. See *Eternal Covenant,* 72–73.

13. For discussions of monism, see Hartshorne and Reese, *Philosophers Speak of God;* Richard R. Niebuhr, "Schleiermacher and the Names of God: A Consideration of Schleiermacher in Relation to Our Theisms," in *Schleiermacher as Contemporary,* ed. Robert W. Funk (New York: Herder & Herder, 1970), 198–201; and Spiegler, *Eternal Covenant,* 94–95.

systems, necessarily involves oscillation. In the opening pages of the *Reden* Schleiermacher first mentions this oscillation between the two opposing drives to draw into oneself and to extend oneself. This recurring theme takes on various forms throughout the *Reden*. In the second speech, religion is found in living oscillations: "While intuiting a universal relationship your glance is so often led back and forth directly from the smallest to the greatest and from the latter back again to the former and moves between the two in living vibrations [*lebendigen Schwingungen*] until it becomes dizzy and can distinguish neither great nor small, neither cause nor effect, neither preservation nor destruction any longer" (Crouter, 126; R^1 102). This is why the ancient dictum *One and All* will remain so important to Schleiermacher: there must be a constant oscillation between unity and multiplicity. The individual is never an isolated thing but can only be understood in terms of relations and of the whole. The whole can only be seen in the particular. Yet more than that, the One *is* only in its individuation.[14] This is also why intuition and feeling are so closely bound with religion, for in intuition and feeling the *One* is recognized in the *All*, and the *All* is recognized as inhering in the *One*.

Schleiermacher's appeal to an oscillating movement between unity and chaos is directed toward the despisers' dislike of deism. Chaos does not eliminate the *One*, because the *One* is not the mechanical universe of the deists; it is neither a precise mechanism nor a positive unity. Chaos is thus the proper symbol for religion because "the perturbations in the course of the stars indicate a *higher unity*, a bolder combination than that which we have already proved true from the regularity of their paths, and the anomalies, the superfluous touches of malleable nature, compel us to see that it treats its most definite forms with an arbitrariness, with an inventiveness, as it were, whose principle we can discover only from a higher standpoint" (Crouter, 117; R^1 84, emphasis added). This unity, however, must be properly understood. Recall that in the earlier Spinoza essays Schleiermacher criticized Kant for positing a plurality of noumena. That is one point at which Schleiermacher used Spinoza to modify his Kantianism: there is only one substance, an infinite not outside the totality of finite things. At the same time, Kant's critical philosophy served to modify his Spinozism: this cannot be a positive unity, a substance. Schleiermacher called it *noumenon*, but finding that term insufficient he came up with his own term, *Seyende*, to denote the infinite, living reality that underlies everything finite. Hence

---

14. See Hermann Süskind, *Der Einfluß Shellings auf die Entwicklung von Schleiermachers System* (1909; reprint, Tübingen: J.C.B. Mohr, 1983), 24–25.

the distinction here in the *Reden* between universe and world: the former grounds the latter and is not itself finite or individual. Because "universe" carries the connotation of a positive unity, Schleiermacher was careful in his revision of 1806 to replace (not entirely but significantly) the term *universe* with terms such as *infinite, whole, One,* and *God*.[15]

At the heart of this view is the understanding of nature as organism. This remains for Schleiermacher the best way to explain how the infinite is not outside the sequence of finite, how the infinite and finite are thus related, and how the individual is related to the whole. He writes that nature's "chemical powers, the eternal laws according to which bodies themselves are formed and destroyed, these are the phenomena in which we intuit the universe most clearly and in a most holy manner. See how attraction and repulsion determine everything and are uninterruptedly active everywhere, how all diversity and all opposition are only apparent and relative, and all individuality is merely an empty name. See how all likeness strives to conceal itself and to divide into a thousand diverse forms, and how nowhere do you find anything simple, but everything is ornately connected and intertwined" (Crouter, 118; R^1 86). This organic view of the universe, this *system* of nature, is the organic monism of 1794. Recall how, in *Spinozismus,* the transition from Leibniz to Spinoza consisted in understanding various transformations, not as the hiding and revealing of a personal God, but as the result of destructive and creative forces and processes of nature. Here, too, Schleiermacher retains the principle *nihil ex nihilo:* "Even in the most common things you know the principle according to which like must be related to like and the particular subordinated to the universal" (Crouter, 99; R^1 45). Inherent to this organic view is the modern scientific understanding of nature and the place of humanity in it. This view, moreover, calls for a reinterpretation of such Christian notions as miracle and revelation. Miracle can no longer be understood as a supernatural intervention that disrupts the laws of nature; revelation is not the direct conveyance of information from the divine. The most religious view is to see as miraculous or revelatory what is "most natural and usual" (Crouter, 133; R^1 117). The organic monism of the early essays on Spinoza is thus not only maintained but further developed in the *Reden*. There is an infinite, the absolutely living unity, but it is not to be found outside the totality of finite things. The *All* cannot exist without the *One,* and the *One* is not outside the *All*: "Of course, it is an illusion to seek the infinite precisely outside

---

15. A good example of this shift is found in the revision to manuscript pages 50 and 51. Compare Crouter, 101–2, with Oman, 35.

the finite, to seek the opposite outside that to which it is opposed; but is it not highly natural for those who do not yet know the finite itself?" (Crouter, 146; R^1 145–46).

Complete Determinism: True System versus Morality

The view of nature as a unity, as an organic whole, extends also to Schleiermacher's criticism of the "moralists." Morality fails to recognize that the human is no exception to the unity and system of nature. As the metaphysicians begin and end with their own deductions, so the moralists begin and end with their free will. To compound the matter, morality mistakenly associates itself with metaphysics and religion insofar as, to legitimate free will, the moralists insist that as a faculty it corresponds to a moral order of being, which in turn they personify as a lawgiver: "The practical people, to whom the will of God is the primary thing, are moralists, but a little in the style of metaphysics. You take the idea of the good and carry it into metaphysics as the natural law of an unlimited and plenteous being, and you take the idea of a primal being from metaphysics and carry it into morality so that this great work should not remain anonymous, but so that the picture of the lawgiver might be engraved at the front of so splendid a code" (Crouter, 98–99; R^1 43–44).[16] This, as we shall see, becomes part of Schleiermacher's critique of traditional theism, namely, that God is too often made to be the "genius of humanity" (Crouter, 136; R^1 125).[17]

Religion and Morality

Schleiermacher's evaluation of morality as law and his contrasting it with religion as piety actually begins toward the end of the first Speech, where

---

16. Compare Speech 1, where he criticizes the use of religion as a tool "for maintaining right and order in the world and for coming to the aid of the shortsightedness of human perspective and the narrow limits of human power with the reminder of an all-seeing and infinite power." Crouter, 92; R^1 31.

17. In this general critique Schleiermacher is not far from Spinoza in his suspicion of the transcendental status given terms such as "goodness" and of the human qualities projected onto God. In the preface to part 4 of the *Ethics,* "Of Human Bondage, or the Strength of the Emotions," Spinoza writes, "As for the terms *good* and *bad,* they indicate no positive quality in things regarded in themselves, but are merely modes of thinking, or notions which we form from the comparison of things one with another." Elwes 2:189. This is similar to his evaluation of final causes (see 188) and free will (see *Ethics* 2.35, note; Elwes 2:108). All such notions, Spinoza argues, arise from inadequate ideas, that is, they result because "the human body, being limited, is only capable of distinctly forming a certain number of images." *Ethics* 2.40, note 1; Elwes 2:111. With too many images, the "powers of imagination break down," distinctions thus break down, and general ideas are formed. Regarding how we conceptualize

it becomes evident that, beneath his criticism of conventional morality, the debate with Kant still continues. Religion, as Schleiermacher presents it, not only does not serve, but should in fact challenge, the very idea of an omnipotent and autonomous moral law: "You have heard this enough from those who defend the independence and the omnipotence of the moral laws, but I add that it also shows the greatest contempt for religion to wish to transplant it into another realm and expect it to serve and to work there" (Crouter, 94; R^1 35). Schleiermacher seems to be doing two things. While making a claim for the independence of religion from morality, he is also implicitly calling for a new model of morality.

Most certainly, he calls for the independence of religion from morality. He thereby completes his critique of Kant's second *Critique*, which makes God a postulate of practical reason. Schleiermacher insists that religion cannot be used by morality. Religion has nothing to do with action, only with innermost feeling. Religion can even be said to thwart morality since, when confused with morality, it produces a bellicose zeal that Schleiermacher joins with the despisers in rejecting. Any combination of metaphysics, morality, and religion (especially the latter two), he argues, leads to superstition and intolerance. Consequently many crimes are committed in the name of religion. Schleiermacher emphasizes the contemplative side of religion and upholds tolerance as a mark of true religion. In fact, his appeal to Spinoza is directly related to the issue of toleration. Spinoza was "full of religion," yet because of that, was condemned and left "without disciples and without rights of citizenship" (Crouter, 104; R^1 55).[18] Furthermore, Schleiermacher's insistence on the separation of religion and morality can be said to be Spinozan insofar as it is a call for the examination of the emotions that motivate our actions. He writes, one "must first master himself and his pious feelings before they press actions out of him" (Crouter, 110; R^1 69).[19]

God, Spinoza writes to Oldenburg that when Scripture says God is angry or acts as judge, it is "speaking humanly, and in a way adapted to the received opinion of the masses, inasmuch as its purpose is not to teach philosophy, nor to render men wise, but to make them obedient." Spinoza to Oldenburg, 7 February 1676; Elwes 2:306.

18. Spinoza, too, distinguished between *superstition*, fed by ignorance, and *piety*, led by the dictates of reason. Indeed, the whole intention of the *Theologico-Political Treatise* is a call for religious toleration. Only reason, he argues, leads to truth, and thus it does not really matter which revealed religion one adopts. We are free to choose our own creeds, since we are judged by our fruits. In the *Ethics*, Spinoza directly relates piety to action: it is "an activity or virtue." *Ethics* 5.4, note; Elwes 2:249. It is "the desire of well-doing, which is engendered by a life according to reason." Ibid, 4.37, note 1; Elwes 2:212; cf. 2.49.

19. This sentence could just as well be a summary remark on Spinoza's *Ethics*, one purpose of which (particularly parts 3–5) is to understand our emotions so that, through

Beyond just separating morality and religion, Schleiermacher also presents a revised understanding of morality, although only indirectly so. True moral action, he suggests, arises not from obedience to law, since there is neither an independent moral order nor a corresponding faculty of will. Religion encourages the cultivation of religious affections rather than merely respect for law. Like Spinoza, Schleiermacher views freedom not in terms of a free will but in terms of an "intellectual love of God."[20] In appealing to the ancients' (i.e., Cicero's) understanding of piety, Schleiermacher begins to identify some peculiarly religious sentiments:

> Morals do not like *love* and *affection,* but activity, which proceeds wholly from within and is not produced by considering its external object; they know no other *awe* than that for their own law; they condemn as impure and self-seeking whatever can occur out of *compassion* and *gratitude;* they abase, indeed despise, *humility;* and if you speak of *remorse,* they think of lost time that you unprofitably prolong. Your innermost feeling must also assent to morality's view that all of these sentiments are not intended to produce action; as functions of your innermost and highest life they are self-contained in their own coming and going. (Crouter, 130; R^1 111–12; emphasis added)

Schleiermacher's point is that the motivations of the moral life are not to be found outside ourselves in autonomous laws; they arise properly from within, from a faculty of desire. He thereby continues the line of thought he had developed in *Über die Freiheit,* namely, that the moral life consists in cultivating our moral sentiments, relating them to each other and to corresponding concepts, so they form a coherent whole. The affections Schleiermacher refers to do not belong to conventional morality, nor do they belong to conventional religion; rather, Schleiermacher holds them up as the ideal, already present to some degree in the despisers, of the truly religious life.[21]

---

reason, we may control them, rather than letting them control us, and thus may we enjoy freedom, or blessedness.

20. See *Ethics* 5, props. 32–37, 10.

21. Note in this discussion of affections the parallels with *Spinozismus,* where Schleiermacher explains how, even though for Spinoza there is no free will and the mind cannot thus be a cause of a bodily transformation (i.e., an action), still, contrary to Jacobi's assessment, the mind is not a mere spectator. There is, Schleiermacher argues, *Entschluß,* which, as judgment combined with desire, mediates between transformations of thought and of extension, between the intellect and action. *Entschluß* is reason occupied with pain and pleasure and thus includes

The essence of religion, as described by Schleiermacher, necessitates a new conceptualization of morality that rejects both a rigid moral order and the notion of free will. The difficulty is that, although this is implied in the *Reden*, Schleiermacher continues to insist on a separation of religion from morality altogether. Yet precisely because they are functions of one's innermost life, affections and desires cannot fail to be manifested in various ways. Piety and law certainly have nothing to do with each other, but it is not clear that the same can be said of religion and morality (as Schleiermacher wants each understood). Whatever ethics of life Schleiermacher may develop elsewhere, or even imply here, his concern in the *Reden* is to ensure that religion "must not use the universe in order to derive duties and is not permitted to contain a code of laws" (Crouter, 98; R^1 43). In relation to morality, religion can at the most be considered only as a possible accompaniment, "like a holy music" (Crouter, 110; R^1 68), but should never be understood as either the essence or cause of any moral action. Schleiermacher warns, "If you still hold this to be religion, however rational and praiseworthy your action may appear, you are absorbed in an unholy superstition.... [W]e should do everything with religion, nothing because of religion" (ibid.).

Religion and Determinism

Religion, when contrasted with metaphysics, is that which gives system; when contrasted with morality, this system is best understood as a determinism insofar as in its critique of both conventional and Kantian understandings of freedom it recognizes the limits, dependency, and passivity of the human. Schleiermacher explains that "morality proceeds from the consciousness of freedom; it wishes to extend freedom's realm to infinity and to make everything subservient to it. Religion breathes there where freedom itself has once more become nature; it *apprehends man beyond the play of his particular powers and his personality, and views him from the vantage point where he must be what he is, whether he likes it or not*" (Crouter, 102; R^1 51–52; emphasis added). The latter part of this text suggests two aspects of passivity which characterize both religion and determinism. First, religion is a viewing, a discovering. It recognizes real existence—the infinite and the universal relationship of all that is finite. It views, it feels, it intuits, but it does not itself create. Second, and this is

---

various affections. In the 1799 edition of the *Reden* Schleiermacher describes this desire in terms of "religious sentiments" that, in varying intensities and combinations, constitute

where determinism enters in, religion involves another, more existential kind of passivity, namely, the awareness that where we are, what we are, and so on, is not determined by us. There is in all of life a certain necessity of givenness that we may or may not like, but which we must nonetheless accept. This givenness has two aspects. It is a givenness by the *One*, since everything is "'cut out of' the infinite." At the same time, it is a givenness by the *All*, insofar as everything has a like cause: "You shall recognize the path of the universe and the formula of its laws from the various causes through which the moment has now been produced" (Crouter, 125; R^1 101). Religion alone not only recognizes this "dependence" but also consents to it. The distinction between recognition and consent is crucial, since piety is more than knowledge of a certain fatedness; it is a joyful acceptance and affirmation of the activity of the world spirit. For Schleiermacher, "To love the world spirit and joyfully observe its work is the goal of our religion, and in love there is no fear" (Crouter, 115; R^1 80).[22] As indicated by the phrase "world spirit," what religion recognizes and consents to are not mechanical and dead forces but the living unity that grounds the organic whole: "But only the person who in fact sees it everywhere, who, not only in all alterations but in all existence, finds nothing else but a production of this spirit and a representation and execution of these laws, only to him is everything visible really a world, formed and permeated by divinity, and is one" (Crouter, 118–19; R^1 87).[23] This closely parallels what in *Spinozismus* he referred to as the transition to Spinozism and is thus a development of the organic, monistic worldview.[24] "System" means in part that there is only *one* set of laws for *all* things; therein rests the unity of nature. This unity of nature, however, this natural law, is not a static set of laws but is always, everywhere dynamic.

---

one's individuality.

22. See also Crouter, 129–30; R^1 110. In this Schleiermacher shows a certain affinity to Spinoza, who writes, "we should wait and endure fortune's smiles or frowns with an equal mind, seeing that all things follow from the eternal decree of God by the same necessity." *Ethics* 2.49, note; Elwes 2:126.

23. In the same paragraph Schleiermacher writes, "See how everything living nourishes itself and forcibly draws dead matter into its life, how on all sides there presses in upon us the stored-up supply for everything living, which does not lie there dead but is itself living and everywhere reproduces itself anew. . . . What infinite fullness is revealed there, what superabundant riches!" Crouter, 118; R^1 85 (cf. Crouter, 116–17; R^1 82, 83). The infinite for Schleiermacher is always living: "Weil es Euch an dem Grundgefühl der unendlichen und lebendigen Natur fehlt, deren Symbol Mannigfaltigkeit und Individualität ist." R^1 53. Unfortunately, Crouter's translation—"because you lack the basic feeling for the infinite, whose symbol is multiplicity and individuality" (103)—omits *und lebendigen Natur*.

24. "I cannot think to myself other than as alternating production and destruction of the organic components of the [*Umfang*]." *Spinozismus*, 532.

Individuality and Freedom

When this unity *is* resisted and the individual asserts its independence, for instance, by clinging to the empty notion of free will, the whole nevertheless has its way. The moralists wrongly attempt to oppose the infinite, living unity; they look to the individual (whether person, deed, or thing) apart from and opposed to its relation to others and the whole: "We see how they seize and hold on to this and that in order to fortify and surround themselves with many external deeds, so that they might conduct their isolated lives according to their own free choice and so that the eternal stream of the world might not disturb any of it for them. We also see how fate then necessarily makes all of this hazy and wounds and tortures them in a thousand ways" (Crouter, 129; R^1 110). In fact, Schleiermacher argues, "all individuality [*Individualität*] is merely an empty name" (Crouter, 118; R^1 86)—a rather startling claim that raises the question of individuation and, especially for Christian thought, human individuality. Schleiermacher means that any particular thing, including any human individual, can only properly be understood as a part of, and in relation to, the whole. The individual is not lost, yet at the same time it cannot be given an exaggerated status, the result of neglecting the dialectical relation between the individual and the whole. Two explanations of this relation (one philosophical, the other aesthetic) can be found in Schleiermacher's thought.

Philosophically, in the words of Richard Brandt, "the individual self is not an ultimate metaphysical unit and . . . its significance lies in the fact that, though only an evanescent ripple on the surface of the Infinite, it represents the Infinite from an individual point of view" (*Philosophy of Schleiermacher*, 40). The reasons for this had been developed in Schleiermacher's earlier years in Halle and Berlin. Recall how in *Spinozistisches System* his criticism of Kant rested partly in his insistence that there is no plurality of noumena, only a noumenon: *Substance* for Spinoza, the *Actually Existing* for Schleiermacher. This argument constitutes a significant part of his post-Kantian Spinozism in those earlier essays, what I have termed his organic monism and what, in 1799, Schleiermacher himself describes as *system*. One consequence of this argument is that individuality is no longer supported by a plurality of corresponding noumena; rather, everything is related to and a manifestation of the one reality. Individuality is not substantial but relational and dynamic; it is "nothing other than the cohesion, the identical combination of forces of a certain measure in a single point" (*Spinozistisches System*, 573). Far from being a separated existence further reified by separated noumena, the individual receives its individuality precisely in its relatedness and its "taking up" of the universe. Hence the significance of the *One and All:* the infinite only comes to expression in the individual; in fact, its existence *is* its individuation. Whatever is individual is thus necessary to the whole. Religion views reality from both sides: it sees the infinite in the finite thing; it also sees the contribution of the finite thing to the infinite; it looks to the individual not only from the outside but also from the inside outward, thus recognizing the excellence of each individual. Moreover, this view through the *One and All* allows for genuine plurality: "See how all likeness strives to conceal itself and to divide into a thousand diverse forms, and how nowhere do you find something simple, but everything is ornately connected and intertwined" (Crouter, 118; R^1 86).

Aesthetically, the whole, while greater than the sum of its parts, depends on the harmony of all parts and the excellence of each. Individuation therefore consists in the contribution of the part to the whole, a contribution that is always twofold. On the one hand, its contribution rests in its relation to every other part: "But might they just once realize that in order to intuit each thing as an element of the whole, one must have necessarily considered it in its unique nature and in its highest perfection. For it can be something in the universe only through the totality of its effects and connections" (Crouter, 149; R^1 152).[25] On the other hand, its contribution rests in its capacity to manifest the whole in itself: "Thus to accept everything individual [particular, *Einzelne*] as a part of the whole and everything limited as a representation of the infinite is religion" (Crouter, 105; R^1 57).[26] Hence individuation is not minimalized by Schleiermacher but is for him grounded in relation and harmony. The emphasis, again, is dialectical insofar as something is what it is in its relation and contribution to the whole, *and* insofar as that something (to the degree that it is related and does contribute) attains uniqueness and perfection.

The underlying issue, of course, is not individuation in general, for which an aesthetic theory alone might suffice, but specifically human individuality and freedom. In this respect, Schleiermacher indeed shows himself to be Kantian in his undeniably strong sense of the ego, the representing subject. One passage in particular rings with an idealism that Schleiermacher elsewhere claims to resist: "What are individuality [*Individualität*] and one-

25. Cf. Crouter, 117, 121, 122, 157.
26. For consistency with Crouter's translation elsewhere, *Einzelne* should here be translated as "particular." For Schleiermacher, this seems to be the more general term, whereas *Individualität* seems to be the more specific term referring to *human individuality*.

ness? Did you get these concepts, by means of which nature first actually becomes for you an intuition of the world, from nature? Do they not derive originally from the interior of the mind, and are they not first directed from there to nature?" (Crouter, 119; R^1 87). It would seem that for Schleiermacher, as for Fichte, that the mind creates the external world and that, in the end, everything is ego.[27] Yet Schleiermacher's idealism would be better termed an "objective idealism"[28] or, even better, a post-Kantian and critical realism.[29] He reminds the despisers that "even the mind, if it is to produce and sustain religion, must be intuited in a world" (Crouter, 119; R^1 88). He distances himself even further from Fichte in the second edition (1806), where the revisions read, "The universe is reflected in the inner life, and only through the spiritual nature is the bodily understandable. Yet the mind, if it is to produce and sustain religion, must operate on us as a world and as in a world."[30]

Individuality, or more to the point, personality, understood from the view of determinism, arises from "the particular manner in which the universe

27. Andrew Bowie describes the difference between an idealism such as Fichte's and a romanticism such as Schleiermacher's: "The essential thought behind the Romantic, as opposed to the Idealist, view of the post-Kantian situation was present in the implications of Kant's notion of the sublime. The sublime indicated an inability to represent the infinite. At the same time it invoked the infinite via the feeling of finitude it produced. . . . Early Romanticism acknowledges the undemonstrability of the sense of reality as a whole, but, in the manner of Kant's *Schwärmer*, cannot stop the endless attempt to grasp the infinite via the desire to see it in the sensuous." *Aesthetics and Subjectivity: From Kant to Nietzsche* (Manchester: Manchester University Press, 1990), 42–43.

28. Wilhelm Dilthey, *Leben Schleiermachers*, in *Gesammelte Schriften* 13/2: 40. Dilthey maintains that Schleiermacher's objective idealism is influenced by Plato. He explains that whereas for subjective idealism "philosophical knowledge is reduced to the activity of the consciousness," for objective idealism the connection of spirit is based on the explanation of the universe.

29. Hans W. Frei identifies Schleiermacher's realism as a critical realism: "The object of faith is given together with the content of faith in such manner that every attribute of or quality in the object is qualified by its being a content of consciousness." "Niebuhr's Theological Background," in *Faith and Ethics: The Theology of H. Richard Niebuhr*, ed. Paul Ramsey (New York: Harper & Brothers, 1955), 38. Paul Tillich defines a post-Kantian realism as one that still seeks a "union between the knower and the known" but understands the "known" in terms of power rather than being: "Of course, if being is defined as 'object of thought' no matter what content it has, the idea of 'degrees of being' is senseless. But if being is 'power' the assertion of such degrees is natural, and it is a vital necessity for the mind to penetrate into the strata in which the real power of a thing reveals itself." "Realism and Faith," in *Paul Tillich: Main Works / Hauptwerke*, vol. 4, *Writings in the Philosophy of Religion / Religionsphilosophische Schriften*, ed. John Clayton (Berlin and New York: Walter de Gruyter, 1987), 345.

30. R^2 93, my translation; cf. Oman, 71.

presents itself to you in your intuitions and determines the uniqueness [*Eigenthümliche*] of your individual [*individuellen*] religion" (Crouter, 110; R^1 68). In this sense, individuality does not, as the moralists would have it, come through a sheer exercise of the will or an assertion of oneself against nature, since the self is not active solely through its own power.[31] Individuality emerges through, on the one hand, an inner necessity or the inner creative drive (how one appropriates the forces of the universe which converge and recombine in a particular personality), and on the other hand, the striving in relation to other, finite things and the limitations set thereby: "You know that the manner in which each single element of humanity appears in an individual [*Individuum*] depends upon the manner in which it is limited or set free by the rest; only through this general conflict does each element in each individual attain a definite form and magnitude, and this conflict is sustained, in turn, only through the community of [particulars] and the movement of the whole" (Crouter, 145; R^1 143).[32] Thus freedom is not unlimited but is constituted by our immersion in relations and our appropriation of these relations. In more personal and psychological terms, this is reflected in the degree to which one is involved with others and affected by events. The key, again, is not to view other individuals or particulars as isolated, and consequently as obstacles or as dead matter, but to view them as the manifesting actions of the living whole.

Throughout the *Reden,* the imagery used is mystical and sexual. Only in losing oneself in the infinite or in the beloved does one become fully oneself.[33] Only in the recognition of, and consent to, our dependence and limitation, and always in oscillation between the One and All, do we find freedom: "Man has merely stolen the feeling of his infinity and godlikeness, and as an unjust possession it cannot thrive for him if he is not also conscious of his limitedness, the contingency of his whole form, the silent disappearance of his whole existence in the immeasurable. The gods have also punished this crime from the very beginning" (Crouter, 102–3; R^1 52). Individuality and freedom are thus closely bound for Schleiermacher, and both are necessarily a part of religion: "Only the drive to intuit, if it is

---

31. See Crouter, 111; R^1 71. Schleiermacher here is very close to Spinoza, who defines freedom as coming from one's own necessity. Only God can be understood as being free—not in the sense of willing or choosing, but in the sense of acting out of God's own necessity.

32. Cf. Crouter, 155–56. Once again, *Einzelnen* should here be translated as "particulars" not "individuals." The "general conflict" seems to allude to the whole relation of particulars, including human individuality. The human person is not set apart from this interactive system.

33. See Crouter, 82, 156, 113, 139.

oriented to the infinite, places the mind in unlimited freedom; only religion saves it from the most ignominious fetters of opinion and desire" (Crouter, 109; R^1 65).[34] It is in the attempt to separate oneself, to deny relations and dependencies, to exert a will, and worst of all to be too anxious about one's own individuality, that one actually loses both individuality and freedom; it is *then* that one becomes bound and subject to fate: "To know of only one point of view for everything is ... to become a true serf, bound to the place on which by chance one may be standing" (Crouter, 150; R^1 154). Free will is merely an abstraction from the concrete reality of relations and the causal system.

Freedom and Final Causes

Contrary to Jacobi and Kant, then, fatedness comes not through the denial of final causes but through the anxious struggle to insist upon them. In Jacobi's *Über die Lehre des Spinoza*, and consequently in Schleiermacher's *Spinozismus* and *Spinozistisches System,* the ethical dimension of the *Pantheismusstreit* boils down to a debate over determinism and final causes. For Jacobi there was no third alternative to the first two of these. If determinism is granted, then freedom and individuality must be denied. In his response of 1793–94, Schleiermacher in effect attempted to construct that middle ground by defending Spinoza's theory of parallelism, but he remained ambiguous in his stance on final causes. In the *Reden* of 1799, Schleiermacher explicitly rejects final causes. He insists, toward the beginning of the second Speech, that, unlike metaphysics and morals, religion does not "seek out final causes" (Crouter, 98; R^1 43). In the third Speech he denounces the bourgeoisie for having to find purpose and design in everything. Nevertheless, although he wants to criticize the method of and motivation for seeking final causes, and although he would also most likely agree with Spinoza's charge that a belief in final causes arises from ignorance, there is a strong note of progress, direction, and intentionality in the *Reden*. As his reasoning unfolds, it becomes apparent that in this he is

---

34. Schleiermacher changes this definition of freedom in the second edition: "Only when the free impulse of seeing, and of living is directed towards the Infinite and goes into the Infinite, is the mind set in unbounded liberty." Oman, 56; R^2 68. This is followed by another revision in which he tries to clarify what it means to be religious: "The whole religious life consists of two elements, that man surrender himself to the Universe and allow himself to be influenced by the side of it that is turned towards him is one part, and that he transplant this contact which is one definite feeling, within, and take it up [*aufnehmen*] into the inner unity of his life and being, is the other." Oman, 58; R^2 72.

closer to the neo-Spinozism of Herder than to Spinoza himself.[35] Schleiermacher seems to follow Herder in, on the one hand, agreeing with Spinoza that there can be no final causes and, on the other hand, departing from Spinoza in a strong emphasis on the teleological drive of the whole. The point is, a fundamental distinction can be drawn between final causes (as external causation through ideas) and organic teleology (as immanent causation). The term *final cause* usually, but not necessarily, implies an extramundane, purposeful divine causality that distinguishes between ends and means; what Schleiermacher terms *progress* implies teleological thrust of immanent drives and causes. Whereas the former pertains to particulars, the latter pertains to the whole. Hence the movement in thought is twofold: away from an extramundane, transcendent cause, and away from focus on the particular. In the *Reden*, this teleological emphasis can be explained through three aspects of Schleiermacher's thought: the unity of nature, the progress of history, and an aesthetic worldview.

The unity of nature. Throughout the *Reden*, Schleiermacher insists that religion, as opposed to metaphysics and morals, views the universe as an *organic, unified,* and *living* whole. Each of these three adjectives implies and requires the other two, but what is not so immediately obvious is that each also reveals general teleological leanings. For instance, inherent in the metaphor of an organism is the assumption of development: "The vulgar, the barbaric, the misshapen shall be engulfed and transformed in an organic development" (Crouter, 126; R^1 103). And inherent in the unity of nature is the inviolability of its laws and, consequently, "the general tendency toward order and harmony" (Crouter, 117; R^1 83). In this light, the term *living*, which has remained vague, gains further meaning. The livingness of infinite nature means there is direction, order, and even progress. That is why there are not just dead mechanical forces by which the whole operates.

---

35. Herder interprets Spinoza's substance as "substantial force," which acts according to its own necessary law. The doctrine of substantial force, which replaces Spinoza's doctrine of the divine attributes, is that *"the Deity reveals Himself in an infinite number of forces in an infinite number of ways."* Herder, *God, Some Conversations*, 103; cf. 105, 109. The ground of this nexus of active forces is "the primal Force of all forces," and it is because of this primal Force that "order emerges from chaos." Ibid., 104, 190. This order is teleological insofar as there is an inhering, dynamic order that determines the progress of the whole. The three highest determining forces in this order are *power, reason,* and *goodness*. There is thus for Herder a determining, immanent, and necessary intentionality, but it is found only in the whole, not in the particular. Spinoza, of course, also understood there to be immanent, driving forces in nature (*Natura naturans, conatus*), but he did not share Herder's progressive view of history and he would most likely have disapproved of Herder's application of goodness and wisdom to such forces.

There is, Schleiermacher says, a world spirit that animates and directs the whole through its creative drive, and it is religion's chief concern "to divine" (Crouter, 124; R^1 100) that spirit. Nature necessarily includes history.

The progress of history. Where the teleological sense becomes most pronounced is when Schleiermacher speaks of human striving and imagination. This is somewhat surprising given his nonanthropocentric tendencies, but less surprising given the general interest of the time in historical development and the romantic emphasis on the individual. Schleiermacher seems to locate a universal progress or *telos* in human striving and human imagination—a move that runs counter to Spinoza's fundamental criticisms. But Schleiermacher's main focus here is on history, and with the leading German thinkers of his age he views history as something organic, as something that develops and progresses, as something through which humanity continually perfects itself. Humanity has a course "on which it progresses; through its inner alterations it too is perfected into something higher and complete. By no means does religion seek to hasten or direct this progress; it limits itself so that the finite can work only on the finite. Rather, religion only wishes to observe and perceive this progress as one of the great actions of the universe"(Crouter, 124; R^1 99).

An aesthetic worldview. This living unity in which the whole is directed and humanity progresses toward perfection is a harmonious and "eternal work of art" (Crouter, 123; R^1 97).[36] On this point, Schleiermacher's appropriation of Spinoza is infused with a Platonic strain. Schleiermacher has already appealed to aesthestics in order to describe the relation between the individual and the whole. Now, when the teleological vein enters in, the aesthetic becomes for him the redemptive: "The work of the moment and of centuries points in this direction; that is the great, ever-continuous redemptive work of eternal love" (Crouter, 127; R^1 104).[37] Although Schleiermacher does not expand on what he means by either redemption or love, what is indicated is that the livingness and unity of everything in the infinite has to do, if not with final causes for particulars, at least with the progress and teleology of the whole through history. Yet, at the same time that he emphasizes redemption and history, Schleiermacher also shares Spinoza's nonanthropocentric sensibility. Religion, as the system of intuitions, rejects the presumption of metaphysics and morality, which "see in the whole universe only humanity as the center of all relatedness, as the condition of all being and the cause of all becoming" (Crouter, 102; R^1

---

36. See Oman, 74.
37. See Oman, 82.

51). Thus, as was true in earlier essays, for Schleiermacher, as for Spinoza, the human is no exception to the rules of nature but is intricately caught up in the forces of nature. Only religion recognizes this. The false systematizers "place humanity in opposition to the universe and do not receive it from the hand of religion as a part of the universe and as something holy"(Crouter, 103; R^1 53).

Religion pushes beyond the finite, even the finite as human, to the infinite because it "lives its whole life in nature, but in the infinite nature of totality, the one and the all; what holds in nature for every individual also holds for the human being; ... religion wishes to intuit this and to divine this in detail in quiet submissiveness" (Crouter, 102; R^1 51). Religion approaches a "highest philosophy in which these two categories [the theoretical and the practical] unite and are always on the verge of finding it" (Crouter, 100; R^1 46); it seeks the "unity in the whole," the "unifying principle" for "dissimilar material" (Crouter, 99; R^1 45). Before this itself begins to sound too speculative, Schleiermacher reminds the despisers that his system is meant to be a realism, to counter the speculation of German idealism. Only religion gives system: "Why, for so long, did speculation give you deceptions instead of a system, and words instead of real thoughts? Why was it nothing but an empty game with formulas that always reappeared changed and to which nothing would ever correspond? Because it lacked religion, because the feeling for the infinite did not animate it" (Crouter, 103; R^1 54). Religion, then, gives real thoughts and ensures their correspondence to nature.

Feeling, Intuition, and God

A Higher Realism

Although the cast of characters had changed by 1799, the pressing philosophical problem bequeathed by Kant (namely, "how best to account for the ground of unity between the human self and the world" [Crouter, Introduction, 60]) continued to occupy Schleiermacher's attentions. Indeed, it received a new urgency in his polemic against Fichte, whose speculative idealism attempted to solve the problem by eliminating the noumenal realm altogether and positing an absolute ego that constructs its own world and that places nature at its own service. Against Fichte, Schleiermacher continues to maintain the underlying themes of his post-Kantian Spinozism. Not only is nature as real as our thoughts, but there is a correspondence that can be discovered through oscillation between the real and the ideal. Real and ideal (object and subject, extension and thought) are both grounded in the same unity, which is to say that our thoughts are themselves a part of the continuum of nature. Recall that in *Spinozismus* and *Spinozistisches System,* where he first developed his post-Kantian Spinozism, Schleiermacher had to defend Spinoza's infinite from the charge of being a mere universal, a form of idealism. In response, he argued for a realism that he described in terms of two kinds of knowledge. The first kind of knowledge, which has to do with our relation to the finite world of forces, is based on the *receptivity of organs.* There is an essentially passive character to our knowledge insofar as impressions are received from the outside and we are so constituted as to appropriate them in a certain way. This, however, does not preclude the possibility that, granted there are real things external to and independent of us, the notion of a world or a "totality" could still be nothing but a general idea abstracted from finite, concrete things. The second kind of knowledge, which has to do with our relation to the infinite and which is the precondition of any knowledge whatsoever, came as a sudden, breakthrough insight regarding Jacobi's *feeling for being* and Spinoza's *immediate intuition:* there is more to knowledge than just being reasonable; since what is not finite and discrete (i.e., the infinite whole) cannot be represented, it can only be known immediately through feeling or intuition.

In the *Reden* Schleiermacher develops this line of thought further. The realism implicit in the post-Kantian Spinozism of his earlier essays is now explicitly developed in relation to Fichte. Although reference is no longer made to Spinoza's philosophy, a "spirit of Spinozism" still characterizes Schleiermacher's thought. Indeed, Schleiermacher himself associates his realism with Spinoza:

> And how will the triumph of speculation, the completed and rounded idealism, fare if religion does not counterbalance it and allow it to glimpse a *higher realism* than that which it subordinates to itself so boldly and for such good reason? Idealism will destroy the universe by appearing to fashion it; it will degrade it to a mere allegory, to an empty silhouette of our own limitedness. Respectfully offer up with me a lock of hair to the manes of the holy rejected Spinoza! (Crouter, 103–4; R^1 54; emphasis added)

As was true in 1794, so in 1799 Schleiermacher's higher realism depends on the necessary and simultaneous explication of two elements of knowledge, receptivity and immediacy. Yet whereas in 1794 the terms *original feeling* or *immediate concept* had been almost afterthoughts, in 1799 *feeling* and *intuition* become the "hinge" of his whole argument (Crouter, 104; R^1 55).[38] What therefore needs to be examined is what, preliminarily, may be said of Schleiermacher's realism, what role feeling and intuition play, what theory of knowledge is operative, and why this realism is said to be *higher*.

The most evident fact of Schleiermacher's higher realism is presupposed by his monistic worldview in what he calls *system*. Nature is an organic system of forces to which humanity is no exception and which is grounded in and reveals an infinite whole. The religious intuition alone is able to consider finite things from two necessary points of view—in their connection to each other (the *All*) and in their relation to the infinite (the *One*). Central to his *organic monism* or *system* is the conviction that there is an extra-mental world of physical forces which acts upon us, of which we are a part, and which we can know both mediately and immediately. Therefore, *system* opposes any cleavage between mind and nature. There are, Schleiermacher holds, three *orientations of sense:* a sense of oneself, a sense of the world, and an oscillation between the two. There must be an "unconditional assumption of their innermost union" (Crouter, 156; R^1 165). This is the most basic meaning of his realism. Their innermost union is possible because there is an underlying ground to this finite, organic whole, namely the infinite and living nature, the world spirit. Through the finite world the infinite universe is constantly revealing itself to us:

> The same is true of religion. The universe exists in uninterrupted activity and reveals itself to us every moment. Every form that it brings forth, every being to which it gives a separate existence according to the fullness of life, every occurrence that spills forth from

---

38. Schleiermacher's understanding of *Anschauung* and its relation to *Gefühl* has been one of the most controversial issues in the history of Schleiermacher interpretation. See Brandt, *Philosophy of Schleiermacher*, chap. 4 and appendix 1; Beisser, *Schleiermachers Lehre von Gott*, 21–26; Crouter, Introduction to *On Religion*, 58–64; Friedrich Graf, "Ursprüngliches Gefühl unmittelbarer Koinzidenz des Differenten: Zur Modifikation des Religionsbegriffs in den verschiedenen Auflagen von Schleiermachers 'Reden über die Religion,'" *Zeitschrift für Theologie und Kirche* 75, no. 2 (1978): 147–86; Süskind, *Der Einfluß Schellings*, 100–133, 173–93; and Terrence N. Tice, "Schleiermacher's Conception of Religion: 1799 to 1831," *Archivio di Filosofia* 52, no. 1–3 (1984): 333–56.

its rich, ever-fruitful womb, is an action of the same upon us. (Crouter, 105; R^1 56)[39]

That is the spirit of the world that reveals itself in the smallest things just as perfectly and visibly as in the greatest; that is an intuition of the universe that develops out of everything and seizes the mind. (Crouter, 118; R^1 86)

Once again, the infinite *is* only insofar as it individualizes itself into finite things. Only religion, through intuition, sees the infinite in finite things as well as the connection of all things to one another.

Intuition is the "touchstone" (*Prüfstein*) between ourselves and the world, between the finite world and the infinite universe. It is that point of unity which ensures a correspondence and connection between our inner life and external nature, between our spiritual and bodily natures.[40] This correspondence, however, always remains rough. The modifier *higher* in part denotes a distinction from a naive realism: intuition and feeling adhere to the critical principle that we can know nothing of things in themselves, only of their actions upon us. In Schleiermacher's words, "All intuition proceeds from an influence of the intuited on the one who intuits, from an *original* and *independent* action of the former, which is then grasped, apprehended, and conceived by the latter according to one's own nature" (Crouter, 104; R^1 55; emphasis added). In this passage, "original" and "independent" underscore the *realism* of which intuition is an integral part; the universe is not constructed by the ego but has a real existence in itself. The terms *grasped* and *apprehended* underscore the qualification of this realism as *higher:* we do not know the universe as it is in itself but as it acts on us and as our imaginations form ideas out of sensible intuitions.

Schleiermacher offers an example of what he means by an intuition of an independent action. It is, he indicates, an immediate perception: "If the emanations of light—which happen completely without your efforts—did not affect your sense, if the smallest parts of the body, the tips of your fingers, were not mechanically or chemically affected, if the pressure of weight did not reveal to you an opposition and a limit to your power, you would intuit nothing and perceive nothing, and what you thus intuit and perceive is not the nature of things, but their action upon you. What you

---

39. Cf. Crouter, 109; R^1 67.
40. See R^1 87–88. In 1806 Schleiermacher changes "inner life" and "external nature" (*das Innere* and *das Aeußere*) to "spiritual nature" and "bodily nature" (*die geistige Natur* and *die körperliche*). See R^2 93.

know or believe about the nature of things lies far beyond the realm of intuition" (Crouter, 104–5; R^1 56). Hence, there are no intuitions apart from relation with a real world, apart from our active receptivity to the forces that act upon us. According to Schleiermacher, "The universe creates its own observers and admirers, and we only wish to intuit how that happens as far as it allows itself to be intuited" (Crouter, 145; R^1 143).[41] The world is neither contained in us nor projected by us; it is, rather, given previously to and independently of the self. Real objects "are indeed there, a well-acquired, inherited possession. . . . Only take them as life presents them" (Crouter, 148; R^1 148). Knowledge is essentially inductive. Still, although this example helps to illustrate Schleiermacher's realism with regard to our fundamental receptivity to the finite world, it raises an epistemological problem in that it does not sufficiently satisfy the other criterion of his higher realism, namely, how intuition can be an immediate apprehension of the infinite, and how this relates to knowledge of finite causes and relations. If intuition is an immediate perception of something finite and representable, how can it also be an intuition of something infinite and unrepresentable?

This question must be addressed through a consideration of the crucial but ambiguous terms, *Gefühl* and *Anschauung,* which are virtually identified in the first edition: "Religion's essence is neither thinking nor acting, but *intuition and feeling*. It wishes to intuit the universe, wishes devoutly to overhear the universe's own manifestation and actions, longs to be grasped and filled by the universe's immediate influences in childlike passivity" (Crouter, 102; R^1 50).[42] In 1806, however, there is a notable shift in his theory of knowledge, a shift echoed in his application of terms. *Gefühl* (feeling) becomes the primary organ of religion, whereas *Anschauung* (intuition) is more exclusively associated with knowledge of the universe. The fundamental contrast of 1799, that between metaphysics, morality, and religion, is identified in 1806 as that between knowledge, activity, and piety. This alteration reflects a clarification in Schleiermacher's thought regarding different kinds of knowledge and their relations. Of particular importance for the development of Schleiermacher's higher realism is the relation between scientific knowledge and piety, or feeling. Recall that in the essays of 1793–94, the more one understood the complexity of relations of finite things, the more one understood the infinite. The Spinozist worldview thus enabled Herder and Schleiermacher to reconcile the new science with their

41. Cf. Crouter, 119; R^1 88.
42. Cf. Crouter, 105, 109.

understandings of God. For Schleiermacher, this relation between science and religion more or less continues in the first edition of the *Reden*, where science stands with religion against speculation. In fact, science stands as an example of how religion can be said to be a realism, as opposed to Fichte's speculative idealism. Both science and religion want to discover the system already present, not to create and impose an arbitrary system.

Yet while Schleiermacher still maintains that the *One* can only be known in the *All* and the *All* in the *One,* and that science cannot contradict religion, and finally that Spinozism helps reconcile the two, nevertheless he makes it clear in the second edition that scientific knowledge is not religious knowledge. The difference between the two editions is subtle but significant. In 1799 Schleiermacher writes, "Praxis is an art, speculation is a science, religion is the sensibility and taste for the infinite" (Crouter, 103; R^1 53). In 1806 this sentence reads, "True science is complete vision; true practice is culture and art self-produced; true religion is sense and taste for the Infinite" (Oman, 39; R^2 49–50). Science, as "complete vision," involves knowledge of the interconnectedness of nature and its causal network. It still retains an immediacy of perception, but this is now something quite distinct from religion. Religious feeling has more exclusively to do with the infinite. Feeling is piety, Schleiermacher explains, as long as it expresses the being and life shared by oneself and the *All,* and as long as it is "the result of the operation of God in you by means of the operation of the world upon you" (Oman, 45–46; R^2 57). Feeling consists in neither perceptions nor objects of perception, both of which entail a mediated mode of knowing. In his 1806 revision Schleiermacher claims that the task of science is

> to show the peculiar relations by which each is what it is; to determine for each its place in the Whole, and to distinguish it rightly from all else; to present the whole real world in its mutually conditioned necessity; and to exhibit the oneness of all phenomena with their eternal laws. (Oman, 35; R^2 45–46)

This appears to be close to what Schleiermacher would have described, in 1794 and perhaps even in 1799, as religious knowledge. But in 1806 he continues,

> This is truly beautiful and excellent, and I am not disposed to depreciate. . . . And yet, however high you go; . . . though you allege that nature cannot be comprehended without God, I would still maintain that religion has nothing to do with this knowledge, and that, quite

apart from it, its nature can be known. Quantity of knowledge is not quantity of piety. (Ibid.)

The principle *nihil ex nihilo,* which for Schleiermacher ensures that scientific knowledge will not be violated, still holds but is not itself religious. Scientific knowledge becomes a limiting case to what can be said religiously. Piety, or feeling, now has the strictly passive character that knowledge does not. In 1806 Schleiermacher describes the two elements of the religious life as a surrendering of oneself to the universe, thus allowing oneself to be influenced by it, and a taking-up of this contact into the inner unity of one's life (Oman, 58; R^2 72).

In conclusion, Schleiermacher's system is a *realism* insofar as it affirms an extra-mental reality and the rough correspondence between our ideas and the finite world (scientifically speaking), and between feeling and the operation of the infinite upon us (religiously speaking). Intuition and feeling are the touchstone, the point of contact, that guarantees that rough correspondence, which is based on the oscillating movement between what is self and not-self. Morality and metaphysics have no such touchstone, for they anxiously try to construct their own finite systems without recognizing the infinite system. Further, it is a *realism* to a large degree in that it is a rejection of Fichte's speculative idealism. There is for Schleiermacher an ego, but it is not what he takes to be Fichte's absolute and abstracted ego. Schleiermacher's ego exists in intimate connection to the nature it perceives. His higher realism is based on a theory of individuality according to which the individual is a positive presentation of the infinite. Schleiermacher's system represents a *higher realism* insofar as it is post-Kantian—that is to say, it acknowledges the structures of our understanding and the limits of our reason; things are not just as we perceive them to be. It is also a *higher realism* insofar as it rejects all one-sidedness, according to which one element in a pair of polar coordinates would be eliminated (world, object, extension) and the other distorted (self, subject, thought). For Schleiermacher it will not do to hold a simple realism over against idealism. A dialectical relation between the two must be maintained, hence the emphasis on the oscillating movement.

Schleiermacher's *system* remains a form of Spinozism, not only nominally in its direct appeal to Spinoza ("the holy rejected Spinoza!"), but also fundamentally. As was true in his earlier essays of 1793–94, Spinoza still helps him, on the one hand, to overcome Kant's bifurcated reality by insisting on the unity of all that is, and, on the other hand, to avoid Fichte's resolution of that bifurcation by insisting on the reality of nature and our dependence on it. But the appeal in 1799 finds something else in Spinoza: Spinoza's intuition of the infinite is an expression of a pious sensibility.

Imaging God

Inherent in his criticisms of metaphysics and morality and in his insistence that religion is a distinct and indispensable third is Schleiermacher's critique of conventional religion. In its self-serving claims for a personal God and immortality, conventional religion (which in the *Reden* he associates with the "bourgeois life") suppresses the religious capacity with which every person is born. Schleiermacher's own doubt regarding such conventional views had been present in his earlier student days and had led to a rift between him and his father. Recounting those times of troubled questioning, he says that religion had remained the one constant in his life: "Religion was the maternal womb in whose holy darkness my young life was nourished and prepared for the world still closed to it. . . . It guided me into the active life. It taught me, with my virtues and defects, to keep myself holy in my undivided existence, and only through it have I learned friendship and love" (Crouter, 84; R^1 14–15).[43] Schleiermacher's twofold objective in the *Reden* is to convince the despisers that the foundations of conventional religion—namely "fear of an eternal being and reliance on another world" (Crouter, 88; R^1 22)—are not necessarily religious and may even be irreligious, and to present a view of religion that does not depend on concepts but on *piety* (*Frömmigkeit* or *Pietät*). His criticism of the complacent and superstitious nature of conventional religion culminates toward the end of the second Speech in a redefinition of miracle, inspiration, and revelation. "One can," he writes, "have much religion without coming into contact with any of these concepts" (Crouter, 132; R^1 116). The same is true with the concept of God. Schleiermacher proceeds to outline three errors in conventional religion's conceptualization of God.

First, many concepts of God have too anthropocentric an orientation. Schleiermacher charges that conventional religion fashions God after humanity in order to maintain humanity's separate and special status in nature. In his words, "To most people God is obviously nothing more than the genius of humanity. Man is the prototype of their God, humanity is

---

43. For more on Schleiermacher's use of the metaphor of the feminine to describe religion, see Katherine M. Faull, "Schleiermacher—A Feminist? Or, How to Read Gender Inflected Theology," in *Schleiermacher and Feminism: Sources, Evaluations, and Responses*, ed. Iain G. Nicol (Lewiston: Edwin Mellen Press, 1992), 13–32.

everything to them, and in accord with what they consider its events and directives they determine the dispositions and the essence of their God" (Crouter, 136; R^1 125). Against such anthropocentric tendencies, which he thinks trespasses the limits of piety, Schleiermacher develops his organic and aesthetic monism, which sees humanity in its intimate connection with the rest of nature and thus avoids making it an idol. "Humanity," he says, "is not everything to me" (ibid.).

Second, humanity seems to be everything to those who cling nervously to the belief in immortality, another notion steeped in anthropocentrism. The need to assert one's own immortality marks the withdrawal of oneself into the self and the suspension of the religious movement of oscillation between the self and the other, thus severing the awareness of the *One and All*. In our attempt to gain security, we actually lose our individuality. Schleiermacher offers harsh judgment of those who insist on immortality: "But they resist the infinite and do not wish to get beyond themselves; they wish to be nothing other than themselves and they are anxiously concerned about their individuality. . . . But they do not want to seize the sole opportunity death affords them to transcend humanity; they are anxious about how they will take it with them beyond this world, and their highest endeavor is for further sight and better limbs" (Crouter, 139; R^1 131). Schleiermacher takes the desire for immortality to be rooted in an irreverent disposition that misses the essence of religion because its primary intuition is no longer of the infinite.

Third, although in 1799 Schleiermacher does not yet use the term *personal God*, it is clearly implied in his criticism of anthropocentric views of the deity. Recall that in *Spinozistisches System,* he followed Spinoza in refusing the attributes of intellect and will, both because we cannot speak of the divine inner attributes and because to affirm them would result in anthropomorphism. Both of these reasons are still operative in the *Reden,* although the latter is more explicit. At the beginning of the second Speech, he accuses the "practical people" of projecting the idea of good onto the universe and then further projecting human traits, so that they have a metaphysical natural law and a lawgiver. Now, at the end of that same speech, he sternly warns that the God of religion can neither "guarantee our happiness" nor "incite us to ethical life, for he is not considered other than as acting, and there can neither be any action upon our ethical life, nor can we conceive of any" (Crouter, 138–39; R^1 130). God is not always who or what we want God to be.

The problem with anthropocentric and anthropomorphic conceptions of God is that, in addition to being irreverent, they make God into an individual being and thus place God within the realm of opposition. God is beyond all opposition of species, beyond all individuality.[44] Schleiermacher explains,

> There may be minds that are more poetic, and I confess that I believe these stand higher, for whom God is an individual being wholly distinct from humanity, the single example of a particular type. . . . But I strive for even more types of beings than one above and beyond humanity, and every class, with its individual being, is subordinated to the universe. Can God in this sense thus be for me anything else than an individual intuition? Yet these may be only incomplete concepts of God. If we immediately proceed to the highest concept, to that of a highest being, of a spirit of the universe that rules it with freedom and understanding, religion is still not dependent upon this idea. (Crouter, 136; R^1 125–26)

The infinite is that *higher unity* (the *One*) that does not abrogate but grounds and includes genuine multiplicity (the *All*). Schleiermacher implicitly employs an apophatic theology here. He is not so much replacing one concept of God with another as he is reminding us that no concept of God is adequate. Concepts are always mediated, whereas feeling or piety is immediate. This does not mean that we ought to abandon any talk about God, but two elements must always be present—piety and oscillation.

Schleiermacher defines three levels of religious intuition and their corresponding conceptualizations of God.[45] The first arises from a confused and dim presentiment of the infinite whole. It recognizes a unity, but only a unity devoid of any difference, and is thus viewed as chaotic, arbitrary, and blind. The resulting concept of the deity is of an idol or fetish. The second level of religious intuition sees the inverse, namely, a "multiplicity without unity." Blind chance gives way to "motivated necessity," the grounding of which we seek in vain, since there is no unity. The corresponding concept of the deity is characterized by anthropomorphism and plurality, in short, polytheism. The third level of religious intuition, where Schleiermacher locates himself and Spinoza, is "the point where all conflict is again united,

---

44. See Robert R. Williams, *Schleiermacher the Theologian. The Construction of the Doctrine of God* (Philadelphia: Fortress Press, 1978), esp. 14–15. Williams sees Schleiermacher as the heir of Nikolaus Cusanus in that he conceives of God as the bipolar coincidence of opposites.

45. See Crouter 137; R^1 126–27. This scheme is retained in the *Glaubenslehre* as fetishism, polytheism, and monotheism.

where the universe manifests itself as totality, as unity in multiplicity, as system and thus for the first time deserves its name." At this level it does not matter whether one conceptualizes God as personal or as nonpersonal *natura naturans;* what matters is this intuition of the *One and All.* This is why Spinoza is deemed so excellent an example of piety: "Should not the one who intuits it as one and all thus have more religion, even without the idea of God, than the most cultured polytheist? Should Spinoza not stand just as far above a pious Roman, as Lucretius does above one who serves idols?" A particular belief in God "depends on the direction of the imagination" (Crouter, 138; R^1 129)[46] and can therefore not be taught or enforced, only drawn out. Hence Schleiermacher concludes Speech 2 with the controversial claim that "God is not everything in religion, but one, and the universe is more; furthermore, you cannot believe in him by force of will or because you want to use him for solace and help, but because you must" (Crouter, 140; R^1 134).

Such statements proved too controversial to Fr. S. G. Sack, Schleiermacher's superior and censor of the *Reden,* who found the view of God presented in Speech 2 to be an apology for pantheism and a presentation of Spinozism. In his letter to Schleiermacher in 1801, Sack claims that this Spinozistic "system appears to put an end to all that religion has meant and been to me up to now" (Blackwell, "Antagonistic Correspondence," 113). Like Jacobi, Sack sees no compromise, no coexistence, between Spinozism and Christianity. He defines Spinozism as that which deifies the universe and subordinates such concepts as God, providence, and immortality. Spinozism, in short, is a denial of a personal God. For Sack, of course, this last is the crux of the matter. The Christian view must be that of a personal God who is a "self-conscious, wise, and good Being; that makes me the creature of an Omnipotence and Wisdom that is nowhere and everywhere; that would rob me of the exalted joy, the indestructible, sweet need to lift up my eyes in thanksgiving to a Benefactor" (115). This view necessarily includes a belief in immortality, for with this personal God one does not "just vanish into the universe after death" (116), a reference to Schleiermacher's mystical view of death.

In his letter of response, Schleiermacher reminds Sack that he has never spoken of such notions as a personal God with contempt. The point, and it is a significant one, is that the concept of God, whether it be personal or

---

46. He uses this same phrase in *On Freedom* (27). For a closer examination of the role of the imagination or phantasy in Schleiermacher's early thought, see Blackwell, *Schleiermacher's Early Philosophy of Life,* part 3.

nonpersonal, is in fact not what is essential. For the first time, however, he denies that he is a Spinozist and claims that any reference he has made to Spinoza has to do purely with that thinker's piety. He writes, "Though I am as little a Spinozist as anyone, I introduced Spinoza as an example, because throughout his *Ethics* a sensibility prevails that one can only call piety" (118). Indeed, Schleiermacher's position, which he develops further in the *Glaubenslehre,* is that his presentation of religion is independent of any metaphysical system. Although Schleiermacher claimed such charges as Sack's were unfounded, the two revisions he would undertake, in 1806 and 1821, reflect sensitivity to these criticisms. In these revisions Schleiermacher would distance himself from Spinoza and yet continue to appeal to that philosopher's sensibility and to insist on the fundamental continuity between the *Reden* and the *Glaubenslehre.* Most important for determining the extent to which his early post-Kantian Spinozism influenced his later Christian theology are his responses to major criticisms that were written in the decade when he was finishing the final editions of the *Reden* and working on his *Glaubenslehre.*

A Platonized Spinozism

In conclusion, the four themes that had defined Schleiermacher's post-Kantian Spinozism of 1794 (organic monism, ethical determinism, critical realism, and nonanthropomorphism) were carried through to the *Reden* of 1799, Schleiermacher's first major theological work. There are, however, subtle developments, attributable partly to the normal processes of time and maturity, but mostly to his enthusiastic embrace of romanticism and its particular brand of Platonism. As a result, Schleiermacher's post-Kantian Spinozism was infused with Platonism. This is not to say that Plato had not been influential in Schleiermacher's thought before his return to Berlin in 1796. Eilert Herms points out that Plato was present even in the younger Schleiermacher.[47] Yet this is true only in a weak or most general sense. In an essay written in 1789, while still a student at the University of Halle, Schleiermacher devoted a short section to Plato, whose moral philosophy aided him in rejecting Kant's notion of transcendental freedom.[48] But he

---

47. See Eilert Herms, "Platonismus und Aristotelismus in Schleiermachers Ethik," in Sorrentino, ed., *Schleiermacher's Philosophy and the Philosophical Tradition,* 9.
48. See *Über das höchste Gut,* in *KGA* 1/1:81–125; translated by H. Victor Froese under the title *On the Highest Good* (Lewiston: Edwin Mellen Press, 1992).

was not then obsessed with Plato in the way that he had been with other philosophers. In the Spinoza essays of 1793–94, the influence of Plato seems to have been mostly filtered through Herder, Hemsterhuis, and Shaftesbury. Herder, the chief representative of neo-Spinozism, considered the spirit of Spinozism to be consistent with the spirit of Platonism.[49] The Dutch philosopher Hemsterhuis, whom Schleiermacher identified as a contributor to his sudden insight regarding the original feeling for being, was popular in certain German intellectual circles precisely because of his Platonism. The third earl of Shaftesbury, whose "aesthetic pantheism" was supposed to have influenced Schleiermacher,[50] was himself directly influenced by the Cambridge Platonists.[51] To the degree that these three thinkers influenced the Schleiermacher of 1793, his essays on Spinoza can be said to have Platonic undertones. Nevertheless, whatever Platonism was present in the earliest years, it had not yet become Schleiermacher's own. He would later admit to his friend Henriette Herz, "How little I understood Plato on the whole when first I read him at the University . . . , yet even then how I loved and admired him."[52]

The initial wave of an active appropriation of Plato appears in the *Reden* of 1799, where virtually every aspect of Schleiermacher's post-Kantian Spinozism is Platonized. His organic monism becomes more explicitly an aesthetic monism;[53] in turn, also due to the influence of the "divine Plato" (Crouter, 158; R^1 168), the aesthetic becomes for him the redemptive.[54] A parallel development can be found in his ethical determinism. In the essays on Spinoza, Schleiermacher, anticipating criticisms from Jacobi and Kant, was careful to develop a moral anthropology that well accounted for individuality. In the *Reden,* the Platonic aesthetic worldview enables him to further establish the irreducible value of the individual as being grounded

---

49. In the fifth conversation, Theophron says to Theano, "I thank the shade of Spinoza for having provided me with such pleasant hours of conversation with you; . . . these conversations with you afford me a second enjoyment, namely they bring back to me my youthful ideas, with which I spent and surely more than dreamed away many sweet hours at the feet of Leibniz, Shaftesbury and Plato." Herder, *God, Some Conversations,* 191.

50. See Dilthey, "Shaftesbury und Spinoza," 169.

51. See Charles Taylor, "Moral Sentiments," in *Sources of the Self: The Making of the Modern Identity* (Cambridge: Harvard University Press, 1989), 248–65.

52. Schleiermacher to Herz, 10 August 1802, *ASL* 1:312; quoted and trans. in Blackwell, *Schleiermacher's Early Philosophy of Life,* 127.

53. The "alternating production and destruction of the organic components of the whole" (*Spinozismus,* 532) becomes "the harmony of the universe, the wondrous and great unity in its eternal work of art" (Crouter, 123; R^1 97).

54. ". . . the great, ever-continuous redemptive work of eternal love." Crouter, 127; R^1 104.

in the infinite, as contributing to the eternal work of art, and as being itself a microcosm of the whole. In short, Plato helped Schleiermacher in articulating what Gadamer refers to as a "metaphysics of the individual" ("Schleiermacher Platonicien," 37). Finally, Schleiermacher found in Plato confirmation of the critical realism he had begun to develop in the Spinoza essays; hence, what in 1794 was a rather muddled account of an immediate apprehension of the infinite becomes the confident higher realism of 1799. Schleiermacher's enduring commitment to both Plato and Spinoza rested on the fact that each recognized our knowledge of the infinite as being primary and original.[55]

Another major shift occurred in Schleiermacher's relation to Plato, when, upon completion of the first edition of the *Reden*, his friend Friedrich Schlegel convinced him to participate in a translation of Plato's dialogues into German.[56] Eventually, Schlegel would not live up to his part of the bargain, and the undertaking fell entirely onto Schleiermacher, occupying him until 1804. He wrote to his beloved at the time, Eleonore Grunow, "Plato is incontestably the author whom I know best, and with whom I have almost coalesced."[57] This coalescence with Plato, however, did not undermine the affinity he felt with Spinoza. If anything, it only served to reinforce it. Indeed, in his *Grundlinien einer Kritik der bisherigen Sittenlehre* of 1803, Schleiermacher's synthesis of Plato and Spinoza is made more explicit than ever. There he allies himself with the ethical tradition of Plato and Spinoza, which he claims is a third alternative to, on the one side, the eudaemonistic tradition represented by Aristotle and the "English school" (Shaftesbury), and on the other side, the rationalist tradition represented by Kant.[58] In Schleiermacher's theology the synthesis of Plato and

---

55. See Schleiermacher, *Grundlinien*, 35.

56. For more on Schleiermacher's translation and ordering of Plato's dialogues, see Dilthey, "Schleiermachers Übersetzung des Platon," in *Leben Schleiermachers*, in *Gesammelte Schriften* 13/2:37–75, and Hans Joachim Krämer, "The Loss and Recovery of the Indirect Platonic Tradition: The Position of Schleiermacher and Its Consequences," in *Plato and the Foundations of Metaphysics: A Work on the Theory of the Principles and Unwritten Doctrines of Plato with a Collection of the Fundamental Documents*, ed. and trans. by John R. Catan (Albany, State University of New York Press, 1990).

57. Schleiermacher to Grunow, 3 September 1802, *ASL* 1:327; quoted and trans. in Blackwell, *Schleiermacher's Early Philosophy of Life*, 128. According to Blackwell, "this immersion in Plato separates the first edition of the *Speeches* from the second edition of 1806, and because of this alterations in the latter provide a particularly sensitive index of Plato's influence on Schleiermacher's thinking." Ibid.

58. For more on the *Grundlinien*, see Wallhauser, "Schleiermacher's Critique of Ethical Reason," and Herms, "Platonismus und Aristotelismus in Schleiermachers Ethik."

Spinoza is captured in the dialectic of the *One and All*. It was through maintaining this dialectic that he thought he could avoid the dangers of materialism and pantheism about which Jacobi had warned. But the criticisms still came, and in the 1820's he still found himself having to explain his *Reden* and revise his *Glaubenslehre*.

3

SPINOZISM, PANTHEISM, AND CHRISTIAN DOGMATICS
EXPLANATIONS AND REVISIONS, 1821–1830

> *How was I to expect, because I ascribed piety to Spinoza, I would myself be taken for a Spinozist?*
>
> —F.D.E. Schleiermacher, *On Religion*

In 1821 Schleiermacher published two significant works, the first edition of his Christian dogmatics, or *Glaubenslehre*, and the third edition of his *Reden*, which included lengthy notes or "Explanations" (*Erläuterungen*). The timing of the two publications was not coincidental, since, more than being a response to further criticisms of the *Reden*, the Explanations represent an attempt to reconcile the tension (for Schleiermacher, only apparent) between the *Reden* and his *Glaubenslehre*. Of these two theological works, arguably the two masterpieces of his career, Schleiermacher writes, "In form they are very different and their points of departure lie far apart, yet in matter they are quite parallel."[1] Whether or not one agrees with this assessment, the question remains, What happens to Schleiermacher's religious worldview and approach to the question of God when translated into the language and the method of Christian dogmatics? More specific, What happens to those post-Kantian Spinozist themes which Schleiermacher first

---

1. Explanation 5 to the second Speech; Oman, 105. Hereafter, in-text, parenthetical reference to Schleiermacher's Explanations of 1821 will be in the form "Expl. 2.5; Oman, 105." The first number refers to the Speech, the second to the note or explanation.

developed in his early philosophical essays and then carried over into the *Reden?*

This chapter addresses these questions through an analysis of those texts in the Explanations and in both editions of the *Glaubenslehre,* including marginal notes, that relate directly to the subjects of Spinozism and pantheism. These texts reveal a development of Schleiermacher's own subtle understanding of an acceptable form of pantheism, which is, by its very definition, a rejection of any understanding of pantheism as a crass identity of God and nature or as a form of materialism. In the Explanations, Schleiermacher's approach to this issue involves a threefold argument: an explanation of the apparent Spinozism of the first edition; a denial of atheism; a defense of pantheism understood as a type of language about God. In the second edition of the *Glaubenslehre,* Schleiermacher makes revisions that, as his marginal notes reveal, were intended to address charges of Spinozism and pantheism. These revisions do not mark a substantial shift in his position; rather, they serve as important clarifications of what he has already said in the *Reden* and the first edition of the *Glaubenslehre.* Taken together, the Explanations and the revisions of the *Glaubenslehre* indicate that Schleiermacher can be said to be pantheistic in two, very qualified, senses: in his espousal of, or at least tolerance for, a nonpersonal conception of God; and in his own adaptation of the ancient pantheist dictum *One and All.* In both these senses, his pantheism is identical with his Spinozism. His Spinozism, however, which also must be understood in a very qualified manner, is broader than his pantheism.

Explanations to the *Reden*

In his reply to Sack's letter in 1801, Schleiermacher appealed to the notion of a pious sensibility as his main defense against suspicions of Spinozism. His tribute to Spinoza in the second Speech, he insisted, had to do with that man's deep piety, not with his philosophy. Twenty years later, in his Explanations to the third edition of the *Reden,* Schleiermacher continues to argue along the same lines, but the passing of time had suggested additional reasons to him. In retrospect, he claims he had to object to the literalist view of Spinoza, on the one hand, and (he is careful to add) an idolization of Spinoza, on the other. Spinoza, he explains, had been at that time the center of attention because of Jacobi's controversial *Über die Lehre des*

Spinoza. Besides, he himself had been admittedly youthful and had not anticipated that he would be so misunderstood.[2] In fact, his argument is much more nuanced than either Spinoza's piety or these circumstantial reasons would suggest. Although the appeal to piety does indeed play a determining role in these Explanations, it is developed not in relation to Spinoza or Spinozism, but in the context of his discussions on atheism and pantheism.

Atheism Denied

In the first Speech of each edition of the *Reden,* Schleiermacher admits to a time in his youth when traditional understandings of God were empty of meaning for him: "Religion helped me when I began to examine the ancestral faith and to purify my heart of the rubble of primitive times. It remained with me when God and immortality disappeared before my doubting eyes" (Crouter, 84; R^1 15).[3] Such an admission invited strong protests, and he found it necessary to add an Explanation that denied "that there ever was a time when he was an unbeliever or an atheist" (Expl. 1.2; Oman, 23). His denial of atheism rests on the distinction, fundamental to Schleiermacher, between conceptualization and piety. There is, Schleiermacher holds, a "hidden kernel" of piety, described in the *Reden* as sense and taste for the infinite and in the second edition of the *Glaubenslehre* as the feeling of absolute dependence. As children, this is nurtured in us and interpreted by us in highly "sensuous" (anthropomorphic) terms, since "the soul lives entirely in images" (Expl. 1.2; Oman, 22). As we mature, however, we come to recognize the inadequacy of such conceptions. The childish images vanish, but "the unknown greatness remains" (Expl. 1.2; Oman, 23). In other words, through the course of religious development, language about God becomes less and less metaphorical: "The analogy with the human in the conception of the Highest Being and the analogy with the earthly still remains the shell of the hidden kernel. But those who are early absorbed in a pure contemplative endeavour take another way. There is nothing in God . . . opposed, divided or isolated. Wherefore nothing human can be said of Him" (Expl. 1.2; Oman, 22). Metaphorical language thus reaches the limit where it becomes "untenable" and "incapable of living reproduction" (Expl. 1.2; Oman, 22).[4]

    2. Explanation 3 to the second Speech; Oman, 104.
    3. Cf. Oman, 9.
    4. This view of analogy is significant for understanding Schleiermacher's doctrine of God since it shows him coming to terms with, and placing himself in relation to, the traditional ways of attributing names to God. Here, as in $Gl.^2$ §50.3, Schleiermacher rejects the way of

Yet it is just as wrong to take the purely contemplative, negative approach and deny *any* speech about God. Although the lower, more sensuous coefficients should ideally be abandoned, the implicit faith becomes attached to higher and higher coefficients (i.e., more unified, integrated, comprehensive concepts). What Schleiermacher means here is that, as he had argued in *Spinozismus* and the *Reden*, the infinite can never be felt apart from finite things, yet at the same time, the religious consciousness never stays fixed on particular things but pushes beyond to glimpse the wider interconnectedness, and then it pulls back again to the particular in order to glimpse the infinite in it. This is the method of the religious consciousness: an oscillation between the particular and the whole, the finite and the infinite, the One and the Many. "But the Infinite . . . we cannot be conscious of immediately and through itself. It can only be through a finite object, by means of which our tendency to postulate and seek a world, leads us from detail and part to the All and the Whole" (Expl. 2.2; Oman, 103). Consequently, some degree of anthropomorphism is unavoidable in religion, since although religious feeling is immediate, it is always and necessarily accompanied by mediated existence: "I in nowise blame these representations. Rather I acknowledge them as indispensable, for otherwise the subject could not be spoken of in such a way that any distinction could be drawn between the more correct and less correct" (Expl. 2.6; Oman, 107). Still, such representations become "vain mythology" when the aid to religion is mistaken for the essence of religion or for exact knowledge. Not only are the aid and the essence to be distinguished, but when the aid is no longer meaningful, when mythology becomes vain, it must be reworked (re-presented) or eliminated. Piety therefore requires that we be willing to let go of certain concepts of God.

In summary, the fact that certain ideas of God are eclipsed or eliminated from religious consciousness is not necessarily an indicator of atheism. Atheism, as Schleiermacher redefines it, is not a denial of certain traditional and anthropomorphic concepts of God, but a godlessness, a lack of piety at the very core; it is not merely a rejection of a religious tradition, but of

---

analogy, although he does not make a distinction between metaphorical and analogical language. Ironically, although the way of analogy was meant in part to curtail anthropomorphism, both Schleiermacher and Spinoza deemed it too anthropomorphic and beyond the limits of piety. Schleiermacher chooses the *via causalitatis*. He does so explicitly in *Glaubenslehre*, but it is also implicit here in the Explanations to the *Reden*: "Underneath this coherence there is a unity conditioning all things and conditioning our relations to the other parts of the Whole." Expl. 2.5. We can only speak of God insofar as God is the cause. Spinoza rejects the way of causality and espouses instead the more radical approach of univocity.

the living, divine connectedness of all existence. This is the atheism that Schleiermacher rejects, and he takes this atheism to be something categorically different from pantheism. Whereas atheism is for him the absence of piety, pantheism can be as legitimate a way of conceptualizing the deity as theism. Hence, his response to charges of pantheism, such as those advanced by Sack in 1801 and by Delbrück after 1821, is other than his response to the charge of atheism. In both cases, piety remains the determining factor.

Pantheism Redefined

One passage of the *Reden* that attracted charges of pantheism is in the first Speech, where Schleiermacher defines the pious soul as one "surrendered to the Universe" (Oman, 18; R^2 24).[5] His critics, it seems, were alarmed by his use of *Universum* or *Weltall* instead of *Gott*. Beyond replying that what he means is more completely developed in his *Glaubenslehre*, Schleiermacher defends himself, first, by explicitly rejecting two understandings of pantheism (as materialism and as belief in a world soul), and second by describing another way of understanding pantheism that he takes to be fully compatible with piety.

As resolutely as he had in 1793–94, Schleiermacher denies any hint of pantheism interpreted as materialism. Recall that, in his earlier essays, he had refuted Jacobi's interpretation of Spinozism as a rationalism that inevitably results in materialism, that is to say, in the reduction of anything spiritual (intellect, will, the divine) to a physical mechanism. Here, in the Explanations of 1821, he likewise quickly dismisses materialistic pantheism but implies that there may be another understanding of pantheism that could be more appropriately associated with him: "But none who reflect on the little that is said about pantheism will suspect me of any *materialistic pantheism*" (Expl. 2.19; Oman, 115; emphasis added). Any simplified understanding of pantheism, such as a crude identification of God and world or a reduction of the former to the latter, is not even a point of discussion for him.

Schleiermacher also rejects an understanding of pantheism based on the notion of a world soul. Critics thought Schleiermacher approaches this when, in the second Speech, he writes, "To love the world spirit and joyfully

---

5. "... in einem dem Weltall sich hingebenden Gemüth." Cf. Crouter, 92: R^1 30: "eine heilige Seele vom Universum berührt wird."

observe its work is the goal of our religion" (Crouter, 115; R^1 80).[6] In response, Schleiermacher explains that there is a difference between what is usually meant by world soul and what he intends by world spirit. Whereas the former implies a reciprocal relation between God and world, or a certain independence of the world from God, the latter denotes "the object of pious adoration in a way that would include all different forms and stages of religion" (Expl. 2.12; Oman, 111). Evidenced here is a more systematic treatment of the God-world relationship and a certain distancing from the neo-Spinozism of the 1780s and 1790s. Piety, as always for Schleiermacher, is the fundamental criterion of religious language, but what it entails is now more carefully explicated in terms of Christian doctrine. At the very least, the world must be understood as being dependent completely on God, and as effecting no change in God. Such limits, however, do not narrowly confine religion and indeed may include a certain kind of pantheism which, Schleiermacher argues, is as acceptable as traditional theistic conceptions of God and indeed may even be more pious. Three defining characteristics of this pious pantheism can be discerned from Schleiermacher's various Explanations: God is not an extramundane cause; the relation between God and world is best described in terms of the *One and All;* God can be conceived of in nonpersonal terms. Each of these is consistent with his post-Kantian Spinozism.

First, God's transcendence is not understood spatially, therefore God cannot be understood as outside the world. This theme has been central to his understanding of God since his earliest essays and is part of his *organic monism* (1794), what he himself has called *system* (1799); in the *Glaubenslehre* it is perhaps best described as a *causal monism*. Schleiermacher does not identify the world with God, which is the most common understanding of pantheism, yet he continues to insist that God is not an extramundane cause: "What, however, has struck most readers is that the Infinite Existence does not appear to be the Highest Being as cause of the World but the World itself. I do not think that God can be placed in such a relation as cause, and *I leave you to say whether the World can be conceived as a true All and Whole without God"* (Expl. 2.2; Oman, 103; emphasis added).[7]

Second, as this quotation suggests, what distinguishes Schleiermacher's insight from either pantheism (as a simple identification of God and world)

---

6. Cf. Oman, 65; Pünjer, 84–85.

7. He carries this train of thought through into his *Glaubenslehre,* where he argues that there can be no nonreligious interpretation of the nature system, since the unity in plurality requires absolute oneness.

or theism (as positing a personal God as external cause of the world) is his understanding of the dialectical relation between the All and Whole and God. The particular and individual is always a manifestation of the Whole, which is grounded by the One: "We do not feel ourselves dependent on the Whole in so far as it is an aggregate of mutually conditioned parts of which we ourselves are one, but only in so far as underneath this coherence there is a unity conditioning all things and conditioning our relations to the other parts of the Whole" (Expl. 2.5; Oman, 106). Indeed, the highest stage of religious consciousness, what is termed monotheism in the *Glaubenslehre,* is the recognition of the universe "as unity in multiplicity, as system" (Crouter, 137; R^1 128).[8]

Third, Schleiermacher's position differs from conventional Christian theism in that it does not necessarily view God in personal terms. If Schleiermacher can be said at all to be pantheistic, or at least to allow pantheism, it is only so in terms of his tolerance and even preference for a nonpersonal view of God and his appeal to the dictum *One and All.* The real difference between the personal and nonpersonal ways of conceiving God is at the heart of the debate. This was true in Lessing's and Jacobi's conversations in 1780, in Schleiermacher's response to Jacobi in 1793–94, in his correspondence with Sack of 1801, and in his letter to Jacobi in 1818. It remains a heated issue in 1821 when Schleiermacher is working out his Christian dogmatics. In the *Reden* of 1821, a definite clarification of his thought can be detected if we apply a series of four distinctions implicit in both the main text and the Explanations, namely, those between personal and nonpersonal ways of conceiving God, between a nonpersonal and impersonal God, between the idea of a personal God and the personality of God as a metaphysical attribute, and finally, between a personal and a living God.

Imaging God

Personal and Nonpersonal Ideas of God

The theistic (personal) and pantheistic (nonpersonal) modes of conceiving God are not mutually exclusive but are, insofar as each is an expression of piety, two viable alternatives in approaching the question of God. Pantheism is not a lower or less developed form of theism. On the contrary, it exists alongside theism on every level of religious consciousness: "Just as

---

8. Cf. Oman, 97; Pünjer, 127.

little are the personal and the opposing pantheistic modes of conception two such individual forms [of religion]. They go through all three types of religion and, for that reason alone, cannot be individualities" (Oman, 222; R^2 254).[9] As is evident already in the first edition of the *Reden*, Schleiermacher considers there to be three stages of religious consciousness. The first stage is chaos. At this stage of fetishism one finds few conceptions at all, and whatever ones there may be are so undetermined that the personal and pantheistic modes are virtually indistinguishable. At the second stage, the images become more definite but are multiple. Thus, for instance, if one tends toward a more personal view of God, this image may become "higher" and progress to the second level. The image is then more definite and integrative, "but at the same time divides and multiplies, each power and element becomes animate, and gods arise in endless number" (Oman, 96; R^2 126). The result is a polytheism, such as that found in ancient Greece and Rome. If, however, one tends more toward pantheism, God is imaged more as a "higher necessity," which in the first stage is mistaken for blind fate. Thus both pantheism and theism may be present, and both may adequately express the religious consciousness. At this second stage, however, Schleiermacher judges the nonpersonal to be preferable to the personal: "But this stage ... is more perfect than the former, especially if the idea of the Highest Being is placed rather in the eternal unattainable necessity, than in single gods" (Oman, 97; R^3 126). From what he has said elsewhere, this is so because the nonpersonal or pantheistic tendency (at this second stage) lessens the danger of going beyond piety by slipping into too much anthropomorphism, and it thus nurtures a less anthropocentric sensibility.

At the third stage, existence is viewed as "totality, as unity in variety, as system" (Crouter, 137; R^1 128)[10] and "as One and All."[11] This stage, which in the *Glaubenslehre* Schleiermacher identifies as monotheism, seems to be a development from his earlier organic monism. But here, as at the two previous stages, the pantheistic form of imaging (as a rejection of the idea of a personal God) is at least *as viable* as the more personal form. The various revisions Schleiermacher makes in describing this third stage underscore this fact. In the original version, he says little beyond this brief definition except to say that Spinoza, because he recognized such unity, must be considered more religious than, say, a "pious Roman" (Crouter, 137; R^1 127).[12] In 1806, he drops the direct appeal to Spinoza, although

9. Cf. Crouter, 198; R^1 256–57. The text is virtually the same in all editions.
10. Cf. Oman, 97; Pünjer, 127.
11. R^1 128: "als Eins und Alles."
12. This was his second and last direct appeal to Spinoza in the *Reden*.

he still defends a "Pantheist" or "Spinozist" on the grounds, so familiar by now, that "the manner in which the Deity is present to [us] in feeling, is decisive of the worth of [our] religion, not the manner, *always inadequate, in which it is copied in idea*" (Oman, 97; R^2 127; emphasis added). In 1821 he makes the additional claim that the pantheistic view, as a rejection of the idea of a personal God, may be even more adequate, since "the ground of such a rejection might be a humble consciousness of the limitation of personal existence, and particularly of personality joined to consciousness" (Oman, 97; R^3 127). Once again, the criterion is piety.

The idea that one attaches to piety, whether it be described as sense and taste for the infinite or as the feeling of absolute dependence, depends, as Schleiermacher already made clear in 1799, on the "direction of the imagination" (Crouter, 138; R^1 129),[13] that is, on whether one's instincts tend to focus on nature or consciousness, or whether one's imagination tends to be abstract or concrete. The human imagination, Schleiermacher emphasizes in 1806 and even more so in 1821, is the highest and most original of human faculties. In an Explanation to the fifth Speech, he suggests that the more symbolic (abstract) a representation is, the less it will involve (concrete) notions of personality, hence the more pantheistic it will be.[14] Thus for Schleiermacher, the difference between pantheistic and theistic views of God is that between nonpersonal (abstract) and personal (concrete) ideas of God. Neither is right or wrong *per se,* since each attempts to express, although never fully adequately, the *"immediate presence of God in us"* (Expl. 2.18; Oman, 115), and since religion arises from feeling, not from concepts.

Nonpersonal and Impersonal Ideas of God

The significance of this understanding of pantheism and theism is indicated in another, more fundamental distinction that can be made between non-

---

13. Cf. Oman, 98; Pünjer, 128. The term is *die Phantasie* or *Fantasie*. Blackwell prefers to translate it as "phantasy" (see Blackwell, *Schleiermacher's Early Philosophy of Life*). In *Über die Freiheit* (1792) Schleiermacher wrote "the first existential ground of all particular actions of understanding, namely the direction of imagination [*Richtung der Einbildungskraft*], is nothing other than an activity of the faculty of desire, for attention itself can be conceived as nothing other than desire for the completion of a train of representations." *On Freedom,* 27; cf. 11.

14. See Explanation 4 to the fifth Speech; Oman, 256. Describing different religions of the second (pluralistic) type, he says that "in the Egyptian and Indian systems the basis is either symbolic or hieroglyphic, and there is no personality underneath. Such a purely symbolical representation of first causes has properly no conscious gods, but is really pantheistic."

personal and impersonal views of God. Implicit already in earlier editions of the *Reden* and in the Sack correspondence, it is again implied in 1818 in a letter to Jacobi, where Schleiermacher writes, "I have been told that you were of the opinion that I could not think very highly of you, because the foundation of your philosophy was the idea of a personal God, which I denied."[15] Three years later it is made more explicit in Explanation 19 to his second Speech, where Schleiermacher laments that he has been so misunderstood. He insists that comparison with his *Glaubenslehre* will reveal that "it is not necessary for me to enter on a defence of myself against the supposition . . . which men whom I greatly honour, and some of whom have already gone hence, have drawn from this Speech. For myself I am supposed to prefer the *impersonal* [*unpersönliche*] form of thinking of the Highest Being, and this has been called now my atheism and again my Spinozism. I, however, thought that it is truly Christian to seek for piety everywhere, and to acknowledge it under every form" (Expl. 2.19; Oman, 115; emphasis added). At issue is actually a threefold distinction among the *personal, nonpersonal,* and *impersonal* ways of conceiving God.

The difference between *personal* and *nonpersonal* is one of images and language. They are general terms which represent two "opposing" ways of conceiving and speaking about God. Both belong, however, under the rubric of piety. They represent the two poles of one continuum of an infinite number of ways of imaging God, two possible directions of the pious imagination. As long as they express the immediate presence of God in us, both remain within the limits of piety. The personal, theistic view of God tends more toward anthropomorphism in that it takes the "Highest Being . . . as personally thinking and willing," whereas the nonpersonal, pantheistic view resists such anthropomorphism and instead conceives of God "as the universal, productive, connecting necessity of all thought and existence" (Oman, 95; R^3 124). Anthropomorphism, once again, is inevitable in religious language, but piety limits the extent to which it can be applied.

In contrast, an impersonal view of God does not stem from piety. Rather than denoting a different kind of language, it has a different reference altogether and thus belongs under an entirely different rubric. What, specifically, Schleiermacher would consider to be an impersonal view of God remains questionable. Clearly, at the extreme, he would include materialistic pantheism. Yet it is the less extreme and more conventional views that are at issue. By implication, Schleiermacher might also include "modern" Romans (whom he calls "godless") and the complacent middle class (whose orienta-

---

15. Schleiermacher to Jacobi, n.d., 1818, in *ASL* 2:351–52; Rowan, *Letters* 2:282–83.

tions are too anthropocentric). In other words, both, according to his definitions, lack true religion or piety. Although they may perhaps exist on the same continuum as nonpersonal and personal expressions of piety, they verge on impiety. How they conceive of God is the result of mixed motives, not all of which are pious.[16] Since, however, they may not be entirely without a "Christian disposition," Schleiermacher urges that fellowship should still be maintained (Expl. 2.10; Oman, 110). All in all, he seems to prefer Spinoza's nonpersonal but deeply religious sense of the divine to most narrow and conventional Christian views of a God endowed with human personality.

To emphasize how Christian theism, whose God is usually imaged as personal, and pantheism, whose God is nonpersonal, stand together over against impersonal views such as atheism or materialistic pantheism, Schleiermacher makes yet another distinction. Thus far, although he has added more detail to his position of 1799 and 1801, he has not altered it substantially. But in a dense and crucial passage from Explanation 19 to the second Speech Schleiermacher introduces two further distinctions that taken together reveal a significant development in his doctrine of God.

A Personal God and the Personality of God

The passage begins with what seems to be a contradiction of what Schleiermacher has just described as the difference between pantheistic and personal ways of conceiving God: "And if any one look at it rightly, he will find that, on the one side, every one must recognize it as an almost absolute necessity for the highest stage of piety to acquire the conception of a personal God, and on the other he will recognize the essential imperfection in the conception of a personality of the Highest Being, nay, how hazardous it is, if it is not most carefully kept pure" (Expl. 2.19; Oman, 115–16). Whereas before Schleiermacher seems to have viewed the pantheistic and personal as two alternative ways of viewing God, now he claims that *both* are necessary for an adequate conception of God. They are the two outer limits of giving expression to piety and are dialectically related to one another insofar as each enriches, balances, and requires the other. Hence,

---

16. "The usual conception of God as one single being outside of the world . . . is only one manner of expressing God, seldom entirely pure and always inadequate. Such an idea may be formed from mixed motives, from the need for such a being to console and help, and *such a God may be believed in without piety*, at least in my sense, and I think in the true and right sense." Oman, 101; R^2 133; emphasis added.

even if the direction of one's imagination tends toward a nonpersonal conception of God, it must nevertheless contain an element of a conception of a personal God. This new twist to the discussion makes more sense when it is understood that it applies only at the highest level of religious consciousness, where everything is seen as a unity in plurality. At this level, Schleiermacher maintains, to conceive of a personal God is unavoidable because of the immediacy and intensity of the religious feeling. Piety, after all, is the awareness of the immediate presence of God. At the same time, with the necessity of a personal view of God comes also the self-corrective impulse that stems from piety. At the highest level of piety, a certain humility attends all notions of a personal God—a humility ever aware of the inadequacy of all images of God and of the dangers of anthropocentrism.[17] This is the case even with the church fathers, who constantly sought to purify the idea of the Highest Being. In short, at the highest level of piety, both personal and nonpersonal tendencies are necessary and together constitute a system of checks and balances.

With this qualification of the difference between a personal and nonpersonal God we discover what else Schleiermacher meant by the adjective *personal*. On the one hand, it can describe the more concrete, anthropomorphic images we have of God (i.e., a God who wills and thinks as we do and who acts and interferes in natural processes). Its referent, in other words, is sometimes a God conceived of in terms of human personality. On the other hand, it can describe a degree of religious feeling. God can be said to be personal because at the highest level of piety the presence of the divine in us is immediate and thus is taken up into and involves our whole lives.[18] With this second meaning, Schleiermacher introduces yet another distinction, namely, that between a personal God and the personality of God.[19] While these two senses may overlap, the former sense always

---

17. The test case for anthropocentrism is immortality. See the last few paragraphs of the second Speech (Pünjer, 130–33; Oman, 99–101); "Schleiermacher's Sermon at Nathanael's Grave," trans. Albert L. Blackwell, *Journal of Religion* 57, no. 1 (January 1977): 64–75; and letter to the widow Henriette von Willich, in Blackwell, *Schleiermacher's Early Philosophy of Life*, 203–4.

18. As Paul Tillich has it, we can be personally related to a nonpersonal God. See *Systematic Theology* (Chicago: University of Chicago Press, 1951), 1:223, 224–25.

19. The significance of this distinction is perhaps best illustrated by an overview of the evolution of his application of the terms *personal* and *personality*. In the first edition of the *Reden* Schleiermacher does not use the terms *personal* and *personality*, but he clearly rejects any attempt to form too anthropomorphic a view of God as the "genius of humanity" and criticizes the moralists' attempts to make God into a human-like lawgiver. True religion, he tells the despisers, transcends all personality. Yet this does not exclude the concept of a personal God, for depending on its tendencies, an imagination may "personify the spirit of the universe

remains, by definition, within the limits of piety, while the latter can extend beyond such limits. Thus while Schleiermacher can say that the third stage of religious consciousness always necessarily includes an element of the personal view and an element of the nonpersonal view, it does not necessarily include a conception of God as having personality. Schleiermacher has nothing against a personal view of God, and in fact holds it as necessary. What he objects to is making personality an attribute of God. On this point, he stands very close to Spinoza.

A Personal God and the Living God

Schleiermacher seems aware of the confusion involved and offers a "great distinction," which will prove critical in his mature doctrine of God: "As it is so difficult to think of a personality as truly infinite and incapable of suffering, a great distinction should be drawn between a *personal* God and a *living* God. The latter idea alone distinguishes from materialistic pantheism and atheistic blind necessity. Within that limit any further wavering in respect of personality must be left to the representative imagination and the dialectic conscience, and where the pious sense exists, they will guard each other" (Expl. 2.19; Oman, 116; emphasis added). Unlike pantheism and theism, which, as forms of imaging and speaking about God, exist in some form at all three levels of religious consciousness, the concept of a living God exists only at the third level. The *living God* is the referent that both pantheism and theism attempt to explain. Although the term *living God* has been a part of the larger Spinoza debates as well as a part of Schleiermacher's own framework, it is not until the Explanations that

---

and you will have a God." Crouter, 138; R^1 129. Although in 1801 Sack did not use the precise terms, his criticisms of the *Reden* clearly focus on the issue of a personal God, which for him meant a "self-conscious, wise and good being" and an "*existing* and *governing* God." "Antagonistic Correspondence," 115, 116. The expression "personal God" seems to be first introduced in Schleiermacher's response to Sack: "Have I indeed spoken with contempt of religion ... or of belief in a personal God?" Ibid., 118. Schleiermacher does not reject the image of a personal God and grants that anthropomorphism is necessary; yet at the same time this is not "limited to the metaphysical concept of the personality of God." History will bear him out on this, for although "today's common concept of God is composed of the features of transcendence, personality, and infinity," the tradition has not always formulated God thus. In the main text of the third edition, these same themes are continued. A personal view of God assigns human personality to the Highest Being. See Oman, 96, 97. A Spinozist or pantheistic view denies a personal God but not the presence of deity. True to his claim in his letter to Sack (1801), Schleiermacher never denies a personal God. He does, however, take great care to critique the notion of personality: *personality of God* is easily refuted because it is arbitrary and susceptible to corruption. See Explanation 19 to the second Speech; Oman, 95.

Schleiermacher develops it into a more definite and comprehensive term. He seems to mean by it that the immediate presence of God can only be felt as active. He writes, "The existence of God generally can only be active, and as there can be no passive existence of God, the divine activity upon any object is the divine existence in respect of that object" (Expl. 2.18; Oman, 115). The term *living God* points to that higher unity, the "universal, divine connection of all things" (Expl. 2.7; Oman, 107). As beyond all personality, the notion of the *living God* alone can refute atheism and materialism. Last, the idea of the *living God* expresses the love that underlies the unity in plurality, the connecting, living force of all things.[20] This is the teleological element in Schleiermacher's worldview.

Summary Remarks on the Explanations

Schleiermacher walks a careful line between, on the one hand, recognizing the importance and unavoidability of anthropomorphism in religious language and, on the other, the need to resist and limit it. This is precisely what he sees as the dogmatic task. As the systematic treatment of religious concepts, dogmatics must not mistake the conception for what is original and constitutive, and it must ensure that the conceptions remain meaningful. From the Explanations, certain criteria for adequacy in formulating a dogmatic doctrine of God, criteria which set limits and formulate meaningful conceptions, can be teased out. First, the best representations are those which are products of oscillation between the *One* and the *All:* "But the infinite . . . we cannot be conscious of immediately and through itself. It can only be through a finite object, by means of which our tendency to postulate and seek a world, leads us from detail and part to the All and the Whole" (Expl. 2.2; Oman, 103). Second, imagination and piety are reciprocally related and together constitute a system of checks and balances. For instance, the only real restriction against a pantheistic conception of God is that against materialism or blind necessity, both of which are dead conceptions of the infinite. Schleiermacher contends that "within that limit any further wavering in respect of personality must be left to the representative imagination and the dialectic conscience, and where the pious sense exists, they will guard each other" (Expl. 2.19; Oman, 116).[21] Third, there is the criterion of livingness. God can only be conceived of as

---

20. See Explanation 11 to the second Speech; Oman, 111.
21. By "dialectic conscience," Schleiermacher again refers to the necessary oscillation between two polar coordinates, for instance the ideal and the real, the *One and All.*

living, that is, as a unity in plurality, as love and redemption. Language must remain living; to be meaningful, it must represent the immediate presence of God in us by reproducing and nurturing piety.[22] Livingness and piety always imply each another. Fourth, talk about God must respect the limits of other forms of knowledge (especially science) and piety. Although there have been shifts in his thought between 1799 and 1821 regarding the relation between philosophy, science, and morality, Schleiermacher reiterates here what he has insisted on all along, namely, the "eternal unity of Reason and Nature, the universal existence of all finite things in the Infinite" (Oman, 39; R^2 51). Neither threatens or hinders the other: "Piety and scientific speculation share with each other, and the more closely they are conjoined the more both advance" (Expl. 1.6; Oman, 25). Fifth, the tradition must be behind one, if not always with regard to specific formulations, certainly with regard to the underlying piety that seeks articulation: "Yet the profoundest of the church fathers have ever sought to purify the idea.... [I]t would be as easy to say that they denied personality to God as that they ascribed it to him" (Expl. 2.19; Oman, 116).[23] Thus to guard against anthropomorphism is not an atheistic impulse: "Such a misunderstanding could only arise in those who have never felt the speculative impulse to annihilate anthropomorphism in the conception of the Highest Being, an impulse most clearly expressed in the writings of the profoundest Christian teachers"(Expl. 1.2; Oman, 23). Sixth, love must be operative.[24] Seventh, the most basic expression is the universal, divine connection of all things.[25]

Revisions to the *Glaubenslehre*

The natural first step in determining the degree to which Schleiermacher's Christian doctrines, particularly those regarding the doctrine of God, are influenced by Spinoza or neo-Spinozism is to examine those texts in the *Glaubenslehre* where Schleiermacher explicitly addresses either Spinozism or pantheism. How does he define pantheism? Does he continue to pay tribute to Spinoza as he had in the *Reden*? The texts commonly appealed

---

22. See Explanations 9 and 10 to the second Speech and Explanation 2 to the first Speech.
23. Cf. *Gl.*² §§15, 16.
24. See Explanation 11 to the second Speech; Oman, 111.
25. See Explanation 7 to the second Speech; Oman, 107.

to in addressing such questions are the four places in the second edition of the *Glaubenslehre*, as well as the section in his first letter to Lücke, where he explicitly addresses pantheism.[26] Taken alone, these texts give a fair summary of Schleiermacher's view of the matter, but they do not reflect the full extent to which the question of pantheism was problematic in the preparation of his Christian dogmatics. In that regard, the marginal notes Schleiermacher made as he wrote his revisions are far more revealing.[27] These notes and revisions make clear that the development of the key term *feeling of absolute dependence* (*das schlechthinnige Abhängigkeitsgefühl*) arises directly from Schleiermacher's concern to free himself from charges of pantheism. Moreover, they reveal that Schleiermacher takes the formula *One and All* to be an expression of an acceptable form of pantheism which is not unreconcilable with monotheism and which, in fact, is closely related to his own doctrine of God as that is presented in his Christian dogmatics. Contrary to some interpreters, Schleiermacher did not make an about-face in his second edition, nor are his changes superficial. He does, however, offer significant revisions, which serve to clarify his original intentions.[28]

Dependence and Pantheism

The common element in all pious emotions, hence the essence of piety, is this: that we	The common element in all howsoever diverse expressions of piety, by which these are conjointly

---

26. See *Gl.*² §§8 p.s., 46.2, 49.2, 53.2, and *On the "Glaubenslehre,"* 47–53. Focus here shall be on the revisions in *Gl.*² §§4 and 8.

27. Schleiermacher's handwritten notes are given in Redeker. Redeker annexes the marginal notes to the leading propositions of *Gl.*¹ at the end of his second volume, where he arranges the corresponding propositions of both editions side by side. These marginal notes *(Randbemerkungen),* Redeker explains, "are found in the first margin of one copy of the first edition, are interweaved with notepaper, and were employed by Schleiermacher apparently for his lectures and for the preparation of the second edition. This copy is in the Schleiermacher Archives in Berlin." Redeker 2:497. They complement Schleiermacher's notes to the Introduction and part 1, which C. Thönes published in 1873. The copy used by Thönes has since been lost. Other notes *(Anmerkungen)* to *Gl.*¹ are given in Peiter.

28. For more on the changes between the two editions of the *Glaubenslehre*, see Richard Crouter, "Rhetoric and Substance in Schleiermacher's Revision of *The Christian Faith* (1821–22)," *Journal of Religion* 60, no. 3 (1980): 285–306; Maureen Junker, *Das Urbild des Gottesbewußtseins: Zur Entwicklung der Religionstheorie und Christologie Schleiermachers von der ersten zur zweiten Auflage der Glaubenslehre* (Berlin: Walter de Gruyter, 1990); and Chang Kyun Mock, "The Development of Schleiermacher's Doctrine of God: A Comparative Study of the Introduction and Part I of the First and Second Editions of Schleiermacher's *Glaubenslehre*" (Ph.D. diss., Drew University, 1986).

are conscious of ourselves as being absolutely dependent, that is, that we feel dependent on God. (*Gl.*¹ §9)	distinguished from all other feelings, or, in other words, the self-identical essence of piety, is this: the consciousness of being absolutely dependent, or, which is the same thing, of being in relation with God. (*Gl.*² §4)

Schleiermacher gives his famous and controversial definition of piety in §4 of the second edition of the *Glaubenslehre:* "The consciousness of being absolutely dependent, or, which is the same thing, of being in relation with God" (*Gl.*² §4; *CF* 12). This definition, so important for his doctrine of God, has continued to this day to arouse the criticism of subjectivism.[29] Such criticisms were more warranted in his own day than in ours, given his original formulation of piety in §9 of the first edition: "The common element in all pious emotions, thus the essence of piety, is this: that we are conscious of ourselves as absolutely dependent, that is, that *we feel dependent on God*"(*Gl.*¹ §9; emphasis added).[30] The difference between these two formulations, though seemingly minor, is significant. Whereas in the second edition consciousness of absolute dependence marks a relationship with God that is qualitatively different from any other, in the first edition the key term *schlechthin abhängig* seems to be compromised by the last clause of the proposition. In other words, by moving from "absolutely dependent" to "dependent" in the same sentence, Schleiermacher left himself open to the criticism that dependence on God is hardly distinguishable from dependence on the world or, for that matter, any other kind of dependency, feeling, or form of consciousness. It would not be unreasonable, therefore, to interpret the original formulation in terms of "simple" rather than "absolute" dependence. Such ambiguity leaves room for two possible

---

29. See Delbrück, *Erörterungen;* Emil Brunner, *Die Mystik und das Wort: Der Gegensatz zwischen moderner Religionsauffassung und christlichem Glauben dargestellt an der Theologie Schleiermachers* (Tübingen: J.C.B. Mohr [Paul Siebeck], 1924; 2d ed., 1928), cited and responded to in B. A. Gerrish, "Continuity and Change: Schleiermacher on the Task of Theology," in *Tradition in the Modern World: Reformed Theology in the Nineteenth Century* (Chicago: University of Chicago Press, 1978); Barth, *Theology of Schleiermacher;* Felix Flückiger, *Philosophie und Theologie bei Schleiermacher* (Zollikon-Zürich: Evangelischer Verlag, 1947), 36; and Van Harvey, "A Word in Defense of Schleiermacher's Method," *Journal of Religion* 42, no. 3 (July 1962): 161.

30. "Das Gemeinsame aller frommen Erregungen, also das Wesen der Frömmigkeit, ist dieses, daß wir uns unsrer selbst als schlechthin abhängig bewußt sind, d.h., daß wir uns abhängig fühlen von Gott."

unwelcome interpretations: *subjectivism* or *subjective idealism,* insofar as our consciousness of God seems derived from our feeling of dependence, and thus seems to be merely a projection of the ego; *pantheism,* insofar as the way we are dependent on God seems indistinguishable from the way we are dependent on the world, from which it would follow that just as we are dependent on, yet a part of, the world, so in our dependence on God we must also be a part of God.

Schleiermacher was bewildered at the idea of having been accused of both idealism and pantheism. He laments in the his first letter to Lücke, "Yet Delbrück reproduces my doctrine by a completely different chemical process, as a strange distillation of Spinoza and Fichte. . . . My sole consolation is that I have at least as much claim to be called an idealist as a pantheist."[31] Although the revisions made in §4 seem to suggest that his main concern was to free himself from the charge of subjective idealism, the motivating force behind these revisions was in fact Schleiermacher's concern to distinguish his own position from pantheism, which he judged to be the more fundamental issue and possibly the more damaging charge. In his revisions he therefore has a threefold agenda: he develops a precise and consistent use of the term *feeling of absolute dependence;* he offers a careful explication of this feeling of absolute dependence through a comparison of relative freedom and relative dependence; finally, he introduces the term *Whence* as the first "name" he applies to God.[32]

The Feeling of Absolute Dependence

In a marginal note to the first edition Schleiermacher insists that "through the expression—that absolute dependence is the same as dependence on God—the *pernicious pantheism [der verderbliche Pantheismus], which*

---

31. On the *"Glaubenslehre,"* 49; KGA 1/10:330. Gerhard Ebeling makes the case for the opposition between pantheism and subjectivism in "Schleiermacher's Doctrine of Divine Attributes," in *Schleiermacher as Contemporary,* ed. Robert W. Funk (New York: Herder & Herder, 1970), 148. It seems at first strange that one proposition could arouse suspicion of two presumably exclusive and heretical positions. Subjectivism, or in this context subjective idealism, places the ego at the center of everything, thus emphasizing radical individuality and autonomy, whereas pantheism supposedly loses the individual, thus emphasizing nature and determinism. Keep in mind, however, what happens with the German revival of Spinoza in the late eighteenth century. No longer interpreted in materialistic or static terms, but in the dynamic terms of Herder, one strand of Spinozism becomes combined with critical idealism to form what Jacobi termed "inverted Spinozism," whereby consciousness rather than substance becomes the One.

32. See Niebuhr, "Schleiermacher and the Names of God," 184.

places human beings as a part of God, is surely excluded."³³ This could be interpreted to mean that Schleiermacher separates himself definitively from any sort of pantheism insofar as he offers a precise definition of it and then attaches a negative judgment concerning it: pantheism mistakenly holds that we are a part of God, hence it is pernicious. The evidence, however, supports the interpretation that the phrase "pernicious pantheism" suggests a distinction between unacceptable and acceptable forms of pantheism.³⁴ If this is true, then this marginal note implies that an acceptable form of pantheism is one that distinguishes our dependence on the world from our dependence on God. The note is largely a response to Delbrück, his chief accuser of pantheism, who helped convince Schleiermacher of the need for greater precision in his terminology. Ironically, it was also Delbrück who suggested the adoption of the adjective *schlechthinnig,* the modifier of *Abhängigkeitsgefühl,* which provides the basis for the revisions from §9 of the first edition to §4 of the second.³⁵ "All precise definitions," Schleiermacher writes, "must be developed from the concept of the feeling of absolute dependence."³⁶

33. Note to *Gl.*¹ §9; Redeker 2:500; emphasis added. That his refinement of the term *dependence* is due chiefly to the debate on pantheism is further supported by another marginal note: "§40 soll auch meinen Pantheismus beweisen.... Doch wird... hier das Abhängigkeitsgefühl dargestellt als das, durch dessen Entwicklung die Vorstellung von Gott und Welt sich trennen." Note to *Gl.*¹ §40; Redeker 2:510.

34. He indicates a similar distinction in his second letter to Lücke: "If the divine wisdom and love meant no more to me than to a pantheistic dogmatician, to use that term pejoratively as it is used against me and others, then it would not have been possible for me to have given them their present position, since I would have taken care not to present my best at the outset." *On the "Glaubenslehre,"* 59–60; *KGA* 1/10:344. Those, therefore, who defend Schleiermacher against a certain kind of pantheism—a naive or crass understanding of pantheism as simple identity of God and world—are certainly correct, but they hardly penetrate the deeper, and far more interesting, issues. Yes, Schleiermacher rejects an identification of God with the world or universe, or even with the sum of all universes. But for Schleiermacher there are other, more viable definitions of pantheism that cannot, and indeed should not, be so easily rejected.

35. In a note to this note, Schleiermacher claims that *"schlechthinnig gleich absolut."* Redeker 1:23a. Mackintosh and Stewart translate it as *absolute,* but many scholars depart from them in this decision. R. Niebuhr points out that *absolute* carries Hegelian connotations and therefore prefers to translate *schlechthin* as *simple* or *sheer.* See "Schleiermacher and the Names of God," 183–84. Likewise, R. Williams prefers to translate *schlechthin* as *utter.* Although I too prefer *utter* (since it better conveys Schleiermacher's intention and acknowledges the shift in terminology between the two editions), I shall translate it as *absolute* in order to maintain consistency with the English translation.

36. Note to *Gl.*² §4.4; Redeker 1:28–29a. "For the word *schlechthinig,* which occurs frequently in the following exposition, I am indebted to Professor Delbrück. I was unwilling to venture upon its use, and I am not aware that it has occurred anywhere else. But now that

In the first edition of the *Glaubenslehre*, the term *Abhängigkeitsgefühl* is not used as precisely or deliberately as it comes to be used in the second edition. When used as a noun, it is most often modified by either *ursprünglich* (*Gl.*¹ §§37, 39) or *absolut* (*Gl.*¹ §§64, 65, 72) but never by *schlechthinnig*. When *Abhängigkeit* is used without being attached to *-gefühl* (in other words, when the noun is not *feeling* but *dependence*), it is modified by either *rein* (*Gl.*¹ §§9.3, 4) or *gänzlich* (*Gl.*¹ 50). At other times, dependence on God is used with no modification, hence there is nothing to distinguish it from other kinds of dependencies.[37] The only places where some form of the terms *schlechthin* and *abhängig* are used together are in predicative clauses where the former is an adverb and the latter an adjective.[38] In the second edition, this predicative form of these two terms, although maintained, is also translated into a substantival phrase, the result being a more definite terminology.

In the second edition of the *Glaubenslehre*, Schleiermacher consistently uses the term *das schlechthinnige Abhängigkeitsgefühl* when speaking of our immediate self-consciousness of God. He does not, as he did in 1821, refer to a dependence on God that is not an absolute dependence. The only exceptions to this, which are rare, are "being in relation to God" (*Gl.*² §4)[39] and "finding oneself absolutely dependent" (*Gl.*² §32).[40] Even these two exceptions, however, maintain the fundamental distinction: both convey our sheer receptivity and sheer givenness in relation to God; both avoid any confusion of dependence on God with dependence on world.[41] The precise and consistent use of *the feeling of absolute dependence* clarifies a fundamental distinction already operative in the first edition. "Pious feeling," Schleiermacher writes there, "is always a pure feeling of dependence, and never a relation of reciprocity" (*Gl.*¹ §9.3; Peiter 1:32). Toward the end of that same paragraph he expands on this difference between pure and reciprocal feelings:

> If the infinity of what is co-determined is necessarily given along with the being-posited (which distinguishes the pious emotion) of a

---

he has given it me, I find it very convenient to follow his lead in using it." Note to *Gl.*² §4; *CF* 12.

37. See *Gl.*¹ §§42, 63, 70.

38. "Daß wir uns unsrer selbst als *schlechthin abhängig* bewußt sind"; and "wir uns als *schlechthin abhängig* finden." *Gl.*¹ §§9, 36; emphasis added.

39. ". . . in Beziehung mit Gott."

40. "Sich-schlechthin-abhängig-Finden." Unfortunately, in *CF* this is translated only as "the feeling of absolute dependence" (132).

41. Brandt points out, and rightly so, that in making a distinction between God and world Schleiermacher has not dissociated himself from pantheism. See Brandt, *Philosophy of Schleiermacher*, 233.

complete and constant dependence (which is thus in no way limited by reciprocal-relations or ordinary dependence), then this is not the divided and finitely formed infinite of the world, rather the simple and absolute Infinite. And this latter is the sense of the above-mentioned expression, that feeling oneself absolutely dependent and feeling dependent on God is the same thing. (*Gl.*¹ §9.3; Peiter 1:32)

This passage, which forms the basis for his discussion in §4.4 of the second edition, leaves no doubt Schleiermacher had the same intentions in 1821 as he does in 1830: we experience ourselves as given in a world which is itself given; while we experience reciprocity in relation to the world, because we are a part of it, we know no reciprocity, only utter and sheer dependency, in relation to God. The fact that this distinction is inserted into the text of the first edition, and not in his marginal notes, gives yet further evidence that the revisions mark a clarification, not a significant change.

Relative Dependence and Relative Freedom

Nevertheless it remains true that this fundamental distinction was not communicated well in its original form. So, in the second edition, in addition to adopting more precise terminology, Schleiermacher must be conscientious in explaining the significance of his terms. He does this in his exposition to §4, where he begins (as he had in §9.1–2 of the first edition) with an analysis of human self-consciousness as being in relation with an other. This paragraph, along with the explanatory paragraphs of §3, forms the basis of his theological anthropology. The self does not create or project the existence of an other. On the contrary, this other is always already presupposed: it is that which is co-posited with the self; it is the very source and context of the self; it is that which partially defines the self. There are two constituent elements in human self-consciousness, the self-caused and non-self-caused or having-by-some-means-come-to-be. This latter element is a presupposition of his critical realism, clearly meant to oppose Fichte's notion of the transcendental ego. There is, Schleiermacher insists, "another factor besides the Ego, a factor which is the source of the particular determination, and without which the self-consciousness would not be precisely what it is" (*Gl.*² §4.1; *CF* 13). This awareness of an other, and of being partially determined by another, corresponds to what Schleiermacher calls our "receptivity" (*Empfänglichkeit*), which exists together with our (spontaneous) "self-activity" (*Selbsttätigkeit*) (13). The choice of each term is significant and underscores the relation between his monism, realism, and determinism. *Receptivity* implies a dynamic, internal relationship between the self and the non-self; the self receives into itself, not just endures, influences of the non-self. Moreover, we are so constituted that we are aware of an other through receptive organs; it is an organic relation. *Spontaneous activity* implies much more than a free will able to exert itself over and against what is other; it includes all affectivities and experiences of the self, including the unique way in which we receive and appropriate outside influences into ourselves and let them determine ourselves.[42]

Thus far his exposition of the proposition is virtually the same as it is in the first edition. The revisions begin in §4.2, where Schleiermacher describes our receptivity and activity in terms of the antithesis between freedom and dependence. This allows him to distinguish relative dependence from absolute dependence. The former exists always in relation to freedom, whereas the latter does not. This is not just a difference in degree, as might be inferred from the first edition, where Schleiermacher tried to distinguish ordinary or limited dependence from pure dependence. In comparing the two kinds of dependence, Schleiermacher seemed to place them on the same spectrum, according to which the difference between pure and ordinary feelings of dependence would only be a matter of intensity. If relative dependence can be defined *only* in its relation to freedom, and if absolute dependence means the absence (not just the diminishment) of freedom, then our dependence on the world and our absolute dependence on God are utterly incommensurate, and thus there should be no confusion between the world and God.

We are relatively dependent not only insofar as we are influenced and determined by something other than ourselves, but also insofar as "we could not so become except by means of an other" (*Gl.*[2] §4.2; Redeker 1:25).[43] In other words, our being influenced by (i.e., our dependence on) an other, is not necessarily life-restricting but must also be viewed as life-enhancing. Similarly, we are free not only insofar as we influence what is other but also insofar as we actively receive influences upon us. In §4.2 (of the second edition) Schleiermacher therefore challenges the usual connotations of the words *dependence* and *freedom*. The antithesis between them is not that "between gloomy or depressing and elevating or joyful feelings"

---

42. This appeal to the interrelation of receptivity and self-activity in the process of knowledge was not unique to Schleiermacher. Karl Leonhard Reinhold, for instance, in his response to Kant, described the faculty of desire *(Vorstellungsvermögen)* as being constituted by *Receptivität* and *Spontaneität*. See *Versuch einer neuen Theorie des menschlichen Vorstellungsvermögens* (Prague/Jena, 1789), 264ff.

43. The English translation is misleading on this score. See *CF* 14.

($Gl.^2$ §4.2; CF 14). The feelings of dependence and freedom are not in opposition but are, in his word, *"one"* (14). This relation between dependence and freedom describes our relation with other finite beings: there is always *reciprocity* (*Wechselwirkung*). We can always influence, and we are always determined. This remains true even when we move beyond the particular relations to the whole of finite relations, in other words, when we form the idea of the *World,* defined by Schleiermacher as the "field of equal reciprocity" (15). Even if this world, this whole of finite things, be infinite, our dependence on it would remain relative because we are a part of it and thus have some influence on it. Even when our freedom is imperceptible, for instance in relation to the stars, we nevertheless continue to "exercise a counter-influence, however minute" (15).[44]

The 'Whence' of Our Existence

In a note to the next expositional paragraph, Schleiermacher asks, "How can the feeling of dependence be absolute?" The reply: "Only exclusively, and not in opposition to freedom."[45] In the main text he explains that the consciousness of absolute dependence is "the consciousness that the whole of our spontaneous activity comes from a source outside of us in just the same sense in which anything towards which we should have a feeling of absolute freedom must have proceeded entirely from ourselves" ($Gl.^2$ §4.3; CF 16). Absolute dependence, once again, is not on the same continuum as relative dependence. In relation to God we, along with the world, are entirely given, entirely determined; we know only sheer receptivity, not the receptivity mutually determined by freedom. For this very reason, "a feeling of absolute dependence, strictly speaking, cannot exist in a single moment as such, because such a moment is always determined, as regards its total content, by what is *given,* and thus by objects towards which we have a feeling of freedom" (16). The feeling of absolute dependence cannot exist in a discrete moment alongside other moments, just as God is not a discrete object alongside other objects, to be known like other objects. While we are in one sense given by the world, the world itself, with ourselves as a part of it, is itself given. "Any possibility," however, "of God being in any way *given* is entirely excluded, because anything that is outwardly given

---

44. In a note to this text, Schleiermacher explains that our tendency to deify nature or even some persons results when we do not recognize our relative freedom and thus mistake our relation to these as sheerly dependent. See Redeker 1:27b.
45. Note to $Gl.^2$ §4.3; Redeker, 1:27c.

must be given as an object exposed to our counter-influence, however slight this may be" (*Gl.*² §4.4; *CF* 18).

Hence the importance of the exposition in §4.4: God is the "*Whence* [*Woher*] of our receptive and active existence" (16).[46] The world cannot evoke a sense of *Whence* because we exist in reciprocal relation with it and are given as a part of it: "This *Whence* is not the world, in the sense of the totality of temporal existence, and still less is it any single part of the world" (16). God, as the Whence of our existence, is that alone with which we stand in a relation of utter dependence. God, as the "co-determinant" in our feeling of absolute dependence, is not an idea or a projection. With the term *feeling of absolute dependence* Schleiermacher exonerates himself from suspicion of subjectivism and pantheism, since world and God are so definitively distinguished. He expresses his exasperation at the end of his note to this text: "So inconceivable, how Pantheism could have been attributed to me, since I entirely separate feeling of absolute dependence from relation to the world."[47] In the first edition, he intended the same distinction, but again, his terminology was inconsistent; he also tried to state the difference more in terms of the relationship between the finite and the infinite; he further confused the issue by offering a distinction between the infinity of the world and that of God. While Schleiermacher grants a possible infinity of the universe, this would only be a totality, an infinite whole of finite things which exist in the field of reciprocity, whereas God, the Whence, is the infinite One.

Schleiermacher thought he had made this perfectly clear in a marginal note to §9 in the first edition: "This equivalence of absolute dependence and dependence on God is at the same time the formation of the concept of God. God is the *One*, to which the absolute dependence is connected, opposed to *all* that is partial."[48] This note, a description of the relationship between God and world in classical pantheistic terms of *One and All*, is not merely a passing thought. In another important proposition of the Introduction, where he offers his most lengthy discussion of pantheism in the *Glaubenslehre*, Schleiermacher again uses the formula *One and All* to describe an acceptable understanding of pantheism and to show that it is not contradictory to monotheism. This text, a postscript to §8 of the second edition, is particularly important. In it Schleiermacher expands his defini-

---

46. This expositional paragraph is an extensive expansion of *Gl.*¹ §9.4. For more on what Schleiermacher means by *Whence*, see "Receptivity in Relation to God" in Chapter 5.
47. Note to *Gl.*² §4.4; Redeker 1:29a (Thönes).
48. Note to *Gl.*¹ §9; Redeker 2:501; emphasis added.

tions of pantheism and indicates which definitions are acceptable and which are not.

Monotheism and Pantheism

It should be noted from the start that the well-known postscript to §8 of the second edition was not added as a conciliatory move in response to criticisms leveled against the first edition of the *Glaubenslehre*.[49] The text does not have a defensive tone. On the contrary, it contains ideas long since articulated. The passage is almost identical, with some reorganization and some omission, to §15.5 of the first edition. The key themes (pantheism's relation to the three levels of piety, the distinction between representation and piety) were present already in the first edition of the *Reden* (1799). Hence, his discussion here should be interpreted in a constructive, rather than re-constructive or defensive, vein. It should also be noted that this relatively lengthy discussion of pantheism occurs in the Introduction, where one of Schleiermacher's concerns is to place Christianity on the map with other religions.[50] Thus the question he is addressing is, How is his conception of Christian piety, as a form of monotheism, related to pantheism? Pantheism, he answers, is not itself a religion, rather it "crept in as a taunt and nickname; and in such cases it always remains difficult to hold consistently to any one meaning" (*Gl.*² §8 p.s. 2; *CF* 39).[51] Because no consistent meaning can be assigned to it, and consequently confusion inevitably arises, Schleiermacher again offers different definitions and, once again, distinguishes between acceptable and unacceptable forms of pantheism.

In its acceptable form, pantheism is neither a materialism nor a negation of theism.[52] As long as this is kept in mind, pantheism can be considered truly pious, for it would then be recognized as a form of theism. As Schleiermacher puts it in the second edition: "But it may be asked whether, having once arisen in some other way—by the way of speculation or simply of

---

49. Brandt argues the contrary: "In his later years Schleiermacher became quite anxious to be as conciliatory as possible to the church. . . . [H]e was particularly careful to avoid being called a pantheist. As a result, he went out of his way to conform his language . . . as much as possible to the views accepted by contemporaries." *Philosophy of Schleiermacher*, 232.

50. See Gerrish, *Tradition in the Modern World*, 38.

51. Cf. *Gl.*¹ §15.5; Peiter 1:54.

52. Recall that in *Spinozismus* and *Spinozistisches System* he also argued against Jacobi's interpretation of Spinoza's philosophy as a materialism; in his Explanations to the *Reden* (1821) and his letter to Sack (1801), he argued that pantheism is not to be confused with materialism and that his notion of "world spirit" is not to be confused with the pantheistic "world soul."

reasoning—it is yet compatible with piety. To this question an affirmative answer may be given without hesitation, provided that Pantheism is taken as expressing some variety or form of Theism, and that the word is not simply and solely a disguise for a materialistic negation of Theism" (*Gl.*² §8 p.s. 2; *CF* 39). Pantheism, in other words, stands with theism over against atheism. He argued this in his Explanations to the *Reden,* and he further expands on it in §33, where he describes three kinds of godlessness.[53] Pantheism, in its acceptable form, would not be a "childish" lack of God-consciousness; nor would it be a "sensual" godlessness that mistakenly associates the codeterminant of our feeling of absolute dependence with some finite thing; nor finally would it be an atheistic, outright denial of God. At this point Schleiermacher makes yet another distinction, namely, that between two kinds of atheism. Pantheism, as he defines it, certainly does not arise from an atheism that is "a wicked fear of the sternness of God-consciousness" and that is "a product of licentiousness and thus a sickness of the soul" (*Gl.*² §33.2; *CF* 135). There is, however, another side to atheism that can also be attributed to pantheism. This kind of atheism, Schleiermacher says, is a "reasoned opposition to the current and more or less inadequate representations of the religious consciousness. Moreover, the atheism of the eighteenth century was, for the most part, a struggle against the petrified, anthropomorphic presentations of doctrine, a struggle provoked by the tyranny of the Church" (136). Here are echoes of the young Schleiermacher trying to convince his Berlin friends, the cultured despisers of religion, that what they reject is not true religion but only a distorted view of it. At that time, the appeal to Spinoza had been direct. It was not the holy and infinite God that Spinoza had rejected, only impious representations of God and their concomitant intolerance. The rejection of certain concepts of God itself stems from piety.

Since pantheism is not in opposition to theism—indeed, it is even "compatible with piety" (*Gl.*² §8 p.s. 2; *CF* 39) and therefore traceable at each level of piety—care must be taken to distinguish its different manifestations from one another. The distinctions Schleiermacher makes in the second edition are similar to those found in the *Reden* and its Explanations. At the lowest level of piety (idol-worship), pantheism would manifest itself as a confusion "between what is assigned to God and what is assigned to the world" (39). This is exactly the simplistic understanding of pantheism most often given. There is an identity or confusion between God and world, to

---

53. See *Gl.*² §33.2; *CF* 135. Schleiermacher does not discuss pantheism *per se* in *Gl.*² §33, but the implication seems clear.

the point where there is no need for God. In the *Reden* Schleiermacher described this as a state of chaos. The pantheistic tendency here would be as inadequate and confused as any other. This form of pantheism is related to what Schleiermacher describes in a note as a misunderstanding of our dependence on the world. At times we are not cognizant of a reciprocal relation: "Hence our propensity to deify natural bodies (stars) and natural powers (elements) against which our feeling of freedom is minimal becomes comprehensible. Likewise we deify persons who have shown a constant, creative and formative force."⁵⁴ The last line of this note applies more to the polytheistic level of piety.

At the second level (polytheism), pantheism would be manifested as the impulse to nonanthropomorphism. Once again, Schleiermacher suggests that the pantheistic representation of the divine is more abstract, and less anthropomorphic, than the gods of Greek mythology. If the argument in the Explanations is carried through to the second edition of the *Glaubenslehre* (and it not only can be but should be), then *at this level* the pantheistic tendency would be more pious than the tendency toward concrete representation. Schleiermacher poses the question, "And why could not a Hellenic polytheist, embarrassed by the entirely human shapes of the gods, have identified his great gods with the evolved gods of Plato, leaving out the God whom Plato represents as addressing them, and positing only the enthroned necessity?" (*Gl.*² §8 p.s. 2; *CF* 39).⁵⁵ Note that if the kind of pantheism that is an identity or confusion of God and world corresponds to the first level of piety, the kind of pantheism that is a fatalism corresponds to this second level. Note also that, again as in the *Reden,* what is pantheistic is the representation, here an abstract one, rather than the underlying instinct of piety: "This would not imply any change in his piety, yet his representation of it would have become pantheistic" (*Gl.*² §8 p.s. 2; *CF* 39).⁵⁶

At the highest level (which in the *Glaubenslehre* is termed monotheism), pantheism should be held "fast to the usual formula of One and All" (*Gl.*² §8 p.s. 2; *CF* 39).⁵⁷ This formula captures for Schleiermacher the proper understanding of the God-world relationship, which includes within itself the human-world relationship. The *All* expresses the interrelatedness of

---

54. Note to *Gl.*² §4.2, Redeker 1:27b.
55. This suggestion hints at Schleiermacher's rather unlikely blending of Spinoza and Plato. See Blackwell, *Schleiermacher's Early Philosophy of Life,* 123–36.
56. Cf. *Gl.*² §3.2; *CF* 7.
57. In *Gl.*¹ §15.5, this formula is given in the Greek, *hen kai pan,* whereas here it is in the German *Eins und Alles.* Also note that the One-All formula is used in another discussion on pantheism in *Gl.*² §46.2.

nature, including ourselves as a part of that whole of nature. This indeed is essential to Schleiermacher's post-Kantian Spinozism: it is an expression of his dynamic, organic monism, what is referred to in the *Glaubenslehre* as the nature system; it explains the deterministic strain in his ethics, which preserves the value of the individual while it reminds us that there is no absolute autonomy, that freedom is always relative, and that we are thus always affected by our (past and present) relations; it is the basis for his higher realism, which requires, if there is to be a rough correspondence, that there be an organic receptivity, a touchstone with what is other than oneself. At a lower level of religious consciousness, the world is perceived as sporadic and separated existences with which there is no true reciprocity precisely because our own existence is not recognized as being inherently and necessarily related to them. As a result, at that level, there is perceived a fatedness to all existence; all is moved by mechanistic causes over against which we have no influence, no freedom. At the highest level of religious consciousness, however, we recognize our reciprocity (relative dependence and relative freedom) with the world, and the world is thus experienced by us as an *All*. This is not the referent of our feeling of absolute dependence, but no feeling of absolute dependence can occur outside of such relations: "No Christian religious emotion can be imagined in experiencing which we do not find ourselves placed in a nature-system" ($Gl.^2$ §34.3; CF 139). Hence the "All" aspect of the preferred pantheistic formula: individuals are so constituted and related that together they form a whole; each individual is also a compendium of that whole. This form of pantheism is indistinguishable from monotheistic piety.

Taken by itself, of course, Schleiermacher's understanding of the *All* is not objectionable. It becomes problematic only in its relation to the *One* and in how that *One* is defined. From one side, it can be objected that if the *All* is granted, the *One* can easily be reduced to it and would therefore be an empty idea.[58] From the other side, it can be asked why this has to be considered a religious view at all. This can just as well be a nonreligious interpretation of the world, an interpretation compatible with many scientific and aesthetic sensibilities. The *One* is not only not needed, it is not desired. For Schleiermacher, the answers to both objections run along the same line: the *All* cannot exist without the *One*. The formula stands together, with emphasis on the conjunction *and*. Both terms of the formula are distinct, just as for Schleiermacher God and world are distinct. The

---

58. This is what is considered so dangerous about Spinoza's dictum *deus sive natura*—it does not matter which term is used, God *or* Nature, because they are one and the same thing.

unity of the world is "a divided and disjointed unity" (*Gl.*² §32.2; *CF* 132) upon which, as he explains in §4, we can be only relatively dependent. This disjointed unity cannot support our feeling of absolute dependence. The only *Whence* of the feeling of absolute dependence is the "absolute undivided unity" (132)—God. It follows that a "non-religious explanation of this sense of absolute dependence" can only be a "misunderstanding" (132). Although the feeling of absolute dependence is a "universal element of life" (*Gl.*² §33; *CF* 133), the interpretation of it is necessarily religious because there can be no *All*, no disjointed unity of the world, without a *One*. God, represented as the *One*, is the very "basis of this togetherness of being [*Zusammensein*] in its various distributions" (*Gl.*² §30.1; *CF* 126).[59] Similarly, the feeling of absolute dependence does not abrogate the feeling of freedom but is its necessary presupposition.[60]

Returning then to §8, Schleiermacher concludes that at the highest level of religious consciousness, pantheism—understood in terms of *One and All*—means that "God and World will remain distinct at least as regards function, and thus such a man [who operates at the highest stage of religion], since he reckons himself as belonging to the world, can feel himself, along with this All, to be dependent on that which is the corresponding One" (*Gl.*² §8 p.s. 2; *CF* 39). This insistence on the necessity of the *One* and its fundamental distinction from the *All* is not a qualification merely added to ward off accusations of pantheism. Much to the contrary, it is a description of what he takes to be an acceptable form of pantheism, namely, his own post-Kantian Spinozism. As the essays on Spinoza (1793–94) reveal, Schleiermacher found Spinoza so attractive because his thought requires the unconditioned, the infinite, and because he explains its relation with the finite in a way that leads neither to a bifurcation of noumenon and phenomena (Kant) nor to an elimination of noumena (Fichte). In the first edition of the *Reden*, the "holy, rejected Spinoza" was hailed for the very reason that he intuited, that he lived in and for, the infinite. Therefore, *One and All*, the classical formulation of pantheism that Lessing also found so attractive, is an expression that Schleiermacher adapts in terms of his own post-Kantian Spinozism, the second way in which Schleiermacher's thought can be fairly said to be pantheistic, and thus is neither a weak qualification of pantheism nor an expression of crude pantheism.

---

59. Recall what he says in his Explanations: "I leave you to say whether the world can be conceived as a true All and Whole without God"; "underneath this coherence there is a unity conditioning all things." Explanations 2 and 5 to the second Speech.

60. See *Gl.*² §§32.2 and 4.3,4.

Dogmatics and Dialectic

The year 1821 marked not only Schleiermacher's transition to Christian dogmatics and the new methodology required by it, but it also marked the midpoint in a series of lectures on his work, the *Dialektik*. Over a twenty-year period at the University of Berlin Schleiermacher taught six courses on dialectics—in 1811, 1814, 1818, 1822, 1828, and 1831. Unfortunately, he did not live long enough to organize his lectures into a form suitable for publication. His intention had been to structure his *Dialektik* much as he had his *Glaubenslehre* (a series of propositions with expositional paragraphs), but the task of preparing his lectures for publication fell instead to his friend and one-time student, Ludwig Jonas. The unfinished state of his lectures has resulted in a twofold controversy over interpretation: Which, if any, of the lectures on the *Dialektik* can be considered definitive? and How is the *Dialektik*, a speculative philosophical work, related to the *Glaubenslehre*, a Christian dogmatics supposedly uninfluenced by any philosophy? Those scholars who have undertaken an intensive study of the *Dialektik* usually argue that it is the necessary key to understanding the *Glaubenslehre*.[61] Most recently, Thandeka has argued that "much of the Protestant world has yet to understand his most basic standpoint [the *Dialektik*], without which it is *impossible* to grasp the principles of Schleiermacher's *Christian Faith*."[62] Friedrich Beisser, whose own study of Schleiermacher's doctrine of God focuses almost exclusively on the *Reden* and *Glaubenslehre*, concedes that if one wants to consider Schleiermacher's entire system, then the *Dialektik* must be taken into account; he defends his choice of texts by explaining that his study is only "a fragment."[63] Yet

---

61. Paul Mehl argues that "no one can understand Schleiermacher's view of the Christian's relation to God on the basis of *The Christian Faith* alone. That work must be supplemented by the *Dialektik*." "Schleiermacher's Mature Doctrine of God as Found in the *Dialektik* of 1822 and the Second Edition of *The Christian Faith* (1830–31)" (Ph.D. diss., Columbia University, 1961), 284. Gerhard Spiegler claims that "*The Christian Faith* is not and cannot be independent from his own speculative philosophy presented in the *Dialectic*"; he takes this even further when he writes, "If we look at the dogmatics from its fundamental theoretical base in the *Dialectic*, we are able to understand its general character more clearly." *Eternal Covenant*, 145, 152. John Thiel's entire project is "to demonstrate the extent to (and the senses in) which the doctrinal criticism issuing from Schleiermacher's methodological procedure in the *Glaubenslehre* was governed by the philosophical principles outlined in his lectures on *Dialektik*." *God and World*, 4.
62. "Schleiermacher's *Dialektik*: The Discovery of the Self that Kant Lost," *Harvard Theological Review* 85, no. 4 (1992): 433; emphasis added.
63. See Beisser, *Schleiermachers Lehre von Gott*, 9–10.

Beisser's choice of texts is more defensible than he himself allows. In the most general sense, it is of course true that, in order to ensure a thorough grasp of any major thinker such as Schleiermacher, one must have intimate knowledge of the entire corpus. That does not mean, however, that an individual work, or a group of related works, does not have its own internal coherence and cannot therefore be taken on its own terms.

There is a further case to be made. The contention that the *Dialektik* is the methodological key to the *Glaubenslehre* is faulty on two counts: it presumes that the dialectical method is new and unique to the *Dialektik*, and it presumes that the relation of influence between the two works is one-directional, from the *Dialektik* to the *Glaubenslehre*. In fact, the rudiments of Schleiermacher's dialectical method are found as early as 1790–92 in his first constructive, full-length essay, *Über die Freiheit,* the purpose of which is to seek the "determining ground of choice" (*On Freedom*, 19). Freedom, Schleiermacher writes, is attained through an "attunement of the soul" (51)—an attunement which involves a dialectical movement between infinite diversity and highest perfection, between impulses and maxims, between the faculty of desire and the faculty of representation. This oscillating movement played an increasingly important role in the development of his anthropology and epistemology, and eventually Schleiermacher captured the sense of this dialectic in his rendition of the ancient dictum *One and All*. The *One and All*, a mark of his simultaneous appropriation of Spinoza and Plato, functioned for Schleiermacher as the fundamental regulative principle for all knowledge, including religious knowledge. Philosophically, his transposition of the Platonic dialectic became formalized in the ongoing project of the *Dialektik*, but it was not unique to that work. Theologically, the notion of the *One* came to represent an outer limit in how our imaginations re-present the fundamental feeling. The conclusion is not that God *is* the One. That in itself is an empty concept and is not to be confused with the *Whence* of the feeling of absolute dependence that (for the Christian) occurs only simultaneously with the concrete experience of having been redeemed by Jesus of Nazareth.

In the *Glaubenslehre*, therefore, the living God is the content given in experience, and the dialectic of the *One and All* guides us in determining how that content can be thought. Thought cannot begin with a transcendental formula of the absolute and then translate that into a concept of a living God. Hence, at least with respect to the doctrine of God, the *Glaubenslehre* yields what the *Dialektik* cannot. Indeed, what is lacking in the *Dialektik* forms the core of the *Glaubenslehre*, which really begins in part 2 (in the experience of redemption and, concomitantly, in the living conceptions of God as love and wisdom) and then proceeds through applications of the dialectic of the *One and All* through part 1 to the more abstract propositions of the Introduction. The methodological key to his Christian doctrine of God is therefore given internally in the *Glaubenslehre* itself.

4

LIMITS AND METHOD
THE COINCIDENCE OF DIVINE CAUSALITY AND THE NATURE-SYSTEM

> ... one and the same thing simply from different points of view.
>
> —F.D.E. Schleiermacher,
> *The Christian Faith*

Amidst all the controversy regarding the "orthodoxy"[1] of Schleiermacher's doctrine of God, no other portion of his writing has attracted so many charges of pantheism as his propositions on divine preservation and omnipotence in part 1 of the *Glaubenslehre*. Nor has any revision or explanation served to satisfy his critics, who to this day continue to claim that Schleiermacher's "doctrine of creation was the same as Spinoza's";[2] that, insofar as his dogmatics reduces divine omnipotence and the doctrine of creation to preservation, it is a direct expression of his pantheism;[3] that his God is not the Christian God because he "fails to make any radical distinction between the Creator and the creation";[4] and finally, that because of its "immanentism," the *Glaubenslehre* "lacks an adequate expression of the transcendence of God."[5] These critics concur in recognizing a continu-

---

1. I use Schleiermacher's definition of that term. "The name of orthodox is then given to what is in unmistakable conformity with the matter fixed in the confessional documents; and what is not thus in conformity is heterodox." *Gl.*² §25 p.s.; *CF* 110; cf. *On the "Glaubenslehre,"* 53.

2. John Hunt, *Pantheism and Christianity* (1884; Port Washington, N.Y.: Kennikat Press, 1970), 313.

3. See Nelson Pike, *God and Timelessness* (London: Routledge & Kegan Paul, 1970), 110–11, and Hugh Ross Mackintosh, *Types of Modern Theology: Schleiermacher to Barth* (New York: Charles Scribner's Sons, 1937).

4. Smith, "A Study of the Relation," 143; cf. 164–65.

5. Niebuhr, *Schleiermacher on Christ and Religion*, 191.

ing affinity with Spinoza or a tendency toward pantheism, but they incorrectly identify this as a materialistic pantheism, as a form of reductionism, or as a borrowing of the specific content of Spinoza's own formulations. Against such critics, I argue that Schleiermacher's doctrine of preservation does contain certain traces of pantheism, *but* only pantheism in the acceptable form he describes in his Explanations to the *Reden* and his Introduction to the *Glaubenslehre;* it also has certain parallels with Spinoza, but the contents, rather than deriving directly from Spinoza, are determined by the particular Christian religious consciousness of his day as well as by the limits set by piety. The general themes that characterize Schleiermacher's early post-Kantian Spinozism (monism, determinism, realism, and nonanthropomorphism), although no longer explicit in their appeal to Spinoza, can nevertheless be traced through to the second edition of the *Glaubenslehre,* especially in part 1, which describes the relation between God and the world. These themes aid Schleiermacher in addressing the major inconsistencies of certain traditional Christian doctrines and in making revisions that although not perhaps in his time orthodox, he deemed more intelligible and reverent.

Schleiermacher's criteria for reverence are that any religious utterance about God should be traceable to the feeling of absolute dependence, that God be "regarded as the sole determinant" (*Gl.*² §38; cf. §37.1), and that God's activity not be "thought of as resembling human activity" (*Gl.*² §41; *CF* 152). Related to these are his criteria for intelligibility, which require that theology not step beyond the limits set by critical philosophy on the one hand and modern science on the other, and which also require that the "dialectical character"[6] of dogmatics be maintained throughout. Language about God must derive from the *Whence* of the feeling of absolute dependence, namely, the divine causality; it denotes "not something special in God, but only something special in the manner in which the feeling of absolute dependence is to be related to him" (*Gl.*² §50; *CF* 194). The doctrine of God, therefore, can only arise out of the feeling of absolute dependence and the manner in which it is related to the divine causality; we can never try to define who God is in Godself, but only who God is for us. In this, Schleiermacher understands himself to enjoy a firm grounding in the wider theological tradition.

The challenge is not unlike what it had been in 1793, when Schleiermacher had responded directly to Kant and Jacobi, or in 1799, when he

---

6. "The dialectical character of the language therefore consists simply in its being formed in a technically correct manner, that it may be used in all intercourse for the communication and correction of the knowledge in question." *Gl.*² §28.1; *CF* 118. Cf. *Gl.*² §16.

was in conversation with the cultured despisers: How can the "relation between the finite being of the world and the infinite being of God" (*Gl.*² §35; *CF* 140) be explained in a postcritical context so that the infinite is not rendered meaningless and yet so no bifurcation of the infinite and finite, hence no necessity for a *salto mortale,* results? As in those earlier works, it is Schleiermacher's own adaptation of a neo-Spinozist worldview that aids him in formulating an answer. The context (Christian dogmatics) and the method (expression of the religious subjective self-consciousness) are, however, significantly different from the contexts and methods of 1793 and 1799.

Part 1 of the *Glaubenslehre* articulates a worldview insofar as it describes the "religious feeling of nature in general, apart from the specifically Christian content which is always attached to it" (*Gl.*² §34.3; *CF* 140; emphasis added). It is somewhat surprising that Schleiermacher would admit that part 1 is a worldview, given the possible interpretation that it connotes a nonreligious (or worse, pantheistic) interpretation of things. In his first letter to Lücke, however, Schleiermacher expands on the purpose of part 1: "In acknowledging our dependence we also specify our view of the world. And I hope that a large part of my *Glaubenslehre* is nothing other than a description of this world view."[7] There can be no danger of this being a nonreligious worldview for at least two reasons. First, there is no world-consciousness without a God-consciousness, since the unity of the world is dependent absolutely on God as the "absolute undivided unity" (*Gl.*² §32.2; *CF* 132). Second, part 1 cannot be a nonreligious worldview because it is an abstraction from part 2, which describes the "specific content of the particular Christian experiences" (*Gl.*² §32.1; *CF* 131). This suggests that careful attention must be given to Schleiermacher's intentions regarding the structure of his dogmatic system. Two mistakes commonly made in examining Schleiermacher's *Glaubenslehre* and its doctrine of God must be avoided: the tendency to give exclusive attention to part 1 as though it were separable from part 2; and the tendency to give exclusive attention to the divine attributes, thus ignoring their dependence on and derivation from the first form of proposition.

Since part 1 is an abstraction from part 2, it follows that the general religious consciousness developed in the former is "always both presupposed by and contained in"[8] the latter. They cannot be read as separate or separable parts, one pantheistic or Spinozist and the other Christian. It is

---

7. *On the "Glaubenslehre,"* 44; *KGA* 1/10:322.
8. Title to part 1 of the *Glaubenslehre* (*CF* 131).

well known that in his *Two Letters to Lücke* Schleiermacher insists that the order between the two parts could be reversed, since part 2 is the heart of his dogmatics and is the most concrete expression of the Christian religious consciousness. His "strong dislike for such an anticlimax"[9] caused him to retain the original order of the first edition. The two parts, however, cannot be so readily switched as Schleiermacher suggests. In the order of experience, the affections described in part 2 are prior, since it is only through our experience of redemption that we come to view the world as created. In the order of logic, however, the world as a nature system, created and preserved by God, is prior, for otherwise there could be no experience of redemption.[10] Although part 2 is indeed the heart of his dogmatics, part 1 sets the limits to what can be said theologically: metaphysics and speculation must be excluded as alien; science, morality, and piety cannot be compromised; religious language and images must be demythologized and made intelligible in the context of the dogmatic system.

Careful attention must also be given to the more concrete descriptions of the religious consciousness when examining Schleiermacher's doctrine of God. Dogmatic propositions are divided into three forms: descriptions of human states, conceptions of divine attributes, and utterances about the world.[11] The first of these is the most "fundamental dogmatic form; while propositions of the second and third forms are permissible only in so far as they can be developed out of propositions of the first form" (*Gl.*² §30.2; *CF* 126). The doctrine of God, Schleiermacher informs us, is "set forth in the totality of the divine attributes, [and] can only be completed simultaneously with the whole system"(*Gl.*² §31.2; *CF* 128). Yet it is a mistake, on the basis of this, to suppose that Schleiermacher's doctrine of God can be explicated by focusing exclusively on the divine attributes as the second form of proposition.[12] The *whole system* has to be taken into account. Because Schleiermacher thinks that the divine attributes cannot "be understood without previous knowledge of" (*Gl.*² §31.2; *CF* 128) human states (the first form of proposition), the danger in focusing exclusively on the

---

9. On the "*Glaubenslehre,*" 59; *KGA* 1/10:344.
10. See B. A. Gerrish, "Nature and the Theater of Redemption: Schleiermacher on Christian Dogmatics and the Creation Story," *Ex Auditu* 3 (1987): 120–36.
11. See *Gl.*² §30; see Diagram 1.
12. Gerhard Heinrich Grau, for example, argues that "Schleiermacher develops the doctrine of God *only* through the divine attributes." "God in Experience: An Interpretation of Schleiermacher's Doctrine of God Concluding with a Reappraisal of His Understanding of the Doctrine of the Trinity" (Ph.D. diss., Princeton Theological Seminary, 1976), 46–47; emphasis added.

divine attributes is that we will move into the realm of speculation. More generally, the second and third form of propositions "must be reduced to propositions of that first form before we can be safe from the creeping in of alien [metaphysical, speculative] and purely scientific [objective] propositions" (*Gl.*² §30.3; *CF* 126). The requirement that every utterance must be traced back to the feeling of absolute dependence serves therefore as a methodological limit for Schleiermacher. At the same time, there are three compelling reasons for questioning Schleiermacher's claim that everything necessary is contained in the first form of proposition: he himself admits that dogmatics is not yet ready to eliminate the secondary forms of proposition since the attributes more adequately explain how divine causality is not external yet completely other; the attributes are structured according to the dictum *One and All;* and the attributes are necessary because they explain how God is living. Schleiermacher therefore protested when F. Ch. Baur established the "structure [of the *Glaubenslehre*] upon the principle of consciousness and resolutely subordinate[d] the other two forms of dogmatic statements to the first form."[13]

I attempt to resolve this dilemma by focusing initially on the first form of proposition (namely, the doctrines of creation and preservation) and then by tracing Schleiermacher's underlying concerns through the propositions on the divine attributes. This approach illuminates the fact that most of what is said concerning the divine causality under the rubric of the divine attributes is an expansion on what is already said in the propositions on divine preservation. The exposition of the divine attributes restructures, refocuses, and reformulates what has already been established under the first form of proposition. Schleiermacher retains the traditional terminology (omnipotence, omniscience, omnipresence, eternity), but he redefines these concepts according to the limits set in the Introduction and under the first form of proposition.

Piety and Its Limits

For Schleiermacher, the "original expression" of the relation between the infinite being of God and finite being is "that the world exists only in

---

13. Sergio Sorrentino, "History and Temporality in the Debate Between F. Ch. Baur and Schleiermacher," in Sorrentino, ed., *Schleiermacher's Philosophy and the Philosophical Tradition,* 118.

absolute dependence upon God" (*Gl.*² §36; *CF* 142). This original expression arises from the Christian religious affections, which contain the immediate feeling of absolute dependence to the degree that "we become conscious that we are placed in a universal nature-system, i.e. in proportion as we are conscious of ourselves as part of the world" (*Gl.*² §34; *CF* 138). In order to express adequately the relation between God and the world, a doctrine must address both the world's absolute dependence on God and our interdependence with the nature system. Schleiermacher argues that, ideally, such a doctrine can be developed from either the concept of creation or that of preservation, as long as God is regarded as the sole determinant.[14] In order to ensure that God be regarded as the sole determinant, Schleiermacher sets up science and morality as two limits. If the doctrines of creation and preservation soundly reflect the original expression of absolute dependence, they must withstand the problems posed by these two limits. Hence, Schleiermacher sees it as "supremely important here to show the harmony between the interests of piety and science on the one hand and morality on the other" (*Gl.*² §49 p.s.; *CF* 193). The door must be left open to whatever science discovers, and God must be understood to be above and to embrace the antitheses of good and evil.

Science as Limit

Schleiermacher's concern, as it had been in his earlier years, was to guarantee a conciliatory relation between ways of knowing and ways of being religious so that the bifurcation Jacobi said we have no choice but to accept may be avoided. In his essays on Spinoza (1793–94), Schleiermacher suggested that the more we understand the causal relations of things, the more religious we are; in the first edition of his *Reden* (1799), he was very careful to insist that morality, science, and piety are distinct realms which are nonetheless inseparable; in the first revision of the *Reden* (1806), he tried further to clarify the difference between scientific (objective) and religious (subjective) knowledge; in the *Glaubenslehre*, his concern is to show there is no contradiction between science and religion. Science, he says, sets certain limits to what can be said in the dogmatic enterprise.

---

14. See *Gl.*² §38. A doctrine of the relation between God and the world must contradict "every representation of the origin of the world which excludes anything whatever from origination by God, or which places God under those conditions and antitheses which have arisen in and through the world." *Gl.*² §40; *CF* 149–50.

First, the religious self-consciousness is such that it necessarily includes the recognition of the system of nature: "In each and every situation we ought to be conscious of, and sympathetically experience, absolute dependence on God just as we conceive each and every thing as completely conditioned by the interdependence of nature" ($Gl.^2$ §46.1; CF 170–71). It is inconceivable to Schleiermacher that the more we know of nature, the less we need God, or that the more we know of God, the less we need to know of nature. God, as the undivided unity, is not the God of the deists that becomes more remote the more we can explain the causes of things. Nor can the appeal to the mystery of God be used to cover our ignorance: "It can only be a false wisdom which would put religion aside, and a misconceived religion for love of which the progress of knowledge is to be arrested" ($Gl.^2$ §46.1; CF 171). After all, our feeling of absolute dependence never occurs by itself but is only "aroused through stimulations of our sensuous self-consciousness" ($Gl.^2$ §46.2; CF 173). Schleiermacher here seems at last to have resolved the tensions in his earlier writings: science coincides with and limits religion but does not itself lead to the feeling of absolute dependence, just as it should not contradict or inhibit it.

Second, as conventionally understood, miracles must be rejected. If a contradiction has arisen between religion and science, it is because religion has left piety for speculation: "It can never be necessary in the interest of religion so to interpret a fact that its dependence on God absolutely excludes its being conditioned by the system of Nature" ($Gl.^2$ §47; CF 178). Again, a belief in miracles betrays piety since the latter necessarily interprets every event with respect to the interdependence of nature. Consequently, belief in miracles also betrays reverence due to God: "If such an interference be postulated as one of the privileges of the Supreme Being, it would first have to be assumed that there is something not ordained by Him which could offer Him resistance and thus invade Him and His work; and such an idea would entirely destroy our fundamental feeling" ($Gl.^2$ §47.1; CF 179). If miracles are to be maintained in Christian dogmatics, they must be understood within the context of natural causation—that is to say, explained in terms of the dynamic character of nature and the "possibility of extension or deviation" ($Gl.^2$ §47.3; CF 184)—but never as a divine suspension of natural order.

Third, this means that any notion of the divine causality as "supernatural"—as somehow a usurpation of, or even as supplement to, the natural "ordered power" ($Gl.^2$ §54.4; CF 215)[15]—must be rejected. The interests

15. Cf. $Gl.^2$ §§13, 54.

of natural science and religion entirely agree "that we should abandon the idea of the absolutely supernatural because no single instance of it can be known by us, and we are nowhere required to recognize it" (*Gl.*² §47.3; *CF* 183). It is because natural causality completely coincides with divine causality that there is a "possibility of pious self-consciousness in every moment of the objective consciousness" (*Gl.*² §46.2; *CF* 173). There can be no experience of God apart from the world, just as, if we were properly aware, there could be no experience of the world apart from God, since the world is absolutely dependent upon God.

Fourth, it would be against piety, the consciousness of our absolute dependence, to look for individual causes and not to recognize "the universal relatedness in which the true causes really lie hidden" (*Gl.*² §46.1; *CF* 172). Also, to ascribe each individual cause to God as an intermediary cause is at root irreverent, since it makes "the radical error of conceiving the dependence on God of what happens as dependence on particular finite causes"; God, however, can never be understood "in the manner of a finite free cause."[16] The divine preservation is a universal, not a particular, cause. This emphasis on the whole pertains to morality as well as science.

Morality as Limit

Unless attention is given to the whole when reflecting on moral issues, we will either run the danger of anthropomorphism by ascribing the "smallest detail" to God "in too human fashion," or be tempted to reject the relation of absolute dependence for fear "our free choices in little things" will be vitiated (*Gl.*² §46.1; *CF* 172, 173). Schleiermacher's concern is that in our attempt to vindicate God by somehow detaching evil or "sad and unhappy experiences" (*Gl.*² §48.1; *CF* 184) from the God-consciousness, we actually posit the divine causality as somehow sporadic and inactive,[17] and thus our feeling of absolute dependence is threatened, and our understanding of God irreverent. Evil, therefore, "is just as much wholly dependent upon God as" (*Gl.*² §48.1; *CF* 185) good is, for four reasons.[18]

---

16. Note to *Gl.*² §47.2; *CF* 182. This is why creation cannot be understood in temporal terms as a first originating cause. For God, in one divine decree, has ordained and continually preserves this ordered power, and it is irreverent (i.e., it tends toward anthropomorphism) to think that God acts in discrete and isolated moments.

17. "The same result [as when the miraculous is regarded as entirely supernatural] follows if we believe that evil was less ordained by God than other things, because, in that case, of the things equally created by Him, He would leave some in the lurch rather than others." *Gl.*² §49 p.s.; *CF* 192.

18. In this section I address only those texts that deal with the question of evil in general and how it must be understood in relation to the divine causality: "Thus [evil] is to be

First, the causal nexus needs and includes both good and evil. "Individual beings belong to the transitory in the form primarily of a vital activity" (*Gl.*² §48.2; *CF* 186) that includes progression and regression. Life consists in the fluctuation between the two, so much so that there can be no progress without arrest. Second, evil never exists by itself but always stands in relation to good: "Evil as such is not ordained by God, because evil in isolation is never found, and the same is true of good, but each thing or event is ordained by God that it should be both" (187). The antithesis is always present. Third, life's repressions cannot be denied. The tendency to deny life's repressions and evil as being dependent on God is due to our misunderstanding: we view them "apart from their natural conditions" (186);[19] we consider them as isolated and assume that they can be eliminated, as if "the world could exist apart from evil" (187). The imperfect emotions are a given in human life and do not derive from a source other than that of the more perfect ones.

Fourth, evil is necessary for the development of the good. This is quite different from saying that evil is justified because it can bring about good. The reason for this reiterates Schleiermacher's reason for rejecting final causes. To distinguish between ends and means implies that, to some degree at least, God thinks and wills in human fashion. Schleiermacher grants no such distinction *in God,* unless the end is the Kingdom of God and the means is redemption, but that is a far from conventional understanding. Although such a claim may be true, it is true only accidentally. The argument for *development* has to do with the very nature of being human: "Everything inward becomes, at a certain point of its strength or maturity, an outward too" (*Gl.*² §6.2; *CF* 27). Schleiermacher takes this drive toward and capacity for expression (central to the structure and contents of the *Glaubenslehre*) to be something of great value that is undiminished by the fact that it is also the occasion of and reason for sin: "Sin only comes to be done by reason of that capacity of man to express his inner nature outwardly which is the source of all good" (*Gl.*² §48.2; *CF* 187).[20]

Morality, then, is a second limiting factor for the doctrines of creation and preservation. If a contradiction arises in which God is placed within a moral antithesis, dogmatics has overstepped its bounds. The antitheses of

---

considered now apart from ethics, and only as it appears and is given as a state affecting the self-consciousness as one of life's obstacles." *Gl.*² §48.1; *CF* 185. §49 is also an important source for Schleiermacher's understanding of human freedom and moral evil; the relevant texts for that discussion will be considered in Chapter 5.

19. Cf. *Gl.*² §46.1,2.
20. Cf. *Gl.*² §§81.2, 84.3.

progress and arrest, good and evil, imply and require one another. If Schleiermacher's doctrine does not meet the challenges of science and morality, "then the main proposition of the doctrine itself would fall to the ground" (*Gl.*² §49 p.s.; *CF* 193). It remains to be seen whether these limits required by piety are indeed met in the propositions regarding creation and preservation, that is, whether they are related to the "original expression."

Causality and Coincidence: The First Form of Proposition

Creation

Because of the challenges posed by morality and science, Schleiermacher maintains that many interpretations of the relation between God and the world prove to be inadequate, insofar as the act of creation has become separated from divine preservation.[21] Indeed, Schleiermacher would be all too happy to dismiss the whole concept of creation, but he did not deem the time ripe for that dogmatic move.[22] Until such a time, creation can only be described in conjunction with preservation because, by itself, it does not fully reflect the religious self-consciousness of our interdependence with the world, and it runs the risk of using dependence on God "as an explanation of the course of the world where the causal nexus is concealed" (*Gl.*² §38.2; *CF* 148). Preservation rather than creation thus becomes for Schleiermacher

---

21. The division between the originating and sustaining activity of God, which came relatively late in the history of Christian thought, became further reified in the contentious debate between Protestant orthodoxy and deism. It is in the context of this debate that Schleiermacher's discussion needs to be understood. According to Jaroslav Pelikan, "The net result of the controversy over deism was an impairment of the doctrine of creation that rendered it largely incapable of coping with even pre-Darwinian evolutionism." "Creation and Causality in the History of Christian Thought," in *Issues in Evolution*, ed. Sol Tax and Charles Callender, vol. 3 of *Evolution After Darwin*, ed. Sol Tax (Chicago: University of Chicago Press, 1960), 38.

22. "I can only anticipate that we must learn to do without what many are still accustomed to regard as inseparably bound to the essence of Christianity. I am not referring to the six-day creation, but to the concept of creation itself, as it is usually understood.... How long will the concept of creation hold out against the power of a world view constructed from undeniable scientific conclusions that no one can avoid." *On the "Glaubenslehre,"* 60–61; *KGA* 1/10:345–46.

the "essential doctrine,"[23] since it more fully expresses the feeling of absolute dependence.

Yet this is not, at least for the time being, to subsume creation under preservation. Together, they fully express the fundamental feeling. The doctrine of creation serves a negative function in that it "is to be elucidated pre-eminently with a view to the exclusion of every alien element" ($Gl.^2$ §39; CF 148).[24] Because it does not express divine causality as experienced in the feeling of absolute dependence, it serves as a "precaution"[25] and cannot be taken literally. This means in part that the formulation *creatio ex nihilo* can be retained only with strict qualifications. Since it is pious in its intentions, insofar as it "excludes the idea that before the origin of the world anything existed outside God" ($Gl.^2$ §41.1; CF 153) and thus guards God's aseity, Schleiermacher does allow it a place in his dogmatics and is tolerant of those who retain it. He is, however, clearly ambivalent about the formula: it trespasses the limit set by natural science, which "may lead us back to the forces and masses that formed the world, or even further still" ($Gl.^2$ §40.1; CF 150); it tends to divorce creation from preservation, even though our feeling of absolute dependence on God always experiences creation as continuous and nature as dynamic;[26] finally, it calls to mind human means of construction and formation and, by suggesting that "there are two divine activities" ($Gl.^2$ §41.1; CF 154), seems to place God under the contradictions of time.[27]

Schleiermacher avoids such contradictions by defining creation as "a single divine act . . . [which includes] the whole system of nature . . . [and which] we do not conceive . . . as having ceased" ($Gl.^2$ §38.2; CF 147). We have no experience of any type of creation outside of the usual system of causal relations, which is to say that we have no experience of an origination without continuity.[28] Creation expresses God's "absolute approval"

---

23. Note to $Gl.^2$ §46; Redeker 1:224a: "Der eigentliche Lehrsatz" (Thönes). Hereafter, I shall refer to §46 as the "essential doctrine."

24. Cf. $Gl.^2$ §41.1.

25. Note to $Gl.^2$ §40.1; Redeker 1:198. Cf. $Gl.^2$ §40.2.

26. "But to acknowledge another creation here is either again entirely to abolish the difference between creation and preservation or to assume different kinds of matter devoid of inherent forces, which is surely meaningless." $Gl.^2$ §41.2; CF 154; cf. $Gl.^2$ §§38.2, 36.1.

27. Against Schleiermacher, Pike argues that "a timeless being could not only not be omnipotent on the traditional interpretation of 'omnipotent,' such a being could have no creative ability whatsoever." Pike, *God and Timelessness*, 110; cf. 175–76.

28. See $Gl.^2$ §§36.1, 38.1, 39.1, 40.1

and not some contemplation of possible worlds ($Gl.^2$ §55.2; CF 226).[29] Schleiermacher views himself not as departing from the theological tradition but rather retrieving a fundamental insight that had become clouded in Protestant orthodoxy, and he is careful to cite the relevant sources. Some confessions of the Evangelical Church, he admits, do indeed place sole emphasis on creation as origination, but there are other confessions that emphasize divine preservation; all of them, however, "belong under our formulation" ($Gl.^2$ §37.1; CF 144). What he means by so bold a claim is that they all intend to describe God as the "sole original activity," which is the only way "that the relation of absolute dependence can be expressed" (ibid.). The emphasis is on one continuous act, one divine decree, and thus approaches the doctrine of divine preservation.

Preservation

In the first edition of the *Glaubenslehre,* Schleiermacher formulates his understanding of the divine preservation in two separate propositions:

> All that affects and determines our self-consciousness persists as such through God. ($Gl.^1$ §59; Peiter 1:168)[30]

> The consciousness so described and insight into the determination of that which affects us through the nature-system are also everywhere completely reconcilable in their greatest perfection. ($Gl.^1$ §60; Peiter 1:173)[31]

Somewhat predictably, these propositions were interpreted as being pantheistic, since, as Schleiermacher paraphrases it, "if the operation of things and the efficacy of God are the same, then the world and God are also the same"; this interpretation, however, is "clearly false."[32] The efficacy is the

---

29. Cf. $Gl.^2$ §57.2. Once again, as in 1793–94, this reflects a preference for Spinoza over Leibniz.
30. "Alles was unser Selbstbewußtsein bewegt und bestimmt, besteht als solches durch Gott."
31. "Das eben beschriebene Bewußtsein und die Einsicht in die Bestimmtheit dessen, was uns bewegt durch den Naturzusammenhang, sind auch in ihrer größten Vollkommenheit überall vollkommen vereinbar."
32. Note to $Gl.^1$ §60; Redeker 2:518. "Der pantheistische Schein: wenn Wirkung der Dinge und Wirksamkeit Gottes dasselbe ist, so ist Welt und Gott auch dasselbe, was aber offenbar falsch ist. Sondern die Wirksamkeit ist dasselbe, weil auch das Sein der Dinge als die Quelle ihrer Tätigkeiten durch die schaffende Wirksamkeit Gottes ist."

same only "because the being of things as the source of their activities is through the creative efficacy of God" (*Gl.*¹ §60; Redeker 2:518). What Schleiermacher means, in part, is that the two propositions cannot be separated. Divine causality and natural causality are "completely reconcilable" (§60) precisely because everything exists through God (§59).[33]

Given that everything persists (*bestehen*) through God (or, viewed from the other side, because God sustains [*erhalten*] everything), it follows that nothing, including natural causality, can be in any way independent of divine causality. This view of the continuance or persistence (*Bestehende*)[34] of all things in God is not entirely unlike the notion of *participation* as a way to explain divine immanence: God, as Being-itself, is the source of the being of all things, and all things continue to exist so long as they continue to participate in the being of God. It is just such an understanding, however, that Schleiermacher deliberately intends to avoid. In the marginal note to §59 of the first edition, he expresses his discomfort with various "scholastic" positions, because they rely on the notion of cooperation (*Mitwirkung*). This, he insists, suggests "a trace of something independent from God."[35] Although he does not elaborate on this further in this note, he does so in his postscript to §46, the corresponding proposition in the second edition. The danger, he there explains, is that a split occurs according to which "some connect the expression 'preservation' only with matter and form, and 'co-operation' with powers and actions; others again connect preservation with the existence and powers of things, and co-operation only with activity" (*Gl.*² §46 p.s.; *CF* 176). In other words, preservation is too often relegated only to the essence of things, which is viewed as being other than their activities; consequently, activities have a different (less dependent) relation to divine causality. This view is unacceptable both in its understanding of nature and in its understanding of God.

Schleiermacher's departure from the notion of participation reflects an interpretation of nature fundamentally different from that assumed by the scholastics. For Schleiermacher, nature, as a system (*Naturzusammenhang*) of organic and dynamic forces, is essentially active. Being is not separable from its active and passive forces, the totality of which constitutes the *All*.[36]

33. Since *Gl.*¹ §60 cannot be properly understood except in light of *Gl.*¹ §59, and consequently since their separation led to an interpretation of his doctrine of divine preservation as pantheistic, Schleiermacher was careful to combine them in §46 in the second edition.
34. See note to *Gl.*¹ §59; Redeker 2:518. Note here the parallel between *persistence* and what in 1793–94 Schleiermacher termed *inherency*.
35. Note to *Gl.*¹ §59; Redeker 2:518.
36. See *Gl.*¹ §59.1; Peiter 1:170.

It is the power of things, not some static substance, that is sustained by the divine preservation, insofar as "things" are defined precisely as "centres of power" (*Gl.*² §46 p.s.; *CF* 178). As a center of power, a thing coexists with, is dependent on, and is partially determined by "the activity of the rest of things" (177), all of which are equally and absolutely dependent on God. Further, to separate *being* from *activity*, and to claim that God preserves the former but only cooperates with the latter, implies that divine causality is not all-embracing, hence that some activity can arise independently of God, or more accurately, would be only relatively dependent on God. This in turn implies a division in divine activity, a division that borders on anthropomorphism and irreverence. The creative efficacy of God can only be expressed as a continuous, rather than intermittent, activity. Just as God did not create the world *ex nihilo* at some point in time and then proceed to preserve it, neither does God preserve the being of things and, in some other mode, cooperate with their activity.[37] Note that the emphasis here is on the divine causality as *sustaining* rather than as efficient or transitive.

There is yet another reason for his rejection of the scholastic notion of participation, namely, its inadequacy for a postcritical interpretation of divine causality. Stricter limits, Schleiermacher cautions, must be placed on our understanding of divine preservation, "since we are not immediately affected by the being of things, but always only by their activity and change" (*Gl.*¹ §59, Anmerkung (b); Peiter 1:168).[38] This, at least in part, accounts for his employment of *via causalitatis*, which better recognizes the limits of reason. He explains in a marginal note, "We first perceive the connecting of things and then call to mind the relation of dependence. The activity of the thing on every occasion is quite certainly the persistence in dependence on God; [and what] is willed by God is just the activity of the thing itself."[39] Because activity itself persists through the divine activity, we can have no knowledge, including knowledge of God, apart from our experience of the activity of finite things. Therefore, the other two ways of speaking about God, *via eminentiae* and *via negationis*, are judged to be inadequate.[40]

---

37. "For being posited for itself can only exist where there is also power, just as power always exists only in activity; thus a preservation which did not include the placing of all the activities of any finite being in absolute dependence on God would be just as empty as creation without preservation." *Gl.*² §46 p.s.; *CF* 176.

38. "Anmerkungen" are not marginal notes, but part of the text of the *Glaubenslehre*.

39. Note to *Gl.*¹ §59; Redeker 2:518.

40. See *Gl.*¹ §64.3; Peiter 1:191; also *Gl.*² §50.3. Schleiermacher actually uses the *via negationis* more than he admits. This is reflected in the order and structure of the section on the divine attributes: he first develops Eternity and Omnipresence (*Gl.*² §§52, 53), both of

Although his orginal intentions are carried through into the second edition, Schleiermacher again finds it necessary to clarify his argument (and also to free himself of charges of pantheism) by adopting more precise terminology: *to persist* in God becomes *to be absolutely dependent* on God;[41] *reconcilability* becomes *coincidence*.[42] The latter revision presupposes the former. Since *absolute dependence* is Schleiermacher's own term, it does not need the qualification and exposition that *continuance* or *persistence* does; in fact, the only way to describe Schleiermacher's use of *Bestehende* (thus to distinguish it from both pantheism and what he refers to generally as "scholasticism") is in terms of absolute dependence. Everything, including natural causality, is absolutely dependent on God. Absolute dependence on God is thus the basis and presupposition for every other relation; as the fundamental relationship of all that is, it includes within itself, and never occurs apart from, the interdependence and interrelatedness of all things (*Naturzusammenhang*). The significance of the term *coincidence* follows from this, and indeed is but another expression of the relation between relative and absolute dependence, with special regard to natural and divine causality.

In the second edition of the *Glaubenslehre*, the doctrine of divine preservation is reformulated under one "essential doctrine": "The religious self-consciousness, by means of which we place all that affects or influences us in absolute dependence on God, *coincides* entirely with the view that all such things are conditioned and determined by the interdependence of Nature" (*Gl.*² §46; *CF* 170; emphasis added). The first expositional paragraph to this proposition, Schleiermacher notes, is meant "as explanation of the difficult expression 'to coincide.'"[43] It is meant, in other words, to explain how natural causality, which belongs to the nature system, can coincide with, yet not be identical to, divine preservation. In fact, §46.1 is more precautionary than constructive insofar as it focuses on certain dangers, limits, and fallacies. For instance, a fallacy results from granting exclusive weight to either the objective or the subjective consciousness when actually

---

which emphasize how divine causality is *not* to be confused with natural causality, i.e., how it is completely other. Gerhard Ebeling, too, recognizes Schleiermacher's indirect use of negation: "As modifications of causality [attributes] can be properly understood only when the two other procedures, distriction and negation, are brought into play as correctives." "Schleiermacher's Doctrine of the Divine Attributes," 139.

41. Compare *Gl.*¹ §59 with the first part of *Gl.*² §46: *from* "Alles . . . besteht als solches durch Gott" *to* "alles . . . in die schlechthinnige Abhängigkeit von Gott stellen."

42. Compare *Gl.*¹ §60 with the second part of *Gl.*² §46: *from* "überall volkommen vereinbar" *to* "fällt ganz zusammen."

43. Note to *Gl.*² §46.1; Redeker 1:224c.

there is a continuity, a necessary correlation, between them: "In each and every situation we ought to be conscious of, and sympathetically experience, absolute dependence on God just as we conceive each and every thing as completely conditioned by the interdependence of nature" (*Gl.*² §46.1; *CF* 170–71). There can be no contradiction, although they may not both come to clarity at the same time. This relationship of correlation requires an oscillation between the two forms of consciousness: "In the one case, through absorption in ourselves, we lose consciousness of the object affecting us, just as in the other case we are entirely merged in the object. But this in no way prevents the one activity, after having satisfied itself, from stimulating and passing over into the other" (171). Such oscillation is by now a familiar theme in Schleiermacher's thought. It demands a turn to the "wider scope," in order that "we identify ourselves in our self-consciousness with the whole world and feel ourselves in the same way as not less dependent" (*Gl.*² §46.2; *CF* 173).[44] We must turn our attention from the particular to the whole in order that, in turn, we may better grasp the particular. In doing so, we can recognize the coincidence between absolute dependence and interdependence.

Schleiermacher pursues this more constructive vein in the second expositional paragraph, where it becomes apparent that it is in terms of the dictum *All-One* that the coincidence of divine preservation and natural causality is best explained: "For the most complete and universal interdependence of nature is posited in this 'All-One' of finite being, and if we also feel ourselves to be absolutely dependent, then there will be a *complete coincidence* of the two ideas—namely, the unqualified conviction that everything is grounded and established in the universality of the nature-system, and the inner certainty of the absolute dependence of all finite being on God" (*Gl.*² §46.2; *CF* 173; emphasis added). The *All,* as the system of finite relations and causes, is absolutely dependent on the *One,* as the absolute causality. That is to say, preservation is the universal cause and ought not be misunderstood along the lines of some powerful particular cause. This is an important text in Schleiermacher's doctrine of God, especially when the concern is to determine the extent to which it may be influenced by pantheism or Spinozism. First, Schleiermacher adopts the term *coincidence* to respond to charges of pantheism; he is not, however, entirely successful, insofar as *coincidence* itself, if not properly understood, raises the same suspicions. Second, it cannot be accidental that Schleiermacher defines *coin-*

---

44. Recall that in the *Reden,* oscillation described the movement of the pious soul between the particular and the whole, between the One and the Many.

cidence in terms of the dictum *One and All,* which for him represents an acceptable form of pantheism, namely, that inspired by Spinoza.[45] This supports the thesis that there are pantheistic themes explicit in the second edition of the *Glaubenslehre* and that, in a sense, critics are right, but they misunderstand and thus misjudge the fundamental insight operative here.

Schleiermacher's well-known conclusion to his doctrine on divine preservation is that "divine preservation, as the absolute dependence of all events and changes on God, and natural causation, as the complete determination of all events by the universal nexus, are *one and the same thing simply from different points of view,* the one being neither separated from the other nor limited by it" (*Gl.*² §46.2; *CF* 174; emphasis added). This claim, so central to Schleiermacher's doctrine of God, is made prematurely here in §46.2, insofar as it is not yet fully explicated and will remain incomplete until the exposition of §54. In other words, the one "point of view" (that there is no relation in the nature system that is not absolutely dependent on God) is surely clear enough by now. But the other "point of view" (that there is no divine causality apart from that exercised within the nature system) is not explained until his exposition of the divine attribute of omnipotence. The reason for this is in part that divine causality has not yet been described. The subject matter of §46, since it falls under the first form of proposition, is religious consciousness; the subject matter of §51, since it belongs to the second form of proposition, is Absolute Causality; both propositions argue the same thesis, although from different vantage points. The description of the relation between divine and natural causality derives from that between the feeling of absolute dependence and the relative feelings of dependence and freedom; that is to say, they completely coincide, but they are not identical. Divine causality, or the continuous act of preservation, *is* the *Whence* of our feeling of absolute dependence when described in more concrete terms than in the Introduction (§4).[46] It is thus necessary to direct attention to the divine attributes, where Schleiermacher further develops his understanding of *coincidence.*

---

45. "But let us think of the highest stage of religion, and let us accordingly hold Pantheism fast to the usual formula of One and All: then God and world will remain distinct at least as regards function, and thus such a man, since he reckons himself as belonging to the world, can feel himself, along with this All, to be dependent on that which is the corresponding One. Such states of mind can scarcely be distinguished from the religious emotions of many a Monotheist." *Gl.*² §8 p.s.; *CF* 39.

46. In the words of Richard R. Niebuhr, "The feeling of simple dependence is one member of a binary. The other is simple productive power or causality." "Schleiermacher and the Names of God," 186.

The Dialectic of One and All: The Second Form of Proposition

The divine attributes are not to be interpreted apart from the first form of proposition, because, if taken alone, they are mere speculation.[47] Little is contained therein that cannot be found, at least implicitly, under the first form of proposition. Nevertheless, while the fundamental principles for the coincidence of divine and natural causality are given in §46, expanded explanations are reserved for the propositions on the divine attributes. The divine attributes can be understood as qualifiers, which in part mark a departure from Spinozism, and as correctives, which explain how the traditional doctrines may be maintained. Roughly speaking, God's eternity explains how God is distinct from the world, God's omnipresence how God is everywhere active, God's omnipotence how God preserves the whole as well as the individual, and finally God's omniscience how God is a *living God*. The structure of Schleiermacher's presentation of these divine attributes is based on the dictum *One and All*. Eternity and omnipresence describe for Schleiermacher the divine transcendence: *One* refers the absolute inwardness of God that distinguishes God from the natural order. Omnipotence and omniscience describe the divine immanence: *All* refers to the absolute vitality of God, which is coextensive with the natural order. Under each of these four attributes Schleiermacher offers further clarification of what he means by a *living God*. Where he departs most decisively from his earlier affinities with Spinoza is in his exposition of the attributes of *omniscience*, which understands the divine knowledge as the productivity of God, and *omnipotence*, which Schleiermacher claims avoids pantheism because it does not mix the divine being with the finite.

The Divine Causality

The "chief attributes"[48] of part 1 of the *Glaubenslehre* (eternity, omnipresence, omnipotence, omniscience) are ways for us to describe the divine causality, the *Whence* of our feeling of absolute dependence. The proposition that formulates the doctrine of the divine causality (§51) puts forth the same thesis as the "essential doctrine" (§46), although from a different vantage point. Compare the two propositions:

47. See Gl.² §50.
48. See note to Gl.² §51; Redeker 1:263a: "Die Haupteigenschaften."

The religious self-consciousness, by means of which we place all that affects or influences us in absolute dependence on God, coincides entirely with the view that all such things are conditioned and determined by the interdependence of Nature. (§46)

The Absolute Causality to which the feeling of absolute dependence points back can only be described in such a way that, on the one hand, it is distinguished from the content of the natural order and thus contrasted with it, and, on the other hand, equated with it in comprehension. (§51)

The latter proposition should be interpreted as an elaboration of the former, since it presupposes the relation of coincidence between absolute dependence on God and the interdependence of nature. At the same time, insofar as it offers a more complete explanation of the relationship of *coincidence,* the doctrine of absolute causality is necessary for understanding the doctrine of divine preservation. Yet, it itself requires the further elaboration given under Schleiermacher's reformulation of the traditional attributes, most especially eternity and omnipotence.[49]

The attribute of *omnipotence* (§54) describes how divine causality remains equal in scope with natural causality. There is no gap in the *All;* everything finite is, by definition, subject to a "condition of mutual relation of differently distributed causality and passivity [which] constitutes the natural order" (*Gl.*² §51.1; *CF* 201). Consequently, divine causality "extends as widely as the order of nature and the finite causality contained in it" (201) and "can never in any way enter as a supplement" (*Gl.*² §54.1; *CF* 212). Nothing exists or acts independently of the divine causality. Precisely because all causality depends absolutely on the divine causality (*One*), it can be explained in terms of its relations in the nature system (*All*); conversely, because it exists within the system of finite causes (*All*), it necessarily is the effect of the divine omnipotence (*One*).

49. The method of approach to be employed here will be to trace the key idea of the "essential doctrine" (§46, namely, the coincidence of divine causality and the nature system) as that is expanded and developed in §51, which in turn is expanded in §52 and §54, which in turn are expanded in §53 and §55, respectively. Let "⟶" mean "expanded in"; let "< ⟹ >" mean "there is a dialectical relation between"; then, the flow of Schleiermacher's argument goes as follows:

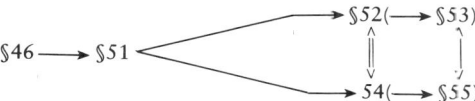

The attribute of *eternity* (§52) describes how divine causality is contrasted with the nature system. Since divine causality stands in equal relationship to activity as to passivity, and since "finite causality is what it is only by means of its contrast with finite passivity, so it is to be inferred that the divine causality is contrasted with the finite" (*Gl.*² §51.1; CF 201). This argument follows from that already given under the first form of proposition and in the Introduction: relative dependence and relative freedom exist in relation to one another on a spectrum that absolute dependence establishes but does not share. When applied to the question of causality, this basic principle means that divine causality, as absolutely timeless and spaceless, not only conditions what is temporal and spatial, but conditions time and space themselves. There can be no analogy between finite and absolute causality.[50]

Therefore, whereas the nature system is defined by its oppositions, by the dynamic relations between passive and active forces, divine causality is absolute, sheer causality. Absolute causality could perhaps be better explained in terms of the *coincidence of opposites,* but Schleiermacher cannot explicitly use this term since it cannot be traced directly to the Christian religious consciousness.[51] He does, however, imply it on several occasions. All antitheses disappear in the absolute unity of the One: "The temporal oppositions of before and after, older and younger disappear in coincidence when applied to God" (*Gl.*² §52.1; CF 204).[52] Indeed, such coincidences of opposites underlie Schleiermacher's presentation of the divine attributes with regard to both content and structure. For instance, the attributes eternity and omnipotence aid Schleiermacher in explaining how *coincidence* means a complete inherence without identification. Yet careful formulations

---

50. "For since here we have to do only with the causality of God, the conception of the infinity of God is useful only as warding off analogy with finite causality." *Gl.*² §53 p.s.; CF 211. There is no analogy because the idea of divine causality is not abstracted from our experience of finite causality, rather it is given immediately in the feeling of absolute dependence. The fact that divine omnipotence and omniscience are fully presented in the nature system (and in that sense that divine causality is fully immanent) allows Schleiermacher to speak of "finite causality" and "infinite causality" without resorting, he thinks, to analogy. The two have something in common in that they fully "coincide," but the realization of this fact is not reached through abstraction from experience; it is given in experience itself.

51. See *Gl.*² §16 p.s. and §33 p.s. Robert R. Williams interprets Schleiermacher's entire doctrine of God in terms of the coincidence of opposites, comparing Schleiermacher with Nikolaus Cusanus. His examination is interesting in its examination of both the *Dialektik* and the *Glaubenslehre;* unfortunately, he narrows his discussion too much to the divine attributes. See *Schleiermacher the Theologian.* See also Thiel, *God and World,* 72–73.

52. Cf. *Gl.*² §§51.1, 55.2.

of these attributes do not alone suffice, since they accurately express the Christian religious consciousness if and only if they are held together in a dialectical relationship: "Instead, therefore, of saying God is eternal and almighty, we should rather say He is almighty-eternal and eternal-almighty, or God is eternal omnipotence or almighty eternity" (Gl.² §51.1; CF 202). This dialectical relation reflects that between the *One* and the *All:* divine causality cannot be understood to be absolutely opposed to natural causality unless it is at the same time coextensive with it, and it cannot be all-powerful unless it transcends the antithesis of activity and passivity. More to the point, eternity, when qualified by omnipresence, expresses the Absolute Inwardness of God (God as the *One*); omnipotence, when qualified by omniscience, expresses the Absolute Vitality of God (God in relation to the *All*).

Hence critics are wrong in charging that his doctrine of God can be reduced entirely to one attribute, namely omnipotence, and consequently that what results is an abstract or pantheistic notion of God. Responding to one such critic in a marginal note to the first edition, Schleiermacher defends himself,

> Röhr . . . chiefly criticizes my handling of the divine attributes, that everything refers to omnipotence and becomes a modification of this, and that I want nothing left of God but the abstract representation that makes God the primordial ground of all being. —This can only be said, if one forgets that the second part follows the first. In this cycle, however, he could not himself build another foundation, and he must yet commend me because I nevertheless put eternity and omnipotence on the same footing.[53]

This note underscores several important working assumptions in Schleiermacher's development of his doctrine of God. First, no attribute can be isolated from the others; the sets of dialectical relations must be maintained. Since the attributes represent nothing in God and are only intended to aid our own understanding, any isolation would lead to speculation. Second, God is not some pantheistic deity, *if* that is understood as something lacking any transcendence or as only an abstraction or generalization. The dialectic between eternity and omnipotence maintains that divine causality is omnipotent (immanent or coextensive) only insofar as it is eternal (transcend-

---

53. Note to Gl.¹ §65; Redeker 2:520.

ent or opposite in kind), and vice versa.[54] As Schleiermacher proceeds to argue, especially under the corollary attributes of omnipresence and omniscience, what is being expressed is nothing less than the *living God*. Third, what he means by the *living God* can be understood only in light of part 2 of the *Glaubenslehre*, which expresses the specifically Christian religious consciousness. Schleiermacher thus suggests in this marginal note what he explicitly argues in his second letter to Lücke: omnipotence *is* an abstraction from the doctrine of preservation as well as from the attributes of wisdom and love, just as part 1 is an abstraction from part 2, and thus should not be read apart from the other chief attributes, most especially those in part 2.[55]

Omnipotence and Immanence

In all of this, Schleiermacher's argument is well taken. Nevertheless, the focus must remain on the doctrine of divine omnipotence. It is, after all, the more constructive, whereas the doctrine of divine eternity is the more cautionary.[56] Moreover, omnipotence is without doubt the more controversial of the two insofar as it makes two claims that may fairly be called Spinozan: first, God is the indwelling or immanent cause of all things; second, there is no mere possibility in God, hence the divine causality is completely presented in the nature system. Both claims require substantial explanation on Schleiermacher's part, since they mark a significant revision of a central Christian doctrine. Because his proposition on the divine omnipotence explicitly correlates the two ideas implied under the divine pres-

---

54. How one describes the relation between God's transcendence and immanence is perhaps the central issue of any doctrine of God. On this point, Schleiermacher is closer, for instance, to Meister Eckhart than to Thomas Aquinas, insofar as the divine immanence explains transcendence. See Bernard McGinn, introduction to *Meister Eckhart: The Essential Sermons, Commentaries, Treatises, and Defense*, trans. Edmund College, O.S.A., and McGinn (New York: Paulist Press, 1981), 33–34.

55. See *On the "Glaubenslehre,"* 55–60. The "part" referred to in the marginal note addressed to Röhr may not have to do with the overall structure of the *Glaubenslehre*. It *could* refer to the two attributes in question, eternity and omnipotence. When Schleiermacher bids Röhr remember that "the second part follows the first," he could mean that omnipotence follows eternity, and it has thus been properly qualified. Such an interpretation would certainly follow from Schleiermacher's overriding structure: the more constructive propositions are almost always preceded by a precautionary one (e.g., preservation follows creation). In this sense, he does indeed employ the *via negationis*, although perhaps more with structure and organization than with content.

56. According to Ebeling, omnipotence "is the basic attribute of God—and this in the sense of perfectly real causality." "Schleiermacher's Doctrine of the Divine Attributes," 142.

ervation and absolute causality, it offers the most comprehensive explanation of *coincidence* given in the *Glaubenslehre*.

From the View of the Nature System

The first idea expressed in §54, which really adds nothing novel, defines *coincidence* from the side of nature: "First, that the entire system of Nature, comprehending all times and spaces, is founded upon divine causality, which as eternal and omnipresent is in contrast to all finite causality" ($Gl.^2$ §54; CF 211). This is really a reiteration of previous key propositions.[57] Nevertheless, precisely because it is cumulative, the expositional paragraphs to this proposition lend some clarity and coherence lacking in previous discussions. For instance, since he has already established how divine omnipotence is opposed to any finite power or efficacy in the two preceding propositions, Schleiermacher can now conclude that "through omnipotence everything is already posited which comes into existence through finite causes, in time and space" ($Gl.^2$ §54.1; CF 212). Building thus on the doctrines of eternity and omnipresence, he tries to settle the confusion over his understanding of the relationship between the divine preservation and the nature system. In a second marginal note addressed to Röhr, Schleiermacher insists that there is no identification. He asks, "But then how could I say that the omnipotence establishes the nature-system"?[58] His line of thought is such that it avoids any suggestion of independence from God, which would be implied if we were to interpret some events, to the exclusion of others, as belonging specially to divine causality. There is necessarily a coincidence between the nature system and divine omnipotence; there can be no identification, since one establishes the other.

Once again, he appeals to the dictum *One and All* to describe this coincidence: "Rather everything is and becomes altogether by means of the natural order, so that each takes place through all and all wholly through the divine omnipotence, so that all indivisibly exists through One" ($Gl.^2$ §54.1; CF 212).[59] In terms of causality, this means that divine omnipotence is the underlying, inherent causality. In his marginal note to the second edition,

---

57. See $Gl.^2$ §§4, 46, 47, 51–53.
58. Note to $Gl.^1$ §68; Redeker 2:522.
59. Cf. $Gl.^2$ §46.2 He closes his first expositional paragraph to $Gl.^2$ §54 with this text, but it is taken virtually intact from his marginal note to the first edition. Note to $Gl.^1$ §68; Redeker 2:522. This, then, is more evidence that he deliberately chose this dictum, along with the term *coincidence*, to correct misinterpretations of his first edition, especially those regarding pantheism and identity.

he writes, "Power and inhering causality are the same."[60] This claim is noteworthy both because it is strikingly close to Spinoza's own claim that "God is the immanent, not the transitive, cause of all things"[61] and because Schleiermacher opts not to use words such as *immanent* or *internal* for the reason that they do not meet the limits set by piety. In his discussion of pantheism in the postscript to §8, Schleiermacher argues that the relation of God and world cannot be described in terms of internal or external, since to do so would bring God under an antithesis.[62] The connection with Spinoza, however, is reinforced when, two notes later, Schleiermacher explains that "nothing is, before it is an object of divine omnipotence."[63] This is not unlike Spinoza's own proof that "all things which are, are in God, and must be conceived through God."[64] For Schleiermacher to define the divine causality in terms of power and inherent causality serves to underscore his organic monism, now perhaps better referred to as his causal monism. Divine activity does not occur over and apart from natural causality; God is not found outside of the totality of finite things.

From the View of Divine Causality

Schleiermacher also comes strikingly close to Spinoza in his insistence that divine causality, as inherent causality, is entirely presented in the system of natural causes. This is the second idea contained in the doctrine of divine omnipotence, "that the divine causality, as affirmed in our feeling of absolute dependence, is *completely presented* in the totality of finite being, and consequently everything for which there is a causality in God happens and becomes real" (*Gl.*² §54; emphasis added).[65] In other words, coincidence

---

60. Note to *Gl.*² §54; Redeker 1:279a. "Macht und innewohnende Ursächlichkeit ist dasselbe" (Thönes).

61. *Ethics* 1.18; Curley 1:428. See also his letter to Oldenburg: "My opinion concerning God differs widely from that which is ordinarily defended by modern Christians. For I hold that God is of all things the cause immanent, as the phrase is, not transient." Spinoza to Oldenburg, n.d., in Elwes 2:298.

62. "The distinction (always rather a curious one, and, if I may so say, roughly drawn) between a God who is outside of and above the world, and a God who is in the world, does not particularly meet the point, for nothing can strictly be said about God in terms of the antithesis between internal and external without imperilling in some way the divine omnipotence and omnipresence." *Gl.*² §8 p.s.; *CF* 39.

63. Note to *Gl.*² §54.1; Redeker 1:279c. "Nichts ist, ehe es Gegenstand der göttlichen Allmacht ist" (Thönes).

64. *Ethics* 1.18, proof; Elwes 2:62.

65. Compare *Spinozistisches System*, 563–64: there are no potentialities apart from actualities.

needs to be explained from the side of the divine, so to speak. That is why, as argued above, the conclusion to his proposition on divine preservation is prematurely given under §46, for it is not until now, under the second part of §54, that both "points of view"[66] are fully explicated. In his marginal note to §54, Schleiermacher admits that this second idea of the doctrine is "new and will be taken for heresy."[67] By "new," however, he does not mean new to the revised edition, since the corresponding proposition in the first edition is for all purposes the same.[68] What he evidently means is that it is new to the system itself; in other words, that although it is implied by the doctrine of divine preservation, it can only be developed under the divine attributes. Because he (rightly) anticipates charges of heresy, he is very careful to anticipate and address his opponents' arguments. In each edition, one paragraph addresses the "conventional" view, while another addresses the "scholastic" view.[69]

Schleiermacher begins his argument for why divine omnipotence is presented "completely and exhaustively in the totality of finite nature" ($Gl.^2$ §54.2; CF 213) by admitting it seems to go beyond what can be traced to the feeling of absolute dependence. Since "what we call 'all' consists of the actual and the potential," it seems to follow that "omnipotence must therefore embrace both of these" (213). Schleiermacher rejects such an analogy, but for unexpected reasons. He argues that there is no potentiality even in the natural order, hence limits are crossed, not in denying possibility regarding the divine omnipotence, but in affirming any possibility at all: "The idea of a potentiality outside the sum of the actual has no validity even for our minds" (213–14). If we examine how we ourselves arrive at the idea of possibility, we will also see how meaningless it is to attribute a difference between actuality and potentiality to God. Our notion of possibility derives mainly from our narrow focus on the particular as isolated rather than as interdependent or as part of the whole. Schleiermacher concludes, "If we could have taken into account for each point the influence of the whole system of interaction, we should then have had to say that what was not actual was also not possible within the system of nature" ($Gl.^2$ §54.2; CF

---

66. The conclusion reads, "The divine preservation, as the absolute dependence of all events and changes on God, and natural causation, as the complete determination of all events by the universal nexus, are one and the same thing simply from different points of view, the one being neither separated from the other nor limited by it."
67. Note to $Gl.^2$ §54; Redeker 1:279a.
68. Cf. $Gl.^1$ §68a.
69. Compare $Gl.^1$ §68a.4, 5 (Peiter 1:208–9) with $Gl.^2$ §54.3, 4

213).⁷⁰ Beyond the fact that there is nothing possible in the nature system, another reason for not attributing possibility to the divine causality is simply that, "however we arrived at it, we should then have to accept a self-limitation of the divine omnipotence which can never be given in experience" (*Gl.*² §54.2; CF 214). We are bound by the limits set by piety and by the limits of our knowledge. Schleiermacher's response to the "conventional" view, therefore, is that the distinction between what God could do and actually does do, while intended by "popular explanations" to affirm God's freedom and power, actually limits it, since "the very separation of each in itself, as though, that is, ability were a different condition from will, is an imperfection" (*Gl.*² §54.3; CF 214). In other words, it implies some division in God, analogous to human ways of acting, and is thus too anthropomorphic.⁷¹ The emphasis is on the absolute unity of divine causality. God acts through one divine decree. There is no opposition in God, no "waxing and waning"; rather "the entire omnipotence is, undivided and unabbreviated, the omnipotence that does and effects all" (*Gl.*² §54.3; CF 215).

Schleiermacher's response to the "scholastic" theological tradition, while longer and more thorough than his response to conventional understandings, follows one basic line of argumentation: in making any distinctions concerning divine omnipotence, the points of reference cannot be to one particular as opposed to another, but only to particulars as opposed to the whole or *All*. For instance, the "contrast between a mediate and immediate ... exercise of the divine omnipotence" (*Gl.*² §54.4; CF 215) cannot be applied to two different events, as though in one case, as opposed to another, God acted without intermediate causes. Everything without exception happens by means of the nature system, and thus all events are equally and absolutely dependent on God. The divine omnipotence cannot be related to one event in a way it is not related to another. The most that can be said, if one insists on some distinction, is that only the whole is the immediate object of divine omnipotence. Likewise, it cannot be the case that some things are absolutely, and other things are only conditionally, willed by God. If such terms apply at all, they describe only a difference

---

70. This is a controversial claim because, insofar as it raises questions concerning determinism and the status of the individual, it suggests another aspect of Schleiermacher's Spinozist tendencies. It will be addressed in more detail in Chapter 5.

71. Recall Schleiermacher's method and his concern for piety as a limit to what can be attributed to God: it is "the business of Christian Dogmatics to regulate these representations, so that the anthropomorphic element ... may be rendered as harmless as possible." *Gl.*² §50.1; CF 195.

between a particular and the whole: "It is the divine will embracing the whole framework of mutually conditioning finite being: and this naturally is the absolute will, because nothing conditions it. In this way everything individual would be willed by God conditionally, but the whole willed absolutely as a unity" (216). Or, if "absolute" can be applied to particulars at all, it can only be done in such a way that everything is absolutely willed in the same way everything else is absolutely willed, and conditionally willed the way everything else is conditionally willed.

And last, for Schleiermacher, it is most important to be clear on the usual distinction between a free and necessary divine will. The notion of a necessary self-willing of God, as opposed to the divine free will to create everything that is not God, is purely speculative "hair-splitting" and can never be traced to the feeling of absolute dependence. More to the point, even if a fallacious distinction between divine essence and divine activity is not made, it is wrong to apply either side of the contrast to God. Those who emphasize the freedom of the divine will are just as mistaken as those who emphasize necessity, since each represents an imperfection, and thus each has meaning only in the finite order. If the contrast is to be used at all with regard to the divine omnipotence, it must be used dialectically: "We must therefore think of nothing in God as necessary without at the same time positing it as free, nor as free unless at the same time it is necessary.... [T]hat is to say, the necessary will is included in the free, and the free in the necessary" (217). In this, Schleiermacher is not unlike Spinoza.[72] There is no possibility in the divine omnipotence. God's eternal power is fully actual in the nature system. This is perhaps best summarized under the doctrine of the divine omniscience, the corollary proposition to the divine omnipotence: "There is nothing left in the divine knowledge to which there is no correlative in existence, or which stands in a different relationship to existence.... Or, to put it briefly, God knows all that is; and all that God knows is, and these two are not twofold but single; for His knowledge and His almighty will are one and the same" (*Gl.*^{2} §55.1; *CF* 222).

Schleiermacher is close to Spinoza on at least five counts. First, he rejects anthropomorphic views of divine will and intellect. Spinoza, too, argues that "neither intellect nor will appertain to God's nature."[73] Second, he

---

72. "That thing is called free, which exists solely by the necessity of its own nature, and of which the action is determined by itself alone." *Ethics* 1, definition 7; Elwes 2:46.

73. *Ethics* 1.17, note; Elwes 2:60. "Will and intellect stand in the same relation to the nature of God as do motion, and rest, and absolutely all natural phenomena." *Ethics* 1.32, cor. 2; Elwes 2:70.

insists that there is no possibility in God. Likewise, Spinoza maintains that "God's intellect is entirely actual, and not at all potential."[74] Third, Schleiermacher recognizes no distinction between being and activity: "Just as little, however, can we think of God's willing Himself, and God's willing the world, as separated the one from the other" (*Gl.*² §54.4; *CF* 217). Along the same lines, Spinoza writes, "God's power is identical with his essence."[75] Fourth, God is the immanent or inherent cause of all that is. Fifth, God's freedom is related to God's necessity. Schleiermacher, however, distinguishes himself from Spinoza concerning the spirituality and intentionality of divine causality.

Spirituality and Intentionality

Omniscience and omnipresence are corollary propositions insofar as they can be understood only in terms of omnipotence and eternity, respectively. They are closer to the first two levels of discourse, namely "popular, poetical, and religious teaching" (*Gl.*² §51.2; *CF* 202),[76] than to the descriptively didactic; when carefully explicated, however, they do have a place in dogmatics, since eternity and omnipotence both need further qualification. Insofar as eternity emphasizes the opposition of divine causality to the nature system in terms of time alone, it needs to be complemented by omnipresence: God is opposed to (transcends) the nature system not only with regard to God's timeless causality, but also with regard to God's spaceless causality. Insofar as omnipotence stresses the coextensiveness of the divine and natural causalities, and thus runs the risk of appearing as some dead force, it needs to be complemented by omniscience: God is a living God. Yet again, it is necessary to keep in mind that such distinctions and qualifications are for the purpose of aiding our understanding and to ensure that we remain within the limits of piety in our language concerning God. In order to safeguard this, the terms are best used in compounds: "And thus omnipresence too, when ascribed to the divine causality, is itself eternity, and omniscience is itself omnipotence" (*Gl.*² §51.2; *CF* 203). Both corollary attributes, omnipresence and omniscience, underscore the "absolutely living" character of divine causality (*Gl.*² §55.1; *CF* 219).[77]

74. *Ethics* 1.33, note 2; Elwes 2:73.
75. *Ethics* 1.34; Elwes 2:74.
76. Cf. *Gl.*² §16.1.
77. While omniscience explicitly describes the livingness of the divine causality, omnipresence only does so implicitly. First, whereas finite causality stands in relation to "'dead' forces," because the divine causality is absolutely spaceless, it cannot be understood as in any way

The attribute of *omnipresence* (§53), understood in its compound form and defined as "the abolutely spaceless causality of God, which conditions not only all that is spatial, but space itself as well" (*Gl.*² §53; *CF* 206), serves to explain *coincidence* while emphasizing the *One,* or how God is other. Schleiermacher thinks that the attribute of omnipresence captures what he means by the inwardness or otherness of the divine causality. Indeed, he suggests that omnipresence, more than eternity, is a "living idea" because it is more frequently evoked by the pious affections; it seems more immediately relevant than that of time. It also explains why every experience is possibly a religious experience, since at every moment we can feel the absolute causality underlying the finite causality: "The equivalence of divine causality with the whole content of the finite enables every act to excite the religious consciousness, every act, that is, in which we take up into ourselves a part of the natural order or identify ourselves with such a part, every moment of our self-consciousness as it extends over the whole world" (*Gl.*² §53.1; *CF* 207). Perhaps more important, it preempts suspicions of a naive form of pantheism, for if the divine omnipresence means the absolutely spaceless causality of God upon which space itself is absolutely dependent, it is to be completely distinguished from finite causality, which is concentrated in varying degrees throughout the nature system: "least, i.e. where the space is occupied with so-called 'dead' forces, and greater where there is a greater development of life, and greatest where clear human consciousness is active" (207). Divine omnipresence, the absolute spaceless causality, is not "greater or smaller at different places" (208). God is not more or less remote, depending on the causality or mass of finite things, and this "negation of all remoteness expresses the contrast with finite causality" (*Gl.*² §53.2; *CF* 208). Absolute divine causality is uniform throughout space and time, but this is not to be mistaken for some inert or dead force, for two reasons. First, the active, dynamic nature system is absolutely dependent on the absolute livingness of God: "Finite causality is nowhere without the divine, but [this does not mean] that the divine with the finite

---

inactive or dead. *Gl.*² §53.1; *CF* 207. Second, since "finite causality is nowhere without the divine," it follows that God is the living and nonremote God who is active in each event. *Gl.*² §53.2; *CF* 208. Third, since the divine omnipresence is "the maintenance of things in their being and in their powers," God cannot be understood as some static substance from which all derives its existence; all is actively sustained by God's own *power. Gl.*² §53.2; *CF* 208–9. Fourth, the doctrine guards against any understanding of inactive attributes: "If this omnipresence be thought of as inactive instead of active, nothing almost remains except that God is that which is in itself empty." *Gl.*² §53.2; *CF* 209. Therefore, similar to the function of the attribute of eternity in relation to omnipotence, omnipresence plays a negative, precautionary role in relation to omniscience.

is in space" (208). Second, divine omnipresence is precisely the "maintenance of things in their being and in their powers. Any other explanation would find it difficult to avoid the suspicion of a mixture of the divine being with the finite, and therefore a semblance of pantheism" (208–9). There is no mixture of being or of space analogous to finite existence. Nor can it be said that God "universally includes all things even spatially" (209). It is not some pantheistic or even panentheistic spatial inclusion. The relationship is one of absolute dependence: one establishes the other through sustaining it.

The attribute of *omniscience* (§55), understood in its compound form and defined as the "absolute spirituality of the divine Omnipotence" ($Gl.^2$ §55; CF 219), serves to explain the intentionality of the immanent, absolute, divine power. It, better than the attribute of omnipotence, captures the livingness of divine causality: "The possibility is still not excluded (if once, rightly or wrongly, 'dead' forces are assumed) of conceiving the idea of omnipotence itself after the analogy of 'dead' forces. Since consciousness is the highest form of life known to us, this danger is averted by the idea of omniscience. . . . [I]f the term 'omniscience' well emphasizes the fact that omnipotence is not to be thought of as a 'dead' force, the same result would be reached by the expression 'Absolute Vitality'" ($Gl.^2$ §51.2; CF 203). The spirituality, livingness, and vitality of divine causality all indicate the intentionality underlying divine omnipotence. Schleiermacher's causal monism, together with its concomitant nonanthropomorphic tendencies, precludes the possibility of final causes. This rejection of final causes reaches back to the early essays on Spinoza: final causes, or causation through ideas, presume some causality external to the natural system of causes; they also presume a distinction between the divine will and intellect. Schleiermacher warns that such a distinction "is inapplicable to God, for there are no objects of observation for Him other than those which exist through His will, but the divine knowledge is exclusively a knowledge of the willed and produced" ($Gl.^2$ §55.1; CF 220). This in itself marks no radical departure from Spinoza. The departure is found in Schleiermacher's insistence that divine omnipotence, as omniscient and utterly spiritual, means that God is a living God with whom we stand in real relation, and that there is direction.[78] Here again, Schleiermacher stands closer to neo-Spinozism than to Spinoza himself: not only nature, but also history, is

---

78. There is also "purpose," but what Schleiermacher means by the term is not made clear until his exposition of the divine wisdom in the closing propositions of the *Glaubenslehre*. See Chapter 6.

dynamic, is alive; the *telos* of both history and nature is an internal one that allows for novelty and genuine multiplicity. Nevertheless, the full meaning of the spirituality and omniscience of God cannot be fully developed at this point in the system. It is only in light of the experience of redemption, when divine omniscience is recognized as divine wisdom and government, that the world can be viewed aesthetically. Schleiermacher writes to his friend Lücke, "Indeed, an omnipotence, the aim and motive force of which I do not know, an omniscience, the structure and value of its contents I do not know, and an omnipresence, of which I do not know what it emits from itself and attracts to itself, are merely vague and barely living ideas."[79]

---

79. On the *"Glaubenslehre,"* 57; KGA 1/10:340.

5

THE FIRST PART OF THE *GLAUBENSLEHRE* AND SCHLEIERMACHER'S POST-KANTIAN SPINOZISM

> *My philosophy and my dogmatics are thus firmly determined not to contradict each other, but for this very reason, neither pretends to be complete.*
>
> —F.D.E. Schleiermacher to F. H. Jacobi, 1818

Having examined the underlying principles and structure of part 1 of the *Glaubenslehre*, and having traced Schleiermacher's continued appeal to the dictum *One and All*, I now turn to examine whether or not the post-Kantian Spinozism of his earlier works of 1793–94 and 1799 is carried through into his mature Christian dogmatics of 1830–31. The same criteria applied in Chapters 1 and 2 will apply here: (1) Is it Spinozist? Does it reflect the seven characteristics described by Jacobi during the Spinoza conversations? (2) Is it neo-Spinozist? How close does it come to the neo-Spinozism of late-eighteenth-century Germany, as that was defined by Herder (substantial force) and Lessing (nonanthropomorphism, *hen kai pan*)? (3) Is it a post-Kantian Spinozism? Do the four post-Kantian Spinozist themes (monism, determinism, realism, and nonanthropomorphism), which are uniquely Schleiermacher's own and which were developed out of his concern to take seriously critical philosophy and modern science as well as to meet the requirements of piety, continue to influence how he understands God and God's relation to the world and to the individual? (4) Is it Spinozan? Are there any parallels between Schleiermacher's doctrines and Spinoza's own propositions, whether or not they are historical, intentional, or explicit? In fact, as a close exposition of the text will show, many of these criteria are indeed met in the the second edition of the *Glaubenslehre,* although just how that is so must be carefully specified.

Causal Monism

The terms *pantheism, Spinozism,* and *monism* are usually intended as synonyms that refer to a worldview in which transcendence is completely collapsed into immanence; there is only one reality, whether understood as God or nature, which is judged to be without purpose or ultimate value. Schleiermacher himself collapses these three terms in his first letter to Lücke: "Would you have thought that, after the way I had challenged [Delbrück] to prove that charge of *Spinozism,* which he had in general so well described, he would not honestly admit that my *Speeches* do not at all teach such pantheism, but would instead repeat the same unspecified insinuations of *pantheism* and *monism* [*All-Eins Lehre*] about which I had already expressed myself?"[1] There is a general consensus among scholars that there are indeed monistic tendencies in the *Glaubenslehre.* Wilhelm Dilthey recognizes Schleiermacher as the heir of the *aesthetic pantheism, pantheistic monism,* and *mystical pantheism* of Shaftesbury and Spinoza.[2] Another biographer, Martin Redeker, contends that "the *Christian Faith* has a monistic tendency because of its view of God; the omnipotence of God is understood . . . in the universalistic sense that in reality he is the cause of everything."[3] Richard R. Niebuhr grants that "what may be done in good faith is to attempt a demonstration that [Schleiermacher's] thinking about God does not in practice significantly differ from immanentism or monism, so that he stands in the history of modern Western theology as a key figure in the process of the dissolution of the Christian notion of God transcending the world";[4] he is careful, however, to note where Schleier-

---

1. *On the "Glaubenslehre,"* 49; *KGA* 1/10:330; emphasis added.
2. "Shaftesbury und Spinoza," 166–77.
3. *Schleiermacher: Life and Thought,* trans. John Wallhausser (Philadelphia: Fortress Press, 1973), 109.
4. "Schleiermacher and the Names of God," 198.

macher differs from what he refers to as "technical monism."[5] Gerhard Spiegler, on the basis of his comparison of the *Glaubenslehre* and *Dialektik*, describes Schleiermacher as a monist insofar as for him the transcendent is the transcendental.[6]

Of course, a monistic tendency in itself is not necessarily problematic. Grace Jantzen notes that "in this sense [that God is the being of all things] every Christian theist is bound to be a monist, and it was this aspect of *Spinozistic monism* which was so attractive to the writers of the Romantic movement who reacted against the Enlightenment ideas of a mechanistic universe and the Deistic compromise which coupled such ideas with a doctrine of a remote, monarchical God."[7] The problem enters when, as Niebuhr points out, the notion of transcendence is forsaken through reductionism. Jantzen suggests a resolution to this problem: *Spinozistic monism* is not a reduction to materialism or blind necessity. On the contrary, for those involved in the late-eighteenth- and early-nineteenth-century debates, it better than other models could correlate an experience of nature as dynamic with the biblical notion of a living God who operates through the powers of nature and history. For Schleiermacher, it also allows for a higher unity that includes a genuine plurality.

Recall that Schleiermacher's original attraction to Spinoza in 1793 had to do with the fact that, for Spinoza, the infinite does not exist outside the finite, but the finite cannot exist without the infinite. Schleiermacher translated this monistic relation of inherency into a dynamic, organic monism. In the *Reden*, "system" became his preferred way of describing this monistic worldview. Schleiermacher used the term in deliberate opposition to the arbitrary system of "rounded idealism," which imposed its view on nature and assumed a dualism of ego against nature. Schleiermacher took *system* to be a more adequate term than *monism* insofar as it better accounted for the status of finite things. Whereas *monism* implies, as Jacobi would say, materialism and determinism, *system* better describes the worldview Schleiermacher shared with his cultured despisers: an interdependent system of finite organic (as opposed to efficient or mechanistic) causality that yields diversity and novelty. This system, this *All*, is possible only because of the *One*, the absolute unity, in which it inheres. This "system" appears in the *Glaubenslehre* as "nature system" *(Naturzusammen-*

---

5. Ibid., 200.
6. See *Eternal Covenant*, 58; cf. 94–95.
7. *God's World, God's Body* (Philadelphia: Westminster Press, 1984), 149; emphasis added.

hang): the interdependence, system, or connection of nature. By this Schleiermacher means that everything finite is held together in the "universal connexion of things" wherein everything acts according to and is conditioned by the "laws of Nature" (*Gl.*² §14 p.s.; *CF* 72). Nor are human beings an exception to this causal nexus; failure to recognize our interdependence with nature only reflects a lower stage of religious self-consciousness. Thus the fundamental insight of his "essential doctrine" (§46) is that "we consider each and every thing as completely conditioned by the interdependence of nature" (*Gl.*² §46.1; *CF* 171). This view of the nature system assumes a *causal monism*. In Schleiermacher's words, there is a complete *coincidence* between natural and divine causality, a coincidence that is best explained in terms of the dictum *One and All*. That this is a development of the organic monism of 1793–94 is evident from three factors: it continues to meet many of the same characteristics of Spinozism and monism set forth by Jacobi in *Über die Lehre des Spinoza;* it roughly parallels Spinoza's own rejection of anthropomorphism, final causes, and *creatio ex nihilo;* it remains close to neo-Spinozism, especially with regard to Herder's translation of Spinoza's substance into substantial force.

Jacobi's Monism

A chief characteristic of this nature system is what Jacobi had recognized as the Spinozist principle *ex nihilo nihil*. According to this principle, everything has a like cause and stands in relation both to what is prior and what is contemporaneous. While Schleiermacher is more explicit in his defense and adoption of this principle in his two early essays on Spinoza, it remains a working assumption, however implicit, in the *Glaubenslehre:* "Every effect within the natural order is also, in virtue of its being ordained by the divine causality, the pure result of all the causes within the natural order" (*Gl.*² §54.1; *CF* 212).[8] If no cause can be found, this must be attributed to our (temporary state of) ignorance. It is a "confused world-view," he writes, "where the causal nexus is concealed, and thus makes use of [dependence on God] mostly where something severed from what went before it as well as separated from its context, appears as either a beginning or in isolation" (*Gl.*² §38.2; *CF* 148). Followed to its logical conclusion, the principle *nihil ex nihilo* implies an infinite regress of finite causes. While Schleiermacher dares assert neither that there is such an infinite regress nor

---

8. Cf. *Gl.*² §51.1. In reflecting on the heavenly bodies, he insists that "their successive origination must obviously be also conceived as the active continuance of formative forces which must be resident in finite existence." *Gl.*² §38.1; *CF* 146.

that there is a definite beginning, he does admonish us to remain open to both possibilities: "Natural science ... carrying its researches backward into time, may lead us back to the forces and masses that formed the world, or *even further still*" (*Gl.*² §40.1; *CF* 150; emphasis added). Science may eventually show us that there was no beginning to the universe, but even if we can trace the causal line back to some beginning, even then there must still be a natural, causal explanation. Schleiermacher further entertains the possiblity of an infinite regress in his exposition of divine eternity in §52, where he maintains that, given the fact that God's eternity cannot be separated from God's omnipotence, it still does not follow that "the temporal existence of the world *must* reach back into infinity" (*Gl.*² §52.1; *CF* 204; emphasis added).[9]

On the one hand, Schleiermacher cannot deny that the world might have had a definite beginning, but he wants to ensure that the precautions and limits regarding what can be said about divine causality are met, and in this he succeeds: God is not brought within the contradictions of time; God's activity remains unified; God's creative activity is not interpreted in human terms; God remains the sole determinant. He concludes, "For as what now arises in time is yet grounded in the omnipotence of God, and therefore willed and enacted by Him in an eternal, i.e. timeless, manner, the world also could be timelessly willed to emerge in time" (*Gl.*² §52.1; *CF* 204). On the other hand, he wants to observe the limits set by science. We must acknowledge at least the possibility of an infinite regress of natural causes: "We need not be anxious lest, if the world is given no beginning or end, the difference between divine causality and causality within the natural order should be cancelled, and the world be as eternal as God" (204).[10] Again, the doctrine of creation expresses a relation of absolute dependence, not a theory about a beginning in time that may conflict with scientific theories. Piety permits either theory (the world as having a beginning in time or as being the result of an "infinite duration of time" [205]),[11] as long as both are kept within the limits defined. In the final analysis, piety requires an agnostic moment.[12]

9. Cf. *Gl.*² §51. The implication is that, because divine causality is fully exhaustive in the nature system, the nature system must thus be coeternal with God.
10. Cf. *Gl.*² §54.1.
11. It does not threaten piety if the world has always existed with God, because it would not therefore be eternal, only infinitely enduring and always absolutely dependent. In his exposition of the doctrine of creation he writes, "It is impossible to see how the idea that God does not exist without something absolutely dependent on Him could weaken or confuse the religious self-consciousness." *Gl.*² §41.2; *CF* 155–56.
12. Aquinas also holds that, although creation as a relation of dependence is open to reason, creation as a beginning in time is not. Yet Aquinas holds the principle *creatio ex nihilo*

In his continued appeal to the *One and All,* Schleiermacher meets yet another of Jacobi's definitions of Spinozism: there is no transition between the natural and the supernatural.[13] Schleiermacher would not object to such an assessment of his worldview, since he is very explicit in rejecting supernaturalism as an irreverent attitude. "We should," he says, "abandon the idea of the absolutely supernatural because no single instance of it can be known by us, and we are nowhere required to recognize it" (*Gl.*² §47.3; *CF* 183). At the same time, such a denial of the absolutely supernatural is not a denial of transcendence *per se,* only of a certain understanding of transcendence that pulls God into the categories of finite existence. Schleiermacher's own understanding of transcendence is captured in the dictum *One and All:* God is the absolute living unity on which the nature system is utterly dependent; God is absolutely inward and thus stands in stark contrast to the finite world or its totality, without at the same time being outside that totality.

Spinoza's Monism

Since the principle *nihil ex nihilo* is a direct contradiction of the Christian doctrine *creatio ex nihilo,* and since Schleiermacher retains the latter in his *Glaubenslehre,* it could be argued that he has abandoned adherence to the former (Spinozist) principle. Such an argument would support the thesis that a substantial shift in thought occurred between the two editions.[14]

---

to be true because of revelation: "That the world did not always exist we hold by faith alone: it cannot be proved demonstratively." *Summa Theologica,* I, Question 46, Article 2. Schleiermacher's agnosticism concerning creation is not unlike his discussion, toward the end of his second Speech on religion, on immortality. We have no experience of life after death and thus should at least leave open the possibility that there will be no continuance of our personality after death. Indeed, the willingness to "annihilate your individuality and to live in the one and all" may be more religious a sentiment than to be "anxiously concerned about [one's] individuality." Crouter, 139; R^1 132, 131. No representation is fully adequate, but if one's representation remains within certain bounds, it is expressive of the essence of religion.

13. According to Vallée, *Hen kai Pan* "embodies a protest against any separation between natural and supernatural. It does not include, though, a clear denial of their distinction." Vallée, Introduction, 13.

14. See for example Edith Sandbach-Marshall, who argues that there is a "revolution" in thought between the *Reden* and *Glaubenslehre,* and that in the later work Schleiermacher avoided all pantheistic phrases and suggestions of identification and describes God as first cause. "The Religious Philosophy of Herder and Schleiermacher: Studies in Relation to the Influence upon them of Leibniz, Spinoza, and Kant" (M.A. thesis, University of London, 1926); quoted in Mock, "The Development of Schleiermacher's Doctrine of God." See also Brandt, who argues that Schleiermacher did an "about-face" so as to "avoid any appearance of pantheism." *Philosophy of Schleiermacher,* 241.

This, however, is not the case. On the contrary, his strict qualification of *creatio ex nihilo* arises in part from his continued adherence to the principle *nihil ex nihilo*, which incidentally parallels Spinoza's own rejection of *creatio ex nihilo* in at least three ways.

First, Spinoza adheres strictly to the principle of necessary causation (*nihil ex nihilo*), according to which everything not only has a cause, but a like cause. There are no gaps between modes, or particular things.[15] This means neither that finite things are not caused by God nor that God is a remote cause. For a remote, or transient, cause is not joined to its effect, whereas God, as supreme cause, *is* joined to God's effects. Everything is dependent on God not remotely but immediately. God, in other words, is the immanent cause of all things.[16] Similarly, Schleiermacher rejects any notion of divine causality as being external or remote.[17] That is why he finds the doctrine *creatio ex nihilo*, when interpreted as a first efficient cause and not as a continuous act of divine preservation, so unacceptable.[18] The principle *nihil ex nihilo* is thus present in Schleiermacher's insistence that origination cannot be so interpreted as to annul the system of causes and that origination is never experienced apart from continuance: "Yet their successive origination must obviously be also conceived as the active continuance of formative forces which must be resident in finite existence" (*Gl.*² §38.1; *CF* 146).[19] It follows from this that creation is not origination as change, but origination as novelty: "There is always something new implied either in the beginning of each series of activities or in the effects produced by a subject—something which was not formerly contained in that particular thing" (146).[20] This still guarantees that everything is nevertheless interpreted in terms of the "processes of nature" (*Gl.*² §§41.1, 2; *CF* 153, 154).[21]

---

15. "Every individual thing, or everything which is finite and has a conditioned existence, cannot exist or be conditioned to act, unless it be conditioned for existence and action by a cause other than itself, which also is finite, and has conditioned existence; . . . and so on to infinity." *Ethics* 1.28; Elwes 2:67.

16. See Chapter 1, note 31.

17. See *Gl.*² §§8 p.s., 53.2.

18. "But to acknowledge another creation here is either again entirely to abolish the difference between creation and preservation or to assume different kinds of matter devoid of inherent forces, which is surely meaningless. . . . We must refer these definitions back to a time when men delighted in such abstractions because there was then no question of a dynamic aspect of nature." *Gl.*² §41.2; *CF* 154–55.

19. Cf. *Gl.*² §§40.1, 36.1.

20. This is also suggestive of why his Spinozism is not blind determinism.

21. "Because a thing can be recognized as having happened through finite causation, it is not on this account the less posited through the divine omnipotence." *Gl.*² §54.1; *CF* 212.

Second, Spinoza insists that God acts according to God's own nature, and "neither intellect nor will appertains to God's nature."[22] God does not act in discrete choices, through separate acts; rather, the "omnipotence of God has been displayed from all eternity, and will for all eternity remain in the same state of activity."[23] God cannot be inactive, and God's power cannot be confused with human power.[24] Similarly, Schleiermacher rejects any interpretation, whether "popular" or "scholastic," that describes divine will and intellect in too anthropomorphic a way. In fact, as his revisions of the attributes of omnipotence and omniscience reveal, he prefers to avoid the very words *will* and *intellect,* because they suggest a change or wavering in God and the possibility that God can be viewed as inactive: "Therefore just as the divine will must not be thought of as a faculty of desire, so the divine omniscience must not be considered as a perceiving or experiencing, a thinking together or a viewing together" (Gl.² §55.1; CF 220). There is no exercise of divine omnipotence or omniscience outside the nature system; both are fully and completely presented. God does not consider possible worlds, choose between them, and then proceed to create.

Third, Spinoza's understanding of the divine causality as immanent (*immanens*) rather than transient (*transiens*) underscores at least three important assumptions. God is not an external cause, a prime mover, and is therefore not separated from God's effects; the relation between the infinite substance and finite modes is one of immanence, or inherency: "All things which are, are in God, and must be conceived through God."[25] Moreover, this understanding of God as immanent cause does necessarily exclude God's being understood as *transcendent cause,* if transcendent is taken *not* as meaning above or external to the universe as its effect; for God, as transcendent cause, is prior in God's causality, which is to say that, as the cause of both existence and essence, God differs from God's effect but is not separated from it.[26] Finally, in describing God as immanent cause, Spinoza means that there is a *relation of dependence:* "All things depend on the power of God."[27] Similarly, Schleiermacher thinks the divine causality is better understood as immanent rather than as efficient.[28] Yet he obviously

22. *Ethics* 1.17, note; Elwes 2:60
23. *Ethics* 1.17, note; Elwes 2:61.
24. See *Ethics* 2.3, note; Elwes 2:84–85.
25. *Ethics* 1.18, proof; Elwes 2:62.
26. See *Ethics* 1.17, note; Elwes 2:61. See Wolfson *Philosophy of Spinoza,* 1:299, 301, 323–25.
27. *Ethics* 1.33, note 2; Elwes 2:73.
28. Schleiermacher does not differentiate types of causality as subtly as Spinoza does; rather, he seems to divide causes into two general camps—that of immanent, internal, organic forces, and that of external, mechanistic, efficient causes. Spinoza makes a further distinction

does not consider *immanence* to be an adequate term and therefore carefully develops his own term, *coincidence,* which can better be traced to the feeling of absolute dependence.[29] Any assignment of the term *immanence* to his doctrine of God must therefore be done cautiously.[30] The term *coincidence* at once expresses how divine causality is not external to finite causality, how the two cannot therefore be collapsed into one another,[31] and how the nature system is absolutely dependent on God. Once again, the key to explaining *coincidence* and the immanent power of God is found in the dictum *One and All.*

Neo-Spinozism's Monism

All of these parallels, however, must be put in the context of late-eighteenth-century Germany, both in terms of its scientific worldview (with its discoveries in chemistry and biology), and its neo-Spinozism (with its translation of substance into force).[32] In other words, Schleiermacher's mo-

---

between transient and efficient causes. He acknowledges God as the efficient cause of all things, but he means by this both that God is the cause "not only of the existence of things, but also of their essence" (*Ethics* 1.25; Elwes 2:66), and also that "God is not only the cause of things coming into existence, but also of their continuing in existence" (*Ethics* 1.24, cor. Elwes 2:65). This is precisely Schleiermacher's point in his insistence that creation and preservation must not be separated.

29. See note to *Gl.*[2] §54; Redeker 1:279a (Thönes). The placement of the reference cannot be overlooked, insofar as it occurs (1) in a marginal note, (2) under the second form of proposition, and (3) after he has already established the contrast between the divine and natural causalities (§§52, 53). See Chapter 4.

30. Schleiermacher was obviously sensitive to charges of pantheism and Spinozism and tried to distance himself from both. Nevertheless, he did not dismiss either out of hand; indeed, he argues in the Introduction to the *Glaubenslehre* for an acceptable form of pantheism which comes close to his own interpretation and adaptation of Spinoza. Further, where he thinks it is required, he does not hesitate in adopting what he knows will be taken as heresy but what he insists is only heterodoxy. See, e.g., *Gl.*[2] §§21.1, 25 p.s.; *On the "Glaubenslehre,"* 68.

31. "But this expression [*co-operation*] requires at least to be treated very cautiously if the differences of finite being are not to be placed within the Supreme Being and thus God Himself appear as the totality, a view which can scarcely be differentiated from that of Pantheism." *Gl.*[2] §49.2; *CF* 192.

32. In the words of Peacocke, "The scientific perspective of a cosmos in development introduces a dynamic element into our understanding of God's relation to the cosmos which was, even if obscured, always implicit in the Hebrew conception of a 'living God,' dynamic in action." A. R. Peacocke, *Creation and the World of Science* (Oxford: Clarendon Press, 1979), 80. Referring to Herder's connecting the divine *Kraft* with *organische Kräfte* of nature, Nisbet concludes, "This pantheistic resolution of the old dualism of God and nature, creator and created, is again thoroughly typical of his whole way of thinking." *Herder and the Philosophy and History of Science,* 13.

nism is an organic monism, according to which efficient causality, characteristic of both premodern theology and the deistic worldview, loses prominence with respect to both natural and divine causality.

In terms of natural causality, the *All* is a dynamic system of internal, living relations: it "is perceived as a totality of living forces" (*Gl.*¹ §40.2; Peiter 1:131) the interconnection of which is abrogated "when we posit either dead mechanism or chance and arbitrariness" (*Gl.*² §34.2; CF 139).[33] A dead mechanism would be one in which causes are all externally imposed rather than being actively appropriated from within: "The expression 'nature-mechanism' is not used as our own, for we should be wrong to reduce anything which stimulates our self-consciousness and thus influences us to mere mechanism, to active points of *transition*" (*Gl.*² §49.1; CF 191; emphasis added). In other words, although he does not use the terminology, Schleiermacher rejects *transient causality* as the primary relationship among finite things, since that would posit a universe made up of separable, independent, static substances that are only externally related to other substances. In reality, the nature system is a system of forces,[34] variously described as "centres of power" (*ein Ort für Kräfte*) (*Gl.*² §46 p.s.; CF 178; Redeker 1:233), "bodily forces of nature" (*leibliche Naturkräften*) (*Gl.*² §14 p.s.; Redeker 1:100), "inherent forces" (*einwohnende Kräfte*) (*Gl.*² §41.2; Redeker 1:202), and "universal powers" (*allgemeine Potenzen*) (*Gl.*² §46.1; Redeker 1:226). Activity and relations are not secondary but define individuality, which occurs where powers coalesce, are appropriated, and are transformed. This in part explains why divine causality can no longer be understood as somehow external. The divine and the finite fully *coincide,* insofar as all activity and relationality are absolutely dependent on divine activity and the fundamental relation: "For being posited for itself can only exist where there is also power, just as power always exists only in activity; thus a preservation which did not include the placing of all the activities of any finite being in absolute dependence on God would be just as empty as creation without preservation" (*Gl.*² §46 p.s.; CF 176).[35]

33. Cf. *Gl.*² §§47.1, 49.1.
34. According to Brandt, "Schleiermacher says that the universe is composed of 'forces.' In this he may have had in mind Schelling's view (close to Kant's) of the nature of matter; but his view is also illuminated by comparison with Plato's ideas (which Schelling had connected with his work), Aristotle's essences, Kant's discussion of the use of the notion of pure elements in chemistry, and perhaps even with Spinoza's idea of the 'infinite immediate modes.' *Ultimately irreducible kinds of reality (e.g., the elements) are a part of what is denoted by the word 'force.'*" Philosophy of Schleiermacher, 85; emphasis added.
35. Nisbet explains that for Herder *Kraft* is the "dynamic power behind all natural phenomena, and in particular, the numerous individual 'Kräfte' into which the universal

Just as, in his earlier work, Schleiermacher maintained that the infinite *is* only insofar as it differentiates itself in the finite, so here he argues that divine causality exists *only* in and through finite causality.

In terms of divine causality, as becomes evident in his postscript to his "essential doctrine," Schleiermacher's preference for preservation over creation reflects a preference for sustaining causality over efficient causality. All causality is absolutely dependent on the sustaining divine activity, and God acts only "by means of the powers distributed and preserved in the world" (177). Sustaining causality is given new meaning in the context of a vitalistic view of nature; it is active, not abstract, and has to do with power rather than structure. It is for this reason that Schleiermacher rejects the scholastic interpretation of the Platonic notion of participation as well as the notion that the miraculous activity of God can be separated from the "sustaining activity of God" ($Gl.^2$ §47.2, note; CF 181). Through this modern version of sustaining causality, the divine omnipresence and omnipotence are to be understood and differentiated from materialistic pantheism. The attribute of omnipresence, which together with divine eternity expresses the absolute inwardness of divine causality, explains sustaining causality negatively, that is, in terms of what it is not. First, it is the "negation of all remoteness" and thus stands in "contrast with finite causality" ($Gl.^2$ §53.2; CF 208). Second, to say that all activity is absolutely dependent on divine activity, consequently "nowhere without the divine," is not to say that the divine and the finite are together in space (208). As the absolute spaceless causality, "the divine omnipresence [is] the *maintenance of things in their being and in their powers*. Any other explanation would find it difficult to avoid the suspicion of a mixture of the divine being with the finite, and therefore a semblance of pantheism" (208–9; emphasis added). Divine causality is immaterial but not extramundane, hence the term *causal monism*.

Divine omniscience, which along with omnipotence expresses the absolute vitality of divine causality, explains sustaining causality in more constructive terms than does the attribute of omnipresence. Although the latter is a "living idea" ($Gl.^2$ §53.1; CF 207),[36] it is only under the attribute of

---

'Kraft' differentiates itself.... [T]he same concept admirably illustrates his characteristic endeavours to reconcile disparates. For it fulfills many functions which are at bottom discrete, although Herder's customary and even intentional vagueness often disguises their separate identity." *Herder and the Philosophy and History of Science*, 8.

36. In the following expositional paragraph he writes, "If this omnipresence be thought of as inactive instead of active, nothing almost [sic] remains except that God is that which is in itself empty." $Gl.^2$ §53.2; CF 209.

omniscience that he can develop what he means by that. Divine omniscience, understood as "absolute spirituality" (*Gl.*² §55; *CF* 219), expresses the "absolutely living" (*Gl.*² §55.1; *CF* 219) nature of divine sustaining causality: "For a lifeless and blind necessity would not really be something with which we could stand in relation; and such a necessity, conceived as equal to the whole of finite causality yet contrasted with it, would really mean positing the latter alone, and thus declaring an absolute dependence unreal" (219). There is direction and life; nothing is attributed to blind fate. Divine omniscience is therefore better understood as the "very productivity of God" (221)—a productivity never separated from the activity of the nature system: "It is, however, equally implied that every effect within the natural order is also, in virtue of its being ordained by the divine causality, the pure result of all the causes within the natural order, according to the measure in which it stands in relation with each of them" (*Gl.*² §54.1; *CF* 212). Schleiermacher maintains that it is precisely this dynamic view of the interconnection of everything that differentiates his position from a materialistic form of pantheism.

Schleiermacher's causal monism rejects any extramundane cause, transitive or final. As he had in his early essays on Spinoza, so now he continues to assert that there can be no distinction between ends and means. From his argument that divine causality and the system of nature fully coincide (§§46, 54), that divine omnipotence is completely and exhaustively presented (§54), and that divine omniscience cannot be conceived anthropomorphically (§55), it follows that, for God, there can be no "purposive thought-activity" (*Gl.*² §55.1; *CF* 220)[37] preceding divine productivity. In an annotation to §59 of the first edition and in his postscript to §46 of the second, Schleiermacher rejects the notion of divine ends, *if* by that is meant either a division in divine will or some external cause, but he does allow the notion of divine government: "But if by [divine *government*] is meant the fulfilment of divine decrees or the guidance of all things to divine ends, and if it be taken as signifying anything else than that everything can happen and has happened only as God originally willed and always wills, by means of the powers distributed and preserved in the world—this is already included in our proposition" (*Gl.*² §46 p.s.; *CF* 177).[38] He allows the notion of divine ends, or rather *end* (singular), but that one "goal" is decreed once and for all time and is nothing other than continual divine activity.[39] The

---

37. "*Zweckbildende Denktätigkeit.*"
38. Cf. *Gl.*¹ §59, Anmerkung (c); Peiter 1:168–69.
39. His rejection of any distinction between ends and means is most explicit in his exposition of the divine wisdom in part 2. See *Gl.*² §§164, 168, 169; also see Chapter 6.

emphasis, in other words, is on the eternal divine decree. Any suggestion of final causes that violates the unity of this decree arises from an analogy with human states and cannot be traced to the feeling of absolute dependence: "We distinguish between the purposive activity of thought upon which production follows, and the observing activity which relates to something already present. But this last distinction is completely inapplicable to God" (Gl.² §55.1; CF 220). This is not to say that there is no purpose or direction in the course of the nature system, only that such divine purposes cannot be understood as individualized or as operating outside the nexus of natural causes.

In his attempt to avoid anthropomorphism and in his rejection of final causes, Schleiermacher seems to fall into determinism. The Spinozist principle of *nihil ex nihilo* may be acceptable as an interpretation of the natural world, but when applied to the ethical and anthropological it seems incompatible with Christian dogmatics. And make such an application Schleiermacher does. There is, he notes, an "equality between free and natural causes."[40] In Schleiermacher's causal monism, according to which no final causes are allowed, everything, including human decisions and actions, is determined by the nature system, and thus would appear to be blind. This is true even if one accepts the neo-Spinozist espousal of a dynamic nature and its rejection of materialism.

Complete Determinism

The controversy over Schleiermacher's Spinozist, monistic, and pantheistic tendencies has to do not only with his understanding of God but also with the implications these tendencies have for the individual. As with any form of pantheism, there is a danger of the particular becoming lost in the whole, thus losing any special status. It appears that, for Spinoza, "no real distinction exists in the universe.... [T]here are no real individuals in the world except the world as a single totality, and all differences must be dismissed."[41] Even Charles Hartshorne, generally sympathetic to pantheistic tendencies, identifies this as a problem in Schleiermacher's thought:

---

40. Note to Gl.² §49; Redeker 1:249. "Gleichheit der freien Ursachen und der natürlichen" (Thönes).
41. Yirmiyahu Yovel, *Spinoza and Other Heretics*, vol. 2, *The Adventures of Immanence* (Princeton, N.J.: Princeton University Press, 1989), 36.

"Schleiermacher had indeed turned decisively away from classical theism toward pantheism, but he failed to safeguard the full reality of the Many, as free and temporal, within the One."[42] This problem regarding the status of the individual becomes an ethical problem insofar as it is fundamentally a question about freedom, and consequently about human individuality. When the individual is taken to be yet another part of the whole and as being determined by that whole, and when God is viewed neither as acting purposively in discrete ways nor as being personally related to each individual, the individual person seems to lose freedom as well as uniqueness. In addressing this issue, two tasks must be undertaken. First, it must be determined whether the charges of determinism are fair. Does the problem exist? Second, if the problem is real, Schleiermacher's attempted resolution of it—the reasons he gives and limits he sets—needs to be examined. Does his form of determinism warrant rejection? Or, if the charges are unfair, why is it he is always so misunderstood?

The Problem

In the *Glaubenslehre,* the problem of the individual presents itself most conspicuously under the doctrines of divine preservation (§46) and justification (§109).[43] In his exposition of the former, the problem is so acute that Schleiermacher finds it necessary to address it in his marginal notes and to add a lengthy postscript on the issue in the second edition.[44] For in de-emphasizing the doctrine of creation and making the doctrine of preservation the "essential doctrine," Schleiermacher also revises the usual understanding of how God is related to the particulars of the nature system: divine causality is no longer understood as creating individual things; divine preservation is not related to one individual in a way different from any

---

42. Hartshorne and Reese, *Philosophers Speak of God,* 269. The authors differentiate theism and pantheism on this very issue: "The difference between the two is that theism admits the reality of plurality, potentiality, becoming—as a secondary form of existence 'outside' God, in no way constitutive of his reality; whereas pantheism . . . supposes that, although God includes all within himself, still, since he cannot be really complex, or mutable, such categories can only express human ignorance or illusion. Thus, common to theism and pantheism is the doctrine of the invidious nature of categorial contrasts." Ibid., 2.

43. Discussion of the problem of the individual with regard to the doctrine of justification will be reserved for the next chapter.

44. See note to $Gl.^1$ §60; Redeker 2:518. The lengthy postscript to $Gl.^2$ §46 reorganizes what had been included in the first and second expositional paragraphs of $Gl.^1$ §59. Recall that it is in the same marginal notes and exposition that he addresses the charge of pantheism. See Chapter 3.

other. How, then, can God be said to be related to the individual? How are we to understand human nature? Schleiermacher's answers to these questions mark a shift to a modern theological anthropology, a shift that challenges some traditional views of the human person.[45]

We must, Schleiermacher holds, abandon the view that God acts in each and every little event and is the cause of each thing, and instead we must shift our view to the "wider scope" in such a way that we "identify ourselves in our self-consciousness with the whole world" ($Gl.^2$ §46.2; CF 173). Our understanding becomes too narrow when we concentrate on the individual apart from its place in the whole, since an individual is what it is only through its interaction with all the rest. There is thus no absolute individuality. No individual is set apart from, or in that sense free from, the nature system. In short, for Schleiermacher, everything is "only relatively individual and is conditioned in its individuality by the universal co-existence" ($Gl.^2$ §46 p.s.; CF 178). This relative individuality is only underscored when attention is turned from our position in the nature system to our relation to the divine causality. God preserves, not in the fashion of some powerful individual cause, but as the universal cause—which means in part that "the universal causality attaches *only* to that on which the totality of this partial causality is itself dependent" ($Gl.^2$ §46.2; CF 175; emphasis added). This calls into question more conventional ways of understanding the individual person as a distinct object of divine love and concern: "But with regard to God such a distinction between the general and the individual is not applicable; in Him the species exists originally as the sum-total of its individual existences, and these in turn are given and established together with their place in the species" ($Gl.^2$ §54.2; CF 213). God does not "know" individuals in some anthropomorphic sense. God does not respond piecemeal to isolated events in a person's life. God does not have discrete intentions.

Largely because of this intense concern to avoid any humanization of God, Schleiermacher departs from dogmatic theology's usual anthropological starting point, the *imago Dei*: "If we ask whether the designation, 'image of God' (which indisputably denotes the superiority of human nature over the other creatures described), is in harmony with the conception we have set forth, we can only answer 'yes' with great caution" ($Gl.^2$ §61.4;

---

45. Wolfhart Pannenberg traces modern theological anthropology to Herder. Even if Pannenberg's assessment is correct, it nonetheless remains the case that Schleiermacher was the first to develop a modern anthropology in Christian dogmatics. See Pannenberg's *Anthropology in Theological Perspective* (Philadelphia: Westminster Press, 1985), 43–79.

CF 252). Such caution is inspired by his deep suspicion of analogy. Inevitably, he warns, in positing the *imago Dei* we "argue regressively . . . to God Himself" (252). The result is a departure from piety and a movement toward either pantheism (as an identification of God and world, analogous to that between soul and organism) or anthropomorphism (as an ascription of human characteristics to God). Schleiermacher prefers locating his anthropological starting point in the human "predisposition to God-consciousness ($Gl.^2$ §60; CF 244), which exists only in connection to our interdependence with the nature system. He maintains that for anthropomorphism to be avoided, *some determinism is required:*

> If then we say . . . that the perfect knowledge of a thing's existence for itself is the same as the knowledge of the inner law of its development, and the perfect knowledge of a thing's place in the sphere of universal interaction is one with the knowledge of the influence of all other things on it, but that both these perfect kinds of knowledge form in God one and the same timeless knowledge, determining the existence of the object, . . . then we have at least an indication as to how to avoid as far as possible too great a humanizing of the divine knowledge. ($Gl.^2$ §55.2; CF 222–23)[46]

What is separated in us is unified in God as the coincidence of all opposition. In the end, Schleiermacher must grant that the uniqueness or "particularity of the individual" ($Gl.^2$ §54.2; CF 213) can never be fully solved. His concept of individuality is therefore not unambiguous; nor, consequently, is his concept of freedom.

As was true in his earlier writings, Schleiermacher's view of the human individual is inherently related to his understanding of freedom. This is true on several levels: (1) rather than being considered as exempt from nature or as having itself created nature, the human person is recognized as being an intricate part of the ordered power of nature; (2) final causes are denied on the human side, which means that transcendental freedom is also denied; (3) final causes are also denied on the divine side, which means that there are no external causes that will interfere with the course of

---

46. Niebuhr claims that Schleiermacher's concern with anthropomorphism is unwarranted: "If one looks at his theology in the perspective of the long continuum of Christian thought about God, his doctrine of God seems poor indeed and his fear of anthropomorphism misplaced. A man of Schleiermacher's intellectual gifts ought to have seen that anthropomorphism is inevitable in any case, and is not necessarily a blemish in Christian theological thinking." *Schleiermacher on Christ and Religion*, 16.

nature; (4) sheer possibility is denied for finite things as well as for divine causality. All of these claims do indeed indicate a preference for a position of determinism. Thus critics are correct in recognizing a certain determinism in Schleiermacher's thought, and they are even partially correct in recognizing in Schleiermacher an echo of Spinoza. The critics, however, do not play the scene out. Spinoza did not deny freedom; a denial of Kant's notion of transcendental freedom is not a denial of freedom; Schleiermacher's concerns have fundamentally to do with the limits set by piety. In describing the divine preservation in terms of *coincidence,* Schleiermacher implies that, since the "unity and completeness of the relation of dependence" ($Gl.^2$ §46.1; CF 172) applies as much to the human person as to any other part of the nature system, the principle *nihil ex nihilo* applies also to human action. In other words, human will can override neither the course of the nature system nor its own previous decisions and actions. There is no freedom that is immune to finite relations and dependencies: "But however much *freedom resides in determination of will and resolution* [*Entschluß*], action, emerging as it does under influences beyond itself, is always so conditioned that it only becomes what it is because it belongs to the very same universal system which is the essential indivisible subject of the feeling of absolute dependence; and this would lose its significance in the whole province of history if we should think of free causes as excluded from this system" ($Gl.^2$ §49.1; CF 189; emphasis added).[47] Of special note here is his use of the term *resolution.* Recall that it is this very term that, in his early essays on Spinoza, he employed in order to reject Kant's transcendental freedom.[48] Freedom is never will alone as a separate faculty but is always judgment combined with desire. It is thus rooted in the context of a particular human life—that is, within a complex configuration of concepts, affections, dispositions, inclinations, and experiences that together compose a personal history. In other words, even with human actions and decisions, there are none whose cause cannot be traced in the system of finite causes. Freedom is never a freedom-from, rather always freedom-in-relation-to. Human choices are themselves "grounded and established in the universality of the nature-system," and thus there is a "complete deter-

---

47. "In our use of the idea of absolute dependence we have annulled every distinction between human freedom and subordinate forms of finite being, while yet the God-consciousness surely . . . has a content which relates exclusively to human freedom and presupposes it." $Gl.^2$ §62.2; CF 260–61.

48. See, for example, *Spinozismus,* 528. His use of the term *Entschluß* was new to *Spinozismus* and *Spinozistisches System* and marked a terminological shift from his earlier essay *On Freedom.*

mination of all events by the universal nexus" (*Gl.*² §46.2; *CF* 173, 174). This is the ethical side of the denial of final causes: there are no causes, including free causes, external to the causal system of nature. And this is precisely what Jacobi had found so threatening about Spinozism: if there is no freedom, then the mind is merely a spectator of the body and can enforce no will.

Of course, there is the other side of the debate, namely, the position of those Christian thinkers who deny human freedom because everything is (pre-)determined by God. Indeed, on this point Schleiermacher's theological lineage is evident in his Reformed emphasis on the one divine decree and the doctrine of election: "Through omnipotence everything is already posited which comes into existence through finite causes, in time and space. Similarly, because a thing can be recognized as having happened through finite causation, it is not on this account the less posited through the divine omnipotence" (*Gl.*² §54.1; *CF* 212). Yet Schleiermacher's understanding of the divine decree is as unacceptable to this side of the debate as it is to the other side since his exposition of divine omnipotence is not modeled on human intelligence and does not operate through final causes. Schleiermacher rejects the partiality such a model suggests.[49] Schleiermacher is not unlike Spinoza in maintaining that all talk about God's freedom must also include the necessity of divine causality; he undoes the usual distinction between what is free and what is necessary in God.[50] Moreover, Spinoza himself speaks of one divine decree, and therefore the term by no means belongs exclusively to Christian dogmatics.

The problem that follows from applying Schleiermacher's religious view of nature to human existence is thus twofold: it seems to lose sight of the individual in its emphasis on the whole, and it seems to espouse a blind determinism in its denial of final causes and transcendental freedom. Schleiermacher's response to such charges in the *Glaubenslehre* follows from his earlier responses, which had themselves developed as part of his post-Kantian Spinozism: individuality is not lost, but neither is it absolute; the denial of transcendental freedom is not a denial of freedom *per se*; freedom is never freedom from or over, but thrives only and always in relation to dependence; freedom involves both judgment and desire and thus is always relative; true individuality and freedom make sense only in a movement of oscillation.

49. See *Gl.*² §§46.2, 55.1, 55.2.
50. See *Gl.*² §54.4; *CF* 216–17.

The Resolution

Schleiermacher does offer a nonconventional view of the individual in his *Glaubenslehre*—a view that is an extension of that developed in his early work, particularly the essays on Spinoza and the *Reden,* and is thus influenced by his post-Kantian Spinozism. As was true in those earlier works, the individual is by no means lost. Indeed, Schleiermacher's vitalistic, holistic interpretation presents an even more powerful and profound interpretation of the individual, but one which requires some revision of Christian dogmatics. As is true for his predecessors Augustine and Calvin, individuality is understood in terms of one's relation with God.[51] But for Schleiermacher, this relation, the feeling of absolute dependence, must coincide with the relation of interdependence between self and world.[52] That is the central insight of the "essential doctrine": interdependence and absolute dependence are not identical, but they cannot be separated. In the postscript to that same doctrine, Schleiermacher launches his criticism of the customary view of the individual. While generally directed against both popular and theological interpretations, it focuses on the "scholastics" and their distinction of "the *general*" (the whole), "the *special*" (species), and "the *most special*" (individuals) (*Gl.*² §46 p.s.; *CF* 175). Schleiermacher contends such distinctions are arbitrary and speculative, hence "quite superfluous" to Christian dogmatics (175).[53] For him, the three categories collapse from

---

51. "Man's original perfection is primarily meant rather in relation to God, i.e. to the presence in him of the God-consciousness, and his endowments relative to the world belong here only insofar as they awaken the God-consciousness." *Gl.*² §58.2; *CF* 237. Since it is only through Jesus of Nazareth that "the human creation is perfected," his redemptive activity is "person-forming." *Gl.*² §89.2; *CF* 367; *Gl.*² §100.2; *CF* 427. For Schleiermacher, then, the more our persons are formed, the more profound is our individuality because we have thereby appropriated and integrated those forces with which we are in "living connexion" and have united them with our God-consciousness. *Gl.*² §59.1; *CF* 239.

52. "All the impressions of the world we receive, as well as the particular way (consequent on human nature) in which the predisposition towards God-consciousness becomes realized, include the possibility that the God-consciousness should combine with each impression of the world in the unity of a moment. . . . [I]n all excitations of the religious consciousness, the consciousness of God, as united with consciousness of the world, is related to One, so the latter belief asserts that in every such excitation the world-consciousness as united with the God-consciousness is related to All." *Gl.*² §57.1; *CF* 234.

53. According to Yovel, Spinoza also found them to be superfluous: "Spinoza was a proponent of the new science in that in his thought too, the causal, mechanistic laws of nature have replaced genus and species as the universal principles by which science proceeds. This abolishes universal essences—but not the concept of essence as such." *Spinoza and Other Heretics,* 1:162. Schleiermacher rejects such distinctions for similar reasons—modern science and a new worldview—except that the science and worldview of his day supersedes that of Spinoza's day.

both points of view—from that of the nature system and from that of divine causality.

From the View of the Nature System

Just as the nature system is constituted by forces, so individuality is defined by the coalescence and intensity of forces, or powers. The continuance or "duration of individual as well as of universal things is simply an expression for the degree of their power as each co-exists with all the rest" ($Gl.^2$ §46 p.s.; CF 176).[54] Several points are of special note in this brief text. First, individual existence and universal existence are described in the same terms, namely *power*. For Schleiermacher, this fact contributes to the breakdown of the debate over which is more real, the universal or the particular. Under the corresponding proposition in the first edition, Schleiermacher argues that the medieval scholastic "realist" views particulars as actions of universal things and prefers to describe divine activity as cooperation; the "nominalist" views the species as dependent on the powers of particular things and prefers to describe divine activity as government.[55] It is not so much that either side is wrong as it is the case that neither is quite right; each loses sight of the dialectic between the universal and the particular, and for that reason each becomes too arbitrary in its claims of reality.[56] Second, the borders or extremities of what is individual are not unambiguous. The organic view of nature as a system of interactive forces (by definition a rejection of an atomistic and mechanistic view of reality) means in part that there are permeable boundaries. Consequently, descriptions of what is individual involve relativity, since conceivably another interpretation could always be given that would choose to include more or less within those borders, depending on the point of view. Third, existence is derived from coexistence.[57] Power, that which defines an individual and that through which the individual is sustained by God, is drawn from the powers of

---

54. Compare Spinoza's notion of perseverance: "For although each particular thing be conditioned by another particular thing to exist in a given way, yet the *force whereby each particular thing perseveres in existing* follows from the eternal necessity of God's nature." *Ethics* 2.45, note; Elwes 2:118; emphasis added.

55. See $Gl.^1$ §59.1; Peiter 1:170–71.

56. His comments here echo, although perhaps less judgmentally, his refutation of the systematizers in the *Reden*.

57. This is related to Schleiermacher's view of the relationship between the Redeemer and the individual person. According to his own distinction in §24 (whereas Protestantism "makes the individual's relation to the Church dependent on his relation to Christ," Catholicism "makes the individual's relation to Christ dependent on his relation to the Church"),

other things and combinations of things. This, however, ought not be interpreted in competitive terms of survival. According to Schleiermacher, we cannot "set ourselves over against any other individual being, but, on the contrary, all antithesis between one individual and another is in this case done away" (*Gl.*² §5.1; *CF* 19). His organic view of nature looks more to what each does for the other and the whole, it assumes a fundamental relation of responsiveness, it involves process and growth, and it assumes the perfectibility of human nature.

The very power that defines an individual is based on the oscillation between the individual and the *All*. The individual receives its power from its dependence on "the activity of the rest of things" (*Gl.*² §46 p.s.; *CF* 177)—that is, from the *All*. These received powers cohere in a unique way and, through that active coherence, a new combination of powers emerges that is more than the sum of its parts. This newly formed power is further individuated to the degree that it in turn influences the *All*. Hence, the individual is by no means lost to the system of nature. Although the individual is indeed dependent on and determined by the totality, the totality requires (is itself dependent on and determined by) the forces of individual things: "Everything is referred to the ordered exercise of power which establishes the dependence of each individual on the totality of existence eternally, and for the maintenance of the general interaction makes use of the forces of individual things" (*Gl.*² §54.4; *CF* 215). The totality is therefore not something abstracted from, or independent of, finite things. There is no generalized, indifferent force of nature, rather it is always particularized and concretized in individuals and in relations. Human existence, particularly, is "an integral part of the world" (*Gl.*² §58.1; *CF* 236) insofar as it is so constituted as to enjoy God-consciousness,[58] and as such it is the point at which "history and nature converge."[59] Nature for Schleiermacher necessarily stands in relation to history and is thus, in the words of one interpreter, "only one pole of the comprehensive process which constitutes the world."[60] The usual dichotomy between the two dissolves within the

---

Schleiermacher is more Catholic than he would ever dare acknowledge, since faith in the Redeemer is dependent on belonging in a community of believers where the Word of God is preached. The individual is possible only within the context of a community.

58. "Along with the absolute dependence which characterizes not only man but all temporal existence, there is given to man also the immediate self-consciousness of it, which becomes a consciousness of God." *Gl.*² §4.4; *CF* 18.

59. Niebuhr, *Schleiermacher on Christ and Religion*, 104.

60. George N. Boyd, "Schleiermacher's 'Über den Unterschied zwischen Naturgesetz und Sittengesetz,'" *Journal of Religious Ethics*, 17, no. 2 (Fall 1989): 47. Boyd expands on this: "As to the comparison of moral law with laws of nature, Schleiermacher's thoroughgoing

framework of an organic worldview. The distinction between organic and inorganic itself becomes superfluous in that both history and nature are formed according to forces. Nature, like history, is progressive and cumulative, and in turn history is rooted in and corresponds to dynamic structures given in nature.

On this point, neo-Spinozism takes its most definitive departure from Spinoza. Whereas for Spinoza nature is not blind, since thought is an attribute of God, neither can it be said to have purpose or even direction, since God cannot be said to have volition. Such ideas as *purpose, goals, goodness,* or *beauty* are "mere human figments."[61] Following Spinoza, neo-Spinozism denies final causes: there can be no appeal to ends and means; there can be no distinction between divine will and divine intellect; divine causality operates in relation to the whole, not particulars; there is nothing external to the dynamic system of nature.[62] Yet neo-Spinozism, unlike Spinoza, maintains that there is indeed direction and purpose: the coalescence of finite forces produces a harmonious whole (and thus includes such notions as *goodness, beauty,* and *wisdom*); there is telos, an ordered progress directed toward an end (although that end is internal to the nature system and does not exist as some external, final, or formal cause); this intentionality is the result of the divine benevolence that works immanently through history as well as nature.[63] Niebuhr explains that for Schleiermacher "human his-

---

teleology allows him to assert a fundamental continuity between the two concepts.... [H]e does assert a fundamental continuity regarding the meaning of law in each concept—moral law, like natural law, describes and determines being, however imperfectly as to degree.... [W]ithin the single organic process and unity known as 'world,' moral law (laws of reason) is the designation for the determinative principles controlling that level of development which we distinguish as conscious/intelligent/rational, just as natural law (laws of nature) is the designation of the principles controlling all those aspects of the world which are not conscious." Ibid., 46.

61. *Ethics,* part 1, appendix; Elwes 2:77.

62. Herder writes, "Now I see also, my friend, why Spinoza is so much opposed to purposes, and ostensibly speaks severely against them. For him, they are the wishes and arbitrary choices which the artist makes yet need not have made. What God effected, He could not first deliberate and choose. The effect flowed out of the nature of the most perfect Being. It is unique, and nothing else is possible." *God, Some Conversations,* 124.

63. "But with every activity [a force] makes its subsequent activity easier. And, since it cannot do this otherwise than by implanted, internal laws of harmony, wisdom and goodness which ... are benevolently forced upon every creature, impressed upon it, and which assist it in every one of its activities, therefore you see everywhere a progress out of chaos into order, an inner increase and enhanced beauty of forces in ever-widening limits according to ever more observed laws of harmony and order. Every blind force is infused with light, every lawless power with reason and goodness. None of its operations, no activity in creation was in vain. Thus there must be progress, advance in the realm of God." Herder, *God, Some Conversations,* 189.

tory is not the devolution of a pure and undifferentiated power. It is better compared to an organism wrought by the power of formation, and this power of formation gives shape and impetus to the processes of history solely in and through personality. Consequently the object of Schleiermacher's ethical inquiry is not the naked energy that posits the cosmos but the creative logos as it indwells mankind and its members."[64] As was true in the *Reden,* so here in the *Glaubenslehre* each person is a compendium of the whole, but not statically so and not exactly as any other person is a compendium. Schleiermacher writes in his Introduction that "every man has in him all that another man has, but it is all differently determined" (*Gl.*² §10.3; *CF* 47).[65] All share certain transcendental structures; that is, we are so constituted as to be predisposed to world- and God-consciousness. The significance of Schleiermacher's adaptation of the dictum *One and All* is that it explains the relation (of inherence and coincidence) of the absolute unity and genuine plurality.

From the View of Divine Causality

The dissolution of the scholastic distinction between whole, species, and individual also applies to divine causality. This follows from Schleiermacher's causal monism, which describes the absolute causality of God primarily in terms of sustaining, rather than efficient or transitive, causality. God actively and continually sustains the whole, and through the "ordered power" of the nature system, God "sustains individual things in their existence and their powers as long as He wills" (*Gl.*² §46 p.s.; *CF* 175). In relation to God, the individual is still defined in terms of power and the degree to which power in every and any configuration is absolutely dependent on the sustaining power of divine preservation. Divine causality is thus immediately and actively related to each individual. Yet this only in part solves the problem. For divine sustaining power is related to the individual just as it is related to the whole. There is no distinction between general and individual (see *Gl.*² §54.2; *CF* 213). The problem therefore remains: Is this not a distant or indifferent relationship of the individual to God? How Schleiermacher answers this question is yet another example of

---

64. Niebuhr, *Schleiermacher on Christ and Religion,* 109.
65. One parallel to this is his insistence that there can be no religion in general, only particular historical religions. A central point of dogmatics is that we are radically historical creatures, and we must therefore continually revise dogmatics in terms of language and present consciousness.

how, under the divine attributes, he expands on what is implicit in the doctrine of divine preservation: "In the region of absolute dependence on God, everything is equally direct and equally indirect, some in one relation and some in another" (*Gl.*² §46 p.s.; *CF* 177).

Divine omnipotence cannot be divided into mediate and immediate operations of divine causality. If such terms are to be applied at all, then only the whole, the *All*, can be interpreted as the immediate effect of divine omnipotence, whereas individuals are preserved through the "ordered exercise of power which establishes the dependence of each individual on the totality of existence eternally" (*Gl.*² §54.4; *CF* 215).[66] The same holds true for any distinction between absolute and conditional divine will. The most Schleiermacher will allow is that the whole is absolutely willed, and the individual only conditionally so. However, the individual is thereby not "any the less willed" insofar as everything, "so far as it is itself effective, and in various ways conditions other things, is absolutely willed by God" (216).

Under divine omniscience, the solution to the problem of the individual's relation to God in Schleiermacher's thought is once again to be found in his appropriation of the dictum *One and All*. If the problem seems exacerbated by that dictum, it is also resolved by it. The individual remains an object of divine knowledge, and thus has uniqueness and value, insofar as "God knows all that is; and all that God knows is" (*Gl.*² §55.1; *CF* 222). But God's knowledge is not piecemeal; rather, it is "related to the object in an eternal and omnipresent way" (*Gl.*² §55.3; *CF* 227). Thus, the relationship is to be understood in terms of the *One and All*: "God knows each in the whole, as also the whole in each—a formula which utterly abolishes the contrast between great and small, and which alone is correct because already given in the idea of a settled natural order" (227). Again, appeal is made to the necessary oscillation between the *One and All*. Individuality only makes sense in terms of the whole; the individual always and only comes from the community. Individual identity is the result of the intensity and complexity involved in the oscillation between self and the whole. This will not completely satisfy those who want an absolutely personalized and individualized God, but it is a necessary consequence of Schleiermacher's method and limits. It arises out of a concern for both reverence and intelligibility, and, what cannot be overlooked, it remains incomplete in part 1. The full description of the relation between God and

---

66. This is really only an expansion of the *coincidence* of the *One and All*, described under the "essential doctrine."

the individual can only be given in part 2, where the focus is on the Christian experience of redemption.

Freedom

To a large extent, Schleiermacher anticipates and addresses this problem in the Introduction. In §4, Schleiermacher makes it very clear that our freedom and dependence (determination) are always relative and always reciprocally related. Our freedom and individuality are found in the creative reciprocity of our receptivity and spontaneity, not in some victory of spontaneity over receptivity. In other words, they have to do with how we receive, or actively take up, the influences upon us; the manner in which we respond to these influences determines our individuality.[67] Therein lies our freedom: "For thus the receptivity of man [with regard to the divine presence] is greater for it than that of any other earthly being, but amongst men it is greatest in the religious" (*Gl.*² §53.1; *CF* 208). Activity is not always better, and receptivity becomes for Schleiermacher almost a virtue. Furthermore, we are never absolutely determined by the world. Even in relation to stars we always have some reciprocal influence, however minimal.[68] When that fact is overlooked, when the nature system is not seen as a living, interconnected whole, only then would there be a blind materialism (at the first level of religious consciousness) or a fatalism (at the second level).[69] At the highest level of human consciousness, where the religious worldview is of the *All-One*, we recognize that we are only relatively determined by the *All*, and absolutely determined, along with the *All*, by the *One*.

As Schleiermacher makes clear in the second edition, there can be no freedom in relation to the *Whence* of our absolute dependence since in that fundamental relationship we know only sheer receptivity. To say this, however, does not abrogate freedom. On the contrary, the *Whence* of our feeling of absolute dependence is experienced as the very source of our freedom, as that which establishes our freedom. Our feeling of absolute

---

67. He defines the feeling of freedom as "the common element in all those determinations which predominantly express spontaneous movement and activity." *Gl.*² §4.2; *CF* 13–14. Pannenberg mistakenly interprets receptivity in negative terms, even though Schleiermacher makes it very clear that is not the case; Pannenberg also makes the mistake of confusing absolute dependence with relative dependence. See his *Anthropology in Theological Perspective*, 253.

68. See *Gl.*² §4.2; *CF* 15; see also the marginal notes to *Gl.*² §4.2,3; Redeker 1.27b and c (Thönes).

69. See *Gl.*² §8 p.s.

dependence includes the immediate awareness that "the whole of our spontaneous activity comes from a source outside of us" (*Gl.*² §4.3; *CF* 16)— a source that is not the *All*, since the *All* itself is absolutely dependent on the *One*. God sustains everything, including freedom. That we are conscious of ourselves as having received our freedom makes us capable of the feeling of absolute dependence. More to the point, the feeling of absolute dependence presupposes freedom: "We are capable of the feeling of absolute dependence as freely active agents—that is to say, that we are conscious of our freedom as something which is received and is gradually developed in a nature-system" (*Gl.*² §49.1; *CF* 190).[70] It is the nonreligious view that, in rejecting the *One* and in misinterpreting it as the *All,* denies freedom. According to Schleiermacher's view, freedom only thrives when it is attached to the feeling of absolute dependence, and "true causality exists only where there is life" (191). It is the very livingness of the nature system, in absolute dependence on the absolute livingness of God, that precludes any possibility of blindness or fatedness.

The consciousness of our feeling of absolute dependence is the consciousness "of being in relation with God" (*Gl.*² §4; *CF* 12). Such a "relation" cannot refer to nature or some indifferent force.[71] On the contrary, because we experience the *Whence* of our feeling of absolute dependence as absolute freedom and the source of our own finite freedom, the relation is fundamentally a communicative one. This, however, cannot be fully developed until part 2. In the Introduction, the relation is described in the most general terms (everything stands in the relation of absolute dependence on God, but only humans are aware of that relation). In part 1, the relation intended by Schleiermacher is more specifically oriented toward humanity: "For a lifeless and blind necessity would not really be something with which we could stand in relation" (*Gl.*² §55.1; *CF* 219). The finite without the infinite would be fatalistic, and freedom would be impossible. In part 2, the relation is described in terms of *impartation:* the divine love imparts itself through its redeeming activity. The relation, therefore, is experienced as the communication of love, and love can only be recognized and received in freedom.

Schleiermacher's understanding of freedom is already given in his monistic worldview. It presupposes that the nature system is not some static

---

70. Cf. *Gl.*² §4.4; *CF* 18.
71. He expands on this in his letters to Lücke: "Pious feeling is not derived from a representation, but is the original expression of an immediate existential relationship." *On the "Glaubenslehre,"* 40; *KGA* 1/10:318. "Is there any phrase which expresses less what is essential to my work than that I deduce Christianity from the feeling of dependence?" *On the "Glaubenslehre,"* 70; *KGA* 1/10:360.

mechanism, that free causes operate by the same rules as natural causes, and that there are no extramundane causes: "But none of us understands by 'the world' which is the object of the divine preservation a nature-mechanism alone, but rather the interaction of the nature-mechanism and of free agents" (*Gl.*² §47.1; *CF* 180). He thus continues a theme he had developed in the early 1790s, namely, that determinism denies not freedom, but the "customary conception" that there is "no causality apart from free causes" (*Gl.*² §49.1; *CF* 190).[72] Such a conception, he argues, derives from a worldview according to which "causality is only applicable to the first mover existing outside this sphere" (*Gl.*² §49.1; *CF* 190). Divine causality is irreverently viewed as an external first efficient cause; human causality, modeled on that, is mistakenly viewed as an independent choice to bring about some definite effect. Schleiermacher argues throughout the *Glaubenslehre* that such assumptions destroy the feeling of absolute dependence. In conclusion, freedom arises from a dynamic system of internal causes and relations. It is not an illusion, nor is it categorically different from other types of causality. Indeed, Schleiermacher goes so far as to say that there is an "equality of natural and free causes": "We assume no sharp antithesis between freedom and natural necessity in finite being, since anything which actually has a being for itself moves itself in some sense or another, even if it has no part in spiritual life; but even in the most free cause its range is ordained by God" (192).[73] Freedom is not given an exclusive status. Both causal monism and perfect determinism assume Schleiermacher's higher realism in that both rest on that universal element of life, the feeling of absolute dependence.

Higher Realism

Schleiermacher's post-Kantian realism, which he first struggled to articulate in the Spinoza essays and further developed in various editions of the *Reden*, continues to play a central, albeit implicit, role in the second edition of the *Glaubenslehre*. Indeed, it is one of the two main presuppositions of

---

72. As Wallhauser describes it, Schleiermacher protests against "the isolation and separation of the rational moral self from the empirical self and the historical world.... The empirical and the rational need to be brought into harmonious relation with one another." "Schleiermacher's Critique of Ethical Reason," 30.

73. Cf. *Gl.*² §32.2 (*CF* 133), and note to *Gl.*² §49 (Redeker 1:249a).

his entire system insofar as it is precisely what Schleiermacher means in defining piety as the *feeling of absolute dependence*.[74] As had been true in *Spinozistisches System, Spinozismus,* and *Reden,* Schleiermacher here describes his post-Kantian realism in terms of *Gefühl,* although *Gefühl* is now more precisely defined and consistently applied. Also like the realism of the earlier works, the realism implied here is defined in part by a rejection of critical idealism's dualism of subject and object, its emphasis on spirit over nature, and its appeal to transcendental freedom. It is "higher" in that it is not a realism placed in stark contrast to idealism, since Schleiermacher resists all dualities; yet, although he can correctly be associated with German idealism or critical idealism, he also makes his own departures, departures which form the basis of his realism. His realism can also be said to be "higher" in that it respects the limits of critical philosophy (i.e., it is post-Kantian) without at the same time rejecting the infinite (i.e., it is Spinozan); it is a refutation of pre-Kantian forms of realism.[75] Finally, his is a "higher realism" in that, as in the *Reden,* it is described in terms of Schleiermacher's distinct adaptation of the dictum *One and All.* What is new to its development in the *Glaubenslehre* is the very precise way in which *Gefühl* is defined and the careful analysis which is given of the transcendental structures of human experience.

Receptivity in Relation to Nature

In a passage that echoes his earlier refutations of subjective idealism, Schleiermacher reminds us that "our knowledge does not determine the existence of a thing, but is determined by it" ($Gl.^2$ §55.2; CF 223). Thus, as was true in his earlier writings, his realism must first establish the reality of "another factor besides the Ego" ($Gl.^2$ §4.1; CF 13). In the *Glaubenslehre,* this means the real and independent existence of the nature system. It is precisely because of the universal connection of the nature system that we are able to know anything at all, whether ourselves, the world, or its absolute, underlying unity. This underscores the interrelatedness of the three post-Kantian Spinozist themes: although his higher realism is a key presupposition for his whole dogmatic system, it itself presupposes Schleier-

---

74. *Piety* is "the consciousness of being absolutely dependent, or, which is the same thing, of being in relation with God." $Gl.^2$ §4. The other presupposition for Schleiermacher's dogmatic system is the experience of having been redeemed by Jesus of Nazareth.

75. According to Frei, "Schleiermacher rejected out of hand the externality or duality upon which pre-Kantian natural religion and rational orthodoxy had insisted. In this rejection he paralleled the Idealists of his day." "Niebuhr's Theological Background," 37.

macher's causal monism and complete determinism.[76] In other words, all knowledge presupposes a relation of reciprocity "inasmuch as it expresses our connexion with everything which either appeals to our *receptivity* or is subjected to our *activity*" (*Gl.*² §4.2; *CF* 14; emphasis added).[77] This notion of reciprocity signals a departure from idealism with regard to both the status of the extra-mental world and the extent of our freedom.[78]

There is always something real, given to us, which stimulates our self-consciousness.[79] Because we have emerged from and with the world, we are so constituted as to receive and organize these stimuli in a certain way.[80] Consequently, there is no irreparable breach between the ideal and the real, since "the two together are one: the knowability of existence is the ideal side of the original perfection of the world, and the natural subsistence of the human organism is the real side of the same perfection as directly related to human receptivity" (*Gl.*² §59.1; *CF* 239).[81] Both a duality of subject and object and an identity of them are thus overcome: duality,

---

76. Recall that science (which corresponds to causal monism) and morality (which corresponds to complete determinism) are two limits to what can be said in dogmatic propositions.

77. I take Tillich to be saying the same thing when he describes subjective reason as "the structure of the mind which enables it to *grasp* and to *shape* reality on the basis of a corresponding structure of reality." Paul Tillich, *Systematic Theology*, 1:76; emphasis added.

78. According to Brandt, "The use to which [Schleiermacher] puts his contentions is quite different from Kant's. For on the basis of his realism and his correspondence theory of truth, he goes on to urge that unless the structure of the real world is such as to conform to these laws of thought, there cannot be science. Kant, in contrast, made no such assumption about the independently real world; he found it necessary to assume only that the mind-constructed phenomenal world must answer to the demands of thought, and the responsiveness of this phenomenal world to the forms of thought, he believed, implies nothing about the character of the independently real." *Philosophy of Schleiermacher*, 211. Reciprocity holds for moral as well as scientific knowledge: "The antithesis between good and evil goes back to the greatest and least in the harmony of universal reciprocal activity with the independent being of the individual." *Gl.*² §49 p.s.; *CF* 193. Because Schleiermacher viewed ethics as being a distinct systematic undertaking from dogmatics, he does not develop it fully here, and perhaps his *Glaubenslehre* is the weaker for it.

79. "For every impulse directed towards perception and knowledge which yet has the qualities, essence, and being of things as its object, begins with a stimulation of self-consciousness which thus accompanies the process of apprehending." *Gl.*² §46.1; *CF* 170. Cf. *Gl.*² §§33.1, 34.1, 46.1, 53.1.

80. "It could of course be said that man himself, with his constitution, is an integral part of the world, and that it is only in virtue of this constitution that he is precisely the part he is; and hence that the original perfection of man is already included in the original perfection of the world. This is quite correct." *Gl.*² §58.1; *CF* 236.

81. "The knowability of the world would be empty if it did not include in itself the expression of its being known; and the human organism would be lost among the more imperfect kinds of existence as similar to them, . . . if there did not proceed from it a new power of organization into which everything else could be taken up." *Gl.*² §59.3; *CF* 240.

because within the organic worldview relations are essentially internal rather than external; identity, because each represents opposite poles of a dialectical relation which is grounded in the absolute unity of the *One*.[82] Life consists in "an alternation between an abiding-in-self [*Insichbleiben*] and a passing-beyond-self [*Aussichheraustreten*]" (*Gl.*² §3.3; *CF* 8).[83] Both moments are necessary since we become a self, and knowledge is made real, only in relation to an other, only in extending beyond ourselves to what is other.[84] In this passing-beyond-self, we realize that, although we are so constituted as to be able to act on the world, our freedom is never absolute.

Therefore, the oscillation between receptivity and activity yields some correspondence between human consciousness and the real. All knowledge is grounded in this reciprocity, which is to say that all existence is coexistence:

> The system [of relations] is seated in the spirit as its original possession, original just because there is a system of nature. It exists in our self-consciousness always as influenced by being other than itself and thus as co-existent with such being in the system of nature.... Even if we were known to ourselves only as presentational activity—that is to say, as being centres for ideas—even so the self-consciousness is a centre for truth; and *that implies a relation of being in the self-consciousness, corresponding to the relation of ideas in the objective consciousness*. (*Gl.*² §34.1; *CF* 138; emphasis added)

This correspondence, however, is always only a rough one. Schleiermacher continually cautions that one must be careful "not to extend too far"[85] by going beyond the proper limits of knowledge. In an annotation in the first edition, he concedes that "through the expression *Alles* the proposition

---

82. Recall that in *Spinozismus* and *Spinozistisches System* he appealed to Spinoza's notion of parallelism in order to explain this continuum between thought and nature. In the *Reden*, he did the same by arguing for the underlying unity of subject and object in the infinite.

83. The world is also receptive to us, making this alternation possible. See *Gl.*² §59.2; *CF* 239–40.

84. "Our whole existence does not present itself to our consciousness as having proceeded from our own spontaneous activity." *Gl.*² §4.3; *CF* 16. "But when we become such-and-such from within outwards, for ourselves, without any Other being involved, that is the simple situation of the temporal development of a being which remains essentially self-identical, and it is only very improperly that this can be referred to the concept 'Freedom'." *Gl.*² §4.2; *CF* 14.

85. Note to *Gl.*² §46.1; Redeker 1:224d (Thönes).

seems to go further than our proper self-consciousness reaches."[86] Although we do not actually "visualize the interrelatedness of nature," we "assume" it extends universally ($Gl.^2$ §46.1; CF 170). We experience only continuity. Any experience to the contrary can only be attributed to a lack of full consciousness: "In every full act of reflection we should recognize ourselves as thus involved in continuity, and should extend the same thought to the whole of finite being" ($Gl.^2$ §36.1; CF 142).

Receptivity in Relation to God

At issue, of course, is not just the reality of the nature system and our capacity to gain knowledge of it. Clearly Schleiermacher's higher realism refers to the reality of God and our capacity, rooted in immediate self-consciousness, to be aware of God. This, however, brings the discussion back to accusations of subjectivism (God as a projection of the ego) and pantheism (God as indistinguishable from nature), as well as to Schleiermacher's insistence that there can be no nonreligious interpretation of the nature system. It might prove helpful to reexamine these issues in light of Schleiermacher's realism.

Receptivity, a basal element of Schleiermacher's realism, is fundamentally an experience of ourselves as having by some means come to be, as having been posited. Unfortunately, Schleiermacher can easily be misunderstood in his discussion of this givenness. In his first expositional paragraph to §4, which according to his marginal note is an analysis of the self-consciousness in terms of its coexistence, he describes an "other."[87] There is, he says, "another factor besides the Ego, a factor which is the source [*woher*] of the particular determination, and without which the self-consciousness would not be precisely what it is.... In self-consciousness there are only two elements: the one expresses the existence of the subject for itself, the other its co-existence with an Other" ($Gl.^2$ §4.1; see CF 13).[88] Karl Barth interprets this "other," this "source" [*woher*] of §4.1, to be identical with the *Whence* [*Woher*] of §4.4: "The 'something other' of §4.1, first boldly

---

86. Anmerkung (a) to $Gl.^1$ §59; Peiter 1:168.
87. See note to $Gl.^2$ §4; Redeker 1:24a (Thönes). "Analyse des Selbstbewußtseins in Beziehung auf das Mitgesetztsein eines Anderen."
88. "Das letzte [Irgendwiegewordensein] also setzt für jedes Selbstbewußtsein außer dem Ich noch etwas anderes voraus, woher die Bestimmtheit desselben ist, und ohne welches das Selbstbewußtsein nicht grade dieses sein würde.... Sondern in dem Selbstbewußtsein ist nur zweierlei zusammen, das eine Element drückt aus das Sein des Subjektes für sich, das andere sein Zusammensein mit anderem." Redeker 1:24.

characterized as neuter, now turns out to be God, *the* origin of our existence. Is this neuter really God, the God of piety, the God of which the doctrine of faith treats, . . . ? Schleiermacher never tires of assuring us that this is so. . . . But surely a neuter that is posited and given is obviously not Spirit, not God, but, no matter how abstract, a thing."[89] According to Barth, Schleiermacher's seemingly smooth transition from the "other" of our feeling of relative dependence to the *Whence* of our feeling of absolute dependence is evidence of the fact that, however the idea of *Whence* is arrived at (whether through subjectivist or pantheist tendencies), it remains nothing but a "neuter" and is not therefore the living God of Scripture.

Barth's interpretation, however, is unfair in that it ignores both terminology and context. In §4.1, *woher* is a relative pronoun that is given no special emphasis. In §4.4, *Woher* is a noun; the fact that it is italicized serves to underscore its importance and uniqueness. It cannot be mistaken for some "neuter." Moreover, the context of the first two expositional paragraphs of §4 indicates that Schleiermacher is describing that with which we are coposited and share some reciprocity and that "to which we can trace the origin [*worauf*] of our particular state" (*Gl.*² §4.1; *CF* 13). For Schleiermacher, we do experience ourselves as having come from the world, and (according to the principle *nihil ex nihilo*) we can trace our origin, the reasons for our particular determination, through the system of finite causes. In the fourth expositional paragraph, however, Schleiermacher is unambiguous about the fact that, while we can trace our origin back through the system of natural causes, the *Whence* of our existence "is not the world, in the sense of the totality of temporal existence" (*Gl.*² §4.4; *CF* 16). The world itself is experienced as having been posited. In relation to this *Whence*, unlike in our relation to our finite origins, we know only a sheer, nonreciprocating receptivity.

Therefore, as is true of his earlier works, Schleiermacher's realism in the *Glaubenslehre* is based on two kinds of receptivity, which are not identical but are fully coincidental. Both are rooted in the organs of receptivity that are susceptible to the impressions of the nature system and consequently to its absolute, infinite ground of unity. The one kind of receptivity, which corresponds to the nature system, is not limited strictly to the empirical. Schleiermacher includes under this relative receptivity the unifying impulse

---

89. Barth, *Theology of Schleiermacher*, 217. For more on Barth's interpretation of Schleiermacher, see *Barth and Schleiermacher: Beyond the Impasse?* ed. James O. Duke and Robert F. Streetman (Philadelphia: Fortress Press, 1988). Note that, in choosing to capitalize *Other*, when the word is neither emphasized nor capitalized in German, the translators of *The Christian Faith* share Barth's biased reading of this expositional paragraph.

of the objective self-consciousness, namely, the "intuition of being."[90] The other kind of receptivity, sheer receptivity, includes the other basal element of Schleiermacher's higher realism: immediacy. Both these elements, receptivity and immediacy, define the all-important term, *das schlechthinnige Abhängigkeitsgefühl:* "God is *given to us in feeling in an original way;* ... along with the absolute dependence which characterizes not only man but all temporal existence, there is given to man also the *immediate self-consciousness* of it, which becomes a consciousness of God" (*Gl.*[2] §4.4; *CF* 17–18; emphasis added). "What I understand as pious feeling is not derived from a representation, but is the original expression of an *immediate existential relationship.*"[91] As immediate and utterly receptive, the feeling of absolute dependence is what in the *Reden* Schleiermacher called the "touchstone" between our finite existence and the infinite existence of God; it is an awareness, in other words, of the "co-existence of God as the absolute undivided unity."[92] Just as natural causality and divine causality are not identical but completely coincide, so relative and absolute receptivity are not identical but completely coincide. The former is dependent on, yet also presupposed by, the latter. Logically, the feeling of absolute dependence is prior and fundamental: like freedom, all knowledge is grounded in the feeling of absolute dependence; our relationship to the *One* establishes the possibility of any relationship with the *All.* Noetically, the feeling of absolute dependence can be realized only because of its physical and intellectual basis in the human organism.[93]

90. *Gl.*[2] §16 p.s.; Redeker 1:111: "Anschauung des Seins." Cf. *Gl.*[2] §33 p.s.; *CF* 137. Curiously, the translators chose to translate *Anschauung,* a term which plays an important role in the development of Schleiermacher's thought, as "contemplation" rather than as "intuition" (whereas under *Gl.*[2] §5 they translate it as "perception"); in thus translating this phrase as "contemplation of existence" (*CF* 81), they obscure a potentially crucial distinction. In using *Anschauung* here, Schleiermacher carries through the distinction he began to make in the *Reden* of 1806 (although not entirely successfully) between two terms he had identified in 1799, *Anschauung* and *Gefühl.* He also identified them in 1793–94, before either term had taken shape for him: Jacobi's *Gefühl* seems to have conveyed for him the same meaning as Spinoza's *immediate intuition.*
91. On the "*Glaubenslehre,*" 40; *KGA* 1/10:318; emphasis added.
92. *Gl.*[2] §32.2; Redeker 1:173: "ein Mitgesetztsein Gottes als der absoluten ungeteilten Einheit." Once again, the English translators are inconsistent: "An awareness of the existence of God, as the absolute undivided unity." *CF* 132. The context suggests that coexistence is meant: two sentences later the translation reads "the realization of oneself as absolutely dependent is the only way in which God and the ego can co-exist in self-consciousness." *CF* 133. And a few pages earlier the same phrase, *Mitgesetztsein Gottes* is translated as "a co-existence of God in the self-consciousness." *Gl.*[2] §30.1; *CF* 126; emphasis added.
93. Its *physical basis* is given in "the fact that the spirit, become soul in the human body, acts also on the rest of the world ... and asserts its nature, just as the other living forces

The "seat of God-consciousness" is thus found in the human organism's openness to all existence and its "new power of organization" (*Gl.*² §59.3; *CF* 240). This capacity is what Schleiermacher means by the original perfection of the world: "In it there is given for the spirit such an organism as the human body in living connexion with all else—an organism which brings the spirit into contact with the rest of existence" (*Gl.*² §59.1; *CF* 238–39). It follows that the feeling of absolute dependence can never occur apart from our experience of the nature system, but for that very reason is possible in every sensible experience. This is the crux of Schleiermacher's "essential doctrine" (§46). There is a continuum (or better, a *coincidence*) between God-consciousness and world-consciousness rooted in the human subject as an organism with the capacity for self-awareness. We are so constituted as to enjoy both forms of consciousness: "Now, as the human soul is just as necessarily predisposed towards a knowledge of the world as towards a consciousness of God, it can only be a false wisdom which would put religion aside, and a misconceived religion for love of which the progress of knowledge is to be arrested" (*Gl.*² §46.1; *CF* 171). Just as Schleiermacher's causal monism argues for a coincidence of causality (natural and divine), so his higher realism argues for the other side of the same coin, namely, the coincidence of feeling (relative and absolute) and the coincidence of consciousness (sensible and immediate).

To say that, for Schleiermacher, God-consciousness always coincides with self- and world-consciousness, is to say that, like the coincidence of divine and natural causality, it can best be described in terms of the dictum *One and All:* "For, as the former belief [divine omnipresence] expresses the fact that in all excitations of the religious consciousness, the consciousness of God, as united with consciousness of the world, is related to One, so the latter belief [divine omnipotence] asserts that in every such excitation the world-consciousness as united with the God-consciousness is related to All" (*Gl.*² §57.1; *CF* 234). Our consciousness of God does not present itself to us as an external fact: "Any proclamation of God which is to be operative upon and with us can only express God in His relation to us; and this is not an infra-human ignorance concerning God, but the essence of human limitedness in relation to Him" (*Gl.*² §10 p.s.; *CF* 52). God is not, as are

---

assert their nature relatively to it." Its *intellectual basis* is given in "the fact that the spirit by means of sense-impressions can obtain that knowledge of existence which is one element in its own nature, ... and can express this knowledge with actual consciousness in the most varied degrees of general and particular ideas, and that thereby it arrives at the accompanying consciousness of a natural order in connexion with which the God-consciousness develops." *Gl.*² §60.1; *CF* 245–46.

our own selves and the world, "in any way *given*" by another (*Gl.*² §4.4; *CF* 18), which is to say, God is not an object alongside others, even (and perhaps especially) if imaged as some infinite supreme individual external to the nature system. God is immediately *given in* the feeling of absolute dependence, but is not *given by* it. Consequently, there is never an isolated moment of God-consciousness, rather "God signifies for us simply that which is the co-determinant in this feeling [of absolute dependence] and to which we trace our being in such a state" (17).

The term *feeling of absolute dependence* is deliberately post-Kantian insofar as it "entirely takes the place, for the system of doctrine, of all the so-called proofs of the existence of God" (*Gl.*² §33; *CF* 133–34). Any attempt to undertake such proofs is, of course, rendered "superfluous" by Kant and, besides, would only "produce an objective consciousness" (*Gl.*² §33.3; *CF* 136), whereas Schleiermacher's concern, in the *Reden* and *Glaubenslehre,* is for piety. Revelation, in other words, is essentially noncognitive: "But I am unwilling to accept the further definition that it operates upon man as a cognitive being. For that would make the revelation to be originally and essentially *doctrine;* and I do not believe that we can adopt that position" (*Gl.*² §10 p.s.; *CF* 50). Hence ideas of God can vary, can be more or less adequate, and yet can still be pious. This is another reason why pantheism, when defined according to "the usual formula One and All," is as acceptable an expression of the feeling of absolute dependence as certain formulations of theism (*Gl.*² §8 p.s.; *CF* 39; see Chapter 3). The feeling of absolute dependence is the awareness of a relation—not just an awareness of the self, or of a relation with the world, but the self in a relation of absolute dependence: "To feel oneself absolutely dependent and to be conscious of being in relation with God are one and the same thing; and the reason is that absolute dependence is the fundamental relation which must include all others in itself" (*Gl.*² 4.4; *CF* 17). This feeling of absolute dependence is part of the necessary and universal structures of human existence, of the human constitution; it is an "inward permanent datum" that makes God-consciousness possible. In the words of Frei, "Schleiermacher's Realism is thus not only nonmetaphysical but critical, i.e., the object of faith is given together with the content of faith in such manner that every attribute of or quality in the object is qualified by its being a content of consciousness. To distinguish between such qualities or attributes and those in God apart from the relation to faith is impossible."[94]

---

94. Frei, "Niebuhr's Theological Background," 38.

Nonanthropomorphic Images of God

Given what has been argued above, it should now be evident that the final post-Kantian Spinozist theme, namely, a tendency toward nonanthropomorphism, is carried through to the second edition of the *Glaubenslehre*. Indeed, Schleiermacher continues to maintain the solution he had reached in his Explanations to the *Reden* in 1821 when he was simultaneously preparing the first edition of the *Glaubenslehre*. When dealing with the religious consciousness, anthropomorphic ideas cannot be completely avoided, since God-consciousness can only be developed according to "particular formations" and will thus "carry with it such determinations as belong to the realm of the antithesis in which the sensible self-consciousness moves. And this is the source of all those anthropomorphic elements which are inevitable in this realm in utterances about God" (*Gl.*² §5 p.s.; *CF* 25). There is perhaps a place for anthropomorphic images at the level of the poetical and rhetorical. Yet all tendencies toward anthropomorphism must be tempered through a dialectical movement in relation to the more abstract, less symbolic utterances about the divine—hence Schleiermacher's defense of what he considers an acceptable form of pantheism. For instance, since we cannot properly speak of "the origin of the world but of its coexistence with God and its relatedness to God" (*Gl.*² §46.2; *CF* 174), it is inevitable that we will tend either toward identifying the world and God (pantheism) or totally opposing them (supernaturalism). "We cannot," Schleiermacher says, "avoid an oscillation between [these] formulas" (174). Yet because such oscillation is necessary, because pantheism as identity is never acceptable, the abstract side of the spectrum is best described in terms of the pantheistic dictum *One and All*, which guarantees that God will never "appear as the totality" (*Gl.*² §49.2; *CF* 192).

The limit set by piety once again plays a central role by turning the critics' charges around and levying the very same charge at them. If either side of the dialectic were dropped or neglected—if the divine activity were made plural, if there were individual, identifiable divine acts interpreted as being alongside (or outside) of the natural order—then several things would have to be granted. God's activity would be considered merely another part of the whole, rather than the undivided, unifying source; God would thus be depicted as acting discretely and arbitrarily through nature; the whole unity of nature would be threatened; not all finite causality would be absolutely dependent on the divine causality, and degrees of dependence would be introduced. The result would be a placing of the relationship between the finite and the infinite on the same spectrum as that between the finite and the finite.[95]

The comparison between Schleiermacher's nonanthropomorphic God and that of Spinoza presents itself easily enough. Schleiermacher's "essential doctrine" maintains that the divine causality fully coincides with the scope of natural causality. Schleiermacher grants that what he means by the omnipotence of God is the immanent causality of God. Schleiermacher refuses to apply the attributes of will and intellect to God, and he links freedom with necessity. Schleiermacher denies final causes, although he departs most decisively from Spinoza in that, with his organic view of nature and his dynamic understanding of history, he still allows for direction, novelty, and *telos*. The comparison, however, cannot end with part 1, since Schleiermacher insists that it is an abstraction of the Christian religious consciousness expressed in part 2. He reminds his critics of this in his letters to Lücke: "If the propositions now in the first part, which in their present form serve only as an external work, were to follow the Christology, the doctrine of the church, and the exposition of the divine love and wisdom, they would certainly take on a warmer tone and likewise appear in their specifically Christian perspective."[96]

The second main part of his *Glaubenslehre*, Schleiermacher insists, is the heart of his dogmatic system. The opening propositions of part 2 reiterate that part 1 is an abstraction and can only be understood in the context of the specifically Christian religious consciousness:

> For the former propositions [in part 1] are in no sense the reflection of a meagre and purely monotheistic God-consciousness, but are abstracted from one which has issued from fellowship with the Redeemer. (*Gl.*[2] §62.3; *CF* 262)

> All doctrines properly so called must be extracted from the Christian religious self-consciousness, i.e. the inward experience of Christian people. (*Gl.*[2] §64.1; *CF* 265)[97]

Descriptions of the *telos* of divine causality can only "attain to perfect precision and vivid clearness" (*Gl.*[2] §64.2; *CF* 267–68) in light of our

---

95. "For the divine causality is only equal in compass to the finite in so far as it is opposite to it in kind, since if it were like it in kind, as it is often represented as being in anthropomorphic ideas of God, it too would belong to the sphere of interaction and thus be a part of the totality of the natural order." *Gl.*[2] §51.1; *CF* 201–2. Cf. *Gl.*[2] §55.3; *CF* 227.
96. *On the "Glaubenslehre,"* 58; *KGA* 1/10:342.
97. Cf. *Gl.*[2] §94.2; *CF* 387.

experience of the Redeemer and our appropriation of the redeeming power of God. Immediately with this transition to part 2 is a notable shift in Schleiermacher's description of religious awareness. Terms such as *divine preservation*, the *feeling of absolute dependence*, and *awareness of the interrelatedness of the nature system* are translated into the more concrete and personal terms of *communion* and *alienation*. The "absolute facility in the development of the God-consciousness from any given stimulus and in every situation, which is proposed as the end, is equivalent to constant communion with God, while every retrograde movement is a turning away from God" (*Gl.*² §62.2; *CF* 261).[98] This emphasis on the more concrete is only a shift, not a break, from the description of the general religious consciousness. In other words, the two main parts of the *Glaubenslehre* are not two separate works, one Spinozist and the other Christian.

That part 1 is deliberately left open is not a weakness of Schleiermacher's organization. He had forewarned his readers in the Introduction that part 1 would be fairly limited in what it could say and that we would have to wait until part 2 for the whole doctrine of God to unfold. The limits and possibilities having been set in part 1, he can now complete the picture. Yet this is not to say that with the shift to the concrete religious experience of redemption goes an abandonment of methodological principles or theological emphases. On the contrary, the principles and emphases established in part 1 are carried over into part 2. I offer two examples. First, the organic view of nature and the principle *nihil ex nihilo* continue to operate: "In accordance with the laws of organic nature the true life of Christ in us announces itself at first only in weak and intermittent impulses, and then gradually a unified activity emerges" (*Gl.*² §108.2; *CF* 486). Second, Schleiermacher's emphasis on the whole continues to operate: "If we regard the individual as the proper object of the divine justice, we degrade that attribute to the status of a mere counterpart of civil justice" (*Gl.*² §84.2; *CF* 348). Our vision becomes skewed when it focuses exclusively on individuals. A world order can only be discovered in the context of a corporate life. Thus the relationship between the individual and the divine causality, while more concrete, is still not anthropomorphized. This continued emphasis on the whole and its problematic consequences for the status of the individual is only partially resolved in the Christological propositions.

---

98. "The distinctive feature of Christian piety lies in the fact that whatever alienation from God there is in the phases of our experience, we are conscious of it as an action originating in ourselves, which we call Sin; but whatever fellowship with God there is, we are conscious of it as resting upon a communication from the Redeemer, which we call Grace." *Gl.*² §63; *CF* 262.

Fellowship with God, given through "a living fellowship with the Redeemer" (*Gl.*² §91; *CF* 371), is given through the community which he formed (and its preaching of the Word) and no longer through "His personal influence" (*Gl.*² §88.2; *CF* 363).[99] Thus even with regard to our relation to Christ the emphasis remains on the whole: "And just as creation is not concerned simply with individuals . . . , but it is the world that was created, and every individual as such was created only in and with the whole, . . . in the same way the activity of the Redeemer too is world-forming, and its object is human nature" (*Gl.*² §100.2; *CF* 427). The object of Christ's priestly and kingly powers is the whole community, not the individual.

It therefore remains the case that the best way to describe the individual's relation to the divine, even in terms of the specifically Christian religious consciousness, is through the dictum *One and All*. Just as in part 1 the individual is related to the divine causality only by being a part of the nature system, so in part 2 the believer is related to Christ only by being a member of the corporate life and "there can be no talk at all of any special intercession and representation on the part of individuals in the community of the perfected" (*Gl.*² §104.6; *CF* 465). At the same time, the individual is not insignificant because, as is true according to the general religious consciousness, the corporate life depends on the concrete experience and thriving character of its members—that is, on the "regeneration of individuals" (*Gl.*² §106.2; *CF* 477).

---

99. The corporate life in which we participate is traced "back to the influence of Jesus, [and] redemption is effected by Him through the communication of His sinless perfection." *Gl.*² §88; *CF* 361.

6

THE SECOND PART OF THE *GLAUBENSLEHRE* AND SCHLEIERMACHER'S LIVING GOD

> *There is only one eternal and universal decree justifying [us] for Christ's sake.*
>
> —F.D.E. Schleiermacher,
> *The Christian Faith*

In turning to part 2 of the *Glaubenslehre,* and consequently to the conclusion of my argument, I find it necessary to return to those questions raised by Schleiermacher's critics which launched this project. Those who accuse Schleiermacher of pantheism or Spinozism tend to see three issues as being at stake: the notion of a transcendent, personal God; the special status of the individual person in relation to God; the stability of central Christian doctrines. Of these three issues, the first is the determining one. The other two, those having to do with individuality and orthodoxy, depend entirely on whether God is understood as personal and transcendent (as defined by Jacobi and Sack) or as nonpersonal and immanent (as implied by Spinoza's *natura naturans*). Yet Schleiermacher refuses to be forced into this dichotomy and opts instead for a third position, according to which God is understood as the *living God*. This, however, has done little to assuage his critics. Friedrich Beisser, for instance, in his study of Schleiermacher's doctrine of God, reaches the conclusion that "the 'livingness' of God ... is nothing other than the wondrous life of the world, for which God is the determining but undifferentiated impulse. In a word, for Schleiermacher God ceases to be a person. Such a God is for him dead."[1] If we were to take into account only those texts that I have examined thus far (the *Reden* and part 1 of the *Glaubenslehre*), this might be a fair assessment of Schleiermacher's doctrine of God. Such an assessment is unwarranted, however, given that Schleiermacher's entire dogmatic system is structured such that the climax is really the starting point[2] and that therefore the full content of what he means by the *living God* is not given until the closing propositions of part 2 of the *Glaubenslehre*. But even to examine the propositions on divine love and wisdom is not sufficient, since it must be recalled that the divine attributes are derived from, and serve as crystallizations of, the first form of proposition.

According to his methodological principles, Schleiermacher cannot describe what he means by the *living God* until he has first described the concrete experience of the individual in relation to God. In part 2, this means that the notion of the *living God* stems from the experience of having been redeemed by Jesus of Nazareth, as that is described under the propositions on Christology, regeneration, and sanctification. Since the latter two doctrines highlight the issue of the individual's relation to God,[3] they become the test case by which to judge Schleiermacher's doctrine of God: insofar as Schleiermacher's exposition of regeneration includes the doctrine of justification by faith, the defining point of Protestant dogmatics, it raises the question of his orthodoxy; insofar as the doctrine of justification expresses the most concrete Christian religious consciousness of divine causality, it more than any other addresses the religious concern for the fate of the individual.

I therefore begin my conclusion with an examination of Schleiermacher's exposition of the doctrine of justification. While Schleiermacher does indeed undertake a substantial revision of that key doctrine—a revision that is related to aspects of his post-Kantian Spinozism—he does not thereby undermine it but instead seeks to render it more intelligible and reverent. I then proceed to examine the propositions on the divine attributes of love

---

1. Beisser, *Schleiermachers Lehre von Gott*, 250.
2. "But here [under the second aspect of the antithesis of sin and grace] we have not only to supply what before was lacking, but also, as we have remarked above, to give their full content (since we are only now for the first time moving in the sphere of the potent God-consciousness) to all those manifestations of the feeling of absolute dependence which could only be indefinitely described in the first part." (*Gl.*² §90.2; *CF* 370. Cf. *On the "Glaubenslehre,"* 57–60.
3. They describe the "Manner in which Fellowship with the Perfection and Blessedness of the Redeemer Expresses Itself in the *individual Soul*" (Heading to Part 2, Second Aspect, First Section, Second Division). *CF* 476; emphasis added.

and wisdom in order to determine what further light they may shed on the correlated issues of the relation of the individual to divine causality and the notion of the *living God*. Finally, I turn to Schleiermacher's understanding of the *living God*. Through this approach to part 2 of the *Glaubenslehre*, three things should be clarified: the extent of Schleiermacher's affinities with Spinoza and neo-Spinozism; the degree to which his post-Kantian Spinozism continues to function in his Christian dogmatics; the point at which he departs from Spinoza. Schleiermacher departs from Spinoza most notably in his understanding of divine intentionality as that is developed in *both* parts of the *Glaubenslehre,* and as that culminates in the divine attributes of love and wisdom.

Justification of the Ungodly

Martin Luther, in his 1545 "Preface to the Latin Writings," recorded what he took to be the decisive theological insight of his career. Concerning Romans 1:17 he wrote, "There I began to understand that the righteousness of God is that by which the righteous lives by a gift of God, namely by faith. And this is the meaning: the righteousness of God is revealed by the gospel, namely, the passive righteousness with which merciful God justifies us by faith."[4] This religious insight came to be known theologically as the doctrine of justification by faith alone—for Luther the central doctrine of Christianity. It is that doctrine which "creates true theologians" and which "is indispensable in the church."[5] It is, in short, that doctrine upon which all doctrines and the Christian life itself hinge. In Luther's view, "If we lose the doctrine of justification, we lose simply everything. Hence the most necessary and important thing is that we teach and repeat this doctrine daily. . . . For it cannot be grasped or held enough or too much."[6] Justification by faith is the "principal doctrine of Christianity."[7] John Calvin followed Luther in recognizing justification by faith as the defining

---

4. *Martin Luther: Selections from His Writings,* ed. John Dillenberger (Garden City, N.Y.: Anchor Books, Doubleday, 1961), 11. Although Luther claims to have made this discovery in 1518, it can be found as early as 1515–16 in his *Lectures on Romans.*

5. Martin Luther, "The Disputation Concerning Justification" (1536), in *Luther's Works,* vol. 34, ed. Lewis W. Spitz (Philadelphia: Muhlenberg Press, 1960), 157.

6. Martin Luther, *Lectures on Galatians* (1535), in *Luther's Works,* vols. 26–27, ed. Jaroslav Pelikan (St. Louis: Concordia Publishing House, 1963), 26:26.

7. Ibid., 26:106.

doctrine of Christian theology. In his *Institutes of the Christian Religion* he described justification as "the main hinge on which religion turns"[8] and complained that "the schools of the Sorbonne, mothers of all errors, have taken away from us justification by faith, which is the sum of all piety."[9] Despite its centrality, however, even Luther admitted that the doctrine of justification is "an elusive thing—not in itself, for in itself it is firm and sure, but so far as we are concerned."[10]

Schleiermacher is keenly aware of this elusiveness, just as he is aware of the fact that in Protestant dogmatic theology the doctrine of justification is the touchstone of orthodoxy. He is thus concerned to demonstrate how his own exposition of justification stands in relation to this theological tradition. After highlighting the inconsistent applications of the term in various confessions and declaring a preference for a definition that includes a "positive element" because "justification includes something more than forgiveness" (*Gl.*² §109.1; *CF* 497), Schleiermacher concedes that his exposition has the "drawback" that it will appear to diverge from more familiar presentations. Indeed, Schleiermacher's reformulation of the doctrine of justification by faith in some ways seems to undermine the three most fundamental aspects of the doctrine—namely, the systematic priority of justification, Christocentrism, and individual justification. Schleiermacher insists, however, that "this difficulty [of apparent divergence] vanishes as soon as the actual interrelations of the subject are understood" (497). Indeed, an analysis of his propositions under "The Manner in which Fellowship with the Perfection and Blessedness of the Redeemer Expresses Itself in the Individual Soul" in the *Glaubenslehre* shows that, with regard to the systematic priority of justification over sanctification, Schleiermacher is fully consistent with Luther's teaching; with regard to the complexities of the relation between what he terms justification and conversion, Schleiermacher comes closer to Calvin than to Luther, but for that reason he stands squarely within the Reformed tradition; and with regard to the Christocentrism of the faith that justifies, he stands close to both reformers. Nevertheless, he departs significantly from both Reformers over the issue of individual justification.

At first glance, the fact that there is no tight correspondence in terminology between Luther and Schleiermacher suggests that the latter does not

---

8. John Calvin, *Institutes of the Christian Religion*, 2 vols., ed. John T. McNeill and trans. Ford Lewis Battles (Philadelphia: Westminster Press, 1960), 1:726.
9. Ibid., 1:794.
10. Luther, *Lectures on Galatians*, 26:63.

Diagram 2. Part 2 of the *Glaubenslehre*: Propositions on Justification

First Aspect of the Antithesis: Explication of the Consciousness of Sin
   First Section: *Sin as a State of Man*
   Second Section: *The Constitution of the World in Relation to Sin*
   Third Section: *The Divine Attributes which relate to the Consciousness of Sin*
      First Doctrine: God is Holy
      Second Doctrine: God is Just

Second Aspect of the Antithesis: Explication of the Consciousness of Grace
   First Section: *The State of the Christian as Conscious of the Divine Grace*
      First Division: *Christ*
         First Doctrine: The Person of Christ
         Second Doctrine: The Work of Christ

      Second Division: *The Manner in which Fellowship with the Perfection and Blessedness of the Redeemer expresses itself in the Individual Soul*
         *First Doctrine: Regeneration
            §108 *Conversion: Repentance and Faith*
            §109 *Justification: Forgiveness and Adoption*
         Second Doctrine: Sanctification
            §111 *Sins of the Regenerate*
            §112 *Good Works of the Regenerate*

   Second Section: *The Constitution of the World in Relation to Redemption*
      First Division: *The Origin of the Church*
      Second Division: *The Subsistence of the Church alongside of the World*
      Third Division: *The Consummation of the Church*

   Third Section: *The Divine Attributes which relate to Redemption*
      *First Doctrine: The Divine Love (§§166–67)
      *Second Doctrine: The Divine Wisdom (§§168–69)

*Denotes propositions on which this study focuses

give justification the same systematic priority that the former does. Whereas for Luther *justification* functions as an umbrella term under which many elements—such as repentance, forgiveness, faith, and imputation—are included, for Schleiermacher *regeneration* functions as the umbrella term under which are included justification (forgiveness and adoption) and conversion (repentance and faith) (see Diagram 2). Schleiermacher's purpose in giving *justification* a more narrow meaning is not to diminish the term but to protect it and at the same time to clarify the various moments of the experience of being assumed "into living fellowship with Christ." (*Gl.*² §107; *CF* 478). At second glance, it thus becomes apparent that what

Luther termed *justification* corresponds closely to what Schleiermacher terms *regeneration*. In this sense, Schleiermacher is consistent with Luther in giving systematic priority to justification/regeneration over sanctification and in viewing justification as an actually making righteous on account of our embracing Christ in faith. Like Luther, Schleiermacher deliberately distances himself from what he perceives to be the Roman Catholic conception. He insists, in other words, that justification is in no way dependent on sanctification, that grace is not cooperative, and that "the state of grace leaves no room for reward" (*Gl.*² §112.3; *CF* 521). He achieves this in two ways. First, having distinguished justification and conversion as two interdependent moments of regeneration, he identifies conversion (*not* justification) as "the beginning of sanctification" (*Gl.*² §112.2; *CF* 520), thereby guaranteeing some sort of distance between justification and sanctification. Second, he orders the propositions such that the propositions on sanctification (§§110–12) are derived from those on regeneration (§§107–9). Not only do the propositions on regeneration, which include justification, come first, but the propositions on sanctification cannot stand on their own insofar as their expositions are really expansions of what has already been developed under conversion and justification. The reasons Schleiermacher offers for retaining the doctrine of sanctification at all are that it is biblical and is a defining point of distinction between Protestant and Roman Catholic dogmatics.

Any comparison between Luther and Schleiermacher on grace would of course disintegrate if Luther's notion of justification by faith were interpreted as being merely a forensic imputation.[11] If, however, one reads Lu-

---

11. According to this line of interpretation, put forth by both Lutheran and Catholic scholars, justification by faith is a forensic or external form of grace; that is, it is not sanative, renewing, or transforming. For example, Jared Wicks, a Jesuit scholar, concludes, "Luther's stress on certitude completely relativized the cleansing work of grace in making us over in charity. Charity is now on the fringe of things valued, for one must be above all certain of God's consoling gift, which then turns out to be not transforming charity but the conscious certitude itself of forgiveness." *Man Yearning for Grace: Luther's Early Spiritual Teaching* (Washington, D.C.: Corpus Publications, 1968), 272. Although Wicks intends this as a criticism, Uuraas Saarnivaara, a Protestant scholar, recognizes this point as the mark of Luther's genius: "The basic idea of righteousness before God ... is no longer compatible with the Augustinian view. Luther quite definitely teaches that man is justified through the eternal righteousness of Christ and not through a renewal of becoming righteous through the working of grace. The emphasis is laid in the work of Christ *for* sinners. In Him the believers have an adequate righteousness." *Luther Discovers the Gospel: New Light Upon Luther's Way from Medieval Catholicism to Evangelical Faith* (St. Louis: Concordia, 1951), 94–95; cf. 46, 101. According to this interpretation, imputation became for Luther not the Augustinian notion of healing plus the nonimputation of sins but the "alien, donated, and imputed righteousness of Christ." Ibid., 42.

ther as intending a real renewal, an actually making righteous, a being engrafted into Christ—an interpretation consistent with his later *Lectures on Galatians*—then there are deep affinities between Luther and Schleiermacher, whether focus is on the more circumscribed proposition of justification as forgiveness and adoption or on the umbrella doctrine of regeneration. A textual analysis of Luther's massive *Lectures on Galatians* (1535) reveals that, although he did indeed see faith as confidence, faith cannot be reduced to certitude alone. Faith is a hearing of the Word that is not merely external. Paul, he said, "means a Word that you believe when you hear it, so that the Word is not only the sound of my voice but is something that is heard by you, penetrates into your heart, and is believed by you."[12] This hearing of the Word is faith because it "takes hold of Christ in such a way that Christ is the object of faith, or rather not the object but, so to speak, the One who is present in the faith itself" (*Lectures on Galations*, 26:129). Throughout the Galatians commentary, Luther appealed to a variety of expressions in order to articulate this intimate, internal relationship between the believer and Christ: faith embraces, takes hold of, grasps, and is closely attached to Christ. This relationship is most eloquently expressed in his commentary on Galations 3:28, "For you are all one in Christ Jesus": "Christ and faith must be completely joined. We must simply take our place in heaven; and Christ must be, live, and work in us. But He lives and works in us, not speculatively but really, with presence and with power" (26:357). Luther even granted that the righteousness given by justification can be considered a formal righteousness, not insofar as it contains love but insofar as it beholds and grasps Christ. Consequently, imputation is not merely an external reckoning but has a manifold, nuanced meaning. Imputation is the gift of the righteousness of God given to us freely and necessary for our salvation; in its negative aspect, imputation is the forgiveness of sins as the nonimputation of sin; in its more positive aspect, imputation is the accepting of our faith in Christ as righteousness; it is "that righteousness by which Christ lives in us" (26:166). For Luther, therefore, Christ really works in us, not just for us: "But to put on Christ according to the Gospel is a matter, not of interpretation but of a new birth and creation, namely, that I put on Christ himself, that is, His innocence, righteousness, wisdom, power, salvation, life and Spirit" (26:352).

In all of this, Schleiermacher echoes Luther. For Schleiermacher, too, regeneration is effected through the proclaimed Word. Justification, which Schleiermacher defines as a "transformation of [one's] relation to God,"

---

12. Luther, *Lectures on Galatians*, 26:215; cf. 375.

depends on our faith in Christ and brings forgiveness (*Gl.*² §109; *CF* 496). This forgiveness is due solely to Christ's redeeming activity, and therefore faith cannot be mistaken as our own work or as an instrumental cause of justification. Our faith itself is divinely created, hence justification is entirely passive; we bring with us only our own receptivity, which is itself given by God.[13] Schleiermacher describes the first moment of regeneration, conversion, as "a twofold inactivity, a state of being no longer active in one direction and not yet active in another" (*Gl.*² §108.2; *CF* 484). And much as Luther described faith as our embracing Christ and being engrafted into Christ, so Schleiermacher describes regeneration as a being assumed "into living fellowship with Christ" (*Gl.*² §107; *CF* 478) and a laying "hold believingly on Christ" (*Gl.*² §109.4; *CF* 503). For both as theologians, faith is Christocentric, the believer is passive in justification, and the renewal brought about is an actual one because we live in Christ. For each as believers, however, justification seems to have been experienced differently. For Luther, the Word comes first as law, as a crushing hammer to humiliate, but Schleiermacher notes that "the true change of heart . . . need by no means invariably spring from a flood of regret that almost wrecks the whole being by its painful emotion" (*Gl.*² §108.3; *CF* 487). He thus grants the possibility of a gradual, steady process of conversion, and he cautions that to deny this possibility is to restrict the divine grace. So far, the differences between Luther and Schleiermacher seem to be ones of structure and sensibility more than of theological content. Yet further analysis of Schleiermacher's exposition of the relation between conversion and justification points to a real divergence from Luther's doctrine; this divergence, however, only brings Schleiermacher closer to Calvin.

To the degree that conversion has to do with a "changed form of life" (*Gl.*² §107; *CF* 478) and involves the spontaneous activity of the believer, the question arises whether this is in any way analogous to what is usually referred to as sanctification; if so, the primacy of justification would once again seem to be compromised. There is no easy answer to this question, since Schleiermacher, in developing a schema for the relation between conversion and justification, seems to make three conflicting claims: conversion and justification are interdependent; justification is derived from conversion; and conversion and justification are entirely independent of each other. Such conflicting claims lead in turn to three incriminating questions about Schleiermacher's reformulation of the doctrine of justification: If justification is derived from conversion, does this not abrogate the principal

---

13. See *Gl.*² §108.6; *CF* 493–94.

Reformation doctrine? If the "total effective influence of Christ is only the continuation of the creative divine activity" (*Gl.*² §100.2; *CF* 427), can this justification not be appropriated without Christ? If the divine decree is eternal and universal, in what way is the individual justified?

Schleiermacher describes justification and conversion as being the two aspects of regeneration, "the divine act of union with human nature" (*Gl.*² §110.3; *CF* 509). Whereas conversion has to do with a changed form of life in fellowship with Christ, justification has to do with our changed relation to God. In the two elements of conversion, repentance and faith, Christ's role is central. Christ alone awakens regret and effects change of heart through the impartation of his perfection; Christ alone arouses faith through his Word. The conversion thus brought about is identical to that of the disciples. Hence conversion belongs to the "realm of grace" insofar as the divine workings in it "depend upon and actually proceed from the being of God in the Person of Christ" (*Gl.*² §108.5; *CF* 492). Thus proceeding, the activity is primarily Christ's self-communication, but we are not entirely passive. Conversion, he says, is precisely "the evocation of [our] spontaneous activity in union with Christ" (*Gl.*² §108.6; *CF* 495). Schleiermacher's intention here is to move beyond an understanding of passivity that is "entirely foreign to human nature, in virtue of which a person would resemble a lifeless object in the matter of conversion" (495). He still, however, wants to maintain passivity in our relation to God—passivity not as lifelessness but as sheer receptivity. In the two elements of justification, forgiveness and adoption, Christ's role is not as central as it is in conversion. While justification is traced to the influence of Christ, it has primarily to do with our relation to God and thus belongs to the "realm of power." Schleiermacher explains that the two elements of justification, "like both elements of conversion, [are] dependent on the whole activity of Christ, but [each] directly and for itself expresses merely the relation of the man to God" (*Gl.*² §109.2; *CF* 498). Rather than clarify, this passage only serves to confuse the relationship between conversion and justification, or, in other words, the relationship between the activity of Christ and divine causality.

Overall, Schleiermacher seems to want to claim a relation between conversion and justification wherein the two "are mutually conditioned" (*Gl.*² §112; *CF* 518).[14] Justification or "our relation to God," he writes, "is really an affair of the quiescent self-consciousness, looking at itself reflected in thought and finding a consciousness of God included there" (*Gl.*² §107.1;

---

14. Cf. *Gl.*² §§107.1, 109.2.

CF 478–79). Recognizing the dangers implicit in such a statement, he says that taken apart from conversion "justification would then be a resolve to forgive oneself on the ground that sin is unavoidable.... A new relation can arise only through the union with Christ which effects conversion too"; it follows that "conversion and justification, being thus utterly inseparable, must also be regarded as happening simultaneously, and each is the infallible criterion of the other" (479). He reiterates this relation of interdependence later in his exposition on justification: "We cannot conceive this divine activity as independent of the agency of Christ in conversion, as if one might exist without the other" (*Gl.*² §109.3; *CF* 500). This time, however, the appeal is made in the midst of a very dense discussion in which a second claim is introduced that seems to conflict with the first. More than interdependence, Schleiermacher argues that the relation is a derivative one: "deriving justification entirely as [this exposition] does from conversion" (499); justification "follows only in so far as [one] has true faith in the Redeemer" (*Gl.*² §109; *CF* 496). This, however, is offset by yet a third claim. Schleiermacher argues that there is no dependency of the divine causality on Christ's activity, not even in intermediate form: "For the decision as to *who* is to attain to conversion and *when* we have already assigned, not to the realm of grace, making it depend on Christ, but to the realm of power, making it depend on God" (*Gl.*² §109.3; *CF* 500–501).¹⁵

Three conflicting claims are thus presented. Justification and conversion are simultaneous, nonderivative, and interdependent; justification is dependent on conversion in that it is traced to the influence of Christ; and justification is independent of conversion. There is a tension here that Schleiermacher is almost determined not to resolve. This tension, it appears, ensures that his "exposition of the matter *will not be readily liable* to the misconstruction that each man justifies himself, seeing that it traces everything back to the influence of Christ" (*Gl.*² §109.3; Redeker 2:176; emphasis added).¹⁶ On the one hand, in claiming that justification belongs to the "realm of power" rather than to the "realm of grace," Schleiermacher

---

15. Lest this "decision" sound too anthropomorphic, one must keep in mind two rules regarding the divine decree: no individual becomes anything for itself apart from the whole of relations; everything is a perfect manifestation of divine good pleasure.

16. "Diese Darstellung der Sache wird zwar nicht leicht dem Mißverständnis ausgesetzt sein, als ob jeder sich selbst rechtfertige, indem sie ja alles auf die Einwirkung Christi zurückführt." Ironically, the English edition of the *Glaubenslehre* mistranslates Schleiermacher on just this point: "This exposition of the matter *is indeed readily liable* to the misconstruction that each man justifies himself." *CF* 499; emphasis added. I am indebted to B. A. Gerrish for calling my attention to this error in translation.

protects the divine prerogative. There is no "dependence of the divine activity on the activity of Christ or its result, not even in the intermediate form of its being motived [sic] by Christ" ($Gl.^2$ §109.3; CF 500). Both the activity of Christ and the activity of the believer that it evokes are eclipsed. With justification, Schleiermacher explains, "an activity of God is implied, and man can be conceived only as passive" (500). Being thus passive, we are unable to procure for ourselves divine forgiveness and adoption. On the other hand, in reminding us that justification is traced back to the influence of Christ, Schleiermacher protects the Christocentric character of grace. Justification cannot be appropriated apart from the redeeming and reconciling activity of Christ; it "follows only insofar as [one] has true faith in the Redeemer," that is to say, insofar as one has been converted.[17] Hence, this focus on Christ's activity reinforces the insistence that we cannot effect our own justification. Justification is dependent on, and derived from, conversion, in that forgiveness and acceptance cannot, for Schleiermacher, precede faith.

By thus relating our changed relation to God (justification) with our changed form of life (conversion), Schleiermacher seems to make a significant shift away from the Reformers. Note, however, that his reworking of the systematic status given to justification, and its resulting complex relation with conversion, is reminiscent of Calvin's discussion of *duplex gratia*. According to Calvin, we receive a "double grace: namely, that being reconciled to God through Christ's blamelessness, we may have in heaven instead of a Judge a gracious Father; and secondly, that sanctified by Christ's spirit we may cultivate blamelessness and purity of life."[18] Both graces, justification and sanctification, are essential—they are inseparable, they cannot be collapsed. Perhaps, then, the question is not one of priority, since for Calvin both together are the "whole of the gospel."[19] In this sense Schleiermacher, in making justification and conversion "simultaneous" ($Gl.^2$ §109.2; CF 498), imitates the shift the Genevan Reformer had already made in relation to Luther. Still, perhaps Schleiermacher can be said to depart from Calvin with regard to the *reasons* for the systematic restructuring of the relation

---

17. The propositions on regeneration have parallels in the Christological propositions. Conversion has reference to Christ's redemptive activity ($Gl.^2$ §100), justification to Christ's reconciling activity (§101). Schleiermacher there wants to maintain a balanced mutual relation, "one conditioning the other and each independent of the other" (§101.1 CF 431). Nevertheless, he insists that "the reconciling activity [justification] can only manifest itself as a consequence of the redemptive activity [conversion]" (ibid.).

18. Calvin, *Institutes*, 1:725.

19. Ibid., 1:613.

between justification and conversion. Calvin had a pedagogical reason. When we understand the sanctified life, we are then able to know the meaning of free forgiveness. Other reasons, not made explicit, were polemical in nature. On one side, his concern was to defend against Roman charges of libertinism; on the other side, he wanted to maintain a distance from Luther's principle of *sola fide*. Schleiermacher's restructuring, however, is necessary given his understanding of divine causality. The passive character of the individual's relationship to divine causality is maintained, in that it is actually God, not the individual self, who justifies. God justifies us through "the whole series of gracious workings mediated by Christ" (*Gl.*² §109.4; *CF* 504). Justification derives from conversion not because the divine justifying act depends somehow on "Christ pointing out something to God" (*Gl.*² §109.3; *CF* 500) but because the person-forming activity of the Redeemer is given in the divine decree. Schleiermacher's concern, once again, is to guard against anthropomorphisms, but for him that means "we can as little here as elsewhere admit an act in time eventuating at a particular moment or an act directed upon an individual" (501).

Therefore, although Schleiermacher maintains the integrity of the doctrine of justification as well as the Christocentrism of faith, the question still remains whether for him it is the individual who is justified. On this point, Schleiermacher's departure from the Reformers is marked, but he believes this is required by the limits of piety because "to admit an individual decree . . . would be to subject God to the antithesis of abstract and concrete, or universal and particular" (501).[20] According to Schleiermacher, "There is only one eternal and universal decree justifying [us] for Christ's sake. . . . Thenceforward the promulgation in time of this divine act is really a continuous one, but in its effects it appears to us in as many points separated and (as it were) strung out" (*Gl.*² §109.3; *CF* 501). The decree is directed to the whole of humanity, not to the individual, and is issued once and for all time. We appropriate this decree by being raised to a higher stage of consciousness through the redemptive and reconciling work of Christ. This means that the notion of justification as a declaratory act must be rethought:

> The phrase in question [we are 'declared just'] certainly goes back to what is here denied, namely, a multiplicity of divine justifying

---

20. See B. A. Gerrish, "Theology within the Limits of Piety Alone: Schleiermacher and Calvin's Notion of God," in *The Old Protestantism and the New: Essays on the Reformation Heritage* (Chicago: University of Chicago Press, 1982).

acts or decrees. For in regard to a single universal decree it is not easy to conceive how it could be declaratory in particular cases. God ordained the Redeemer because through Him sin was to be taken away and men become children of God. But in God thought and will are one.... A special act, therefore, by which God—so we should have to state the matter—declared to Himself what He in another act performs, would be an utterly empty thing. This form of representation, so common in the Old Testament, is simply one of its anthropomorphisms. (502)

Recall that for Schleiermacher the divine care for the world, as expressed in the doctrines of creation and preservation, cannot be said to sustain individual things through isolated, particular divine acts but can only be understood as operating within the totality of the nature system. The doctrines of creation and preservation, however, are themselves abstractions from the Christian religious consciousness of redemption, as that is described in the (more concrete) doctrine of regeneration. In part 2, therefore, the themes and limits developed in part 1 of the *Glaubenslehre* are carried through to their full extent. Not only are we *unable* to speak of an individual divine act, but to do so would not even be necessary if we could. There is only one eternal decree which determines our relation with God, and "all that is needful is that the consciousness of its [guilt's] cessation should arise in the individual" (502). Justification can only be understood in terms of the individual on two counts: insofar as in its effects it *appears* to us to be individual; insofar as for dogmatics the "starting-point [is] the self-consciousness of the individual" (501). To claim any more than this would be to revert to figurative language. Once again, justification is not a separate act of God but a recognition of a relationship, a recognition that takes place through the redeeming and reconciling work of Christ.

With this in mind, it should now be clear how Schleiermacher would respond to objections such as "The individual man and particular events are being lost sight of in the execution of the one decree for the world.... Schleiermacher has presented an unconvincing view of the significance of *my personal history*."[21] This objection is valid to the extent that there is indeed to be found in Schleiermacher a shift of focus from the particular to the whole, from the individual to the corporate life. Yet from Schleiermacher's perspective such a shift actually reveals the misguided character of the fearful question, "What about *my* personal history?" Perhaps the

---

21. Moore, "Schleiermacher as a Calvinist," 182; emphasis added.

issue can best be addressed through a consideration of prayer. Does it make sense to pray to a God who does not justify individuals in special divine acts? Schleiermacher replies, yes, of course, as long as prayer heeds the limits of piety. This means, in part, that prayer must always reflect the needs of the whole church:

> For the higher place we give an individual, the more easily we may be seduced to believe that it is a distinct loss for the Kingdom of God that he should be snatched away from his sphere of influence, or hindered in his work. But on closer inspection we shall always be compelled to own that except Christ Himself no individual is indispensable to the Kingdom of God. At a still greater distance stand all wishes relating to our own external welfare or that of others, where too we are less easily deceived. But yet, as long as we have not attained to simple resignation that excludes all wishes, it is natural and wholesome for us even as Christians to combine these wishes with the God-consciousness. ($Gl.^2$ §147.3; CF 675)[22]

Just as in his organic monism the well-being of the particular depends on that of the whole, and *vice versa*, so in his view of the corporate life each individual must be viewed in the context of the whole community, which in turn depends on the regeneration of individuals. Traces of Schleiermacher's philosophy of resignation therefore remain, but it is not a resignation to some blind fate; rather, it is a consent that, because of redemption, recognizes the universe as an "absolutely harmonious divine work of art" ($Gl.^2$ §168.1; CF 733).

The Theater of Redemption

Schleiermacher is unambiguous regarding the limits of the doctrine of the divine attributes as presented in part 1 of the *Glaubenslehre*. The attributes

---

22. Recall Schleiermacher's refutation of the "best friends" and "most zealous defenders" of religion in the *Reden*. The true concern of religion is not the fate of the individual but "the immediate consciousness of the Deity as He is found in ourselves and the world." Oman, 101; R^3 133. In the context of the subject of immortality, Schleiermacher underscores this concern: "If our feeling nowhere attaches itself to the individual, but if its content is our relation to God wherein all that is individual and fleeting disappears, there can be nothing fleeting in it, but all must be eternal." Oman, 100; R^2 131.

relating to our general religious consciousness are "wholly indeterminate in character" and, when interpreted apart from those having to do with the experience of redemption, result in a belief in God that "is nothing more than that shadow of faith which even devils may have" (*Gl.*² §167.2; *CF* 731). Eternity and omnipotence, as the primary correlates in part 1, are only "abstraction[s] from the definite feeling-content of our God-consciousness" (731). He explains in his second letter to Lücke, "Indeed, an omnipotence, the *aim* and *motive* force of which I do not know, an omniscience, the *structure* and *value* of its contents I do not know, and an omnipresence, of which I do not know what it emits from itself and attracts to itself, are merely vague and barely living ideas."[23] He goes on to suggest that the more determinate content can only be given under the attributes of the love and wisdom of God, after the "State of the Christian as Conscious of the Divine Grace" (*CF* 371) has been explicated: "It is quite different when omnipotence makes itself manifest in the consciousness of the new spiritual creation, omnipresence in the activity of the divine spirit, and omniscience in the consciousness of divine grace and favor."[24] This brief text, then, contains the key to what Schleiermacher means by his term the *living God*. His exposition of divine love and wisdom should describe the *aim, motive, value,* and *structure* of divine causality; it should, in other words, describe divine intentionality as experienced by redemption. In describing this divine intentionality, Schleiermacher is also describing what it means to say God is the *living God*.

The attributes of love and wisdom do not just complete the picture, as though all the attributes together play equal and complementary roles.[25] On the contrary, they (and most especially the attribute of love) form the very core of Schleiermacher's whole doctrine of God, in which all the other attributes "merge" (*Gl.*² §167.2; *CF* 731).[26] And so, Schleiermacher concludes, "love alone and no other attribute can be equated thus with God" (*Gl.*² §167.1; *CF* 730). This claim, which recognizes love as the essence of

---

23. *On the "Glaubenslehre,"* 57; *KGA* 1/10:340; emphasis added.
24. Ibid.
25. According to Ebeling, "For if knowledge of God came about by adding up the concepts of divine attributes and were completely attained in this way, then the knowledge of God, and indeed God himself, would be a kind of aggregate." "Schleiermacher's Doctrine of the Divine Attributes," 131.
26. The difference between love and wisdom and the other attributes cannot be explained as merely the difference between parts 1 and 2, since the attributes of holiness and justice also cannot express the divine essence; they can only be understood in terms of the antithesis of good and evil and, indeed, must be "reckoned in as part of the work of redemption." *Gl.*² §167.2; *CF* 731.

God, immediately raises three difficulties that seem in one breath to violate the basic tenets of his *post-Kantian Spinozism*. First, in applying the term *love* to God, and in drawing an analogy to the human disposition in order to describe the relationship between love and wisdom in divine causality, Schleiermacher also seems to forego his own concerns about anthropomorphism; in doing so, he seems to make a clear departure from Spinoza. Second, in daring to speak of divine essence, Schleiermacher seems to suspend his own method and limits; in doing so, he seems to make a departure from the postcritical concerns that informed his doctrine of God for four decades. Third, in claiming that wisdom (as the extension of divine love) is the "comprehensive name for the divine purposes" (*Gl.*² §55.1; *CF* 222), Schleiermacher seems to introduce the notion of final causes; in doing so, he seems to contradict his earlier refutation of the same. The limits set by Schleiermacher's post-Kantian Spinozism thus seem to be transgressed in the closing pages of the *Glaubenslehre,* and thus it is here that a final evaluation regarding his relationship to Spinoza and neo-Spinozism must be made.

Divine Love

The experience of redemption, Schleiermacher says, includes "recognition of the divine love" (*Gl.*² §166.2; *CF* 729). Indeed, it reveals that the very essence of God, or the divine disposition, is love. Schleiermacher recognizes the danger of anthropomorphism here but thinks he can avoid naive or irreverent forms of it, first, by emphasizing "differences which, as being human, depend on some antithesis" (*Gl.*² §165.1; *CF* 726) and then by removing any such antithesis from his description of divine love. In this sense Schleiermacher employs a *via negationis*. Nevertheless, there is a clear divergence from Spinoza insofar as Schleiermacher grants that, although anthropomorphism should be guarded against, when dealing with the subjective self-consciousness it is in the end unavoidable.[27] It is here, at the heart and climax of his doctrine of God, that he finds the risk least avoidable. The issue becomes, therefore, the *degree* of anthropomorphism allowed and whether or not it results in attributing a *personality* to God. Schleiermacher certainly seems to approach attributing a personality to God in the analogy he draws between the "underlying temper or disposition" in human causality and the "underlying disposition" of divine causality (*Gl.*² §165.1; *CF* 726, 727). He develops this analogy further by defining

---

27. See for example *Gl.*² §5 p.s.

human love as "the impulse to unite self with neighbour and to will to be in neighbour" and by claiming that the Kingdom of God involves "the union of the Divine Essence with human nature" (727). The significant difference between the two kinds of love is that, whereas in human life disposition is separable from activity and its impulses are sporadic, in the Divine Essence "no such dualism can be conceived of" (*Gl.*² §165.2; *CF* 727).

Spinoza refuses to apply the attribute of love to God. First, to do so would be against piety, which for him is a life lived according to the "dictates of reason,"[28] because it would bring God into the contradictions and fluctuations of human emotions.[29] Second, love is not a divine attribute because it does not express the essence of God; rather, it belongs to a third category of properties that do not belong at all to God but have to do with how we imagine God.[30] Third, if the term applies so differently to God than to humans, then it would really be meaningless when applied to God. This last point reflects Spinoza's own rules regarding language about God. He rejects both the way of analogy and the way of causality and insists that the attributes of God must be applied univocally. Any term ascribed to God must be understood in the same way as it applies to humans, since analogy actually results in an equivocal application of the terms.[31] Spinoza would in all likelihood say that the definition of love offered by Schleiermacher ("the impulse to unite self with neighbour" [*Gl.*² §165.1; *CF* 726]) describes only a property of love, not its essence, which is *"pleasure accompanied by the idea of an external cause."*[32] This term certainly cannot be applied to God, since there are no causes external to God. We should, of

---

28. *Ethics* 5.4, note; Elwes 2:249; cf. *Ethics* 4.27, note 1, and 2.49, note.

29. "It cannot be said that God loves men, much less that he loves them because they love him, and hates them because they hate him.... Moreover, this would also have to produce a great mutability in God. Where previously he had neither loved nor hated, he would now begin to love and to hate, and would be caused to do this by something that would be outside him. But this is absurdity itself." Spinoza, *Short Treatise on God, Man, and His Well-Being*, part 2, chap. 24; Curley 1:142.

30. See *Short Treatise*, part 1, chap. 7; Curley 1:89. Spinoza describes imagination as "an idea, which indicates rather the present disposition of the human body than the nature of the external body." *Ethics* 4.1, note; Elwes 2:192.

31. This is why he denies that will and intellect appertain to God. If they did, then "we must take these words in some significations quite different from those they usually bear. For intellect and will, which should constitute the essence of God, would perforce be as far apart as the poles from the human intellect and will, in fact, *would have nothing in common with them but the name*." *Ethics* 1.17, note; Elwes 2:61; emphasis added.

32. *Ethics* 3.13, note; Elwes 2:140. See also *Ethics*, part 3, "Definitions of the Emotions"; Elwes 2:175.

course, love God, but not because God is present to us in a particular or personal way, only because God is eternal. This is the intellectual love of God, wherein lies our freedom and blessedness.[33] We cannot endeavor that God should return our love, otherwise we "would desire that God, whom [we love], should not be God."[34] The most that can be granted is that "God, in so far as he loves himself, loves man, and, consequently, that the love of God towards men, and the intellectual love of the mind towards God are identical."[35] Compare this with Schleiermacher's statement that "in virtue of their capacity for the God-consciousness all men certainly are also objects of the divine love" (*Gl.*[2] §166.2; *CF* 729). It is interesting that, for both Spinoza and Schleiermacher, the love of God for us can only be understood as being somehow linked to our capacity to know God.

Schleiermacher, even though he dares to identify love as the essence of God and to speak in terms of an underlying divine disposition, nevertheless continues to share some basic instincts with Spinoza—instincts that prohibit the possibility of God being assigned the characteristics of a human personality. Schleiermacher insists that divine love cannot be understood as being directed toward individuals. He therefore retains his emphasis on the whole to ensure that God not be brought within the realm of antitheses: "Supposing we regard the single life as its object, then, if we are not going to lapse into the grossest particularism, it is impossible from such aids to life to infer the divine love; they involve restraints upon the lives of others; so that the presence of love would always imply the presence of its opposite" (*Gl.*[2] §166.1; *CF* 728). Schleiermacher implicitly warns against the same dangers recognized by Spinoza: emotions cannot be attributed to God; divine love cannot be an excuse for religious intolerance; God cannot be understood except as eternal.[36] Moreover, both Spinoza and Schleiermacher emphasize the one, eternal divine decree that determines the whole course of nature and history and that remains unaltered. For both thinkers, this entails that *intellect* and *will* not be assigned to God, since such terms are too anthropomorphic insofar as they imply some division in God and

33. See *Ethics* 5.29, 5.32, cor.; 5.36, note; Elwes 2:261, 263, 265.
34. *Ethics* 5.19, proof; Elwes 2:256.
35. *Ethics* 5.36, cor.; Elwes 2:265.
36. Indeed, it should be noted that the relationship between the attributes of love and wisdom, respectively, correspond to that between those attributes in part 1 that express the "absolutely inward" character of the divine causality (eternity and omnipresence) and those that express the "absolute vitality" of the same (omnipotence and omniscience). See *Gl.*[2] §51.3; *CF* 203. See also Ebeling, "Schleiermacher's Doctrine of the Divine Attributes," 162. From this it follows that the notion of divine eternity is derived from an experience of divine love, or put another way, divine love is that which conditions all that is.

allow the possibility of a divine usurpation of the natural order.[37] For Schleiermacher, however, unlike Spinoza, a definitive goal is given, namely, the Kingdom of God. The eternal divine decree, it must be remembered, is that which justifies us for Christ's sake (see *Gl.*² §109.3; *CF* 501). Nevertheless, the emphasis remains on the whole: "And thus here, too, we come back to the position that He loves them only as He sees them in Christ, just as it is only when they themselves are in Christ that they come to a knowledge of the divine love" (*Gl.*² §166.2; *CF* 729). Schleiermacher can therefore say that the essence of God is love without falling into the usual contradictions of anthropomorphism, insofar as God loves us not through isolated acts but through the one continuous act of redemption.[38]

Because redemption is part of the eternal divine decree, Schleiermacher does not think his appeal to love as the essential attribute of God is arbitrary or imaginary. The reason for this is related to his higher realism: we recognize divine love as given already; we do not merely project a human characteristic onto God. Schleiermacher's discussion of the feeling of absolute dependence and its *Whence* (§4) is an abstraction from this very concrete experience. The experience is fundamentally one of an utter givenness in relation to which we can only be receptive and exert no counterinfluence; it is a recognition of the reality already and always present. The point that Schleiermacher is making is an important one.[39] Some thinkers, he writes, "recognize the divine love in all those arrangements of Nature and all those dispositions of human affairs which protect life or further it. And yet, apart from redemption, and taken only in this sense, the divine love must always remain a matter of doubt" (*Gl.*² §166.1; *CF* 728). The notion that love alone applies to the essence of God would mean nothing apart from the experience of redemption. It cannot be derived merely from some vague

---

37. Spinoza writes, "All things, I repeat, are in God, and all things which come to pass, come to pass solely through the laws of the infinite nature of God, and follow from the necessity of his essence." *Ethics* 1.15, note; Elwes 2:59. "Wherefore the omnipotence of God has been displayed from all eternity, and will for all eternity remain in the same state of activity." *Ethics* 1.17, note; Elwes 2:61. See also *A Theologico-Political Treatise*, chap. 4, "The Divine Law"; Elwes 1:57–68.

38. Recall his revision of the doctrine of justification by faith: "Thenceforward the promulgation in time of this divine act is really a continuous one, but in its effects it appears to us in as many points separated and (as it were) strung out from one another, as there are different people whose union with Christ is accomplished." *Gl.*² §105.3; *CF* 501. This also relates to his employment of the dictum *One and All*: "God knows each in the whole, as also the whole in each." *Gl.*² §55.3; *CF* 227.

39. Indeed, it is not unlike Spinoza's discussion of the distinctions between *imagination*, *reason*, and *intuition*. See *Ethics* 2.39, note 2; Elwes 3:113.

sense of order or abstracted from some emotion. It can arise only from the concrete experience of having been redeemed: "... recognition of the divine love. *That* only comes with the efficacious working of redemption, and it comes from Christ" (*Gl.*² §166.2; *CF* 729). Therefore, in his exposition of divine love, Schleiermacher does not abandon his Spinozan disdain for anthropomorphism. Nevertheless, the differences are now rendered unambiguous: he departs from Spinoza in his claim that only love expresses the essence of God and that therefore only love can properly be said to be an attribute of God;[40] he also departs from Spinoza in his identification of redemption through Christ with the goal of the eternal divine decree. He maintains his affinities with Spinoza through his refusal to assign personality to God, his suspicion of anthropomorphism, and his emphasis on the whole.

The issue now turns to the other aspect of his post-Kantian Spinozism. In identifying love as the essence of God, or in even allowing himself to speak of the divine essence, does he abandon his own postcritical concerns and methodology? Not exactly. The fact that Schleiermacher dares to say that "love alone and no other attribute can be equated thus with God" (*Gl.*² §167.1; *CF* 730) is actually a consequence, not a violation, of the method he has employed throughout the *Glaubenslehre:* it follows from his appeal to the *via causalitatis;* it is an expression of the Christian religious consciousness. It must be remembered, first, that all utterances concerning God must be traced back to divine causality, since it "stands in the closest connexion with the feeling of absolute dependence itself" (*Gl.*² §50.3; *CF* 197),[41] and second, that being cannot be separated from activity. This applies to God as well as to finite things. God, after all, is the *living God* who can never be understood as inactive.[42] Divine causality, or "divine self-impartation" (*Gl.*² §166.1; *CF* 727), is given to us immediately in the experience of having been redeemed by Jesus of Nazareth, which attaches itself to the feeling of absolute dependence: "If we look at the way in which we become aware of the two attributes respectively, it turns out that we

---

40. Spinoza, of course, claims that, although there are an infinite number of divine attributes (none of which are 'love'), we only have knowledge of two: thought and extension.

41. "We can arrive at ideas of divine attributes only by combining the content of our self-consciousness with the absolute divine causality that corresponds to our feeling of absolute dependence." *Gl.*² §79.1; *CF* 325. The divine causality is "the ground of our feeling of absolute dependence." *Gl.*² §51.1; *CF* 201.

42. "But once the activity of God has been separated from the being of God, and only the latter regarded, there of course remains for this immensity only a negation with no positive substratum which could have emerged from religious emotion." *Gl.*² §53 p.s.; *CF* 211.

have the sense of divine love directly in the consciousness of redemption, and as this is the basis on which all the rest of our God-consciousness is built up, it of course represents to us the essence of God" (*Gl.*² §167.2; *CF* 732). Because of the immediacy, intensity, and uniqueness of this experience of divine causality, and because causality is not to be separated from being, the essence of God can fairly be said to be love. Note, however, the qualification given in this passage: love *represents to us* God's essence. Since the experience of redemption is fundamentally one of a gracious and loving acceptance, forgiveness, and regeneration, the God experienced will inevitably be described in terms of love.

Divine love, which communicates itself through the continual act of redemption, is thus the *content* and *motive* of all the other attributes as well as the presupposition for the divine preservation.[43] Schleiermacher's doctrine of God, therefore, cannot be understood as speculative. It is rooted in the Christian religious consciousness and is, at its core, biblical. Its key proposition is taken from 1 John 4: "God is love" (*Gl.*² §167; *CF* 730). Curiously, although love alone can be described as the essence of God and is that attribute in which all the others merge, what Schleiermacher means by it is best understood in light of his exposition of divine wisdom, "since the two attributes cannot be conceived in separation from each other" (*Gl.*² §167.2; *CF* 732). The *aim* of divine love is expressed as wisdom, "the right outlining of plans and purposes" (*Gl.*² §165.1; *CF* 727). This, however, raises further suspicions since terms such as *plans* and *purposes* ring of anthropomorphism and approach the notion of final causes. If this is the case with Schleiermacher's exposition of divine wisdom, then this would seem to contradict one of the basic tenets of his post-Kantian Spinozism, as that is carried through in part 1 of the *Glaubenslehre,* and thus would indeed support the contention that the two parts are irreconcilable. In fact, his exposition of divine wisdom not only serves as the culmination of what he means by the *living God,* but does so precisely by pulling together vari-

---

43. According to Ebeling, "Love alone can be equated with the nature of God. It is the only attribute of God which can take the place of the name of God himself. This makes it plain once again that Schleiermacher's doctrine of the divine attributes moves in the opposite direction to that of speculative thought. The latter takes those attributes to be the nature of God which . . . are the expression of a mere shadowy faith in God such as devils, too, can have. Christian faith, on the other hand, conceives the nature of God only as self-communicating and therefore as love." "Schleiermacher's Doctrine of the Divine Attributes," 160. According to Niebuhr, "Love, insofar as it names God as power more satisfactorily than does any other quality, names him neither simply as an ethical agent nor simply as an artist but as power akin to both: as an intender embodying his intention beyond himself." "Schleiermacher and the Names of God," 195.

ous strands of his post-Kantian Spinozism: his rejection of final causes, his aesthetic vision, his determinism, and his adaptation of the dictum *One and All*.

Divine Wisdom

The experience of redemption, which results immediately in the recognition of divine love, also leads necessarily to the recognition of divine wisdom as "the principle which orders and determines the world" (*Gl.*² §168; *CF* 732). The attribute of wisdom, in other words, describes the "divine government of the world" (*Gl.*² §164; *CF* 723). This is not the first time that Schleiermacher introduces this idea. Indeed, he lays the groundwork for it in part 1 under the doctrine of divine preservation. There he argues that the idea of *divine government*—as "the fulfillment of divine decrees or the guidance of all things to divine ends"—can be allowed only on the condition that such "fulfillment" and "guidance" be understood in terms of the *one* divine decree, "as God originally willed and always wills, by means of the powers distributed and preserved in the world" (*Gl.*² §46 p.s.; *CF* 177). Beyond this, however, Schleiermacher admits that little more can be said in part 1 regarding divine government, since its *content* can only be understood in terms of "the Kingdom of God, established by means of redemption" (177), and therefore its exposition belongs to part 2. *Wisdom* is the "comprehensive name for the divine purposes" (*Gl.*² §55.1; *CF* 222) and, together with the attribute of omniscience, expresses the livingness of divine causality. The notion of the *living God* therefore has to do with divine intentionality and knowledge.

That this divine intentionality cannot be understood in terms of final causes has already been established under the proposition on divine omniscience, largely through a Spinozan, nonanthropomorphic interpretation of divine knowledge. Divine will cannot be separated from divine knowledge, as though God considers various possibilities and then chooses to act on one;[44] divine will cannot be thought of as a desiring of what not yet is; there is no potentiality apart from what is real, that is, what is already presented. There is, in short, no cause, end, or purpose that is not already immanent in the nature system: "The world as the whole content of the divine formation and production is so self-enclosed that there is nothing external which could gain an influence upon it" (*Gl.*² §55.1; *CF* 221).

---

44. "It can never be said that in [God] the purposive thought-activity precedes the will-activity." *Gl.*² §55.1; *CF* 220.

So far, Schleiermacher remains close to Spinoza in his reluctance to speak of divine will and intellect (hence his preference for the term *omniscience*), as well as in his insistence that there is nothing in divine knowledge that is not fully presented in the nature system. The difference between the two thinkers, however, becomes evident when Schleiermacher continues his discussion of divine knowledge under the attribute of wisdom. There, although he still rejects the notion of final causes, he also wants to develop the notion of divine purposes.[45] This could not have been addressed under the attribute of omniscience, which "looks backward," but it becomes an issue under the attribute of wisdom, which "looks forward" (*Gl.*² §168.1; *CF* 732). Schleiermacher thinks he can have it both ways by interpreting "plans and purposes" aesthetically, an interpretation that he thinks is warranted by the fact that divine love imparts itself through the work of redemption. This aesthetic interpretation of divine knowledge allows him to include such notions as purpose and value without resorting to *more* anthropomorphic notions of choice, ends, and means.[46]

Wisdom, Schleiermacher explains, is "the art (so to speak) of realizing the divine love perfectly" (*Gl.*² §165.1; *CF* 727). Whereas the notion of final causes usually, but not necessarily, rests on a distinction of ends and means, in art there can be no such no distinction: "Every human work of art is the more perfect, the more it conforms to the idea that elements within it should not be distinguishable as end and means, but are all reciprocally related as parts to the whole" (*Gl.*² §168.1; *CF* 733). Just as in his organic monism each part is itself a whole, so in his aesthetic vision of redemptive divine causality nothing is merely an end or a means: "There is nothing outside the world which could be used as means; all things within it, rather, are so ordered that viewed in connexion with one another they each stand related as parts to the whole; while every particular in itself is so entirely both things—means and end—that each of these categories is constantly abrogating itself and passing over into the other" (733). In other words, the aesthetic vision developed in these last few propositions—a vision which tries to account for divine purpose without appealing to final causes—is a rendition of what Schleiermacher has already described through his adaptation of the dictum *One and All*. The absolute unity of

---

45. Spinoza attributes consciousness to God (one attribute is, after all, thought), but he denies that God acts for a purpose or end: "Nature has no particular goal in view, and . . . final causes are mere human figments." *Ethics,* appendix to part 1; Elwes 2:77.

46. "Nor can we easily conceive the determination of means otherwise than in the form of choice, which means reverting to that very mediate knowledge which we discarded." *Gl.*² §168.1; *CF* 734.

the *One*, which would be obscured by the introduction of ends and means, remains intact.[47] Nothing is external to this creative process, nothing is unrelated, and nothing is without value.

This leads to another point of departure from Spinoza. Schleiermacher's aesthetic vision allows him to speak not only of purposes but also of values: "The divine wisdom is the ground in virtue of which the world, as the [theater] of redemption, is also the absolute revelation of the Supreme Being, and is therefore *good*" (*Gl.*² §169; *CF* 735).[48] Whereas Spinoza denies that goodness and beauty have any ontological status, for Schleiermacher "the whole world was so ordered by God that He could say it was all very good" (*Gl.*² §120.3; *CF* 555).[49] In this he is much closer to neo-Spinozism than to Spinoza himself. Recall that Herder, too, uses aesthetic terms to describe the divine force: "Nothing could be dormant in Him, and what He expressed was Himself, an indivisible wisdom, goodness and omnipotence. . . . Therefore all forces exist which could exist, all together forming an expression of the All-wise, All-good and All-beautiful."[50] A whole system of values is attached to this aesthetic vision as Schleiermacher interprets it—complexity, relationality, freedom, novelty, impartation and interdependence. The universe is an "absolutely harmonious divine work of art" (*Gl.*² §168.1; *CF* 733).

This religious experience of redemption, and the recognition of values that accompanies it, is the presupposition for Schleiermacher's causal monism, as that is developed under the doctrines of creation (divine approval) and preservation (divine sustaining activity). There is, he insists, a necessary connection and continuity between creation and redemption: "By creation all things . . . were disposed with a view to the revelation of God in the flesh, and so as to secure the completest possible impartation thereof to the whole of human nature, and thus to form the Kingdom of God" (*Gl.*² §164.1; *CF* 723).[51] There can be no division between the divine causality

---

47. "It is censurable only when we obscure the absolute unity of divine wisdom by introducing the contrast of end and means." *Gl.*² §168.2; *CF* 735.
48. I follow B. A. Gerrish in departing from H. R. Mackintosh's translation of *Schauplatz* as "scene" since "theater" better captures the aesthetic sense of the text.
49. For Spinoza, such notions are merely abstractions, the result of confusion in the human mind. See *Ethics*, appendix to part 1.
50. *God, Some Conversations,* 169–70. "All senseless fear vanishes when on every hand there is discovered the joyous, clear security of a creation in whose smallest point, God with His wisdom and goodness is present in His totality, working according to the nature of each creature with His undivided and indivisible divine power." Ibid., 117.
51. This in part explains why his worldview cannot be considered nonreligious: "The world of nature is not to be considered as going its own way on the strength of the divine

that preserves the nature system and the divine causality that redeems it.[52] This necessary link, and the divine decree that forges it, illustrates that the divine government is "an inwardly *coherent order*" and a "unity, directed towards a *single goal*" (*Gl.*² §164.3; *CF* 725; emphasis added). The end of divine government ("the one object of the divine world-government" [725]) is the Kingdom of God. It is redemption that gives "unity" to all things and is the "goal" of all things.

This serves to clarify what Schleiermacher means when, under the attribute of omniscience, he says that divine causality must be understood as *absolutely living:* "For a lifeless and blind necessity would not really be something with which we could stand in relation; and such a necessity, conceived as equal to the whole of finite causality yet contrasted with it, would really mean positing [a spirit in existence] alone" (*Gl.*² §55.1; *CF* 219). To say that God is living is to say that divine causality is not "blind" but acts with "purpose" and that this divine causality is something with which we stand "in relation" because there is communication, a divine "self-presentation and impartation" (*Gl.*² §168.1; *CF* 733). In other words, with Schleiermacher's exposition of divine wisdom is given the *content* (divine love), the *aim* (the Kingdom of God), the *motive* (redemption), and the *structure* (a harmonious work of art) of divine causality.

It cannot, however, be emphasized enough that all this is given in the one, eternal divine decree. The purpose is one and is unchanging: redemption *is* creation *is* preservation. The impartation is not to individuals, although it is appropriated by individuals. The divine purpose and communication is fully presented: "Our exposition knows of no unconditioned divine decree regarding the individual, for all individuals are mutually conditioned; it knows only a single unconditioned decree by which the whole, as an undivided system, is what it is in virtue of the divine good-pleasure. . . . [E]verything, and in particular the way in which redemption is realized, is the perfect manifestation at once of the divine good-pleasure and of the divine omnipotence" (*Gl.*² §120.4; *CF* 557–58). It is in light of his understanding of the eternal divine decree of the *living God* that Schleiermacher's "determinism" must be understood. He denies that his view can be mistaken for fatalism and appeals to the scriptural terms (emphasized in the Reformed tradition) *predestination* and *foreordination:* "These words express far

---

preservation, the divine government only exerting influence on it through special isolated acts." *Gl.*² §164.1; *CF* 723.

52. "From the beginning the whole disposition of nature would have been different had it not been that, after sin, redemption through Christ was determined on for the human race." Ibid.

more clearly the relation of each single part to the connected whole, and represent the divine rule of the world as an inwardly coherent order" (*Gl.*² §164.3; *CF* 725). Schleiermacher would therefore agree with Spinoza on the limits set by a consistent interpretation of the eternal decree: "Hence it follows solely from the perfection of God, that God never can decree, or never could have decreed anything but what is."[53] But unlike Spinoza, he still wants to retain some notion of *purpose* and *value*. This is not to say that for Spinoza God or *natura naturans* is "blind," since thought is an attribute of God; God just has no volition. On this point, Schleiermacher is closer to neo-Spinozism than to Spinoza himself, but he departs from both neo-Spinozism and Spinoza in his focus on redemption in explaining the eternal divine decree and the aesthetic view of the universe: "Our recognition of *redemption as the real key* to the understanding of the divine wisdom is itself the *specifically Christian view* of this subject" (*Gl.*² §168.2; *CF* 734; emphasis added).

In many ways, therefore, the issue comes down to Schleiermacher's understanding of the eternal divine decree. He maintains affinities with Spinoza in at least three ways: he interprets the individual through the whole; he does not attribute the human characteristics of intellect and will to God, nor does he allow there to be any potentiality or change in divine knowledge; he rejects any notion of final causes understood as some external, intelligent, purposive cause that operates on individuals through the contrast of means and ends. In each of these cases, however, Schleiermacher also makes a significant departure from Spinoza. Although he diverts his attention from the individual, he can nevertheless be said to be anthropocentric in that the one "goal" of the divine decree is the Kingdom of God, or "the planting and extension of the Christian Church" (*Gl.*² §164; *CF* 723). Humanity remains the object of divine love:

> And just as creation is not concerned simply with individuals (as if each creation of an individual had been a special act), but it is the world that was created, and every individual as such was created only in and with the whole, for the rest not less than for itself, in the same way the activity of the Redeemer too is world-forming, and *its object is human nature,* in the totality of which the powerful

---

53. *Ethics* 1.33, note 2; Elwes 2:72. Spinoza avoids the term *decree* wherever possible, since it has anthropomorphic connotations of volition. When he does use it (i.e., when he considers other discussions of the same and is forced to use the vocabulary of his opponents), he is always careful to qualify it significantly. There is an ordered process of nature that emerges by the "eternal necessity of nature." Wolfson, *Philosophy of Spinoza*, 2:338.

God-consciousness is to be implanted as a new vital principle. (*Gl.*² §100.2; *CF* 427; emphasis added)

Schleiermacher's understanding of the eternal divine decree is more influenced by the Christian, especially Reformed, tradition than by Spinoza. Furthermore, although he is guarded about it, Schleiermacher does introduce some elements of anthropomorphism in his attributing love and wisdom (understood as purpose, not just consciousness) to God. Finally, although he denies final causes, he nevertheless allows for purpose, but always and only understood as being immanent to the system of nature and history. Once again, in this sense, he is closer to neo-Spinozism than to Spinoza himself. In all these departures from Spinoza, however, Schleiermacher remains within the limits set by his own post-Kantian Spinozism while he tries to describe the Christian experience of redemption.

The Living God

The theme of a *living God* can be traced back at least to the pantheist debate between Jacobi and Lessing. In opposition to what he took to be the Spinozist God, Jacobi sought to defend what he called a living God who "can manifest himself only in *that which is alive* and can make himself known to that which is alive only *through love which has been quickened*" (*Spinoza Conversations,* 121). For Jacobi this meant a transcendent, personal God who thinks, wills, and creates out of nothing. Lessing found such an anthropomorphic view of God boring. Herder offered an alternative view by translating Spinoza's *substance* into *substantial force,* which he described as the unity of all active forces, as the "one necessary law" that is imbued with life and directs all things living. "Life," Herder says, "is movement, activity, the activity of an inner force, united with the deepest enjoyment of, and striving for persistence" (*God, Some Conversations,* 188). Schleiermacher followed suit in *Spinozismus* and *Spinozistisches System* by insisting that activity is the final, irreducible characteristic of the infinite. However the infinite be conceived, it cannot be conceived as inactive. Yet this *livingness* must be understood in terms of a post-Kantian Spinozism: it assumes an organic monism, which views the universe as a living system of dynamic forces that inheres in the infinite; this relation of inherency and immanence requires a nonanthropomorphic God in whom will is not separated from intellect.

Schleiermacher carried these same themes over into his *Reden,* where he gave them romantic expression. There the word *living* runs as a refrain throughout all editions. The divine is described in terms of the "infinite and living nature" (Crouter, 103; R^1 53); religion is the intuition of the "ever-active, ever-living, and serene activity of the world and its spirit" (Crouter, 105; R^1 57); "religion shows you how the living gods hate nothing as much as death" (Crouter, 126; R^1 102); "even God cannot be imagined in religion except as active, and no one has ever denied the divine life and activity of the universe" (Crouter, 138; R^1 130). The *living God* is that higher unity, the "universal, divine connection of all things" (Expl. 2.7; Oman, 107). The idea of the *living God,* insofar as it expresses the love that underlies the unity in plurality, also expresses the teleological thrust of the *One and All,* but it does so in aesthetic terms rather than through an appeal to final causes: "As it is so difficult to think of a personality as truly infinite and incapable of suffering, a great distinction should be drawn between a personal God and a living God. The latter idea alone distinguishes from materialistic pantheism and atheistic blind necessity. Within that limit any further wavering in respect of personality must be left to the representative imagination and the dialectic conscience, and where the pious sense exists, they will guard each other" (Expl. 2.19; Oman, 116).

In the *Glaubenslehre,* the very notion of a "system of nature" obviously assumes that there is some order; the fact that this particular notion of a nature system means to describe an organic whole only underscores the teleological aspect by describing this order as dynamic, as an "ordered exercise of power" ($Gl.^2$ §54.4; CF 215). The term *organic monism* is intended to describe what Schleiermacher sees as a living, organic whole. A whole, as opposed to an aggregate, is structured in such a way that each part contributes to the whole at the same time that it depends on that whole; the parts work together to guarantee the continuing health of the whole and, consequently, of themselves. Taken alone, the notion of a whole does not itself admit of any notion of purpose, since conceivably such a whole could result from either random mutation or blind necessity.[54] Hence

---

54. For example, Charles Hartshorne describes an *inorganic whole:* "The notion of absolutely non-purposive or inorganic wholes throws no light whatever on the existence or nature of purpose. . . . But given mere purposeless stuff or 'matter,' we have not, in so far, any notion of purpose." *The Logic of Perfection* (LaSalle, Ill.: Open Court, 1962), 194.

the importance of the modifier "organic": there is a continual process and striving, the end or purpose of which is *life;* this end cannot be understood in static terms, since the striving is always toward new forms of life that become increasingly complex. The relationality involved in an organic whole is fundamentally internal, hence the emphasis on sustaining, rather than efficient or transitive, causality. There is a real exchange of forces, an exchange which cannot be merely accidental in that it includes the being of a thing, since for Schleiermacher being can never be separated from activity. Thus activity, or power, or force (and, according to their very definitions, the exchange of these) constitutes the very nature of reality. The more intense the exchange of forces and the more complex the immersion into the system of relations, the more life (and wholeness) there is. Thus already, along with ends, a certain understanding of value (another aspect of a teleological view) is suggested in Schleiermacher's *organic monism:* inherency, complexity, interdependence, relationality, plurality, movement, and novelty. This organic monism, however, is necessarily a *causal monism:* the livingness of the *All* is possible only because of the livingness of the *One* on which it is absolutely dependent; the divine causality fully coincides with, and is completely presented in, the whole nexus of natural causality. The livingness of the *One* is not some "blind" force or naked process with which we could not stand in relation, for by *living* Schleiermacher means not only *active* but *communicative.* The *living God* is the redeeming God whose self-impartation is the exchange of life, or better, of love. Yet this love cannot be understood as being part of some divine personality, for not only would such an understanding sentimentalize and trivialize divine love, it would also be irreverent and, in the end, unintelligible. It would, in other words, trespass the limits of piety.

Schleiermacher's *living God,* therefore, is the "third alternative" to Jacobi's personal God and Spinoza's *natura naturans.* While influenced by Spinoza and neo-Spinozism, Schleiermacher's doctrine of God cannot be simplistically interpreted as "Spinozist" or "pantheistic." Nor can the two parts of the *Glaubenslehre* be separated, one being "Spinozist" and the other "Christian." The livingness or intentionality of divine causality is to be found consistently in both parts, although its specific *content, motive, value,* and *aim* is only given in part 2. The most that can be said is that, on the one hand, Schleiermacher's doctrine of God is *in part* a development of his post-Kantian Spinozism that can be traced back at least to 1793, and on the other hand, it could be considered an "acceptable" form of pantheism (i.e., neither a simple identity of God and nature nor a crude materialism) that is best described through his unique adaptation of the ancient dictum *One and All*. For Schleiermacher, the *One and All* is at once an expression of the relation between divine transcendence and immanence and a regulative principle which guides us in our speech about God. The fundamental experience of God is not that of some abstract or lifeless *One;* rather, it is the experience of having been redeemed through the communication and impartation of the divine love. Once understood as he defines them, neither his "pantheism" nor his "Spinozism" is inherently incompatible with Christian dogmatics; neither undermines the notion of the divine transcendence. If anything, for Schleiermacher they function so as to guarantee the stability of Christian doctrine.

Bibliography

Primary Works

Calvin, John. *Institutes of the Christian Religion* (1559). 2 vols. Edited by John T. McNeill. Translated by Ford Lewis Battles. Philadelphia: Westminster Press, 1960.
Herder, Johann Gottfried. *God, Some Conversations* (1787). Translated and with an introduction by Frederick Burkhardt. New York: Veritas, 1940. Reprint, Indianapolis: Bobbs-Merrill, 1962.
Jacobi, Friedrich Heinrich. *David Hume über den Glauben, oder Idealismus und Realismus* (1787). Facsimile of the 1815 edition. The Philosophy of David Hume. Lewis White Beck, general editor. New York: Garland Publishing, 1983.
———. "Open Letter to Fichte" (1799). In *Philosophy of German Idealism*. Translated and edited by Ernst Behler. New York: Continuum, 1987.
———. *Über die Lehre des Spinoza, in Briefen an den Herrn Moses Mendelssohn* (1785, 1789). In Scholz, *Die Hauptschriften*. Translated by G. Vallée, J. B. Lawson, and C. G. Chapple under the title *The Spinoza Conversations between Lessing and Jacobi: Text with Excerpts from the Ensuing Controversy*. Edited by Gérard Vallée. Lanham, Md.: University Press of America, 1988.
Kant, Immanuel. *Critique of Judgement* (1790). Translated by James Creed Meredith. Oxford: Oxford University Press, 1986.
———. *Critique of Practical Reason* (1788). Translated by Lewis White Beck. New York: Liberal Arts Press, 1956.
———. *Critique of Pure Reason* (1781). Translated by Norman Kemp Smith. New York: St. Martin's Press, 1965.
Luther, Martin. "Disputation Concerning Justification" (1536). In *Luther's Works*, vol. 34. Translated and edited by Lewis W. Spitz. Philadelphia: Muhlenberg Press, 1960.
———. *Lectures on Galatians* (1535). In *Luther's Works*, vols. 26–27. Translated and edited by Jaroslav Pelikan. St. Louis: Concordia Publishing House, 1963.
———. *Martin Luther: Selections from His Writings*. Translated and edited by John Dillenberger. Garden City, N.Y.: Anchor Books, Doubleday, 1961.
Reinhold, Karl Leonhard. *Versuch einer neuen Theorie des menschlichen Vorstellungsvermögens*. Prague and Jena: 1789.
Schleiermacher, Friedrich Daniel Ernst. *Aus Schleiermachers Leben in Briefen*. 2d ed. Vols. 1 and 2. Berlin: Reimer, 1860–63. Translated by Frederica Maclean Rowan under the title *The Life of Schleiermacher as Unfolded in His Autobiography and Letters*, 2 vols. London: Smith, Elder, 1860.

―――. *Briefe* (1774–1800). In *KGA* 5/1–3. Edited by Andreas Arndt and Wolfgang Virmond.
―――. *Der christliche Glaube nach den Grundsätzen der evangelischen Kirche im Zusammenhange dargestellt* (1821/22). 2 vols. Edited by Hermann Peiter. Berlin: Walter de Gruyter, 1984.
―――. *Der christliche Glaube nach den Grundsätzen der evangelischen Kirche im Zusammenhange dargestellt* (1830–31). 2 vols. 7th ed. Edited by Martin Redeker. Berlin: Walter de Gruyter, 1960. Translated by H. R. Mackintosh et al., under the title *The Christian Faith*. Edinburgh: T. and T. Clark, 1928, 1976.
―――. *Dialektik*. In *Schleiermachers sämmtliche Werke*. Edited by Ludwig Jonas. Berlin: Reimer, 1839.
―――. *Grundlinien einer Kritik der bisherigen Sittenlehre* (1803). In *Schleiermachers Werke*. Edited by Otto Braun and Johannes Bauer. Leipzig, 1928. Reprint, Aalen: Scientia Verlag, 1967.
―――. *Kritische Gesamtausgabe*. Edited by Hans-Joachim Birkner, Gerhard Ebeling, Hermann Fischer, Heinz Kimmerle, and Kurt-Victor Selge. Berlin and New York: Walter de Gruyter, 1980– . [Cited as *KGA* by part and volume.]
―――. *Kurze Darstellung des Spinozistischen Systems* (1793/94). In *KGA* 1/1:559–82. Edited by Günter Meckenstock.
―――. *Monologen. Eine Neujahrsgabe* (1800). In *KGA* 1/3:1–61. Edited by Günter Meckenstock. Translated by Horace Leland Friess under the title *Schleiermacher's Soliloquies: An English Translation of the Monologen*. Chicago: Open Court, 1926.
―――. *Spinozismus* (1793/94). In *KGA* 1/1:511–58. Edited by Günter Meckenstock.
―――. *Über das höchste Gut*. In *KGA* 1/1: 81–125. Translated by H. Victor Froese under the title *On the Highest Good*. Schleiermacher: Studies-and-Translations 10. Lewiston: Edwin Mellen Press, 1992.
―――. *Über die Freiheit* (1790/92). In *KGA* 1/1:217–356. Edited by Günter Meckenstock. Translated by Albert L. Blackwell under the title *On Freedom*. Schleiermacher: Studies-and-Translations 9. Lewiston: Edwin Mellen Press, 1992.
―――. *Über die Glaubenslehre. Zwei Sendschreiben an Lücke* (1829). In *KGA* 1/10:307–94. Edited by Hans-Friedrich Traulsen. Translated by James Duke and Francis Fiorenza under the title *On the "Glaubenslehre": Two Letters to Dr. Lücke*. American Academy of Religion Texts and Translations. James A. Massey, general editor. Chico, Calif.: Scholars Press, 1981.
―――. *Über die Religion. Reden an die Gebildeten unter ihren Verächtern* (1799). First critical edition, *Friedrich Schleiermacher's Reden Ueber die Religion*. Edited by G. Ch. Pünjer. Braunschweig: C. A. Schwetschke, 1879. Pünjer's edition includes the revisions made in the second (1806) and third (1821) editions of the *Reden*. Second critical edition in *KGA* 1/2:185–326. Edited by Günter Meckenstock. First edition (1799) translated by Richard Crouter under the title *On Religion: Speeches to its Cultured Despisers*. Cambridge: Cambridge University Press, 1988. Third edition (1821) translated by John Oman under the title *On Religion: Speeches to Its Cultured Despisers*. New York: Harper & Row, 1958. Reprint, Louisville, Ky.: Westminster/John Knox Press, 1994.

Scholz, Heinrich, ed. *Die Hauptschriften zum Pantheismusstreit zwischen Jacobi und Mendelssohn*. Berlin: Reuther & Reichard, 1916.
Spinoza, Benedict de. *Ethics*. Translated by R.H.M. Elwes. *The Works of Spinoza*, volume 2. New York: Dover Publications, 1955. Critical edition in English, *The Collected Works of Spinoza*, volume 1. Translated and edited by Edwin Curley. Princeton, N.J.: Princeton University Press, 1985.

———. *A Theologico-Political Treatise*. Translated by R.H.M. Elwes. *The Works of Spinoza*, volume 1. New York: Dover Publications, 1951.

Secondary Works Cited

Allison, Henry E. *The Kant-Eberhard Controversy*. Baltimore: Johns Hopkins University Press, 1973.
Barth, Karl. *The Theology of Schleiermacher: Lectures at Göttingen*. Edited by Dietrich Ritschl. Translated by Geoffrey W. Bromiley. Grand Rapids, Mich.: William B. Eerdman's, 1982.
Bayle, Pierre. *Dictionnaire historique et critique* (5th edition, 1740). Translated by Richard H. Popkin under the title *Historical and Critical Dictionary: Selections*. Indianapolis: Bobbs-Merrill, 1965.
Beck, Lewis White. *Early German Philosophy: Kant and His Predecessors*. Cambridge: Harvard University Press, 1969.
Beiser, Frederick C. *The Fate of Reason: German Philosophy from Kant to Fichte*. Cambridge: Harvard University Press, 1987.
Beisser, Friedrich. *Schleiermachers Lehre von Gott: Dargestellt nach seinen "Reden" und seiner "Glaubenslehre."* Göttingen: Vandenhoeck & Ruprecht, 1970.
Bell, David. *Spinoza in Germany from 1670 to the Age of Goethe*. Biltrell Series of Dissertations 7. London: The Institute of German Studies, University of London, 1984.
Blackwell, Albert L. "The Antagonistic Correspondence of 1801 between Chaplain Sack and His Protégé Schleiermacher." *Harvard Theological Review* 74, no. 1 (1981): 101–21.

———. *Schleiermacher's Early Philosophy of Life: Determinism, Freedom, and Phantasy*. Harvard Theological Studies 33. Greenville, S.C.: Scholars Press, 1982.

———. "Schleiermacher's Sermon at Nathanael's Grave." *Journal of Religion* 57, no. 1 (January 1977): 64–75.
Bowie, Andrew. *Aesthetics and Subjectivity: From Kant to Nietzsche*. Manchester: Manchester University Press, 1990.
Boyd, George N. "Schleiermacher's 'Über den Unterschied zwischen Naturgesetz und Sittengesetz.'" *Journal of Religious Ethics* 17, no. 2 (Fall 1989): 41–49.
Brandt, Richard B. *The Philosophy of Schleiermacher: The Development of His Theory of Scientific and Religious Knowledge*. New York: Greenwood Press, 1968.
Camerer, Theodor. *Spinoza und Schleiermacher: Die kritische Lösung des von Spinoza hinterlassenen Problems*. Stuttgart and Berlin: J. G. Cotta'sche, 1903.
Cobb, John. *Living Options in Protestant Theology*. Philadelphia: Westminster Press, 1962.

Crouter, Richard. "Rhetoric and Substance in Schleiermacher's Revision of *The Christian Faith* (1821–22)." *Journal of Religion* 60, no. 3 (July 1980): 285–306.

Delbrück, Johann Friedrich Ferdinand. *Erörterungen einiger Hauptstücke in Dr. Friedrich Schleiermachers christliche Glaubenslehre.* Bonn: Adolf Marcus, 1827.

Di Giovanni, George. "From Jacobi's Philosophical Novel to Fichte's Idealism: Some Comments on the 1789–99 'Atheism Dispute.'" *Journal of the History of Philosophy* 27 (January 1989): 75–100.

Dilthey, Wilhelm. *Leben Schleiermachers* (1870). In *Gesammelte Schriften*, vols. 13–14. Edited by Martin Redeker. Göttingen: Vandenhoeck & Ruprecht, 1970.

Donagan, Alan. *Spinoza.* Chicago: University of Chicago Press, 1988.

Duke, James O., and Robert F. Streetman, eds. *Barth and Schleiermacher: Beyond the Impasse?* Philadelphia: Fortress Press, 1988.

Ebeling, Gerhard. "Schleiermacher's Doctrine of the Divine Attributes." In Funk, *Schleiermacher as Contemporary.*

Faull, Katherine M. "Schleiermacher—A Feminist? Or, How to Read Gender Inflected Theology." In *Schleiermacher and Feminism: Sources, Evaluations, and Responses.* Edited by Iain G. Nicol. Schleiermacher: Studies-and-Translations 12. Lewiston: Edwin Mellen Press, 1992.

Flückiger, Felix. *Philosophie und Theologie bei Schleiermacher.* Zollikon-Zürich: Evangelischer Verlag, 1947.

Forstman, Jack. *A Romantic Triangle: Schleiermacher and Early German Romanticism.* American Academy of Religion Studies in Religion 13. Missoula, Mont.: Scholars Press, 1977.

Frei, Hans W. "Niebuhr's Theological Background." In *Faith and Ethics: The Theology of H. Richard Niebuhr.* Edited by Paul Ramsey. New York: Harper & Bros., 1957.

Funk, Robert W., ed. *Schleiermacher as Contemporary.* New York: Herder & Herder, 1970.

Gadamer, Hans-Georg. "Schleiermacher Platonicien." *Archives de Philosophie* 32 (1969): 28–39.

Gerrish, B. A. "Faith and Existence in the Philosophy of F. H. Jacobi." In *Witness and Existence: Essays in Honor of Schubert M. Ogden.* Edited by Philip E. Devenish and George L. Goodwin. Chicago: University of Chicago Press, 1989.

———. "Nature and the Theater of Redemption: Schleiermacher on Christian Dogmatics and the Creation Story." *Ex Auditu* 3 (1987): 120–36.

———. *The Old Protestantism and the New: Essays on the Reformation Heritage.* Chicago: University of Chicago Press, 1982.

———. "The Secret Religion of Germany: Christian Piety and the Pantheism Controversy." *Journal of Religion* 67, no. 4 (October 1987): 437–55.

———. *Tradition and the Modern World: Reformed Theology in the Nineteenth Century.* Chicago: University of Chicago Press, 1978.

Graf, Friedrich Wilhelm. "Ursprüngliches Gefühl unmittelbarer Koinzidenz des Differenten: Zur Modifikation des Religionsbegriffs in den verschiedenen Auflagen von Schleiermachers 'Reden über die Religion.'" *Zeitschrift für Theologie und Kirche* 75, no. 2 (1978): 147–86.

Gram, Moltke S. "Intellectual Intuition: The Continuity Thesis." *Journal of the History of Ideas* 42 (1981): 287–304.
Grau, Gerhard Heinrich. "God in Experience: An Interpretation of Schleiermacher's Doctrine of God Concluding with a Reappraisal of His Understanding of the Doctrine of the Trinity." Ph.D. diss., Princeton Theological Seminary, 1976.
Grene, Marjorie, ed. *Spinoza: A Collection of Critical Essays.* Garden City, N.Y.: Anchor Books, 1973.
Grunwald, Max. *Spinoza in Deutschland: Gekrönte Preisschrift.* Berlin, 1897.
Guyer, Paul. "Feeling and Freedom: Kant on Aesthetics and Morality." *Journal of Aesthetics and Art Criticism* 48 (1990): 137–46.
Hartshorne, Charles. *The Logic of Perfection.* LaSalle, Ill.: Open Court, 1962.
Hartshorne, Charles, and William L. Reese. *Philosophers Speak of God.* Chicago: University of Chicago Press, 1953. Midway Reprint, 1976.
Harvey, Van. "A Word in Defense of Schleiermacher's Method." *Journal of Religion* 42, no. 3 (July 1962):151–70.
Herms, Eilert. "Platonismus und Aristotelismus in Schleiermachers Ethik." In Sorrentino, *Schleiermacher's Philosophy and the Philosophical Tradition.*
Hunt, John. *Pantheism and Christianity.* 1884. Port Washington, N.Y.: Kennikat Press, 1970.
Jantzen, Grace. *God's World, God's Body.* Philadelphia: Westminster Press, 1984.
Junker, Maureen. *Das Urbild des Gottesbewußtseins: Zur Entwicklung der Religionstheorie und Christologie Schleiermachers von der ersten zur zweiten Auflage der Glaubenslehre.* Berlin: Walter de Gruyter, 1990.
Krakauer, Moses. "Zur Geschichte des Spinozismus in Deutschland während der ersten Hälfte des achtzehnten Jahrhunderts." Ph.D. diss., University of Breslau, 1881.
Krämer, Hans Joachim. *Plato and the Foundations of Metaphysics: A Work on the Theory of the Principles and Unwritten Doctrines of Plato with a Collection of the Fundamental Documents.* Edited and translated by John R. Catan. Albany: State University of New York Press, 1990.
Krieg, Carl E. "Schleiermacher: On the Divine Nature." *Religion in Life* 42, no. 4 (Winter 1973): 514–25.
Lamm, Julia A. "The Early Philosophical Roots of Schleiermacher's Notion of *Gefühl*, 1788–1794." *Harvard Theological Review* 87, no. 1 (1994): 67–105.
Lermond, Lucia. *The Form of Man: Human Essence in Spinoza's "Ethic."* Brill's Studies in Intellectual History 11. A. J. Vanderjact, general editor. Leiden: E. J. Brill, 1988.
Mackintosh, Hugh Ross. *Types of Modern Theology: Schleiermacher to Barth.* New York: Charles Scribner's Sons, 1937.
Mandelbaum, Maurice, and Eugene Freeman, eds. *Spinoza: Essays in Interpretation.* LaSalle, Ill.: Open Court, 1975.
McFarland, Thomas. *Coleridge and the Pantheist Tradition.* Oxford: Clarendon Press, 1969.
McGinn, Bernard. Introduction to *Meister Eckhart: The Essential Sermons, Commentaries, Treatises, and Defense.* Translated by Edmund Colledge, O.S.A., and McGinn. The Classics of Western Spirituality. New York: Paulist Press, 1981.
Meckenstock, Günter. *Deterministische Ethik und kritische Theologie: Die Auseinandersetzung des frühen Schleiermacher mit Kant und Spinoza, 1789–1794.* Berlin: Walter de Gruyter, 1988.

———. "Schleiermachers Auseinandersetzung mit Fichte." In Sorrentino, *Schleiermacher's Philosophy and the Philosophical Tradition.*
Mehl, Paul Frederick. "Schleiermacher's Mature Doctrine of God as Found in the *Dialektik* of 1822 and the Second Edition of *The Christian Faith* (1830–31)." Ph.D. diss., Columbia University, 1961.
Mock, Chang Kyun. "The Development of Schleiermacher's Doctrine of God: A Comparative Study of the Introduction and Part I of the First and Second Editions of Schleiermacher's *Glaubenslehre.*" Ph.D. diss., Drew University, 1986.
Moenkemeyer, Heinz. *François Hemsterhuis.* Boston: Twayne Publishers, 1975.
Moore, Walter. "Schleiermacher as a Calvinist: A Comparison of Calvin and Schleiermacher on Providence and Predestination." *Scottish Journal of Theology* 24, no. 2 (1971):161–83.
Nicolson, Marjorie Hope. *Newton Demands the Muse: Newton's "Optics" and the Eighteenth Century Poets.* Princeton: Princeton University Press, 1946.
Niebuhr, Richard R. "Schleiermacher and the Names of God: A Consideration of Schleiermacher in Relation to Our Theisms." In Funk, *Schleiermacher as Contemporary.*
———. *Schleiermacher on Christ and Religion: A New Introduction.* New York: Scribner's, 1964
Nisbet, H. B. *Herder and the Philosophy and History of Science.* Modern Humanities Research Association Dissertation Series. Cambridge, Mass.: The Modern Human Research Association, 1970.
Nowak, Kurt. *Schleiermacher und die Frühromantik: Eine literaturgeschichtliche Studie zum romantischen Religionsverständnis und Menschenbild am Ende des 18. Jahrhunderts in Deutschland.* Göttingen: Vandenhoeck & Ruprecht, 1986.
Ogden, Schubert M. *The Reality of God.* New York: Harper & Row, 1977.
Pannenberg, Wolfhart. *Anthropology in Theological Perspective.* Philadelphia: Westminster Press, 1985.
Peacocke, A. R. *Creation and the World of Science.* The Bampton Lectures, 1978. Oxford: Clarendon Press, 1979.
Pelikan, Jaroslav. "Creation and Causality in the History of Christian Thought." In *Issues in Evolution.* Edited by Sol Tax and Charles Callender. Vol. 3 of *Evolution After Darwin.* Edited by Sol Tax. Chicago: University of Chicago Press, 1960.
Pike, Nelson. *God and Timelessness.* London: Routledge & Kegan Paul, 1970.
Redeker, Martin. *Schleiermacher: Life and Thought.* Translated by John Wallhausser. Philadelphia: Fortress Press, 1973.
Saarnivaara, Uuras. *Luther Discovers the Gospel: New Light Upon Luther's Way from Medieval Catholicism to Evangelical Faith.* St. Louis: Concordia, 1951.
Schröder, Winfried. *Spinoza in der deutschen Frühaufklärung.* Würzburg: Königshausen & Neumann, 1987.
Smith, Samuel David, III. "A Study of the Relation between the Doctrine of Creation and the Doctrine of Revelation through the Created Universe in the Thought of John Calvin, Friedrich Schleiermacher and Paul Tillich." Ph.D. diss., Vanderbilt University, 1965.
Sorrentino, Sergio. ed. *Schleiermacher's Philosophy and the Philosophical Tradition.* Schleiermacher: Studies-and-Translations 11. Lewiston: Edwin Mellen Press, 1992.

Spiegler, Gerhard. *The Eternal Covenant: Schleiermacher's Experiment in Cultural Theology.* New York: Harper & Row, 1967.
Süskind, Hermann. *Der Einfluß Schellings auf die Entwicklung von Schleiermachers System.* 1909. Reprint, Tübingen: J.C.B. Mohr, 1983.
Taylor, Charles. *Sources of the Self: The Making of the Modern Identity.* Cambridge: Harvard University Press, 1989.
Thandeka, "Schleiermacher's *Dialektik:* The Discovery of the Self that Kant Lost." *Harvard Theological Review* 85, no. 4 (1992): 433–52.
Thiel, John E. *God and World in Schleiermacher's Dialektik and Glaubenslehre: Criticism and the Methodology of Dogmatics.* Basler und Berner Studien zur historischen und systematischen Theologie. Bern: Peter Lang, 1981.
Tice, Terrence N. "Schleiermacher's Conception of Religion: 1799–1831." *Archivio di Filosofia* 52 (1984): 333–56.
Tillich, Paul. "Realism and Faith" (1948). In *Paul Tillich: Main Works / Hauptwerke.* Vol. 4, *Writings in the Philosophy of Religion / Religionsphilosophische Schriften.* Edited by John Clayton. Berlin and New York: Walter de Gruyter, 1987.
———. *Systematic Theology.* 3 vols. Chicago: University of Chicago Press, 1951–63.
Vallée, Gérard, ed. *The Spinoza Conversations between Lessing and Jacobi: Text with Excerpts from the Ensuing Controversy.* Translated by G. Vallée, J. B. Lawson, and C. G. Chapple. Lanham, Md.: University Press of America, 1988.
Vitiello, Vincenzo. "The Otherness of God: Schleiermacher and Barth." In Sorrentino, *Schleiermacher's Philosophy and the Philosophical Tradition.*
Wallhauser, John. "Schleiermacher's Critique of Ethical Reason: Toward a Systematic Ethics." *Journal of Religious Ethics* 17, no. 4 (Fall 1989): 25–39.
Walzel, Oskar. *Deutsche Romantik.* Leipzig: B. G. Teubner, 1923. Translated by Alma Elise Lussky under the title *German Romanticism.* New York: G. P. Putnam's Sons, 1932.
Wicks, Jared, S.J. *Man's Yearning for Grace: Luther's Early Spiritual Teaching.* Washington, D.C.: Corpus Publications, 1968.
Williams, Robert R. *Schleiermacher the Theologian: The Construction of the Doctrine of God.* Philadelphia: Fortress Press, 1978.
Wolfson, Harry Austryn. *The Philosophy of Spinoza: Unfolding the Latent Processes of His Reasoning.* 2 vols. 1934. Reprint, New York: Schocken Books, 1969.
Yovel, Yirmiyahu. *Spinoza and Other Heretics.* Vol. 1, *The Marrano of Reason.* Vol. 2, *The Adventures of Immanence.* Princeton, N.J.: Princeton University Press, 1989.
Zammito, John H. *The Genesis of Kant's "Critique of Judgment."* Chicago: University of Chicago Press, 1992.

Index of Names

Allison, Henry E., 14n. 5
Aquinas, Saint Thomas, 148n. 54, 163–64n. 12
Aristotle, 29, 41n. 52, 93, 168n. 34
Augustine, Saint, 177

Barth, Karl, 2n. 6, 3n. 7, 111n. 29, 189–90
Baur, Ferdinand Christian, 131
Bayle, Pierre, 3, 16–17, 19
Beck, Lewis White, 17n. 16
Beiser, Frederick C., 17n. 16, 47n. 63
Beisser, Friedrich, 4n. 12, 82n. 38, 124–25, 199–200
Bell, David, 16n. 10
Blackwell, Albert L., 1n. 1, 4n. 11, 5n. 14, 38, 60n. 8, 90n. 46, 93n. 57, 106n. 17, 121n. 55
Böhme, Christian Friedrich, 1n. 2
Bowie, Andrew, 75n. 27
Boyd, George N., 179–80n. 60
Brandt, Richard B., 4n. 11, 33n. 41, 73, 84n. 38, 114n. 41, 119n. 49, 164n. 14, 168n. 34, 187n. 78
Brinckmann, Carl Gustav von, 13n. 2
Brunner, Emil, 111n. 29

Calvin, John, 177, 201–2, 206, 209–10
Camerer, Theodor, 4n. 10
Cicero, 59, 70
Cobb, John, 3n. 9
Crouter, Richard, 74n. 26, 82n. 38, 110n. 28
Curley, Edwin, 27n. 31

Delbrück, Johann Friedrich Ferdinand, 1n. 2, 99, 111n. 29, 112, 113, 160
Di Giovanni, George, 50n. 67
Dilthey, Wilhelm, 4n. 10, 75n. 28, 92n. 50, 93n. 56, 160

Dohna, Count Alexander von, 58
Donagan, Alan, 27n. 31
Duke, James, 1n. 2

Ebeling, Gerhard, 112n. 31, 141n. 40, 148n. 56, 213n. 25, 216n. 36, 219n. 43
Eberhard, Johann August, 14
Eckhart, Meister, 148n. 54

Faull, Katherine M., 87n. 43
Fichte, Johann Gottlieb, 14, 22, 24, 25, 41n. 52, 44, 59, 61, 62, 75, 80, 81, 85, 86, 112, 115, 123
Fiorenza, Francis, 1n. 2
Forstman, Jack, 57n. 1
Frei, Hans W., 75n. 29, 186n. 75, 193

Gadamer, Hans-Georg, 9, 93
Gerrish, B. A., 18n. 16, 24n. 26, 54n. 72, 111n. 29, 119n. 50, 130n. 10, 208n. 16, 210n. 20, 222n. 48
Goethe, Johann Wolfgang von, 18, 20, 21
Goodwin, George L., 25n. 26
Graf, Friedrich Wilhelm, 82n. 38
Gram, Moltke S., 47n. 62
Grau, Gerhard Heinrich, 130n. 12
Grunow, Eleonore, 93
Grunwald, Max, 16n. 10
Guyer, Paul, 37n. 44

Hallet, H. F., 27
Hartshorne, Charles, 3n. 9, 65n. 13, 171–72, 226n. 54
Harvey, Van, 111n. 29
Hemsterhuis, François, 49–50, 51, 54, 92
Herder, Johann Gottfried, 5, 14, 17, 20–21, 22n. 25, 26, 78, 84, 92, 112n. 31, 159,

Index of Names

162, 167n. 32, 168–69n. 35, 173n. 45, 180nn. 62–63, 222, 225
Herms, Eilert, 91
Herz, Henriette, 58, 92
Hume, David, 27n. 31
Hunt, John, 127n. 2

Jacobi, Friedrich Heinrich, 1, 2n. 5, 3, 4, 5, 6, 11, 14, 17–21, 61, 63, 65, 81, 90, 112n. 31, 159, 161, 176, 199, 225, 227
  David Hume über den Glauben, 37n. 43
  "Open Letter to Fichte," 22
  philosophy of faith, 21–24
  Schleiermacher's response to, 25–56, 62, 63, 70n. 21, 77, 92, 94, 99, 101, 104, 119n. 52, 128, 132, 162–64, 191n. 90
  Über die Lehre des Spinoza, 2n. 5, 3n. 8, 13, 15, 17–19, 21, 24, 25, 45, 77, 96–97, 162.
Jantzen, Grace, 161
Jonas, Ludwig, 124
Junker, Maureen, 110n. 28

Kant, Immanuel, 5, 6, 14, 22, 25, 26, 27n. 31, 30, 31, 32, 34, 36, 40, 41n. 52, 42, 43, 44–46, 47, 48, 49, 50, 59, 60, 61, 66, 69, 73, 75n. 27, 77, 80, 86, 91, 92, 93, 123, 128, 168n. 34, 175, 187n. 78, 193
  Critique of Judgment, 40n. 51, 43
  Critique of Practical Reason, 14, 15, 43n. 58, 45n. 59, 69
  Critique of Pure Reason, 15
  Schleiermacher's appropriation of, 9, 66
Krakauer, Moses, 16n. 10
Krämer, Hans Joachim, 93n. 56

Lamm, Julia A., 15n. 8
Leibniz, Gottfried Wilhelm von, 14, 25, 30, 34, 42, 67, 92n. 49, 138n. 29
Lermond, Lucia, 33n. 39
Lessing, Gotthold Ephraim, 5, 17–21, 22, 23, 24, 49n. 66, 55, 101, 123, 159, 225
Lücke, Gottfried Christian Friedrich, 110, 112, 129, 130, 148, 157, 160, 184n. 71, 195, 213
Luther, Martin, 201–6, 209, 210

McFarland, Thomas, 16n. 10, 17n. 15, 18n. 16
McGinn, Bernard, 148n. 54
Meckenstock, Günter, 4n. 10, 14n. 4, 47, 50, 61n. 9
Mehl, Paul Frederick, 10–11n. 18, 124n. 61
Mendelssohn, Moses, 6, 17, 18, 19–21, 22, 24, 25, 48, 53
Mock, Chang Kyun, 110n. 28, 164n. 14
Moenkemeyer, Heinz, 50n. 66
Moore, Walter, 3n. 7, 211n. 21
Moretto, Giovanni, 61n. 9

Nicolson, Marjorie Hope, 33n. 41
Niebuhr, Richard R., 2n. 6, 65n. 13, 112n. 32, 113n. 35, 127n. 5, 143n. 46, 160–61, 174n. 46, 179n. 59, 180–81, 219n. 43
Nikolaus of Cusa, 89n. 44, 146n. 51
Nisbet, H. B., 33n. 41, 167n. 32, 168–69n. 35
Nowak, Kurt, 57n. 1

Ogden, Schubert, 3n. 9, 24–25n. 26
Oldenburg, Henry, 16, 32, 69n. 17, 150n. 61

Pannenberg, Wolfhart, 173n. 45, 183n. 67
Paul, Saint, 205
Peacocke, A. R., 167n. 32
Pelikan, Jaroslav, 136n. 21
Pike, Nelson, 127n. 3, 137n. 27
Plato, 9, 41n. 52, 58, 60, 75n. 28, 91–94, 121, 168n. 34, 125

Redeker, Martin, 110n. 27, 160
Reimarus, Elise, 18
Reinhold, Karl Leonhard, 14, 47n. 63, 116n. 42
Rice, Lee C., 33n. 38
Rust, Isaaco, 1n. 2

Saarnivaara, Uuraas, 204n. 11
Sack, Friedrich Samuel Gottfried, 1, 56, 58–59, 90–91, 96, 99, 101, 104, 107n. 19, 119n. 52, 199
Sandbach-Marshall, Edith, 164n. 14
Schelling, Friedrich Wilhelm Joseph von, 168n. 34

Schlegel, Friedrich, 58, 93
Schleiermacher, Johann Gottlieb Adolph, 13n. 1, 60n. 8
Schleiermacher, Friedrich Daniel Ernst
  Dialektik, 4n. 10, 5, 10, 124–26, 146n. 51, 161
  Glaubenslehre (The Christian faith), 1, 4n. 12, 5, 6–7, 8, 9, 10, 10n. 18, 15, 89n. 45, 91, 94, 95–96, 97–98n. 4, 100, 101, 102, 104, 109–26, 127–57, 159–97, 199–228
  Grundlinien, 10, 93
  Kurze Darstellung des Spinozistischen Systems, 9, 10, 13, 24–56, 61, 73, 77, 81, 88, 119n. 52, 150n. 65, 175n. 48, 186, 188n. 82, 225
  Reden (Speeches), 1, 4n. 12, 5, 6, 10, 38, 54, 56, 57–94, 95–109, 119, 120, 121, 123, 128, 132, 142n. 44, 161, 164n. 14, 177, 178n. 56, 181, 185–86, 188n. 82, 191, 193, 194, 200, 212n. 22, 226
  Spinozismus, 9, 10, 13, 24–56, 57, 61, 67, 70n. 21, 72, 77, 81, 98, 119n. 52, 175n. 48, 186, 188n. 82, 225
  Über die Freiheit (On freedom), 5n. 14, 15, 34n. 42, 37, 38, 39, 41, 45, 52n. 70, 70, 90, 125, 175n. 48
Scholz, Heinrich, 17n. 16
Schröder, Winfried, 16n. 10
Shaftesbury, Third Earl of (Anthony), 4n. 10, 92, 93, 160
Smith, Samuel David, 2n. 6, 127n. 4
Sorrentino, Sergio, 131n. 13
Spiegler, Gerhard, 11n. 18, 64–65n. 12, 65n. 12, 13, 124n. 61, 161
Spinoza, Benedict de
  philosophy of, 15n. 9, 22n. 25, 26–28, 32–33, 37–38, 53–54, 68–70nn. 17–19, 78n. 35, 98n. 35, 122n. 58, 150nn. 61–62, 164–67, 171, 177n. 53, 178n. 54, 215–16, 217nn. 37–39, 221n. 45, 222, 224n. 53

reception in Germany, 9, 16–21, 112n. 31
Schleiermacher's affinity with, 4–11, 13–15, 25–26, 28–29, 35, 37, 39–40, 41, 42–43, 44–46, 55, 63, 77–78, 79–80, 86–87, 88, 89, 96–97, 107, 150, 153–54, 156, 160, 161–62, 164–67, 168n. 34, 170, 175, 176, 188n. 82, 191n. 90, 195, 201, 216–17, 221, 224, 227
Schleiermacher's departure from, 33, 43, 54, 79, 91, 101–102, 144, 154, 156–57, 166–67, 180–81, 195, 201, 214, 217–18, 221, 222, 224–25
Süskind, Hermann, 66n. 14, 82n. 38

Taylor, Charles, 92n. 51
Thandeka, 124
Thiel, John E., 4n. 12, 11n. 18, 124n. 61, 146n. 51
Thönes, C., 110n. 27
Tice, Terrence N., 82n. 38
Tillich, Paul, 75n. 29, 106n. 18, 187n. 77

Vallée, Gérard, 3n. 8, 16n. 10, 19, 20n. 19, 164n. 13
Velthuysen, Lambert de, 16
Vitiello, Vincenzo, 3n. 7, 64n. 12

Wallhauser, John, 41–42n. 52, 93n. 58, 185n. 72
Walzel, Oskar, 57n. 1
Wicks, Jared, S.J., 204n. 11
Williams, Robert R., 89n. 44, 113n. 35, 146n. 51
Willich, Henriette von, 106n. 17
Wolff, Christian, 17, 30n. 35
Wolfson, Harry Austryn, 28n. 32, 166n. 26

Yovel, Yirmiyahu, 17n. 14, 171n. 41, 177n. 53

Zammito, John H. 18n. 16, 33n. 41, 40n. 51, 48n. 64

Subject Index

absolute, the, 28, 36, 46, 50
aesthetic worldview, 34, 74, 75n. 27, 78, 79–80, 92, 122, 159, 220, 221–22, 224, 226
affections. *See* emotion
anthropocentrism, 87, 102, 224
  Schleiermacher's nonanthropocentrism, 6, 7, 79, 88
  Spinoza's nonanthropocentrism, 21, 23
anthropology, 125
  moral, 44–45, 92
  philosophical, 44
  theological, 115, 173–74
anthropomorphism, 2, 7, 21, 88, 89, 97–98, 102, 104, 106–7n. 19, 108, 109, 120, 134, 140, 152, 173, 174, 208n. 15, 211, 216, 219, 221, 225
  nonanthropomorphism, 121, 159
  Schleiermacher's nonanthropomorphism, 5, 6, 15, 26, 91, 128, 153, 156, 166, 170–71, 194–97, 210, 214, 217, 220, 226
  Spinoza's nonanthropomorphism, 28, 153, 162, 218, 224n. 53
atheism, 2n. 5, 16, 17, 19, 21, 22, 25, 26, 29, 36, 55, 96, 97–99, 104, 105, 109, 120, 226
attributes, divine, 7, 26, 29, 129, 130–31, 140–41nn. 37 and 40, 143, 144, 145, 146, 151, 182, 200, 203, 212
  Schleiermacher's doctrine of: eternity, 131, 140n. 40, 144, 145, 146, 147, 148, 149, 154, 155n. 77, 163, 169, 213, 216n. 36; holiness, 213n. 26; justice, 213n. 26; love, 10, 24, 92n. 54, 126, 148, 184, 195, 200–201, 203, 213–20, 221, 223, 224, 225, 227, 228; omnipotence, 2n. 6, 28, 127, 131, 143, 144, 145, 146, 147, 148–54, 155n. 77, 156, 157, 160, 163, 165n. 21, 166, 169, 170, 176, 182, 192, 195, 213, 216n. 36, 217n. 37, 222, 220; omnipresence, 131, 140n. 40, 144, 147, 148, 149, 154–57, 169, 192, 213, 216n. 36; omniscience, 131, 144, 146n. 50, 147, 148, 153, 154–57, 166, 169–70, 182, 213, 216n. 36, 220, 221, 223; wisdom, 9, 10, 21, 126, 148, 156n. 78, 157, 170n. 39, 195, 200–201, 203, 213–14, 219, 220–25
  Spinoza's doctrine of, 27, 32, 34–35, 37, 39, 53n. 71, 78n. 35, 180, 215, 218n. 40, 224

beauty, 9, 21, 37n. 45, 180, 222
being (essence), 22, 46–55, 75n. 29, 89, 177n. 53, 219
  as activity, 140, 154, 226
  as "Actually Existing," 49, 51–52, 73
  as moral order, 68
  "highest Being," 97, 100, 104, 105, 106, 107n. 19, 109
  of God, 35, 139, 154, 214–19
  of things, 36, 139–40, 156, 166, 167n. 28, 226
  "Supreme Being," 222

causality, 27n. 31, 30, 38, 43, 45, 136–43, 145, 184, 185
  divine, 2, 7, 8, 28, 78, 128, 131, 133–34, 137, 139–40, 141, 143, 144–48, 149, 150–54, 155, 156, 163, 165, 166–67, 168, 169, 170, 172, 173, 175, 178, 180, 181–83, 185, 194, 195, 197, 200, 201, 207, 208, 209, 210, 214, 216n. 36, 218, 219, 220, 221, 223, 227
  natural, 7, 45, 134, 139, 141, 145, 146, 150, 151, 162–63, 167, 168, 169, 170, 185

Subject Index

cause(s), 30, 32, 43, 78, 84, 142, 162
  absolute, 143, 145, 146, 149, 155, 181
  efficient, 19, 23, 28, 37, 43, 44, 45, 165, 166–67, 168, 169, 181, 185, 227
  final, 21, 22n. 25, 23, 25, 28, 29, 36, 37–38, 43, 44, 55, 62, 68n. 17, 77–80, 135, 156, 162, 170–71, 174, 176, 180, 195, 214, 219, 220, 221, 224, 225, 226
  external, 166, 168, 174, 180, 215
  extramundane, 7, 26, 28, 29, 30, 37, 47, 53, 78, 100–101, 169, 170, 185
  finite, 27, 36, 38, 145, 146, 149, 155, 175, 176, 190, 194, 223
  free, 185
  immanent or inherent, 19, 23, 27, 34, 43, 148, 149–50, 154, 165, 166, 195
  infinite regress of, 23, 27, 30, 162–63
  infinite, 36, 146n. 50
  mechanistic, 122, 168, 177n. 53
  necessary, 63, 165
  sustaining, 169, 181, 227
  system of, 36
  transcendent, 166
  transitive (transient, transeunt), 27, 150, 165, 166–67, 168, 170, 181, 227
  universal, 134, 142, 173
chaos, 21, 64–67, 78n. 35, 89, 102, 121, 180n. 63
Christ, 125, 177n. 51, 178n. 57, 186n. 74, 195–97, 199, 200, 201–12, 217, 218, 223n. 52, 224
Christianity, 90, 184n. 71
Christology, 7, 8, 195, 196, 200, 209n. 17
church, 178–79n. 57, 195, 201, 203, 212, 224
coincidence, 141–43, 145, 146, 149, 150–51, 155, 166, 168, 175, 177, 181, 182n. 66, 190, 191, 192
  of divine causality and natural causality, 136–43, 141, 144, 154, 162, 170, 191, 192, 195
  of opposites, 89n. 44, 146, 174
  of thought (representation) and extension (presentation), 39, 41
concept, 22, 23, 32, 38, 39, 40, 43, 45, 46, 47, 51, 53, 60, 65, 70, 75, 82, 103
consciousness, 22, 39, 51, 75n. 29, 103, 111, 117, 131, 138, 156, 188, 192, 193, 210, 221n. 45

God-consciousness, 112, 120, 129, 134, 174, 175n. 47, 177nn. 51–52, 179, 181, 192–93, 195, 200n. 2, 207, 213, 219
  immediate, 114, 189, 191, 212n. 22
  objective, 134, 141–42, 188, 191, 193
  of absolute dependence, 184, 186
  religious, 98, 120, 133, 136, 143, 155, 162, 163n. 11, 177n. 52, 181n. 65, 183, 192, 194; Christian, 128, 130, 146, 147, 148, 195, 200, 211, 218, 219; general, 129, 196, 197, 213; stages of, 101–2, 106, 107, 120–23
  self-consciousness, 115, 134, 142, 155, 168, 173, 187, 188–89, 207, 211, 218n. 41; immediate, 44, 179n. 58
  subjective, 141–42
  world-consciousness, 129, 181, 192
conversion, 202–4, 206–10
cosmology, 25, 50
creatio ex nihilo, 7, 23, 29, 55, 137, 162, 163n. 12, 164–65, 225
creation, 20, 30, 132, 134n. 16, 140n. 37, 167n. 28, 168, 169, 223
  doctrine of, 2n. 6, 7, 127, 131, 135, 136–38, 163–64nn. 11–12, 172, 211, 222

decree, eternal divine, 7, 72, 134n. 16, 152, 170–71, 176, 199, 207, 208, 210–11, 216–17, 218, 220, 223–25
deism, 21, 62, 66, 133, 136n. 21, 161, 168
dependence (*see also* feeling of), 7, 72, 76, 77, 110–19, 122, 129, 140, 141, 146, 163n. 12, 166, 175, 176, 179, 183, 194
  absolute (*see also* feeling of), 7, 111, 116, 117, 132, 133, 134, 138, 141, 142, 143, 145, 151n. 66, 152, 155, 156, 163, 164, 167, 168, 169, 170, 175n. 47, 179n. 58, 181, 182, 184
desire, 15, 37, 40, 41, 42, 43, 45, 70, 71, 175, 176
  faculty of, 103n. 13, 116n. 42, 125, 166
determinism, 5, 15, 19, 23, 26, 36, 41, 53, 75, 77, 115, 128, 159, 161, 165n. 20, 171, 185, 220, 223
  "complete determinism," Schleiermacher's, 36, 37–46, 59, 62, 68–80, 171–85, 187

ethical, 6, 7, 15, 26, 37, 41, 44, 91, 92, 122
dialectic
  and dogmatics, 124–26; "dialectical character" of dogmatics, 128
  dialectical movement of religious language, 194, 226
  dialectical relation, 65, 64–65nn. 12–13, 73, 74, 86, 178, 188
  of *One and All*, 94, 144–57
  Platonic, 9
direction, 22n. 25, 38, 77, 156, 170, 171, 180, 195
doctrine
  Christian, 2, 4, 7, 8–9, 10, 59, 100, 128, 144, 148, 199, 201–2, 228
  heterodox, 6, 127n. 1, 167n. 30
  orthodox, 6, 11, 23, 59, 127, 128, 199, 200, 202
dogmatic propositions, Schleiermacher's, 7–8, 127, 129, 130–31, 203
  "first form of proposition," 136–43, 144, 146, 200
  "second form of proposition," 143, 144–57, 167n. 29
dogmatics, Christian, 5, 6, 7, 95, 101, 130–31, 133, 136, 152n. 71, 171, 173, 176, 177, 181, 187n. 78, 204, 228
  Schleiermacher's, 10, 11, 108, 110, 124–26, 129, 130, 137, 154, 159, 186, 195, 200, 201, 211
dualism, 26, 31, 40, 44, 65, 161, 167n. 32, 186, 215

ego, 22, 34n. 42, 44, 74, 80, 83, 86, 112, 115, 161, 186, 189
emotion, 63, 69, 70, 71, 111, 114, 135, 143n. 45, 155, 175, 206, 215, 216, 218
essence. *See* being
ethics (*see also* determinism *and* morality), 7, 41n. 52, 134–35n. 18, 187n. 78
evil, 7, 132, 134–36, 187n. 78, 213n. 26

faith, 2n. 6, 164n. 12, 190, 202, 213, 219n. 43
  Jacobi's philosophy of, 21–24, 54
  Luther's notion of, 205

Schleiermacher's notion of, 75n. 29, 193, 203, 204, 206, 207, 209, 210
fatalism, 19, 21, 22, 36, 37, 39, 41, 43, 45, 73, 77, 121, 170, 183, 184, 212, 223
feeling, 57, 75n. 27
  Barth's criticism of Schleiermacher's notion of, 2n. 6, 189–90
  Jacobi's notion of, 24, 81
  Kant's suspicion of, 45
  Schleiermacher's notion of: in his early philosophy, 15n. 8, 41, 46–55, 92; in the *Reden*, 59, 66, 69, 70, 71, 77n. 34, 80–87, 89, 98, 103, 106; in the *Glaubenslehre* (*see also* feeling of absolute dependence), 121, 123, 129, 143, 184n. 71, 186, 190, 192
feeling of absolute dependence (*see also* dependence, absolute), 97, 103, 110, 112–15, 117–19, 120, 122, 123, 125, 128, 131, 132, 133, 134, 137, 143, 144, 145, 146n. 50, 150, 151, 153, 167, 171, 175, 177, 182, 183–84, 185, 186, 190, 191, 192, 193, 196, 200n. 2, 217, 218
finite existence, 27, 29, 34, 35–36, 48–49, 65, 76, 84, 179
"flux of things," 36, 43, 61
force(s) (*see also* power), 20, 26, 28, 33, 39, 40, 48, 50, 51, 67, 72, 76, 78, 80, 82, 84, 102, 121, 139, 146, 154, 155, 156, 157, 162n. 8, 166n. 28, 168–69, 170, 178, 179, 180, 184, 191–92n. 93, 213, 225, 226
  as constitutive of individuality, 32, 34, 35–36, 42, 43, 44, 73, 178
  infinite or ground Force, 20, 35–36, 42, 44, 50, 168n. 34, 222
  Herder's notion of substantial force, 5, 20–21, 29, 78n. 35, 159, 162, 167, 225
freedom, 3, 16, 22, 24, 34n. 42, 37, 39, 40, 44, 45, 46, 59, 62, 63n. 10, 70, 71, 73–80, 89, 116, 117, 121, 125, 135, 143, 146, 172, 174–75, 176, 183–85, 187, 188, 191, 195, 216, 222
  relation to desire, 37, 40, 41, 44–45
  relative, 7, 112, 115–17, 122
  transcendental, 15, 40, 41, 42, 43, 44, 91, 174, 175, 176, 186

God
  as cause, 98n. 4, 100
  as Creator, 2n. 6, 127, 167n. 32
  as free, 22n. 25, 152, 153, 154, 176
  as immanent (*see also* immanence), 127, 139, 144, 146n. 50, 147, 148–54, 160, 166–67, 199, 228
  as impersonal, 101, 103–5
  as living, 6, 7, 9, 10, 21, 23, 24, 25, 28, 30, 55–56, 101, 107–8, 109, 125, 144, 148, 154, 155, 156, 161, 164, 167n. 32, 170, 184, 190, 199, 200, 201, 213, 218, 219, 220, 223, 225–28
  as nonpersonal, 90–91, 100, 101–5, 106
  as personal, 6, 7, 9, 16, 19, 22, 23, 24, 25, 36, 44, 55–56, 58, 59, 67, 87, 88, 90–91, 101–3, 104, 105–8, 172, 199, 216, 225, 226, 227
  as transcendent (*see also* transcendence), 2n. 6, 6–7, 9, 23, 55, 100, 127, 144, 147–48, 154–55, 160, 161, 100, 225, 228
  as *Whence,* 112, 117–19, 123, 125, 128, 143, 144, 183–84, 189–90, 217
  concept or idea of, 47, 87–91, 97–98, 100, 101–8, 118, 126, 194
  in relation to individuals, 160, 172–73, 177, 181–83, 196–97, 199, 200, 201–12, 216, 217, 223, 224–25
  in relation to world, 20, 47, 88–89, 99–100, 160, 167n. 32
  language about, 96, 97, 104, 108, 128, 154, 211, 215; analogical (*via eminentiae*), 97–98n. 4, 140, 146n. 50, 174, 214, 215; apophatic (*via negationis*), 89, 140–41, 148n. 55, 214; *via causalitatis,* 140, 215, 218
  personality of, 101, 103, 105–8
  proofs for existence of, 193
  Schleiermacher's doctrine of, 1, 2, 5, 7–8, 10, 11, 58–59, 80–91, 105, 108–9, 110, 111, 124, 127–28, 129, 130, 142, 143, 147, 167, 174, 196, 199–200, 213–14, 219, 227
  Spinoza's doctrine of, 16, 27, 150n. 61, 153–54, 165–67
goodness, 21, 37n. 45, 38, 68, 78n. 35, 88, 132, 134–36, 180, 187n. 78, 213n. 26, 222
govenment, divine, 157, 170, 178, 220, 223

grace, 196n. 98, 200n. 2, 203, 204, 206, 207, 208, 209, 213

harmony, 21, 34, 74, 78, 180, 187n. 78, 212, 222, 223
heresy, 151, 167n. 30
history, 63, 78–79, 156–57, 161, 175, 179, 180, 181, 195, 211, 216, 225

idea. *See* concept
idealism, 24, 31, 46–47, 49, 55n. 73, 59, 60n. 7, 74–75, 80, 81, 85, 86, 112, 161, 186, 187
  transcendental, 22, 25, 61
  subjective, 49, 75n. 28, 111, 186
  objective, 75
imagination, 22, 37n. 45, 38, 42, 64, 68n. 17, 79, 83, 90, 103, 104, 106, 107, 108, 215n. 30, 217n. 39, 226
imago Dei, 173–74
immanence, 2n. 6, 20, 21, 65, 225, 226
immortality, 15, 58, 87, 90, 97, 106n. 17, 164n. 12, 212n. 22
individuality, 9, 26, 28, 32, 34–36, 43, 48, 58, 59, 65, 66, 67, 71–72n. 21, 73–77, 86, 88, 89, 92, 93, 112n. 31, 144, 152n. 70, 164n. 12, 168, 172–85, 196–97, 199
individuation, 33n. 38, 36, 44, 51, 65, 66, 73, 74
infinite, the, 23, 26, 29, 31, 36, 48, 50, 51, 52, 53, 55, 57, 62, 67, 71, 72, 73, 76, 77n. 34, 79, 82, 83, 84, 85, 86, 88, 93, 97, 103, 108, 129, 186, 188n. 82, 225
  relation to finite things, 15, 28, 29, 31, 32, 34, 35, 46, 47, 50, 52, 53, 54, 61, 64, 65, 66, 67, 71, 74, 75n. 27, 83, 98, 109, 129, 131, 161, 169, 184, 191, 194–95
  Spinoza's notion of, 15, 26, 123
inherency, 51, 139n. 34, 161, 166, 181, 225–26, 227
  coinherency, 41
  principle of, 26, 28, 29, 31, 32, 34, 43, 50
intellect, 23, 42, 70n. 21, 99, 153n. 73, 216
  divine, 7, 29, 54, 55, 56, 88, 154, 156, 166, 180, 195, 215n. 31, 221, 224, 226
intentionality, 38, 77, 78n. 35, 180

divine, 9, 154–57, 201, 213, 219n. 43, 220, 227
intuition, 47n. 62, 50, 53–54, 57, 59, 64, 65, 66, 67, 71, 75, 76, 79, 81, 82, 83, 84, 86, 89, 90, 191, 217n. 39, 226

Jesus of Nazareth. *See* Christ
judgment, 29, 40, 41, 175, 176
justification by faith, 3n. 7, 8–9, 10, 172, 200, 201–12, 217n. 38

Kingdom of God, 135, 212, 215, 217, 220, 222, 223, 224
knowledge, 24, 31, 53n. 71, 54, 60, 75n. 28, 81, 84–86, 109, 116n. 42, 128n. 6, 132, 140, 152, 153, 174, 187n. 78, 187n. 79, 188, 189, 191, 192, 213n. 25, 217
divine, 56, 182, 220–21, 224

love (*see also* attributes, divine), 70, 72, 79, 87, 109, 173, 184, 215, 226, 227
intellectual love of God, Spinoza's notion of, 216

materialism (*see also* materialistic pantheism), 22, 24, 25, 55, 65, 94, 96, 99, 108, 119, 161, 171, 183, 227
matter, 20, 22, 39, 40, 47–48, 49, 52, 61, 76, 139, 168n. 34, 226n. 54
metaphysics, 29, 40, 59, 61, 62, 63–68, 69, 71, 77, 78, 79, 84, 86, 87, 91, 93, 130, 131
mind, 32, 39–40, 48, 52, 61, 75, 82, 83, 143n. 45, 187n. 77, 216, 222n. 49
and body, 23, 51, 176
miracles, 22, 67, 87, 88, 133
monism, 5, 36, 40, 45, 53, 65, 82, 115, 128, 159, 160, 161
aesthetic, 9, 54, 65, 88, 92
causal, 27, 100, 150, 156, 160–71, 181, 185, 187, 192, 222
organic, 6, 15, 26–36, 43, 44, 54, 55, 59, 63–68, 72, 73, 88, 91, 92, 100, 102, 122, 150, 161, 168, 212, 221, 225, 226–27
pantheistic, 160
Spinoza's, 9, 26–27, 164–67
Spinozistic, 161
technical, 161

monotheism, 89n. 45, 101, 102, 110, 118, 119–23, 143n. 45
moral law, 45, 69, 70, 71, 88, 179–80n. 60
morality (*see also* ethics), 16, 17, 19, 23, 40, 41, 59, 60n. 7, 61, 62, 68–80, 84, 86, 87, 109, 130, 134–36, 187n. 76

natura naturans, 1, 7, 25, 27, 78n. 35, 90, 199, 224, 227
naturalism, Spinoza's, 37
nature system, 2, 67, 68, 100n. 7, 122, 130, 132, 138, 141, 142, 143, 145, 146, 148, 149–50, 152, 153, 154, 155, 161–62, 163, 164, 166, 167, 168, 170, 171, 173, 174, 175, 178–81, 183, 184, 186, 189, 190, 192, 196, 197, 211, 220, 221, 223, 226
nature, 22, 24, 27, 28, 30, 37, 38, 42n. 52, 43, 44, 57, 66, 67, 75, 78–79, 80–81, 82, 88, 103, 109, 117n. 44, 122, 129, 133, 142, 145, 149, 151, 156–57, 160, 161, 165, 169, 176, 178–79, 180, 186–89, 195, 196, 216, 217, 221n. 45, 222–23n. 51, 223n. 52, 224n. 53, 225
as causal nexus, 7, 63, 85, 135, 151n. 66, 156, 161, 176, 227
continuum of, 37–38, 81
deification of, 2
laws of, 27, 28, 36, 43, 67, 78, 80, 88, 162, 177n. 53, 179–80
unity of, 78–79, 194
necessity, 6, 16, 19, 27, 63, 64, 65, 72, 76, 89, 102, 104, 105, 185, 195, 224n. 53
blind, 6, 107, 108, 161, 170, 184, 223, 226
in God, 76n. 31, 153, 154, 176, 217n. 37
in nature, 15
neo-Spinozism, 5, 10, 20–21, 29, 33, 34, 92, 100, 159, 162, 167–71, 180, 201, 214
Schleiermacher's appropriation of, 6, 26, 55, 77–78, 109, 129, 156, 220, 224, 225, 227
nihil ex nihilo, 7, 19, 23, 28, 29, 30, 37, 38, 67, 86, 162, 164–65, 171, 175, 190, 196
nihilism, 22, 23, 24, 61
noumenon, 30, 45, 54, 66, 73, 123
as cause, 40, 41
Kant's notion of, 26, 31

Kant's noumenological interpretation of individuality, 34, 44–45
novelty, 33, 34, 157, 161, 165, 195, 222, 227

One and All, 5, 9, 10, 18, 21, 23, 26, 61, 64, 65–68, 72, 74, 76, 80, 82, 85, 88, 89, 90, 94, 98, 100–101, 102, 108, 110, 118, 121–23, 125–26, 131, 139, 142–43, 144–57, 159, 160, 161, 164, 167, 168, 177n. 52, 179, 181, 182, 183–84, 186, 191, 192, 193, 194, 197, 217n. 38, 220, 221–22, 226, 227, 228
ontology, 46, 222
oscillation, 61, 66, 81, 82, 86, 88, 89, 98, 108, 125, 142, 176, 179, 188, 194

pantheism, 1, 10, 109–10, 141, 172n. 44, 228
　aesthetic, 92, 160
　charges against Schleiermacher of, 1, 3n. 9, 58, 90, 99, 112, 114n. 41, 127–28, 138, 139n. 33, 141, 147, 160, 171–72, 189, 199
　definitions of, 4, 34n, 112–13, 119, 160, 171, 172n. 42; as identification of God and nature, 96, 99, 100, 113n. 34, 120, 121, 164n. 14, 174, 189, 194, 227; Jacobi's notion of, 2n. 5, 22n. 25, 25–26
　materialistic, 99, 104, 105, 107, 128, 169–70, 226
　mystical, 160
　relation to Spinozism, 4, 6, 96, 97, 100
　Schleiermacher's interpretation of, 99–108, 110–23, 150; acceptable form of, 6, 96, 110, 113, 118–20, 121–23, 128, 143, 167n. 30, 193, 194, 227; his doctrine of God distinguished from, 141, 142–43, 144, 149n. 59, 155–56, 164n. 14, 167n. 30, 167n. 31, 169, 172, 174, 194, 227
　Spinoza's, 3n. 9
Pantheist Controversy, 6, 17–21, 77, 225
parallelism, 38–41, 46, 52, 77, 188n. 82
participation, 139–40, 169
particulars, 64, 65, 66, 76, 78, 79, 210, 221

perfection, 37n. 45, 41n. 52, 74, 79, 177n. 51, 179, 187, 192, 197n. 99, 224
personality, 75, 76, 181, 214, 216, 218, 226, 227
　of God, 56
philosophy, 80, 109, 159, 212
　critical, 29, 31, 36, 45, 49, 52, 55, 61, 66, 128, 159, 186
piety, 7, 60, 60n. 7, 68, 70, 71, 72, 84, 85–86, 87, 88, 89, 160, 174, 193, 196n. 98, 202, 210n. 20
　and pantheism, 119–22
　as criterion for religious language, 97–109, 163
　as feeling, 84, 85–86, 89
　as feeling of absolute dependence, 110–11, 186
　as limit, 88, 98, 102, 104, 107, 128, 130, 131–36, 150, 152, 154, 175, 194, 210, 212, 227
　Barth's criticism of, 190
　Schleiermacher's, 60
　Spinoza as example of, 2, 19, 90, 91, 95, 96, 97
　Spinoza's notion of, 69n. 18, 215
Platonism, 50n
　Schleiermacher's, 9, 54, 60, 79, 125; Platonized Spinozism, 7, 9, 91–94; rejection of Platonic notion of participation, 169
plurality, 33, 65, 74, 89, 106, 157, 161, 172n. 42, 181, 226, 227
polytheism, 89n. 45, 90, 102, 121
possibility. *See* potentiality
post-Kantian Spinozism, Schleiermacher's, 5, 6, 9, 10, 14, 15, 26, 31, 42, 58–59, 64, 65, 73, 81, 91, 92, 95, 100, 122, 123, 128, 159, 176, 177, 186, 194, 200, 201, 214, 218, 219–20, 225, 227
potentiality, 148, 150n. 65, 151–54, 166, 175, 220, 224
power (*see* forces):
　and being, 75n. 29, 178
　as causality, 27n. 31, 143n. 46, 150
　as type of force, 78n. 35
　chemical powers, 67
　divine, 16–17, 28, 68n. 16, 152, 153, 154, 156, 166; relation to finite powers, 149

human, 68n. 16, 71, 76, 83
Jacobi's notion of mechanism of efficient powers, 23, 37
of Christ, 205
of things, 75n. 29, 139, 140, 155n. 77, 156, 178–79
"ordered exercise of power," 133, 134n. 16, 168, 174, 181, 182, 226
"realm of power," 207–8
things as centers of, 140, 168
"universal powers," 168
prayer, 3, 17, 212
preservation, divine, 132, 134, 137, 165, 167n. 28, 168, 169, 175, 185, 196, 219, 223
Schleiermacher's doctrine of, 7, 127, 128, 131, 135–36, 138–43, 145, 148–49, 151, 172, 181, 182, 211, 220, 222
progress, 77–79, 180
Protestant orthodoxy, 21, 136n. 21, 138, 186n. 75
providence, 19, 21, 90
purpose(s), 22n. 25, 40, 62, 77, 156n. 78, 160, 170–71, 172, 180, 214, 219, 220, 221, 222, 223, 224, 225, 226

rationalism, 20, 21, 22n. 25, 23, 25, 99
realism, 5, 25, 46–55, 80, 81, 86, 115, 128, 159, 186, 187n. 78, 189, 190, 193
critical, 15, 26, 49, 50, 59, 75, 91, 93, 115
"higher realism," Schleiermacher's, 6, 55, 59, 80–87, 93, 122, 185–93, 217
naive, 49, 83
reason, 30, 41, 42n. 52, 43, 44, 45, 50, 52, 60n. 8, 63n. 10, 69n. 18, 78n. 35, 109, 140, 180n. 60, 187n. 77, 215, 217n. 39
Jacobi's critique of, 21–24
practical, 40, 45, 46n. 61, 50, 69
receptivity, 53, 82, 84, 114, 115–16, 117, 122, 183, 186–93, 206, 207
of the organs, 49, 50, 54, 81, 116
Redeemer, the. *See* Christ
redemption, 79, 109, 125–26, 130, 135, 157, 177n. 51, 183, 196, 200, 203, 206, 209, 212–25, 227, 228
regeneration, 197, 200, 203–4, 205, 206, 207, 209n. 17, 211, 212, 219

religion, 6, 16, 19, 55n. 73, 58, 59–80, 82, 83, 84–85, 87, 90, 91, 97, 98, 100, 102, 103, 105, 106n. 19, 120, 132, 133, 143n. 45, 164n. 12, 181, 186n. 75, 192, 202, 212n. 22, 226
representation, 22, 23, 24, 29, 31, 38n. 46, 39, 40, 41, 43, 47n. 63, 49, 50, 52, 55, 98, 103, 119, 120, 121, 125, 147, 152n. 71, 164n. 12, 184, 191
resolution (*Entschluß*), 40–41, 46, 70n. 21, 175
revelation, 24, 67, 87, 164n. 12, 193, 222
romanticism, German, 5, 20, 57–58, 60, 65, 75n. 27, 79, 91, 161, 226

sanctification, 200, 203–4, 206, 209
scholasticism, 27, 30n. 36, 139–40, 141, 151, 152–53, 166, 169, 177, 178, 181
science, 33, 36, 42, 61, 67, 84–86, 109, 122, 128, 130, 132–34, 136, 137, 159, 163, 167, 177n. 53, 187n. 76
sin, 3n. 7, 35, 196n. 98, 200n. 2, 203, 205, 208, 211
"Spinozan," 5, 26, 54, 69, 148, 160, 186, 218, 220
Spinozism (*see also* neo-Spinozism *and* post-Kantian Spinozism), 6, 13, 16–21, 25, 26, 46, 48, 55, 96, 97, 99, 109, 112n. 31, 142, 144, 160
charges against Schleiermacher of, 1, 3–4, 6, 58, 90, 96, 160, 199
Herder's, 21, 84
"inverted," 22, 61, 112n. 31
Jacobi's definition of, 19, 20, 21, 22–23, 24, 26, 162–64, 176
Lessing's, 18, 19, 21, 23, 49–50n. 66
Mendelssohn's, 21
relation to Platonism, 91–94
Schleiermacher's, 4, 5, 10, 11, 25–26, 65, 66, 81, 84, 85, 86, 90–91, 96, 104, 142–43, 164, 165n. 20, 167n. 30, 171, 228
subjectivism (*see also* subjective idealism), 111–12, 118
substance, 22, 29, 34, 44, 47, 48, 51, 65, 112n. 31, 140, 155n. 77
infinite, 35–36
Spinoza's doctrine of, 5, 20–21, 26–27, 30, 31, 33, 34–35, 51, 52, 73, 78n. 35, 152, 166, 225

supernatural, the, 133–34, 164, 194
system, 59–80, 82, 85, 100, 102, 161
   dogmatic, 130, 157

teleology, 78–79, 108, 157, 180, 195, 226–27
theism, 2n. 5, 3n. 9, 19, 21, 22, 24, 26, 29, 68, 99, 101–3, 104, 107, 119, 120, 172, 193
"third alternative," Schleiermacher's, 24, 40, 41–42n. 58, 77, 93, 199, 227
totality, 47, 48–49, 54, 55, 66, 67, 80, 81, 90, 102, 118, 150, 151, 164, 167n. 31, 168, 171, 179, 182, 190, 194, 195n. 95, 211, 224
transcendence, 65, 164

universe, 20, 30, 32, 33, 36, 58, 61, 62, 63, 66, 67, 71, 72, 74, 75, 76, 77n. 34, 78–79, 80, 82, 83, 84, 86, 89, 90, 99, 101, 113n. 34, 118, 163, 168, 171, 212, 222, 225, 226
   soul of , 23, 36

value, 157, 160, 182, 213, 222, 224, 227

whole and part, relation of, 32–33, 34, 36, 48, 49, 73, 74, 98, 142, 151, 152–53, 155, 171–72, 173, 180, 181, 182, 196–97, 211–12, 216, 217, 221, 224, 226
will, 23, 28, 42, 45, 53, 70, 76, 77, 90, 99, 153n. 73, 175, 176, 216
   free, 17, 21, 23, 25, 26, 40, 42, 68, 70, 71, 73, 77, 116, 153
   divine, 7, 29, 55, 56, 68, 88, 153–54, 156, 166, 170, 180, 182, 195, 215n. 31, 220, 221, 224, 226
Word, 205, 206, 207
world, 23, 30, 49, 50, 51, 53, 61, 64, 67, 72, 75, 80, 84, 98, 113–19, 121–23, 130, 131–32, 136, 142, 143n. 45, 144, 150, 155, 163, 169, 171, 173, 177, 179–80, 185, 185, 187, 188n. 83, 191n. 93, 193, 194, 197, 203, 211, 212n. 22, 220, 221, 222;
   as dependent, 20, 100, 129, 134, 164
world soul, 48, 99–100, 119n. 52
world spirit, 72, 79, 82–83, 99–100, 119n. 52, 226

BT
101
.S144
L36
1996
40534s

DATE DUE

ILL 3wks

DEMCO 38-297